MORE VOICES OF CIVIL RIGHTS LAWYERS

UNIVERSITY PRESS OF FLORIDA

Florida A&M University, Tallahassee
Florida Atlantic University, Boca Raton
Florida Gulf Coast University, Ft. Myers
Florida International University, Miami
Florida State University, Tallahassee
New College of Florida, Sarasota
University of Central Florida, Orlando
University of Florida, Gainesville
University of North Florida, Jacksonville
University of South Florida, Tampa
University of West Florida, Pensacola

More Voices of Civil Rights Lawyers

Continuing the Struggle

Edited by Kent Spriggs

UNIVERSITY PRESS OF FLORIDA

Gainesville/Tallahassee/Tampa/Boca Raton
Pensacola/Orlando/Miami/Jacksonville/Ft. Myers/Sarasota

Cover: Civil rights lawyer C. B. King with staff and interns, 1967. Courtesy of the author.

Copyright 2024 by Kent Spriggs
All rights reserved
Published in the United States of America

29 28 27 26 25 24   6 5 4 3 2 1

Library of Congress Cataloging-in-Publication Data
Names: Spriggs, Kent, editor.
Title: More voices of civil rights lawyers : continuing the struggle / edited by Kent Spriggs.
Description: Gainesville : University Press of Florida, 2024. | Includes bibliographical references and index. | Summary: "In this book, twenty-three lawyers discuss their experiences in the struggle to advance and maintain civil rights in the United States South, from the 1960s to the 1980s and from Texas to Virginia to Florida"—Provided by publisher.
Identifiers: LCCN 2024016862 | ISBN 9780813079165 (hardback) | ISBN 9780813080741 (pbk.) | ISBN 9780813070841 (pdf) | ISBN 9780813073453 (ebook)
Subjects: LCSH: Civil rights lawyers—Southern States—History—20th century. | African Americans—Civil rights—Southern States—History—20th century. | Civil rights movements—Southern States—History—20th century. | African American civil rights workers—Southern States—History—20th century. | African American lawyers—Southern States—History. | Civil rights lawyers—Southern States—History. | BISAC: HISTORY / African American & Black | LAW / Civil Rights
Classification: LCC KF299.C48 M67 2024 | DDC 342.7308/73—dc23/eng/20240512
LC record available at https://lccn.loc.gov/2024016862

The University Press of Florida is the scholarly publishing agency for the State University System of Florida, comprising Florida A&M University, Florida Atlantic University, Florida Gulf Coast University, Florida International University, Florida State University, New College of Florida, University of Central Florida, University of Florida, University of North Florida, University of South Florida, and University of West Florida.

University Press of Florida
2046 NE Waldo Road
Suite 2100
Gainesville, FL 32609
http://upress.ufl.edu

CONTENTS

List of Abbreviations ix

Editor's Note xi

Introduction 1
   Kent Spriggs

Chapter 1. Law Students Civil Rights Research Council 7
   The Law Students Civil Rights Research Council 7
      Amy Ruth Tobol
   A Transformative Internship with Attorney C. B. King 31
      David Rudovsky
   Clerking in Mobile 39
      James Ayers
   Panola County, Mississippi, in 1966 51
      Stephen Oleskey
   I Don't Want to Die in Vietnam 61
      Paul Harris
   My Dad as a Role Model 64
      Chevene King Jr.
   My Memories of the Civil Rights Movement 71
      Kenneth Cloke

Chapter 2. Southern Legal Action Movement 83
   SLAM: The Organizing Drive and the Summer Institute 83
      Jim Rowan

Southern Legal Action Movement 88
Jack Drake

Chapter 3. North Mississippi Rural Legal Services 96

Bonds, Bridges, and Defining Moments 96
Wilhelm H. Joseph

From the Law School to the Community: The Early Years of North Mississippi Rural Legal Services, 1966–70 103
Michael B. Trister

Holmes County, Legal Services, Summer 1970 111
Kent Hull

Chapter 4. Trying Cases 121

Louie Baeza and the Fork in the Road 121
David Kern

A Sometimes Strange and Unusual Career 133
Gerry Hebert

The Corum Claim: A New Remedy 148
John Gresham

From Wall Street to Occupy Wall Street: A Journey 152
Alan Levine

Chapter 5. Movement Figures 161

Lawyers Constitutional Defense Committee, 1964–66 161
Bruce Rogow

The Civil Rights Movement Comes to an End: The 1966 Meredith Mississippi March against Fear 171
Melvyn R. Leventhal

Why I Went South and What I Did There 185
Charles Stephen "Steve" Ralston

When Lawyers Could Win Civil Rights Suits in Alabama 196
James Blacksher

Chapter 6. New Delivery Systems 233

Life after Passage of the 1964 Civil Rights Act 233
Robert L. Wiggins Jr.

Mississippi Center for Justice: Building Homegrown Capacity to Dismantle Mississippi's Historic Culture of Injustice 245
Martha Bergmark

Conclusion: Where Are We Going? 260

Imagine and Create the Third Reconstruction 260
Barbara Phillips

About the Editor 269

List of Contributors 271

Index 273

ABBREVIATIONS

AAMU	Alabama A&M University
ABA	American Bar Association
ACLU	American Civil Liberties Union
ADC	Alabama Democratic Conference
ASU	Alabama State University
CORE	Congress of Racial Equality
DOJ	Department of Justice
EEOC	Equal Employment Opportunity Commission
FDP	Freedom Democratic Party
FLSA	Fair Labor Standards Act
HBCU	historically black college or university
KKK	Ku Klux Klan
LCDC	Lawyers Constitutional Defense Committee
LDF	Legal Defense and Education Fund, a.k.a. Inc. Fund
LSCRRC	Law Students Civil Rights Research Council
MALDEF	Mexican American Legal Defense and Educational Fund
MCJ	Mississippi Center for Justice
MFDP	Mississippi Freedom Democratic Party
NAACP	National Association for the Advancement of Colored People
NLG	National Lawyers Guild

NMRLS	North Mississippi Rural Legal Services
NYU	New York University
OEO	Office of Economic Opportunity
SCEF	Southern Conference Education Fund
SCLC	Southern Christian Leadership Conference
SLAM	Southern Legal Action Movement
SNCC	Student Nonviolent Coordinating Committee
SSOC	Southern Student Organizing Committee
UC	University of California
VRA	Voting Rights Amendments/Act

EDITOR'S NOTE

For the purpose of clarification, editorial interpolations appear in the text enclosed in square brackets. A measure of purposeful political and social perspective abides in each author's decision about capitalizing the terms "black" and "white." Some capitalize both terms. Some capitalize the word "Black" only. Most use lowercase for both. The University Press of Florida honored my editorial preference to let each author's capitalization preference stand as written rather than to enforce consistency across all of the essays herein.

Introduction

Kent Spriggs

Oscar Adams, whose office was in Birmingham, called LDF one day and told me that he needed help as quickly as possible. Demonstrators in a small city in Greene County had been arrested and mistreated by the local sheriff, and Oscar had been contacted for legal assistance. I checked with Jack Greenberg, and he OK'd me going immediately to Birmingham to meet up with Oscar. I put papers and pleadings together and caught a late plane that arrived in Birmingham at around midnight. Oscar met me, and as I got into the passenger seat of his car he said, "It's in the glove compartment." I asked, "What is?" and he said, "The gun." So, there I was riding shotgun as we drove into the dark night—and I mean dark as only a country night can be. Me, who joined the US Army Medical Corps since, as a nonofficial conscientious objector, I hated guns and had no intention of ever shooting anyone.

* * *

The first appellate case I argued was a voting rights/segregation case that C. B. had brought when an African American woman ran for justice of the peace in one of the small Georgia counties. When she went to the polling places, she found that there were three polling booths—for white men, white women, and colored. She refused to use the "colored" booth and attempted to vote in the white women booth. She was of course arrested, and C. B. brought an action in federal court to enjoin the prosecution, to prohibit future segregation, and to require that a new election be held.

* * *

I immediately drove back to the Miles' farm nervously glancing in my rearview mirrors for any sign of pursuit. There was none. I parked the Freedom Wagon and went into the Miles' house. Seeing Mr. Miles in the living room, I told him what had just happened. He asked me who had sent me to see the

Joneses and I told him. He shook his head in bemusement and said, "Didn't he tell you that the store was the headquarters for the local Klan?" I replied, "No." He added that I had just walked into an informal gathering of the KKK and was very lucky that I had returned unscathed. I asked him if he had a pistol in the house.

* * *

My father C. B. King accompanied me to a town south of Albany near the Florida state line. As we were returning to Albany, he began to give me alternative, if not backroad, directions on where to turn. I asked him for his reasons, and he would only say that he had had an experience or two on certain roads that he wished to avoid. I assumed that his reasons were not to be questioned. Approximately two years later, I was representing an Albany resident who had been arrested along with his girlfriend in Troy, Alabama. While investigating the case, a police officer arrived and stated that he was taking us to jail. No arrest was made. As we began to leave the jail, the sheriff was noticeably absent. And as we began to make our way back to the highway that we had used coming into Troy, we noticed no fewer than four or more police cars positioned along the road and saw two pulling in behind us. At that point, I pulled into a gas station and upon explaining the situation to a black customer there at a nearby gas pump, asked if there was there a "back way" out of town. He thereafter obliged us and got us safely on our way. As we were returning to Albany, an off-duty policeman whom I had hired for extra protection asked me why we were using such a circuitous route back to Albany. My response was clear. "My father said to always know more than one way out of town."

This anthology represents 23 voices, many of which reveal defining moments in the lives of civil rights lawyers. The stories in this book all unfolded as small, singular events in the midst of the large political and social upheavals of the 1960s and 1970s. The temporal scope extends into and beyond the 1980s, in what has been called the second phase of the civil rights movement. The experiences of lawyers in this phase reveal ongoing challenges to basic civil rights, regardless of federal legislation.

Their eyewitness accounts of dramatic moments in the civil rights legacy provide a unique window into history. As Alan Levine succinctly writes in his chapter, "What Black citizens from every walk of life did to secure their rights in the face of physical violence and economic reprisal is a story of popular resistance that became an inspiration for social and political movements throughout the remainder of the twentieth century and into the present."

Just as bus boycotts, sit-ins, and other acts of civil disobedience were the engine of the civil rights movement, there was at all times a litigation context. The lawyers played defense in getting demonstrators out of jail. The lawyers played offense in vindicating constitutional rights to desegregated schools and implementing the new statutory rights to vote and enjoy equal employment opportunity.

The growth of the civil rights movement spawned a new generation of civil rights lawyers, and this work tells the intergenerational stories of these men and women who helped shape southern history. As civil rights lawyers, we plied our trade in a context—and in turn shaped that context. To a person, the clients were remarkable for their bravery and vision. These attorney-client relationships were often extraordinary in their mutual trust and commitment to risk-taking. Many of the clients are not famous. Telling these stories now helps us recognize and remember the ubiquity of injustices in that time.

As civil rights lawyers, we were both handmaidens of change and among those who took a front row seat to the history that unfolded. We thought in strategic terms about the new legal tapestry that was emerging. Without exception, the experience of being in the cauldron dramatically shaped us as people.

After slavery came the hope of Reconstruction. In the latter part of the nineteenth century, there was tremendous backsliding, culminating in *Plessy v. Ferguson,* a decision that enshrined legal segregation. There was little activity until Thurgood Marshall chose litigation to eat at the edges, heightening the contradictions. This multidecade process culminated in *Brown v. Board of Education,* ending legal segregation. This was followed by the Civil Rights Act of 1964 and the Voting Rights Act the following year under the leadership of President Lyndon Johnson.

Some issues have been resolved, such as equal access to public accommodations.

The core legal issues of school desegregation were resolved, but related issues, such as segregated private schools (derisively named "seg schools") and white flight, eroded the desired societal goal, even though legal.

Voting rights were seemingly settled with the 1965 Voting Rights Act, and indeed, it brought about a dramatic increase in black participation. All-white juries are a thing of the past. There is a substantial complement of black judges. But hostility to voting rights resurfaced in other forms.

Most boldly, the 2013 *Shelby County v. Holder* Supreme Court decision dealt a body blow to the Voting Rights Act by eliminating the preclearance that had been so powerful. Additionally, a great many states have passed laws, such as voter ID, with the intent of making voting more difficult with an express intent to limit black participation. Unfortunately, most of these are of a nature that they are not susceptible to litigation, since they are "legal." And, of course, there is still a great deal of racism in the political process, such as the 2023 expulsion of two black legislators, Justin Pearson and Justin Jones, by the Republican-led legislature in Tennessee.

Litigation of employment discrimination has produced great gains against systemic discrimination. It is instructive, however, that there is enough systemic discrimination that successful class actions can still be brought.

The general legal context that affects all these issues is that we are now faced with a less friendly federal judiciary than in the 1960s.

Contributors' narratives are gathered into six thematic chapters. Chapter 1 focuses on the Law Students Civil Rights Research Council to examine the role of LSCRRC and the experiences of some of those who were interns. LSCRRC placed law clerks throughout the South, many of whom became civil rights lawyers upon graduation.

Chapter 2 presents stories from individuals involved with the Southern Legal Action Movement (SLAM), which was a movement of lawyers, law students, and legal workers that grew in response to repressive conditions in the South. The movement was inherently southern, in that it arose from lawyers in the South committed to supporting positive social change without the top-down participation of national groups like the American Bar Association. This grassroots organization encouraged lawyers to share strategies with one another to improve defense outcomes, and it encouraged efforts to educate citizens on basic rights and legal systems.

Essays in chapter 3 discuss North Mississippi Rural Legal Services (NMRLS), which was a civil rights law firm disguised as a legal services program (disguised in the sense that civil rights litigation was not the focal point of most legal services programs). Over time the powers that be curtailed some of the civil rights activities of legal services nationally. The NMRLS program exists to this day.

Chapter 4 presents essays that discuss processes in trying a variety of cases—such as employment, voting rights, library access, and private right of action. Appreciation for the litigation process allows the reader to better understand how the law evolves.

In chapter 5, a number of notable civil rights lawyers and judges are profiled.

Chapter 6 focuses on class action suits. Class actions are integral to civil rights litigation in that they allow the litigation to protect everyone in a class, rather than litigating for an individual person to be benefited.

The volume closes with a thought-provoking essay by Barbara Phillips. To examine where we may be headed, Phillips puts forward ideas and strategies for a third Reconstruction.

1

Law Students Civil Rights Research Council

The Law Students Civil Rights Research Council

Amy Ruth Tobol

As law students, former first lady and secretary of state Hillary Clinton and Supreme Court justice Clarence Thomas received internships through a multiracial, student-run organization called the Law Students Civil Rights Research Council (LSCRRC). In different ways, both Clinton and Thomas have identified those internships as touchstones in their legal careers. On March 10, 1993, as part of her speech at a luncheon held by the NAACP Legal Defense and Education Fund (LDF) in Washington, DC, Clinton noted:

> Twenty-three years ago, in the spring, I received a grant from an organization . . . called LSCRRC, the Law Students Civil Rights Research Council, to be an intern for the blessed Marion Wright Edelman in the old Washington Research Project . . . Elaine [Jones, newly appointed director of LDF] was also a LSCRRC intern that summer. And I remember so well the events of that very active couple of months, the work that the Washington Research Project did with LDF on a variety of issues and all that I learned. And for me it was a singular experience that led me to continue to work on behalf of the issues that I learned about and particularly with Marion and the Children's Defense Fund.[1]

In a speech to Holy Cross College on March 24, 1984, Clarence Thomas noted:

> Through my radical days, through my days at New Haven Legal Assistance, through the summer working under a grant from the Law Students Civil Rights Research Council, I did not forget; through Holy

Cross and Yale, I did not forget; as Assistant Attorney General and Assistant Secretary, I did not forget; as Chairman of the EEOC I cannot and will not forget. I can never forget the agony of discrimination, the humiliation of prejudice.[2]

Clinton and Thomas are two of a distinguished group of close to 5,000 alumni whose lives were influenced in varying degrees by their experiences with LSCRRC between 1963 and 1987. LSCRRC's largest and most successful program was the summer internship program, which placed close to 5,000 law students in civil rights internships throughout the United States over its 24-year history. Besides participating in the legal fight for civil rights by providing much needed interns, LSCRRC demonstrated the power of student organizations and provided a viable framework for future student groups to model.

Between 1992 and 1999, as a PhD student in the American Studies department at the University of Buffalo, I conducted extensive oral history and archival research for my dissertation focused on LSCRRC. I examined LSCRRC's contributions to the civil rights and other movements of the 1960s, '70s, and '80s and to the evolution of the legal profession and legal education. LSCRRC's contributions had gone largely unacknowledged. I had worked as LSCRRC's program director from 1983 to 1986; my experiences in this role were pivotal in my own life story. I wanted to understand my work with LSCRRC in a larger context.

Personal Context

The first I heard about the Law Students Civil Rights Research Council was sometime in 1981 or 1982 when I was a student at the University of Buffalo Law School. As an active member of the Buffalo Law School chapter of the National Lawyers Guild I was asked to participate on the committee that reviewed law student applications for LSCRRC's summer internship program. All I knew is that there was a national organization that sponsored public interest internships around the country and local chapters were responsible for sending applicant recommendations for consideration by the national board. It's an overstatement that we had a "chapter" in Buffalo. In addition to the guild, the other organizations represented on this committee that I remember included the Black Law Students Association (BLSA), OUTLaw (LGBT-identified students), Public Interest Law Program, Women's Law Students Association, and the Asian Law Students Association. There were earlier versions of the current Latin American Law Students

Association and the Native Indigenous Law Students Association represented as well. We interviewed applicants, made our recommendations, and that was it for me and LSCRRC. Until 1983.

In 1983, my last year in law school, a close friend of mine showed me the advertisement for a program director position at LSCRRC at the New York City office. I applied, was interviewed by the board and staff, and started working at LSCRRC in the fall of 1983. The salary was unlivable; I had to move in with family. The opportunity of working for LSCRRC allowed me to meet some of the most preeminent civil rights and public interest attorneys of the twentieth century, which was priceless. I was responsible for running the summer internship program, which included traveling around the country, meeting with supervisors of our placement sites, developing new contacts and running workshops at law schools on pursuing careers in civil rights and public interest law. I became part of a community I had always admired, I was contributing to an ongoing civil rights movement, and was participating in mentoring a next generation of civil rights attorneys.

And I learned that I was a white person. Not that I didn't know I was white. I grew up in a largely white Roman Catholic neighborhood on Long Island and was one of two Jewish teens in my junior high school. There was one African American student. My summers and weekends were spent with an integrated group of teens I met through my years at a progressive summer camp. My family history included socialists, anarchists, conservatives, and rabbis and I prided myself on being race-conscious and understanding privilege. I discovered I knew next to nothing when I arrived at LSCRRC.

From 1983 to 1986 I was often the only white person on staff at the national office, at the workshops I conducted, at LSCRRC board meetings, and at meetings with law students, activists, and lawyers. I often felt out of place and was often challenged in subtle and not so subtle ways to justify why I belonged. The women I worked with in the national office were very patient with my "white girl questions" as I called them, the memory of which embarrasses me today. I loved every minute of this work. I often wondered if others who had been either in leadership or involved with LSCRRC's internship and other law school–based programs were as affected as I was by the experience. I aimed to find that out through my dissertation.

My study was grounded in personal experience, formal oral history interviews, informal conversations, and archival research.[3] What I discovered was that the individual participants I interviewed, as well as the thousands I was able to track down, demonstrated how successful LSCRRC had been in its primary goal of encouraging law students to pursue careers in civil rights and public interest law. Not all the participants went that route for the entirety of their careers. Many of their careers were not spent in one law firm, agency, or even in one area of the law. What I could find out about many of them, though, was some connection between their LSCRRC experience and the trajectory of their working lives over time.

I also discovered that examined collectively, these individual experiences had an impact on legal education and the profession. Finally, examining the opportunities the organization provided for networking with law students and lawyers engaged in the civil rights movement and other movements around the country provided additional information about the cross-fertilization of social movements.

Historical Context

The impetus for the organization's establishment is rooted in the intersection of particular moments in the history of the legal profession, legal education, and the civil rights movement. LSCRRC was founded by a small group of law students who met at law schools and worked with civil rights attorneys in the South in 1963 and on buses traveling to the historic 1963 March on Washington. They were part of a growing movement of northern law students and college students who had begun to travel south in the 1950s and 1960s to add their voices and talents to the civil rights movement. What was particularly significant about the growing numbers of northern students coming south was that they were not deterred by how McCarthyism stifled the few efforts to organize around race issues in the 1950s. Though the fear of being branded "communist" by McCarthy did inhibit many white activists from supporting these struggles, other white activists, including very few lawyers, participated at significant risk to themselves.

Despite this pressure, the newly formed SCLC joined NAACP and the Congress of Racial Equality (CORE) in participating in civil rights protests that generated interest, participation, and support among southern college students. The 1960 sit-in by four black students at the Woolworth's lunch counter in Greensboro, North Carolina, inspired black and white southern students to protest segregation in the South and to establish the Student Nonviolent Coordinating Committee (SNCC) at Shaw University in Raleigh, North Carolina. The Southern Regional Council estimated that in 1960 alone, 70,000 people, mostly college students, participated in the sit-ins and that 3,600 of them were arrested. According to a 1963 Southern Regional Council report, "at least 141 students and 58 faculty members were dismissed by southern colleges and universities" because of their participation in sit-ins and other civil rights activities.

College and law student participants, some of whom came from the North, participated in increasing numbers in the Freedom Rides, which were initiated and led in 1961 by James Farmer, the first African American director of CORE. The Freedom Riders were small, interracial groups of CORE members and sympathizers who traveled in buses in the South, challenging racial segregation in rest rooms, waiting rooms, and restaurants in bus terminals throughout a predetermined route. These students persevered despite being beaten and having their buses burned by local segregationists. Their efforts attracted the attention of the media and inspired northern students and activists to join them.

College and law students from around the country were encouraged to participate in the southern civil rights movement by SNCC's campaigns. SNCC's 1963 "Freedom Vote Campaign" dramatized the exclusion of blacks from the electoral process. Where white students assisted with the campaign, they were attacked by local white southerners who opposed the interracial group as well as their efforts to guarantee equal voting rights to African Americans. Although violence against African Americans had been virulent and constant, it was violence against white students that attracted the kind of publicity SNCC and the civil rights movement could use to further their agendas. SNCC initiated the massive 1964 Mississippi Freedom Summer, which was intended to attract white student participants to voting registration drives in the South. It was hoped that these efforts would bring additional national attention to the civil rights struggles of the South.

By 1963 the movement for desegregation and full participation for all citizens of the South in all facets of American life had grown to the "largest mass movement for racial reform and civil rights in the twentieth century." In 1963, 1,000 desegregation protests occurred across the region in more than 100 cities; some 15,000 men, women, and children were imprisoned as a result of these activities.[4] Some civil rights activists were arrested while participating in boycotts, pickets, or nonviolent marches. Others were charged with alleged traffic infractions, disorderly behavior, and other misdemeanors and violations that amounted to harassment by local law enforcement agencies rather than violations of law.[5] There were few lawyers, especially in the South, willing to risk being associated with communists and fellow travelers when they represented these activists. Many attorneys who represented members of the Communist Party USA, unions, and civil rights activists were routinely attacked by judges and other attorneys and were often faced with contempt charges and the revocation of their licenses to practice or threat of attacks by local bench and bar.[6] The American Bar Association refused to participate in aiding the ongoing legal work of the few attorneys who were representing individuals and communities involved with the civil rights struggles in the 1950s and 1960s.

In response to the increased need for legal support, three legal organizations were established that later formed the nucleus of legal support to civil rights activists in the 1960s. Two of these legal organizations were formed in part in response to the American Bar Association's commitment to segregation and the lack of legal challenges to the status quo: the National Lawyers Guild (NLG) and the NAACP Legal Defense and Education Fund (LDF). A third organization, the American Civil Liberties Union (ACLU), though initially formed as a vehicle for protecting the First Amendment, also participated in efforts to end segregation. The original impetus for the establishment of each of these organizations was markedly different.

The ACLU was established in 1920 and until the 1960s focused on First Amendment litigation. It provided little support to individual litigants whose claims had minimal impact on First Amendment issues. The National Lawyers Guild was founded in 1937, as an integrated progressive alternative to the all-white American Bar Association that was not supportive of Roosevelt's New Deal legislation. The membership of the guild included liberal, progressive, and radical attorneys who identified with the Communist Party, the ACLU, and a diverse array of organizations and issues. The guild provided support and a professional home to those who were ignored by the mainstream bar and provided litigation and political support to the African American community and others not served by the mainstream bar.[7]

In 1940, the LDF was created as a charitable organization to perform the NAACP's nonlobbying activities, including antidiscrimination litigation. The creator of the LDF, Thurgood Marshall, headed a small paid staff of attorneys who along with cooperating attorneys around the country represented communities and individuals in election law, voting rights, and capital punishment cases. Until the early 1960s, only the NAACP was developing broad-based legal strategies to attack institutionalized segregation.[8]

The civil rights era of the '60s transformed the ACLU, which, after much internal debate, decided to break with its tradition of litigating exclusively First Amendment cases and provide legal support to civil rights activists.

Mel Wulf, assistant ACLU legal director in 1960, tried to arrange legal assistance for activists who were arrested as sit-ins spread throughout the South. In 1962, Wulf traveled throughout the South in search of cooperating attorneys. There were very few since some, such as white attorneys Bill Higgs in Mississippi and Chuck Morgan in Birmingham, had been run out of their communities by threats and accusations of criminal behavior. Others were faced with legal challenges resulting from their representation of civil rights activists. Len Holt, a black Virginia attorney, faced a possible ten-year prison term on an incitement charge, and white New Orleans lawyers Ben Smith and Bruce Waltzer were fending off attacks by the House on Un-American Activities Committee (HUAC). The ACLU provided cooperating attorneys and initiated the Lawyers Constitutional Defense Committee (LCDC), which was intended to coordinate legal support offered to civil rights organizations by various legal organizations including LDF and the National Lawyers Guild.[9]

The National Lawyers Guild sponsored the first interracial conference of civil rights attorneys in Atlanta, Georgia, in 1962. Its main objective was to recruit and train attorneys for the guild's Committee to Assist Southern Lawyers (CASL), which provided legal assistance to civil rights activists. The first CASL office was opened in Jackson, Mississippi, in 1962 and was staffed by Claudia Shropshire (now the Honorable Claudia Morkham). Through CASL, whose name was changed to Committee for Legal Assistance to the South (CLAS) in 1964, the National Lawyers Guild recruited almost 100 attorneys on a rotating basis to work on civil rights cases throughout the South.[10]

LDF–cooperating attorneys were also available to represent activists. In 1960, Thurgood Marshall, the legal director of LDF, held an internal LDF conference at Howard Law School to discuss ongoing litigation strategies. During the proceedings, he exhorted conference participants to individually commit to representing demonstrators.

Belatedly, in the summer of 1963, the American Bar Association formed the Lawyers' Committee for Civil Rights under Law (Lawyers' Committee) as a result of pressure levied by President John F. Kennedy. The intent of the Lawyers' Committee was to recruit ABA members to provide legal assistance to demonstrators in the South. Then ACLU executive director Jack Pemberton was concerned that the Lawyers' Committee would do little because of the federal government's history of minimal assistance to civil rights activists. As a way to hold the Lawyers' Committee to its commitment, and to generate coordinated legal assistance for civil rights activists,

Pemberton organized a coalition of civil rights groups under the banner of the Lawyers Constitutional Defense Committee (LCDC). LCDC included the Lawyers' Committee, the guild, ACLU, and LDF. LCDC also recruited northern attorneys who rotated through several offices in the South providing legal assistance to civil rights workers.[11]

This legal coalition was not without its tensions. Conflict between member organizations of the coalition revolved around perceived differences in political affiliation. The tension was generated largely by Jack Greenberg's response to the participation of the guild in the coalition and anticommunist sentiment. Jack Greenberg, then director of LDF, which both supported local southern attorneys directly and participated with LCDC, refused to participate with guild attorneys since the guild had been accused of being a "communist front" during the 1950s by then US attorney general Brownell.[12]

Greenberg's position created conflict within LCDC and to some extent among civil rights groups. Ultimately, Greenberg withdrew from the LCDC board to protest LCDC's work with guild attorneys. Although Greenberg threatened to withhold legal assistance to SNCC if it accepted assistance from the guild, SNCC maintained its policy of accepting assistance from all legal organizations.[13] Regardless of the political tensions, a core group of committed attorneys provided critical support to the civil rights movement. They needed reinforcements and turned to law schools to recruit law students to assist with the volumes of legal work.

As civil rights struggles received increasing publicity in the North and as northern and southern law schools admitted more students who had been involved with the civil rights movement, law students became more aware of the need not only for legal assistance in the South but also for a model of lawyering that focused on social justice. Law students were already developing a social consciousness and interest in being active in the civil rights movement as legal workers and were drawn to opportunities to work with civil rights attorneys and to participate in real legal work.

By the 1960s, law schools and legal education were facing major critiques from law students influenced by the civil rights movement and college-based student movements. Criticisms of legal education had surfaced during the Depression, when social circumstances highlighted the need for representation and protection of individuals who lacked money and had no access to the legal system. Law school curricula did not emphasize the importance of equal access to the legal system, nor were there any courses offered that focused on the representation of poor people. Representing the poor was not considered a viable career option. The few attempts to reform law school curricula to train law students to represent marginalized communities were largely unsuccessful until the 1960s.

Although a few law schools had incorporated clinical legal education as early as 1893, the clinical legal education movement started to pick up steam in the early twentieth century with the development of a few clinics, largely legal aid offices at law schools during the 1920s and 1930s. As a result of growing student demands for relevance as well as a growing critique of legal education, new clinic programs and poverty law courses were incorporated into the curricula of an increasing number of law schools.[14] In 1960, there were 15 such clinics supervised by law faculty that assisted the poor.[15] Law students were ready to respond to the call for legal assistance to the civil rights movement.

The Genesis of LSCRRC: Law Students Respond to Civil Rights Movement

Prior to 1963, law students participated in many ways in the civil rights movement. Some law students had participated in the Freedom Rides of the early '60s and came to law school because of these experiences. Others, such as Marian Wright Edelman, one of LSCRRC's founders, had already gone south to work on civil rights cases. Many students in law school in the '60s who did go south while still in school had been south during their college years.[16]

During the 1962–63 school year, attorneys working with civil rights activists such as Bill Higgs toured northern law schools encouraging law students to become involved. Higgs, an attorney from Mississippi, was one of a handful of white attorneys committed to providing representation to the black community and civil rights activists. To facilitate the work of the few attorneys in Mississippi who were doing similar work, Higgs recruited law students from Yale, Harvard, NYU, and Columbia to come south during the summer of 1963. At Columbia University Law School, second-year law students Steve Antler and Bill Kopit signed up after hearing Higgs speak. They were instructed to report to Medgar Evers, then head of the NAACP in Jackson, Mississippi, for assignments.[17]

At Yale Law School, Marian Wright Edelman, then a third-year law student, arranged for Higgs to visit Yale and to encourage law students to go down south the following summer. On the West Coast, Ann Fagan Ginger, a San Francisco–based attorney active with the National Lawyers Guild, had begun recruiting law students to work with black attorneys C. B. King in Albany, Georgia, and Chuck Connelly in Birmingham, Alabama. Dennis Roberts, then a second-year law student at Boalt Hall [UC Berkeley School of Law] and currently in private practice in Oakland, California, was recruited by Ginger to work with C. B. King.[18]

As law students geared up to go south during the summer of 1963, racist violence continued throughout the South. On the night of June 11, 1963, Mississippi's NAACP leader, Medgar Evers, was shot in front of his home in Jackson, Mississippi. That same evening, the first organized group of law students from the North arrived in Jackson and in other cities throughout the South to aid the few attorneys representing civil rights activists and communities victimized by the widespread violence. Not only had Evers been assassinated, but also Higgs had been run out of state.[19] These law students were committed to their work and persisted in finding ways to participate in the civil rights struggles going on that summer.

Steve Antler, law student at Columbia at the time, noted that as he was unable to arrange working for the three African American attorneys in Jackson, Mississippi, and SNCC did not want white workers at all, he spent the summer running a youth workshop in Jackson. Two NYU students recruited by Higgs to work in Mississippi—Elizabeth Holtzman, former Kings County district attorney and currently in private practice, and Frank Parker, a professor of law at the DC College of Law before his death in 1997, made their way to C. B. King's office in Albany, Georgia. For many of these students, their experiences during the summer of 1963 propelled them to develop plans for an organizational response to the need for law student support. For some law students, it was a transformative summer experience.

By the end of that summer, Roberts, Holtzman, Antler, and Slater as well as other law students who had worked in the South, including Marian Wright Edelman and Eleanor Holmes Norton, had begun to form a loose network. In his interview, Steve Antler stated that he and other Columbia Law School students met the Yale Law School students when the former were thrown out of the house they were renting in Jackson, Mississippi, and moved in with the latter. They kept in touch with one another during the school year as well as with other students who had been working on civil rights issues in the North.

Slater remarked that plans for the council were developed during the bus ride to the historic 1963 March on Washington, organized to call attention to the right of African Americans to political and economic equality. This "nice little Jewish boy from Brooklyn who had no connection to anything until I heard Bill Higgs speak" was drafted by his colleagues to quit Yale Law School for a year and to direct a new organization that would facilitate the participation of law students in the civil rights struggle. By the time Slater arrived in New York City that fall, Marian Wright Edelman and Tom Gilhooly had arranged for office space at the ACLU building. Edelman gave Slater several names of people who might help him raise funds, and, with the help of the networks established in the South among law students, the Law Students Civil Rights Research Council was established.

Startup funds for the organization were easily raised as many foundations in 1963 and 1964 had civil rights high on their lists of funding priorities. Supporters included the LDF and ACLU, as well as the Stern Family Fund, the Marshall Field Foundation, the Taconic Fund, and the New World Foundation.[20]

The contradictions inherent in fundraising for civil rights issues, particularly from foundations and corporations whose policies and actions did not align with civil rights goals, did not go unnoticed. John Brittain, a board member from 1967 to 1968, assisted with fundraising. His reflections evidence this understanding:

> My first impression is money was flowing like water out of a spigot . . . and it took me a long time before [I] asked where'd this money come from? The wealth of the privileged class and their exploitation within the capitalist and indeed the worldwide imperialist structure [made] this guilt money . . . so they carve off a little chunk of the revenue . . . to give to good, worthy things . . . during those days it was the contradiction.

There is no evidence, however, that LSCRRC ever turned down any money offered by any source. As a nonprofit, LSCRRC was able to raise money from a wide range of elite sources as well as governmental and other sources.[21] Many foundation grants, particularly in the late '70s and '80s, were earmarked for specific purposes.[22] To raise unrestricted funds, LSCRRC solicited matching funds from placement sites, conducted direct mail campaigns, and held other fundraisers.[23]

The civil rights legal community was enthusiastic about this new organization and assisted the new group in critical ways. Civil rights attorneys hoped that more law students could be recruited to work on the increasing number of cases generated by the civil rights movement. Jeremiah Gutman, a white LCDC–cooperating attorney and LSCRRC's counsel in the 1970s, had "heard general conversations in the ACLU circles [to the effect] that we had to do something" to get law students involved. Gutman states that he was aware of LSCRRC as a new organization when Father Robert Drinan and Henry Schwarzschild, ACLU legal director, asked him to assist LSCRRC founders with ideas about fundraising, space for the organization, and assistance in connecting students with civil rights attorneys in the South.

Jack Greenberg provided the council with startup funds from LDF, introduced its leaders to foundations, and obtained grants from the Stern and Taconic foundations to hire law students to work in cooperating southern lawyers' offices as part of LSCRRC's summer internship program. Shirley Fingerhood, an Inc. Fund staff attorney at the time and currently in private practice, was paid a minimal sum to serve as counsel for the new organization.[24]

Kent Spriggs remembers the first official organizational meeting of the LSCRRC founders, held after the summer of 1963:

> It was ordained that there was going to be a meeting at the ACLU of law students who wanted . . . to create some kind of group . . . in which law students could use whatever skills we had to assist the civil rights movement. . . . Howie [Slater] . . . says I'm willing to blow off Yale Law School for a year which was unthinkable in those days.

Although this meeting was held in New York City and attracted only local law students, these students were committed to developing an organization with a national presence engaging law students from around the country. In the fall of 1963, LSCRRC founders organized a national conference at Columbia Law School for law students interested in civil rights issues. At this conference, an organizational structure was developed that included law school–based chapters from around the country.

The founders and early LSCRRC members ranged from experienced activists to young people energized for the first time by the opportunity to participate in the major social transformations taking place as a result of civil rights activities in the South. As the focus of a national, organized network and newly developing law student movement, LSCRRC fostered a community of support that sustained and nurtured these law students who were committed to social justice. The founders developed goals for the organization that embodied this energy.

LSCRRC founders' experience in the South influenced the goals they set for the organization. Goals were guided by founders' desires to create an organization that would (1) serve as a catalyst for new models of lawyering; (2) encourage and train law students for civil rights careers; (3) provide needed support to the civil rights movement; and (4) encourage a more relevant, socially conscious culture at law schools. Initially, LSCRRC focused on providing law student assistance to civil rights attorneys in the South.

The reality of law practice in the South contradicted the image of the profession projected by law schools and generated cynicism among these law students.[25] Law students were angry at the reluctance of the legal profession to support equal access to legal assistance for marginalized communities. These law students observed the overt hostility of southern attorneys and judges to civil rights activists and their supporters. Not surprisingly, these observations added to the students' perceptions of the profession. Law students looked for models of lawyering that would prioritize social justice. According to Slater, the vision founders had for LSCRRC was to "[accelerate] the process of people in law school focusing on the possibility that they would make a difference." He discussed how with the election of Robert Kennedy in 1960, there was new energy among law students and that lawyers could be instruments for social change:

> Richie Granat and Phil Hershkop, they both had that same vision, far more than the rest of us. . . . They looked at it as part of a movement. . . . We're gonna change the legal profession by having more people whose hearts are in the right place.

By providing new models of lawyering through matching law students with civil rights attorneys in the South, founders hoped to influence the legal profession to prioritize social justice values in practice.

A second organizational goal, to encourage and train law students to pursue civil rights careers, was to be accomplished by expanding opportunities to work with civil rights attorneys who would model not only realities of lawyering but also career pathways. Their exposure demonstrated an immediate need for civil rights attorneys in the South, and their vision expanded to promote civil rights legal careers throughout the country. Steve Antler noted:

> We went to the south and it really affected us and we [want] other people affected in the same way . . . that was one of the initial . . . purposes of setting up this program.

LSCRRC's primary aim when it was founded was to develop students into lawyers with an interest in public service and to get law students involved in the movement. . . . All the political wrangling was secondary.[26]

Through the summer internship program, LSCRRC founders hoped to encourage law students to pursue civil rights careers by exposing them to the realities of the civil rights struggles and showing them how lawyering could be part of a broader movement for social change.

LSCRRC's third goal, and arguably the most important at the time, to provide needed support to the civil rights movement, was to be accomplished largely through the summer internship program. Organizers would identify attorneys and organizations that needed law student assistance and would then place law students in these offices for the summer. Other LSCRRC programs developed to provide ongoing assistance to civil rights attorneys throughout the school year.

Fourth, LSCRRC founders wanted the organization to participate in reforming law school curricula and promote diversity in law school student and faculty composition through chapter projects and national organizing efforts. Projects such as development of scholarships for African American law students in the South were intended to increase the number of African Americans in the profession.[27]

By 1983 when I arrived at LSCRRC, it was a vibrant organization that continued to provide a substantial number of internships around the country, despite fluctuations in availability of funds. Over 3,000 law students had participated in the summer internship program, chapter activities, and other projects. It was clear to me that LSCRRC had created a bridge between the legal profession, law schools, and the civil rights movement in ways that facilitated new approaches to legal education and the profession. The difference was that law schools and law students were developing their own internship programs (both local and national) that began to account for the slowly decreasing availability of funds, placement sites, and student applicants. Despite these pressures, we were able to keep the summer internship program and several projects functioning until 1987. The longevity of the organization (1963–87) was due in part to its continued relevance to law students facilitated by the organizational structure.

LSCRRC was set up as a 501(c) 3 tax-exempt nonprofit corporation, with a board of directors composed of one member from each law school chapter. Board members generally served terms of 13 months maximum.

One of the board's priorities was to encourage the development of chapters across the country. They traveled to law schools across the country, meeting with students and encouraging them to set up local chapters. LSCRRC became national in scope almost immediately. In the fall of 1963 about fifty law schools had active law student chapters, and the numbers continued to grow. These chapters attempted to influence the direction of law school education and recruited summer interns.

Law school chapters, maximum terms for board members, and rotating leadership of the national organization accounted for LSCRRC's relevance to law students. Rotating leadership was also intended to ensure diversity on the board and in the national office. The national directors could serve a maximum of one year, and then would be replaced by a newly graduated law student. LSCRRC's fifth director, D'Army Bailey, reflected the founders' reasoning behind rotating leadership:

> (It) kept the director more in tune with the law student community, because he was just out of law school, and he became less of . . . a detached organization man. . . . [We were concerned that] we would become so ensconced in our position and begin to develop such a sense of power and authority that we would move away from the goals. . . . I saw it less as a safeguard against the negative, than as a reinforcement of the positive, the connection to the more recent experience of the law school environment.

Though rotating leadership ensured LSCRRC's relevance, it did not provide a solid foundation for the organization. As Wulf indicated in his 1977 evaluation of LSCRRC, the data he collected suggested that "LSCRRC's fortunes would be served by professionalization and continuity of staff." In particular, Wulf pointed to uneven administration of the summer internship program and fundraising as a result of the inexperience of the law graduate directors who turned over so regularly. Yet Wulf concluded that the policy of hiring law graduates for short terms was "an invaluable policy," which he believed accounted for "LSCRRC's effectiveness, its longevity and its singularity of principle across a decade and a half."

Although the limited terms were intended to guarantee diverse leadership and membership, this policy was initially not enough to attain that goal. Though the original group of law students who developed the idea of LSCRRC included women and people of color, most notably Eleanor Holmes Norton, Marian Wright Edelman, and Elizabeth Holtzman, the founders' group were largely white, middle-class, male, and northern law students who in 1963 came face to face with the realities of institutional racism.

The composition of early LSCRRC leadership in part reflected law school enrollments. In 1963, approximately 0.4 percent of the total enrollment in ABA-accredited law schools were women. By the 1969–70 academic year, women accounted for 6.89 percent of the total enrollment in ABA-accredited law schools. During that same year, 4.3 percent of the total enrollment in ABA-accredited law schools were students of color. In contrast, by the 1985–86 academic year, the percentage of minority enrollment had increased to 10.4 percent while the percentage of women enrolled had increased to approximately 38 percent.[28]

LSCRRC directors recognized that they had to remain conscious of the composition of the organization and make special efforts to reach out to law students of color. Interviews with participants who were executive committee and board members in the 1960s revealed consciousness of the problem. Projects were developed to raise money to provide students of color with scholarships so that they could afford to participate in the summer program.

Haywood Burns remarked:

> My recollection [is that] it was not seen as a white organization. though it was overwhelmingly white. It was seen as an integrated organization, as a progressive organization. There were black people and people of color who were interested and active in it. . . . I wasn't the lone person. . . . LSCRRC was a very positive influence . . . because it was a place where people with similar values and similar politics could get together on nonracial lines, enjoy one another and also plan for a better future. . . . It was the . . . only game in town for the law school.

John Brittain agreed that LSCRRC was the only game in town, though he was very conscious of the homogeneity of the board of directors regarding both race and class. Brittain talked about efforts to include law students, particularly black law students, from law schools other than the Ivy League law schools:

> The first time in the history of American legal education that law students of color were . . . admitted into American law schools . . . there was literally no inclusion in the student-ABA organization. . . .

> LSCRRC was a place where white and black students could work around the common denominator of still fighting racial segregation in the South.... I can recall saying: when are we going to bring some brothers and sisters up from the South, or even from Howard. LSCRRC ... was heavy Ivy at the time, Harvard, Yale, Columbia, NYU ... I got on [the board] because of my exposure during the Mississippi poll watching and ... then later [as part of] an effort to bring Howard more into the fold with its larger [pool of] black [law students].

Implicit in Brittain's comments is the sense of elitism that may have permeated LSCRRC in the early years. The majority of founders and early participants were from Ivy League schools, largely in the Northeast.

LSCRRC leadership recognized that economic barriers existed particularly for many people of color who wanted to go to law school and participate in council programs. LSCRRC executive committee minutes dated April 3, 1965, reflected this understanding as members voted to continue providing scholarships to African American law students. The minutes reflect concerns that there was a "danger of having the council's summer activity open only to those who were independently wealthy." Directors also recognized that increasing diversity in the internship pool would require attention to economic barriers to participation.

In addition to increasing the numbers of students of color in the summer internship program, LSCRRC organizers recognized the need to increase the number of African American students in law schools and developed a recruitment and retention program to meet that goal. This program was funded by the Carnegie Foundation for several years and provided scholarships and mentoring support to African American law students throughout the South,

Although LSCRRC organizers were conscious of race and class issues, several male interviewees did not remember a gender consciousness, particularly in the early years.

William Robinson noted that though race consciousness was very much a part of the early LSCRRC experience, gender consciousness wasn't explicitly addressed, though his experience was of an organization that did involve women:

> There wasn't much discussion about gender balance, but there was a sensitivity and a care to make sure that women law students were in-

cluded in the various programs that LSCRRC had.... [I]t was always an organization that was interracial ... though it took a while before Ivy Davis became the first woman director. That could have happened much earlier. So, if Eleanor had been interested, she would have been picked. If Elizabeth Holtzman had been interested, she would have been picked.... There was no focus on discrimination against women. That just wasn't part of the dialogue ... and while I don't recall a lot of gross insensitivity ... the women's liberation movement was in its very early conceptual stages at the time.

William Robinson was the first African American director and assumed that position in 1966. Ivy Davis, the first African American woman director, was not elected to the position until 1970. Out of a total of 18 directors over its 24-year history, six were women and eight were people of color. Out of the six women, four were African American. With one exception, all the women elected as directors served during the last 12 years of LSCRRC's existence, from 1974 to 1986.

It is likely that the representation of women and people of color in leadership positions might have been even more infrequent without the policy of rotating leadership. There was, at the very least, an opportunity for new people to come on to the board or into other leadership positions every year until 1980. At this point, board and director tenure was extended to two years and regional representation replaced individual law school chapter representation on the board. The emphasis on inclusion of all students in law schools and the profession underscored the programs the council developed over the years.

Summer Internship Program

LSCRRC's largest and most widely known national program was the summer internship program, which placed close to 5,000 law students in civil rights internships throughout the United States over its 24-year history. The summer internship program was perhaps the most successful of LSCRRC's programs in supporting its goal of aiding the civil rights movement.[29] The support of foundations, the civil rights legal community, and some law school administrations made it possible for the council to quickly pull together its first summer internship program to coincide with Mississippi Freedom Summer 1964. Placement sites were developed through the contacts law student founders had made when they were down south in the summer of 1963. Contacts were also developed through ACLU and LDF attorneys who provided advice and support to the new organization. The council was a "well connected" organization that provided support to a wide range of civil rights organizations in the South. From the beginning, law students wanted LSCRRC to provide support for civil rights activities throughout the United States.

Although civil rights violations in the South were the impetus for founding the organization, participants understood the critical need for representation in the North. Many of the law students who went south witnessed extreme poverty and returned north with a deeper understanding of the connection between the welfare rights movement as part of the larger struggle for civil rights. The executive committee of LSCRRC's board of directors was interested in funding a northern summer project but stated that:

> Such a program would most likely be on a part-time basis since it was felt that most of the funds collected should go toward the southern summer project. There were two basic approaches suggested for a northern program. These would be to maintain, first, research teams to assist southern lawyers and, second, a full-time clerking program for working with northern lawyers engaged in civil rights work.[30]

Alan Houseman, a 1966 intern and LSCRRC assistant director from 1966 to 1967, remembered the decision that "we had to remain neutral in terms of the skirmishes between various groups and that our job was to get anybody doing effective work down there." Houseman recalled getting a matching grant from VISTA and the American Association of Law Schools to run a summer internship program in Cleveland and the ensuing debate concerning the use of the money:

> Why weren't we putting some [of the money] in the South, because we were putting all the other interns in the South.... [E]ssentially ... it was a poverty [versus] civil rights type of debate.

The discussion on the board was one of priorities; how should limited resources be expended, in the North or in the South. How resources were allocated would indicate the position the council took on what "civil rights" meant. The debate centered on defining "civil rights" narrowly to refer only to the southern experience or to include economic justice issues throughout the country. These discussions led to decisions to expand the summer internship program in the North and out West. The first summer internship program in 1964 funded 115 students around the country in civil rights and related internship positions.

Early organizers were also conscious of race, class, and gender concerns as they developed placements for the summer internship program. In addition to identifying economic justice issues as part of the civil rights movement, organizers' understanding of "race" was more inclusive than traditional formulations. To the general public in the 1960s, "the race problem" referred to tensions between African American and white communities. Although LSCRRC participants acknowledged this understanding of the civil rights movement, the summer internship program, as well as other LSCRRC projects, reflected a much broader understanding of who the movement should serve. William Robinson's comments about race consciousness in the council in the early '60s demonstrate this approach:

> There was ... a sensitivity that this was a racially oriented organization.... [T]he civil rights movement was related to the struggle to end racial segregation ... the system of racial separation in our country was every bit as thorough [as] apartheid.... Later, there was also ... a focus on poverty (which) was viewed as an outgrowth of the concern with racial discrimination.... To be sure there were some concerns about hunger that spilled over into a concern about what was happening on Indian reservations. But the basic hunger study again was focused on Blacks in the South. The report done by the ... medical community ... focused on health needs of Blacks, and malnutrition among Blacks in the Deep South ... there was no significant discussion at all [about] discrimination against Latinos.

In addition to the southern offices, placements were developed to aid other communities with limited access to the legal system. For example, Alan Lerner reported that during his tenure as director from 1965 to 1966, through contacts with organizations addressing Native American issues, summer placements were developed on reservations in North Dakota, South Dakota, Arizona, and New Mexico.

By 1965, the federal Office of Economic Opportunity (OEO) began to fund a new kind of neighborhood legal service program modeled after the Mobilization for Youth (MFY) Legal services office in New York City.[31] LSCRRC-sponsored projects in the North included internships at these new neighborhood legal services programs funded by the OEO.

In a letter calling for student applicants for the 1965 summer internship program, students who participated in the South during the 1964 summer were encouraged to work in these northern offices in 1965.

In later years, as the gay/lesbian/bisexual movement and disability rights movement gained prominence (1970s–1980s), these categories of difference also became important to LSCRRC participants as they reshaped the internship program each summer and developed other programs throughout the school years. Wilhelm Joseph describes the breadth of LSCRRC's commitment in the 1970s:

> We did more than race and class. We'd taken [on] all issues of the day . . . our organizations were about the broadest concept of race. . . . [W]e went out to recruit Native Americans. We went out to recruit Latinos. We went out to recruit Asian Americans . . . we had to sit down and discuss recruiting Native Americans and discuss that it's a priority . . . the conference wasn't held in Albuquerque just because it had hot springs! It was a particular move to say to the Native American law students and the Latinos in the Southwest, but particularly the Native Americans. Use us. We're here. We're not just in New York. We're here in your home base.

Joseph's comments reflect LSCRRC's ongoing commitment to include all voices in its programming and development of policies.

From the beginning, the scope of the summer internship program was very broad. Organizations involved in diverse civil rights activities became placement sites for LSCRRC's summer interns. Through law school chapters, projects addressing local concerns were developed. Just prior to and during my tenure as LSCRRC program director (1983–86), national fundraising became more difficult and we assisted board members and law school chapters in developing internship placements that were often funded with money raised from regional rather than national foundations. Throughout its history, law student applications to the summer internship program far exceeded the number of positions LSCRRC could fund.

Law students applied for internships for a variety of reasons. Some law students had been involved in activist work before law school and wanted to continue that work. Others had had no prior personal connection to the civil rights movement but were moved by the drama and urgency of the historical moment to participate. Others were attracted to the opportunity for an adventure.

Many interviewees had applied to the council because they had some sensitivity to the importance of civil rights issues at the time. D'Army Bailey, the council's second African American national director (1968–69), commented that "LSCRRC applicants had to have some degree of idealism, because the salary was no attraction." At that time, interns received $30 a week and free housing during the course of the internship. African American interns received an additional scholarship that increased the weekly stipend to $60.[32]

Many early LSCRRC participants had already been doing activist work and were looking for a way to continue doing that work in law school. Carol Ruth Silver had participated in the Freedom Rides in the early 1960s and had already been jailed for her activities before going to law school:

> LSCRRC gave me a national organizational umbrella in which to do the kind of student organizing that I possibly would have done myself anyway. That is, to organize people at a time of crisis in the South, at a time when I knew lots of people in the South were in need of this kind of help. LSCRRC gave a name to the organizing of those people, law students and lawyers, to help people in the South.

Amanda Hawes decided to go to law school because of the LSCRRC interns she met in Mississippi when she went down as a college volunteer. As an undergraduate at Wellesley and a volunteer at the NAACP office in Boston, Hawes went to Mississippi and documented violations of the public accommodations section of the 1964 Civil Rights Act. Hawes remembered that what impressed her about the two women law students she worked with were the skills they had because of their training that made them "more effective servant[s] of peoples' struggles . . . and that's what I want[ed] to do."

Luke Hiken knew that he wanted to work with C. B. King in Albany, Georgia, as an intern in 1965. He applied to LSCRRC to secure money for that work.

William Robinson, a 1964 LSCRRC intern, talked about how it was impossible not to be affected in some way by what was going on during those years:

> Civil rights issues were being hotly discussed and debated, certainly in all the Ivy League law schools. . . . Civil rights was *the* most gripping issue *in the country* . . . you would have had to put a sack over

your head to avoid those issues, both as emotional issues and social issues, as intellectual issues, whether you were on a campus or not . . . that summer, while it was indeed the experience I had that gave me firsthand knowledge, it was the experience that gave me my first direct involvement, it was not in my mind a linchpin. . . . It was a part of a . . . continuing set of experiences, processing the information that was coming at you from a lot of different directions.

Others who had had no prior connection to the civil rights movement were inspired by law school speakers, by the experiences of friends who had already been south, and by what they had heard in the news about events in the South. Howard Slater was among the group of participants who heard Bill Higgs speak at their law school and was inspired to participate. Dennis Roberts reported that at least one student who heard him speak about his experiences working with C. B. King in Albany, Georgia, was moved not only to tears but also to participate in LSCRRC's first summer internship program as an intern with C. B. King in the 1964 program. Lorenzo Eric Chambliss was also drawn to participate in the civil rights movement at the same time that he was interested in having an exciting summer. Chambliss participated in the 1964 and 1965 internship programs. He was moved by what was happening in the South, but also wanted the opportunity for an exciting summer:

> I believed in the movement in civil rights and integration. . . . I'd never been out picketing or doing anything. . . . And this was, in one way safe and in another way it wasn't. . . . I wasn't doing anything in my own backyard . . . I was clear across the country . . . I hadn't traveled at all in my life, . . . I wanted the adventure of it too . . . I looked at it as the ancillary to the main civil rights movement . . . [and it was] . . . an amazing period of time.

Those who had internships in the 1970s and 1980s had similar reasons for applying to LSCRRC's summer internship program. Some developed their own projects and applied to the program for funding for these specific proposals.[33] Jerome Paun, a white 1977 intern, developed a proposal for a prisoners' rights project with two other students and presented that to the council for funding. Once assured that the students would be supervised through Prisoners Legal Services of New York, the council funded the project:

[LSCRRC] was a place where you could get money to do some progressive civil rights legal work. It was not perceived as a place at least by me . . . that was going to provide us with particular guidance or leadership or help us to define some politically progressive civil rights–oriented project.

Marlene Archer, a 1979 and 1980 intern and the second African American woman to direct LSCRRC (1981–84), knew of the council even before attending law school:

I'd heard of LSCRRC before I got to law school, and my first year in law school I was extremely hot to get a LSCRRC intern[ship] . . . it was one of those things that had a history . . . it was a big deal and a big honor . . . more importantly, they were doing really good work.

As Chambliss indicated, in the 1960s, the summer internship program was an ideal mechanism for drawing law students into the civil rights movement, particularly those who had not previously been active in social justice issues. For Robinson, Hawes, and Silver, the internship program was a way for them to continue their civil rights activities as legal assistants. Even though in later years, the council was perceived by some as simply a funding source, others identified the council as part of a larger movement. Law students recognized the unique opportunity the council provided for participation in the civil rights work through its summer internship program.

Other Programmatic Work

In addition to the summer internship program, the council sponsored other programs and projects that similarly gave law students opportunities to participate in the legal arm of the civil rights and other social movements. For several years, LSCRRC sponsored school-year research projects, matching law students with civil rights attorneys who needed research assistance. LSCRRC also sponsored a postgraduate program early on that placed newly graduated law students in legal services offices around the country.

During my tenure at LSCRRC, we sponsored a voting rights project in Mississippi, participation in the first American Indian law symposium co-sponsored by the American Indian Law Alliance, a high school speakers program, and various other projects and initiatives.

Conclusion

The council was intended to be a vehicle for law students to engage with the legal arm of the civil rights movement of the '60s. Until its demise in 1987, the council functioned as a civil rights organization, encouraging law students to work on traditional civil rights projects (e.g., voting rights projects). During the 1970s and 1980s, the council also expanded its programs in response to the legal needs of other social movements. In the 1970s, LSCRRC annual reports indicate an increase in summer internship placements in women's rights organizations and environmental groups. In the late 1970s and early 1980s, LSCRRC annual reports indicate a growing number of projects and summer internship placements in gay and lesbian rights projects.

Throughout its history, LSCRRC was arguably the only multiracial, law student–directed national law student organization dedicated to racial, gender, and economic equality. The network of LSCRRC law school chapters and interns initiated a wide range of activities from assistance to the Mississippi Freedom Democratic Party to development of some of the first legal services offices in the country. Over its 24-year history, LSCRRC provided close to 5,000 law students with their first legal experiences as part of the LSCRRC summer internship program and other projects. For some of us, interns and directors, the experience was life-changing. For others, it was simply the next logical step in their evolution as civil rights activists and lawyers. In the end, LSCRRC was one of the forces that shaped a generation of lawyers whose consciousness was raised to the needs of marginalized communities.

A Transformative Internship with Attorney C. B. King

David Rudovsky

The modern civil rights movement had multiple foundations, but two epochal events, the Montgomery bus boycott and the US Supreme Court decision in *Brown v. Board of Education*, are often referenced as the key mutually reinforcing community protest and legal interventions that sparked the civil rights movement. The combination of mass protests and legal intervention eventually ended the 100 years of post–Civil War state-mandated segregation and many—but not all—aspects of Jim Crow racism.

The 1956 Montgomery bus boycott was one of many actions of political and community resistance to racist laws and practices and was the fountainhead for the thousands of demonstrations and protests over the next two decades. The Freedom Rides of the early 1960s revealed both the intensity of the resistance to integration of basic means of transportation and the violence that would be inflicted on those who challenged the status quo. Ultimately, notwithstanding the failure of the national government to fully protect those exercising basic constitutional rights to protest, the sit-ins, civil disobedience, and the compelling moral narrative of racial equality changed the very fabric of our society.

On the legal side, *Brown v. Board of Education* made clear that all mandatory segregation laws relating to governmental operations were unconstitutional and the decision was a significant complement to the political and social struggles being carried out on the streets of the Old Confederacy. Ultimately, after the 1963 March on Washington and the historic speeches of John Lewis and Martin Luther King Jr., the moral force of the movement forced Congress to enact civil rights statutes, including the Voting Rights Act and Title VII prohibiting discrimination in employment. Favorable legal rulings and progressive legislation were not self-enforcing, and continued protests and activism were needed to make these gains a reality.

Much has been written about the political and community efforts that were at the core of the civil rights movement and the organizations and leaders that led the fight for full civil rights and the end of Jim Crow. There have also been insightful histories and critiques of the legal strategies, and in particular the role played by legal organizations, including the NAACP Legal Defense and Education Fund, National Lawyers Guild, ACLU, Emergency Civil Liberties Committee, Lawyers Constitutional Defense Committee, and Lawyers Committee for Civil Rights. This article focuses in part on another important manifestation of the legal attack on racial injustice in the 1960s and 1970s—the support provided by thousands of law students who volunteered to work with civil rights lawyers under the auspices of the Law Students Civil Rights Research Council (LSCRRC). At a time when the political left in the United States was energized by the civil rights and the anti–Vietnam War movements, and found strong support among younger activists, law students joined the struggles in modest numbers but with increasing effectiveness.

The legal arm of the movement developed sophisticated strategies and tactics, litigated key test cases, and provided representation to thousands of protesters and activists who had been subjected to assaults, prosecution, and intimidation. Many of these lawyers worked with the constant risk of serious retribution. They represented the best ideals of a new generation of activists, and they built a model of legal practice and client representation that became a blueprint for later generations of civil rights, civil liberties, criminal defense, legal services, and public interest lawyers. The stories of these lawyers and those who worked with them deserve to be told, not only to chronicle their efforts and accomplishments but also to document their impact on legal institutions and the legal profession. They created new forms of lawyering and new ways of supporting and defending progressive movements. They inspired, and continue to inspire, new generations of progressive lawyers.

Nevertheless, it is important to note that there was no single legal strategy and no single political and community approach to liberation for African Americans. Indeed, on the legal side, there were internal conflicts regarding litigation strategies, political and social policy, and the relationship of lawyers to civil rights organizations. For some legal organizations, support was in the form of appellate advocacy and amicus briefs filed in the Supreme Court in significant civil rights cases. But for others, including the National Lawyers Guild and LSCRRC, there was direct "on the ground" support. They engaged lawyers and law students in the difficult work of local representation in criminal prosecutions of civil rights workers and in the litigation of affirmative civil rights actions against government officials enforcing Jim Crow justice.

At the very core of the debate were the same conflicts over basic strategy that surface in many large-scale social movements: is the goal incremental legal and legislative change or a radical restructuring of social and political institutions? Not surprisingly, these conflicts have surfaced again in the current era in debates about policing, mass incarceration, and other criminal justice issues, where the abolitionists articulate a more radical change of institutions and reformers argue for more pragmatic progressive reforms. Further, some of these conflicts spilled over to issues of legal representation; at one point, the Legal Defense and Education Fund stated that it would not be part of the Mississippi Freedom project if SNCC was represented by the National Lawyers Guild.

The guild was founded in the 1930s as an alternative to the then archly conservative and racially segregated American Bar Association. Guild lawyers defended New Deal legislation and over the years represented radical labor activists. However, during the post–World War II "Red Scare" and Senator McCarthy's reckless attacks on government officials he labeled as communists, J. Edgar Hoover asserted that the guild was the legal arm of the Communist Party and placed the guild on the attorney general's list of subversive organizations. The guild did not recover from that attack until the "New Left" movement of the 1960s and its focus on civil rights and racial equality.

As noted, one of the legal organizations that provided resources to the civil rights movement was LSCRRC, founded in 1963. One of the founders, Kent Spriggs, has chronicled the lives and civil rights work of lawyers and law students in his book, *Voices of Civil Rights Lawyers*. The narratives document the difficulties in practicing law in an openly hostile environment. The stories also provide insight into the creative legal strategies that were developed to further the equality movement. For these lawyers, there could be no other place and no other practice of law.[34]

LSCRRC provided stipends for law students working with civil rights lawyers throughout the nation, with most of the placements for lawyers in the Deep South. Over a 15-year period, thousands of law students volunteered with LSCRRC, and many went on to practice in the civil rights and related fields. As an example, Spriggs joined the Rabinowitz & Boudin law firm in New York City, one of the few offices in the country with an explicitly progressive agenda, representing unions, radical dissidents, and the Republic of Cuba. From there, he transitioned to the Lawyers Constitutional Defense Committee in Jackson, Mississippi, and a lifetime career as a civil rights lawyer.

I was one of the many beneficiaries of this political and legal movement. I started at NYU Law School in 1964 with only a vague idea of how I might translate my political and social views into effective advocacy, but I was fortunate to find among my first-year classmates a small cohort of similarly minded students and among the faculty some support for career choices outside of the traditional large-firm corporate world. We soon learned of the work of LSCRRC, the guild, the Mississippi Freedom Summer Project, and the stellar work of the NAACP Legal Defense and Education Fund, ACLU, Emergency Civil Liberties Committee, Lawyers Constitutional Defense Committee, and the Lawyers Committee for Civil Rights. At the core of each of these national legal movements were the highly courageous black lawyers in the South who had staked their lives and careers on fighting for racial justice, including C. B. King, a remarkable civil rights attorney in Albany, Georgia.

Attorney King was the only black lawyer in southwest Georgia whose practice was devoted to representation of those active in the civil rights movement. In 1963, Dennis Roberts, then a student at Berkeley Law School, interned for King and returned to the C. B. King firm for several years after law school. Their collaboration was quite successful and led to many years of King's mentoring of law students and young lawyers in the continuing legal struggle for equality. King's legal skills, tenacity, and courage in the face of repeated physical attacks and other forms of intimidation by the white power structure are legendary. He represented thousands of protesters, brought class action cases that helped to dismantle segregation in southwest Georgia, and equally important, created a legal practice that inspired and served as a model for many of us who worked for him and others who decided to practice in the civil rights arena.

The LSCRRC placements with C. B. King in the summer of 1965 were representative of several thousand law students who worked that summer and for over an additional decade for progressive lawyers around the country. With me in Albany were Drew Days, who later was solicitor general of the United States in the Clinton administration; Furman Templeton, an outstanding advocate who with just two years of law school training had the skills of an experienced lawyer; Stan Zaks, a community organizer and law student from San Francisco, who worked on both legal and organizing efforts with SNCC and who later practiced civil rights law on the West Coast; Ken Cloke, also from the Bay Area, and a committed civil rights advocate.

We assisted King and Roberts in a range of civil rights and criminal defense cases that arose from the mass protests organized by SNCC and other activists. The experience was transformative. We observed the sheer courage and persistence of those protesting racial injustice, the brilliance of King's legal advocacy, and his absolute commitment to protecting those involved in the movement. In a world that was starkly one of right and wrong, we also understood the utter corruption of the police, the local courts, and the economic power structure. And that short-term experience had an enormous impact on our professional lives and our understanding of the ravages of inequality in America.

One event captured the essence of civil rights lawyering in the South in 1965. That summer SNCC started to organize civil rights protests in Baker

County, likely the most repressive and terrifying area in all of Georgia. Baker County was the location of the infamous shooting death of a black resident by the county sheriff that led to the troubling decision by the US Supreme Court in *Screws v. United States* that imposed a "specific intent" element in federal civil rights criminal prosecutions. Not only did the prosecution have to prove all elements of the criminal offenses but had to show that the conduct was expressly motivated by an intent to deprive the victim of her constitutional rights. In Baker County, the Klan was largely in charge, and those who sought change in the status quo did so at enormous personal risk.

SNCC had targeted Baker County only after it was successful in promoting voting rights and access to public accommodations in other areas of Georgia where repression still reigned, but the fears of the community could be overcome by protests and advocacy. Almost immediately, however, SNCC workers in Baker County were arrested on false charges and in the normal course would surely have been convicted and imprisoned. Fortunately, however, a post–Civil War civil rights statute authorized "removal" of state criminal cases to federal court where the state criminal prosecution was racially discriminatory. And since racial bias was at the root of almost all the mass arrests of civil rights workers, lawyers could invoke the "removal" process and local prosecutors had to convince federal judges that the state prosecutions were not tainted by racism for the cases to proceed in state court.

Over a several year period, thousands of prosecutions were thwarted by the simple filing of the removal petition. And thanks to the creativity of Professor Anthony Amsterdam whose scholarship resurrected the removal statute from its demise in the late nineteenth century, civil rights lawyers and law students had a book of forms and legal briefs to expedite the removal process. Ultimately, the US Supreme Court restricted the use of this statute, but for a critical period in the 1960s criminal prosecutions were stalled.

We filed the petitions with the court in Baker County, but King, who well understood the need to provide more than legal support to the protesters, decided to personally serve the removal petitions on the local state court judge to demonstrate to local law enforcement that there would be resistance to their repressive tactics and to signal to the black community a tangible step of solidarity. The "court" in Baker County for these cases was a rural barn, with proceedings scheduled at night, and we knew that the white locals would not be amused by a black lawyer upending their nighttime entertainment. Yet King took the opportunity with each case to lecture the judge in exquisite detail as to the significance of the removal process. He ended with a powerful statement: the court was now "*without jurisdiction to proceed,*" which means he added "you have no power."

The anger of the white crowd was palpable and as the last case was called, there was the need to get out of that county—and quickly. We did so, followed by several cars of angry whites, and made it back to Albany, which by comparison seemed almost civilized. I recall thinking how calm King appeared even as we made our way out of the zone of danger. Of course, appearances can be deceiving and when King, who had a well-known fondness for "soft" ice cream, stopped at a local stand and ordered two very large cones, I could better understand both his fear and his courage. He could have informed the judge by phone of the filing of the removal petitions, but the personal appearance demonstrated that King would be there whenever needed to defend those who risked their lives seeking change in Baker County. For me, it was a nerve-racking, but essential lesson in lawyering.

In 1967, I started my legal career as a public defender in Philadelphia as part of a clinical fellowship program at Penn Law School. I was supervised by Anthony Amsterdam, the "theoretician" behind the removal strategy, and then and now a legal giant in the civil rights and criminal defense world. As in Albany, the defender experience provided important insights into the relationship of criminal defense and civil rights lawyering. Criminal prosecutions were not infrequently marked by unfair and discriminatory actions of police and prosecutors, and changes in the system could not be achieved even with the best criminal defense practices.

In 1971, my colleague at the Defender, David Kairys, who also was a LSCRRC intern during law school, started a civil rights/criminal defense practice in Philadelphia where for the past 50-plus years we and our law partners have engaged in many of the political and social movements that have marked this half century of political, social, racial, and gender conflict in the United States. We have focused primarily on the injustices of the criminal justice system in litigation involving police and prosecutorial misconduct, prisoner rights, exonerations of those wrongfully convicted, and in defense of those who were arrested or otherwise targeted for the exercise of their constitutional rights. For me, the experience with C. B. King has always been a kind of beacon: if in doubt, do what C. B. would have done. Of course, even that process was easier said than done.

The civil rights movement became a model, both for community organizing and legal advocacy for future liberation movements and in the current era, the campaigns to end mass incarceration, provide competent counsel to criminal defendants, and to end the unconstitutional practices long tolerated in the law enforcement community. We owe much to the pioneering work of the first generation of civil rights lawyers who translated their moral and political beliefs into representation of those most in need of legal services. The fact that today so many public defenders, legal service lawyers, civil rights and civil liberties advocates, and other public interest lawyers are able to provide a broad range of legal services largely free of the great risks faced by lawyers only several decades ago is itself a legacy of the civil rights movement.

Finally, there are three special bookends to my time in Albany. First, in 1992, just a few years after the death of C. B. King, his family invited all of those who had worked in his law office during the civil rights movement, as well as the community activists who were the real catalysts for change, to a celebration in Albany for the opening of the newly named C. B. King Federal Courthouse. Of course, if anyone in the 1960s had suggested that King would be so honored, their sanity would be justly questioned. But there we were, in a very different Albany, now with black political leadership, and notably for me, paved roads, as opposed to the red clay roads that had forever distinguished black from white sections of the city. Hundreds of persons who worked for or were represented by C. B. King attended the celebration, and many had continued to work for social and political change in Georgia and beyond, a testament to King's legacy.

Second, several years ago the Capital Habeas Unit of the Federal Defender in Philadelphia, which has an extraordinary record in attacking capital convictions in federal habeas proceedings, came under attack by the chief justice of the Pennsylvania Supreme Court for allegedly improperly litigating postconviction cases in state court. Critics of the unit were openly resentful of the quality of representation provided by the Defender, and they could not understand why Defender clients were entitled to the same zealous representation large corporations and others with financial resources could demand of their lawyers. Legal proceedings were initiated against the Capital Habeas Unit in state court, and as the president of the board of the Defender Association I well understood that this misguided attack threatened the very existence of this key legal unit.

We were extremely fortunate to gain the support of pro bono counsel, and in our legal response, as a reprise of the strategies used in Albany and elsewhere, we invoked another removal statute that sent state court litigation that addressed issues of federal concern to federal court. Soon thereafter, the case was dismissed, and the work of the Capital Habeas Unit continues to produce scores of reversals and a sharp reduction in the number of persons on death row in Pennsylvania.

Third, about ten years ago, my son, Sam, started college at Wesleyan University in Connecticut. Sam knew of my experiences with C. B. King and late in his first year he introduced me to his friend Wolfie, C. B. King's grandson! I soon reconnected with Wolfie's mother, whom I first met in Albany when she was no more than ten years old. Some days later she sent me a wonderful photograph of a card Wolfie as a child had composed for C. B., stating quite simply: "Everyone is entitled to a good lawyer." So, there it was: three generations of the King family and I could hardly hold back the tears.

Clerking in Mobile

James Ayers

Signing Up

I never paid attention to the civil rights movement while I was at Colgate. I didn't read a newspaper, and the only time I remember watching the news was during the Cuban missile crisis. But by the time I got to Columbia Law School in 1964, I couldn't ignore what was happening any longer.

In the first half of the twentieth century, the movement made little progress. State laws in the South barred Black people from voting, and the white-dominated Democratic Party maintained political control so that passing reform legislation was impossible.

In the 1960s, the movement adopted a new strategy. Instead of just seeking change by lobbying and litigation, the movement turned to direct action. It gathered strength with major campaigns of civil resistance throughout the South including the Montgomery bus boycott, the Birmingham Children's Crusade, the Selma to Montgomery march, the Freedom Rides, and voter registration drives.

But southern resistance to the movement was widespread, stubborn, and violent. In 1963, Medgar Evers was murdered by the head of the White Citizens' Council, and four young Black girls were killed in church by a bomb blast. In 1964, three civil rights workers, Andrew Goodman, James Chaney, and Michael Schwerner, were shot by two carloads of KKK members and buried in an earthen dam.

The Law Students Civil Rights Research Council (LSCRRC) placed law students to work for southern civil rights lawyers during summer vacations. LSCRRC had an information desk at the law school and a sign-up sheet for students to volunteer. While I wanted to do it, the people at the desk and the students signing up were not like me. They were mostly hippies—long hair, beards, funky clothes. The law school didn't have many students like that, but they all seemed to hang out around the LSCRRC desk. I was your typical suburban student—the son of a dentist and a kindergarten teacher. I had never even signed a protest petition. Joining up with this group was not who I was, and I decided not to do it.

But it bothered me. Several days later, I walked past the LSCRRC desk. Suddenly, I turned around, grabbed the pen, and signed my name.

Training in Jackson

Shortly after classes ended in 1966, I took a bus from the Port Authority Terminal in New York City to Jackson, Mississippi, for two days of LSCRRC training. The bus left early in the morning and arrived in the afternoon of the following day.

Toward the end of the trip, we made a meal stop in Clarksdale, a small Mississippi Delta town that was a center of civil rights activism in the 1960s. I didn't want anyone to identify me as a civil rights worker. My jeans and T-shirt blended in with the other riders, but as we got farther south, the new passengers who got on began to sound different. When we stopped at the bus terminal in Clarksdale, I bought two candy bars from the vending machine rather than order a hamburger so I wouldn't have to speak to the cashier.

The LSCRRC training took place at Jackson State College, a Black college in Jackson, Mississippi. The summer interns arrived from law schools all across the country.

Our first meeting was in an auditorium. Marian Wright Edelman began the program by giving us an overview of what would be happening that summer. She practiced law with the NAACP Legal Defense and Education Fund's Mississippi office. Later in life, Marian founded the Children's

Defense Fund and was awarded the Presidential Medal of Freedom in recognition of her efforts on behalf of children and families. She told us about the demonstrations, voter registration drives, and community organizing that would be going on throughout the South that summer. While these activities were important and were what the media would cover, she said the litigation projects we would work on would be critical to making permanent changes.

Several other attorneys gave presentations on various areas of the law we might be dealing with including job discrimination, voting rights, and discrimination in places of public accommodation. We also got some practical tips: if possible, travel in pairs and be careful what you say in restaurants where someone might eavesdrop.

The tips were not reassuring. I suspect I was not the only one who wondered what the hell I was doing there. The summer protest actions had just begun and already James Meredith, the first Black student admitted to the University of Mississippi, had been shot and wounded by a white gunman while on a solo 220-mile march. Civil rights activists from around the country poured in to complete the march for him, and Meredith recovered enough so he was able to join the 15,000 marchers when they entered Jackson at the end of the march. While the ending was a victory for the movement, the beginning was another civil rights worker getting shot.

I didn't know it at the time, but James Meredith had been admitted to Columbia Law School. When I got back to school, he was in one of my classes, Accounting for Lawyers. I wonder if he found it as boring as I did.

What upset me the most was the realization that if I were in trouble and ran up to a cop for help, the cop might just be the brother of the guy who was chasing me. I was scared, though I tried not to show it. Getting to know the other interns during meals and downtime helped. They were anxious too, but no one talked about going home and as a group we made one another braver than we really were.

That evening we got our assignments. My supervisor was D'Army Bailey, who later became a judge and successfully campaigned to transform the motel where Martin Luther King Jr. was assassinated into a civil rights museum. D'Army told me I was going to Mobile, Alabama, to work for a Black lawyer named Vernon Crawford. There were five Black lawyers in Alabama, and he was the only one who practiced in Mobile.

Mr. Crawford was counsel to the Non-Partisan Voters League and had handled a number of important civil rights cases in Mobile. In one case, he represented a Black man who was convicted of rape by an all-white jury and sentenced to death. Mr. Crawford argued on appeal that the systematic exclusion of Black people from the jury pool was unconstitutional. Not surprisingly, the Alabama State Supreme Court dismissed the appeal. However, the federal appeals court reversed the conviction. The decision served as precedent for many other jury integration cases throughout the South.

In 1963, Mr. Crawford filed suit against the Mobile County School Board after the board rejected a petition seeking the desegregation of Mobile schools. A federal judge ordered the schools to be desegregated, which led to years of litigation and confrontation with reactionary white groups formed to oppose integration. Governor George Wallace ordered state police to Mobile to prevent desegregation of the schools. This case became one of the longest-running desegregation cases in American history, finally ending 34 years later with a negotiated settlement.

Vernon Crawford

Another law student, Greg Hren, was also assigned to work for Mr. Crawford. Greg and I took a bus to Mobile early the next morning. When we got there, we called Mr. Crawford, and he told us how to get to his office. It was on Davis Avenue in the middle of the Black business district. The office was on the second floor above a barbershop and consisted of a reception area with worn furniture, and two offices with piles of legal papers covering the desks and much of the floor.

"Welcome. Call me Vernon," he said with a big smile. After we sat down in the two chairs he cleared for us in his office, Vernon wanted to know all about us: where we were from, what courses we were taking, who the members of our family were, and did we have girlfriends. Vernon then told us about his background, his family, and the secretary and paralegal who worked for him. And he told us what we would be doing. He worked on many civil rights cases, including ones involving employment discrimination, voting rights, and school desegregation, but he also had a regular general practice of real estate closings, wills, and criminal defense. We would be helping him primarily on the civil rights cases, but also on a murder case where he was the assigned counsel.

Vernon said the first thing to do was to find a place for us to stay. He got the newspaper and spread it out on a table so that he could go through the apartment listings with us. I told Vernon our pay from LSCRRC was just barely enough to cover our expenses and we would have to find something really cheap. The apartment listings were arranged by price, and we started with the cheapest places. Vernon said some places were in really bad neighborhoods and we shouldn't live there, but he found a few he thought we should check out. He said he'd like to drive us around, but he couldn't do that. No landlord is going to rent to you if you got a Black man with you.

Before we began our apartment hunt, Vernon said he wanted us to meet someone. He took us to a nightclub across the street and introduced us to Tiny, the 300-pound bouncer.

"Hey Vernon," Tiny said. "What can I do for you?"

"Tiny, I want you to meet Greg and Jimmy. They're gonna be working for me this summer. I want you to get the word out—no one's to mess with my boys."

Tiny laughed. "I'll make sure they're OK."

Tiny did get the word out and we never had any problems in the Black part of town.

We found a cheap apartment in a poor white neighborhood. It was in an old Victorian house that had been carved into many small apartments. Ours was one room with a small kitchen and a grungy bathroom. There was a large bed, a couple of chairs, and a small plastic table to eat on.

It seemed odd that the bed legs were sitting in glass bowls, but I didn't think anything of it until later that evening. We got back to the apartment about ten o'clock. When we turned the lights on, there was a scurrying around the room. It was swarming with roaches. The glass bowls must have been filled with insecticide to keep roaches out of the bed. It worked, but we had to change the insecticide every few days because the dead roaches formed a bridge for their brethren to cross. I never quite got used to them, but I learned to manage—I shook my clothes out in the morning and kept my toothbrush in a plastic bag.

The apartment was about a mile from Vernon's office. The only way to get there by bus would be to take one bus downtown to the terminal and then another out to Davis Avenue. So, I walked to the office, except when there was heavy rain. I had to cross a big field with tall weeds growing in it. Although not many people went from the poor white part of the city to the Black business district, there was a path worn across the field.

One day, I met an old Black man coming from the other direction. He was short and stooped over. When we got close, I stepped off the path to let him pass. He stopped and stepped aside for me to pass. I felt uncomfortable having an old man step aside for me, so I stepped farther out of the way and said, "Please go ahead."

He didn't say anything, but he looked anxious and again stepped aside for me. This could have seemed funny, but it wasn't. He must have been afraid I was playing a trick on him, that if he let me step aside for him I would attack him for not knowing his place. I realized I had to let him step aside for me, and I did.

The Straw Boss

The first case Vernon asked me to work on was an employment discrimination complaint against a large company in the Mobile area—large enough that it had its own railroad line.

Vernon's client, Bill (not his real name), was the straw boss (the assistant to the foreman) of the crew that maintained the railroad line.[35] There were six men on the maintenance crew: the foreman, the straw boss, and four other workers. Bill was about 50 years old and had been the straw boss for more than 20 years. A new foreman had been hired, and he was white. Bill and the rest of the crew were Black. Bill had applied for the foreman's job, and this was the third time the company had passed him over and hired a white man instead.

Bill was fed up and went to see John LeFlore, the head of the Non-Partisan Voters League. Mr. LeFlore referred him to Vernon, who was counsel to the league. Vernon filed a complaint on Bill's behalf with the Equal Employment Opportunity Commission. The EEOC had been created two years earlier with the adoption of Title VII of the Civil Rights Act of 1964. The act provided that the EEOC was to solve job discrimination complaints through "conference, conciliation, and persuasion." If the EEOC failed to work out a settlement, it was required to notify the complainants that they were permitted to sue to enforce their rights. Vernon had scheduled a meeting with the lawyer for the company to see if the matter could be settled without litigation. He knew it probably was a waste of time, but it was a procedural step he had to take before he could sue.

Bill came in to meet with Vernon to help him prepare for the meeting. Vernon asked me to sit in. Bill was tall, thin, and jiggled the hat he held in his hands. He said the new foreman and the two prior foremen had all worked in the motor pool before they were promoted to foreman of the railroad maintenance crew.

The prior foremen knew nothing about railroads when they started, Bill said, and he had to train them on everything. He came to an understanding with the foremen. They let him run the crew, and he didn't do anything to make them look bad with their boss.

While the straw boss job paid well enough, Bill was humiliated to have to work under men he had trained to be his boss. He said he'd been passed over twice before and he'd be damned if he'd let it happen again this time.

The day before the meeting with the lawyer for the company, Vernon called me into his office. His wife was sick, and he wouldn't be able to go. Vernon wasn't optimistic that the meeting would be productive, but he didn't want to postpone it. He asked me if I felt comfortable going by myself. Well, the answer to the question was clear. Of course I didn't feel comfortable. I was a second-year law student, and the lawyer I would be meeting with was the general counsel for a large company. But I didn't tell Vernon that; I said I'd be glad to go.

I crammed until midnight reading everything I could find on employment discrimination law. While I was still nervous about the meeting, I realized that because the law was only two years old, I probably knew as much about it as the lawyer for the company.

I caught an early bus that went out to the plant. I was the only person on the bus in a suit. As we got out of the city, the road went in a straight line as far as I could see. I asked the man sitting next to me if he knew where the company's plant was. He pointed out the front window and way off in the distance there were tall smokestacks with several buildings around them.

When I got off the bus, I could feel the sweat running down my side. It was only 9:30, but, like every Mobile morning, it was over 90° and humid. The guard at the gate directed me to the executive offices that were in a brick building near the front entrance. Mr. Edwards, the general counsel, had a large office with the usual lawyer maroon leather and mahogany furniture. He introduced me to the deputy general counsel and the director of human resources.

Mr. Edwards asked me about law school—what courses I was taking and what I wanted to do after I graduated. He told a couple of funny stories about when he was in law school. After a while, it occurred to me that perhaps all this pleasant law school chatter was intended to remind me that I was only a law student. Fully aware of my lowly status, I didn't appreciate Mr. Edwards trying to intimidate me with it. Anger is a great antidote to anxiety.

Mr. Edwards then turned to the reason for our meeting. He said he was very glad to have a chance to meet with Mr. Crawford's assistant. It gave him the opportunity to explain the employment procedures at the company. He was confident that once I understood the procedures, I could explain to Mr. Crawford why there was nothing they could do.

Mr. Henry, the HR director, said that Bill was a good employee. He was hard working, knew how to maintain the railroad, and was respected by management. Mr. Henry said he could understand why Bill felt it was unfair that he had been passed over again for the foreman position, but their hands were tied. Bill was just not eligible for the promotion.

Mr. Henry asked me if I knew what a line of progression was. When I said no, he took out a large chart and spread it out on a table. It contained a listing of all the jobs at the plant and showed what position each employee was eligible to be promoted to. Under the heading for the railroad maintenance crew, starting workers were eligible to be promoted to senior workers. Senior workers were eligible to be promoted to straw boss. The straw boss, however, was not eligible to be promoted to foreman. The only persons eligible to be the foreman were the assistant directors of the motor pool.

The lines of progression had been determined in negotiations with the unions representing the employees, Mr. Henry explained. Since the lines of progression were part of the contract with the unions, management had no authority to promote Bill to be the foreman.[36]

I was furious. I told Mr. Henry that Bill had been a good employee for 25 years. He carried the two prior foremen who didn't know what they were doing. He's the best qualified man to be foreman and this is just blatant discrimination because he's Black. I said you can't hide behind the union contract that protects the white workers. The company agreed to the discriminatory plan, and the company's responsible for it. This is wrong and you know it.

Mr. Edwards must have decided that there was no point in arguing with me. He was not going to convince me, and there really was no reason for him to bother to try. He had done what the law said was necessary. Just having the conference satisfied the EEOC requirement that he make a good faith effort to resolve the disagreement by "conference, conciliation and persuasion." No need to waste any more time.

Mr. Edwards said he appreciated my views, but it appeared we wouldn't be able to settle the matter. He thanked me for making the trip and asked me to give his regards to Mr. Crawford.

Vernon was not surprised. There was no way that the company was going to breach its contract with the white union by promoting a Black man to a position outside his line of progression. This would only be resolved by litigation.

A Visit from Our Neighbors

My roommate, Greg, and I were careful not to let anyone know what we were doing in Mobile. If we were talking in a restaurant, we referred to people by their initials. If we were discussing one of our cases, we spoke quietly and used code words.

There were a few times when a confrontation was unavoidable. Vernon asked me to file some papers for him in the county clerk's office. The clerk was quite friendly when I first stepped up. "Howdy. How can I help you?" When I said I was filing papers for Vernon Crawford, the clerk turned into Mrs. Hyde. She could barely control her rage. A white man delivering papers for a n——. She grabbed my papers and I thought she was going to throw them at me, but she didn't. I left quickly.

I tried not to speak to anyone in the apartment building where Greg and I lived. I didn't want anyone to ask me where I was from and what I was doing in Mobile. I just nodded and muttered, "Hello."

One night, I woke up around 2 a.m. The couple next door was having a fight—screaming, crashing, glass breaking. The walls were thin, and it was like being in the same room with them. Suddenly there was a loud crash, and we were in the same room. One of them had thrown the other through the wall into our closet. Greg and I looked at each other and ran for the door that led to the fire escape. We rushed down the stairs to the backyard.

We sat there for an hour or so. We didn't call the police—we'd been told never to have any contact with them. If they weren't KKK members themselves, they probably had friends who were who would be glad to know where two civil rights workers lived.

After a while, we crept back up the stairs. There were no sounds coming from the neighbors' apartment. We opened the door to our closet hoping we wouldn't find a body. We didn't, but there was a big hole and we could see into their apartment. No sign of anyone, though we weren't about to climb through to make sure.

We got dressed and went to work. I called the landlord, and when I got home that night, the hole had been patched. There were no further signs of our neighbors. They either were arrested or moved out, but, in any event, we never heard from them again.

The Fire

One Sunday morning around 6 a.m., the phone rang. It was Vernon and he was upset. "Jimmy, our house burned down."

He said he and his wife and their kids had gone down to the beach and stayed with friends for the weekend. Around 3 a.m., they got a call from a neighbor who said their house was on fire. By the time they got home, the fire was mostly out, but the house was destroyed. I told Vernon we'd be over as quick as we could.

Greg and I took a bus downtown and then another out to Vernon's place. We ran the two blocks from the bus stop to Vernon's street. As soon as we turned the corner, we could smell the burnt wood. The house was about halfway down the block. There were two fire trucks and the fire marshal's car in front. The front porch was made of brick, and it was still standing. The rest of the house was made of wood, and it had burned and collapsed into a pile of rubble. There was nothing left except some lawn furniture in the backyard.

Vernon was standing near the front porch talking to some of his neighbors. Greg and I waited until the neighbors left.

"It's gone. It's all gone," Vernon said as we walked up to him.

One of his neighbors, he said, drove by about 2 a.m. and spotted the house burning. He called the fire department, but by the time they got there it was too late. The house was engulfed in flames.

The neighbor told Vernon that when he first saw the fire, it was burning near the front door and also in the kitchen in the back of the house. The fire marshal told Vernon it was likely to have been started by a frayed lamp cord in the living room and that the neighbor probably saw a reflection in a window and just thought the fire was burning at both ends of the house. After the fire marshal walked away, the neighbor said, "Bullshit. I know the fire was burning in two places."

Vernon walked over to talk to some other neighbors. Greg and I were standing in the driveway near the front porch. The brick floor of the porch was covered in ash, and there were some burnt boards from the roof. We noticed some pieces of curved broken glass. We went over and asked Vernon if he kept any bottles on the front porch. "No," he said looking surprised. Greg and I spent the next hour putting together a broken glass jigsaw puzzle. The glass pieces were from a whiskey bottle.

I don't believe Vernon ever publicly charged that the fire was started by a Molotov cocktail. Perhaps he was concerned that making the charge might encourage KKK members to torch the homes of other civil rights activists. Also, getting homeowners insurance coverage when he rebuilt might not be easy. If an arsonist burned your old house down, why wouldn't he burn your new house down as well? Not a good insurance risk.

Morrison's Cafeteria

For my birthday, Greg and I decided to go to a nice restaurant for dinner. Vernon recommended Morrison's Cafeteria. I must have looked wary because Vernon said, "No, no, it's not like your school cafeteria." While he had never been there, he said it was supposed to be one of Mobile's finest restaurants.

I was glad I wore my suit because the men all had jackets and ties. The concept was actually like a school cafeteria—you got a tray and went along a line where servers offered you different dishes. But this was a five-star cafeteria: roast beef, steak, ham, oysters, shrimp, and a choice of 15 or so vegetables and salads. The tables had white-linen table clothes, candles, and fresh flowers.

The servers and waiters were all Black, but the hostess and manager were white. Although there was no sign saying, "WHITES ONLY," there were no Black customers. The servers were courteous, but it was as if they wore masks. "Would you like some roast beef, sir?" No expression and no eye contact.

Three weeks later, I came back to Morrison's—this time with three Black men. A state leader of the Non-Partisan Voters League had come to Mobile to meet with Vernon and John LeFlore, the head of the league's local branch. They decided they were going to try Morrison's Cafeteria for lunch. Vernon asked Greg and me to join them. There had been several restaurant sit-ins in other cities in Alabama that summer, but nothing so far in Mobile. Instead of a sit-in, this was a scouting mission. We'd simply go in and see what happened. If they told us to leave, we would do so. This time.

When Greg and I had gone for dinner earlier in the summer, it had been dark by the time we got there. I guess that's why I hadn't noticed the billboard across the street from the parking lot. It had a big advertisement for a KKK meeting that Saturday night. I didn't have any plans, but I thought I'd skip it.

When we walked in, the hostess looked startled, but the boss apparently wasn't there and she didn't know what to do. Vernon just said hello to her and led our group to the beginning of the serving line. The place had suddenly grown quiet. Everyone was looking at us, but no one said anything.

As we started down the cafeteria line, the servers, who had been cold, distant, and polite robots when Greg and I last visited, came to life. They smiled and said things like, Let me get you the best cut of the roast beef.

Wouldn't you like some more shrimp? How about some fresh mashed potatoes?

How could the boss get angry because the servers were being too nice to the customers? They carried our trays to the table and checked back with us every five minutes to see if they could get us anything else.

It was a good meal, especially the server rebellion. But we were concerned that at any moment customers would start yelling at us or the boss would come back. We ate quickly, left a large tip, and got out of there.

Heading Home

At the end of August, it was time to head home. I climbed on a Greyhound bus at 5:30 in the morning and started the 35-hour trip to New York. I felt sad to leave Vernon and the people I'd worked with but excited about seeing my girlfriend. Mostly though, there was just a sense of relief. For the first time in three months, I didn't have to worry about someone figuring out who I was. This time when we stopped for breakfast, I didn't quietly get a candy bar from the vending machine. I ordered ham and eggs in my best Long Island accent.

I had a window seat and, at first, I watched the countryside go by. Rural Alabama heading north looked a lot like rural Mississippi coming south—flat with acres and acres of cotton and vegetable fields. We stopped in Atmore, Andalusia, Enterprise, and, it seemed, every other small town in northern Alabama. They were all at crossroads with a few stores, a traffic light, and sometimes a gas station.

After a while, I stopped seeing the country pass by. Scenes from the summer came to me in a disorganized, dreamlike flow. I knew I was different from the person looking out the window coming south, but I couldn't say how.

Now in my 70s, in writing these stories I see events and connections, unclear at the time, that with a distant perspective, form patterns. There are threads that are discernible even today. Some began in Mobile, while others started many years before. Some are broken. Some have just stopped. And some are woven together and grace me still.

Panola County, Mississippi, in 1966

STEPHEN OLESKEY

What Drew Me to Mississippi in 1966

In the fall of 1965, I entered the New York University School of Law. I had graduated from Wesleyan University in 1964 and spent the following year teaching school in Recife in northeast Brazil. Because I was in Brazil, I had not participated with my fellow students in the "Freedom Summer" voter registration project and related civil rights activities in Mississippi in 1964. But I learned at NYU that the Law Students Civil Rights Research Council was recruiting law students to work on civil rights and economic justice issues in Appalachia and the Deep South in the summer of 1966, so I applied to work in Mississippi. I was excited to be selected to intern there because it would put me at the heart of the long struggle to achieve full civil rights for our African American fellow citizens.

I had scant contact with individual African Americans until that time. I grew up in New Hampshire in the 1940s and '50s, a state that was over 99 percent white. Wesleyan was similarly racially situated, though I had participated in a Wesleyan-Tuskegee Institute weeklong exchange program in 1961.[37] I lived in a dormitory in Alabama with Tuskegee students, shared meals with them, attended classes, and discussed their aspirations and concerns. This brief experience strengthened my conviction that achieving full civil rights for all Americans was the imperative moral and political issue of our time. Yet by mid-1966, despite the passage of the Civil Rights Act of 1964[38] and the Voting Rights Act of 1965,[39] achievement of most civil rights in the former Confederacy was still largely bogged down in political and legal disputes. I believed that as a law student with a growing toolbox of skills I could (and should) begin to take on advocacy of civil rights initiatives beyond participating in marches and demonstrations. Such work was, after all, one of the reasons I had begun to focus on law as a career when I was only 13. I wanted to be a societal change agent, and a legal career seemed to be a promising avenue to achieve this goal.

In June I began a one-week training program with a handful of other law student summer volunteers in Jackson, Mississippi's capital. Our living stipend was $15 a week. While I would be living and working that summer in rural Mississippi, I would be coordinating what I did with the Jackson office of the Lawyers' Committee for Civil Rights under Law. That office was headed by Dennison "Denny" Ray, who had left a white-shoe Wall Street law firm to practice civil rights law full-time in Mississippi. Our training was largely conducted by two colleagues working for the NAACP LDF in Jackson (the "Inc. Fund"): a very talented young lawyer named Marian Wright[40] and another named Henry Aronson.[41] I was impressed and inspired by Ray, Wright, Aronson, and other advocacy lawyers I encountered in Jackson who were working hard to advance the cause of civil rights in Mississippi[42] in the face of widespread opposition.

Substantively, our training largely involved gaining familiarity with federal statutes, programs, and agencies pertinent to our work that summer. Practically, we received a great deal of invaluable advice. I particularly recall two specific pieces of advice from Henry Aronson: "(1) Don't ever get caught out alone at night driving in rural Mississippi. (2) Listen closely to your local contacts and be guided by what they have set as their objectives." This advice was sensible, and I should have followed it more closely.

My Introduction to Panola County

I would be living and working in Panola County and environs in northwest Mississippi about 60 miles south of Memphis, Tennessee, and 150 miles north of Jackson. Batesville was the county seat of Panola County. Panola County at that time was approximately 56 percent African American out of a total population of approximately 30,000. Like the fertile Delta region into which it merged along its western edge, Panola County was still overwhelmingly agricultural. The principal crops were soybeans, corn, and cotton, grown alongside livestock. As had been the case since well before the Civil War, the majority of the landholdings involved large areas, reflecting the former slave economy that rested on the plantation model. In the 1960s the majority of these large former plantations were farmed by African American tenant farmers and sharecroppers who were economically (and therefore politically) wholly dependent on the white men who owned most of this fertile and profitable land.

I would be living on the Miles' family farm on the outskirts of Batesville. At that time, the Miles family on the farm were Robert Miles Sr., his wife, Mona, and their young son, Kevin. Mr. Miles was an established leader in the ongoing struggle for civil rights in the Panola County area going back to the 1950s and was justly respected for his tenacity and courage. In both the Freedom Summer of 1964, as well as in 1965, the Mileses had hosted numerous civil rights volunteers, including Stokely Carmichael, the controversial leader of the Student Nonviolent Coordinating Committee or SNCC. In the summer of 1966, however, I would be the only volunteer staying at the Miles farm. Mr. Miles had loaned the earlier volunteers the farm's dusty white-panel wagon to use for transportation. I learned near the end of my summer there that the truck was widely known in the area as the "Freedom Wagon." Since I had been traveling around the Panola County area by myself all summer in the Freedom Wagon, I was relieved that I had not known earlier that everywhere I drove I was unwittingly proclaiming, here comes another northern civil rights agitator.

The Mileses were warm and gracious hosts. I generally had breakfast and dinner with them. Breakfast was often an African American Mississippi farm meal with some combination of pig's brains with scrambled eggs, sausage, grits, biscuits, and coffee. I dutifully became the newest member of Mona Miles's clean plate club.[43]

Some of My Panola County Projects

I soon accumulated a laundry list of projects to pursue, almost all referred to me by my new local contacts. They ran the gamut in my informal ranking system from lesser to greater importance. Among the former were the still segregated public facilities at the aging Batesville railroad station on the Illinois Central Railroad line running north–south from Chicago to New Orleans. After inspecting the station, and with the typing assistance of the able clerical staff at the Lawyers' Committee Jackson office, I wrote my best version of a lawyerly letter of complaint to the Interstate Commerce Commission in Washington. I received a perfunctory reply from the ICC acknowledging the letter. No doubt the ICC's low level of interest reflected, among other things, the reality that few if any passengers used the station by 1966. Indeed, I do not think there was any longer a scheduled stop at Batesville by any train. Nonetheless, to local African Americans, the signs in the station still proclaiming its segregated facilities (including its separate water fountains!) was rubbing salt in an old and still very much open wound.

I was also enlisted by local African American teenagers to inspect the "public" but wholly segregated whites-only beach on Sardis Lake, a 95,000-acre federal flood-control river impoundment created by the US Army Corps of Engineers (the "Corps") in the 1930s and covering parts of three counties including Panola. By the 1960s, the new man-made lake included many recreational amenities including boating, fishing, and swimming. Access to public amenities was now a controversial issue in the South. It was an especially bitter pill to local African Americans dealing with the high humidity and heat in the Delta region to be excluded from a federally funded and operated public recreational facility. I accompanied some of my new Panola area contacts to the Sardis Lake public beach one sweltering day. I found it, as described, populated only by whites who shouted at us to leave. We eventually left but only after making our point, satisfied that we had successfully integrated the beach. I don't recall whether any of us swam there. Unlike locally owned and operated swimming pools, which could be drained to prevent their integration, the local authorities were in a much weaker position to shut down a federally funded and operated beach to prevent its use by African American citizens. I followed up with a formal written complaint to the district office of the Corps.

I recall two other projects in which I was enlisted by my new clients. One was helping to encourage African American parents to enroll their children in the better equipped local all-white public schools. These schools had far superior facilities, books, and better trained teachers. The public schools were still separate and unequal in Mississippi despite the twelve years that had elapsed since the Supreme Court 1954 decision in *Brown v. Board of Education*[44] mandating integration of segregated public schools with its opaque and elusive mandate to proceed with "all deliberate speed." The federal government by 1966 had developed many freedom-of-choice plans under which African American parents could voluntarily enroll their children in all-white schools. This mechanism was proving wholly inadequate to the task at hand in such staunchly segregated bastions as Mississippi. By the summer of 1966, few if any African American parents had volunteered their children to transfer to white schools in Panola County or indeed elsewhere in Mississippi. I was asked by my local contacts to meet with parents who were thought to be potentially interested in electing such transfers. I met with all parents I was directed to but with a marked lack of success. The implacable local white resistance to school integration coupled with the power held by whites over African American laborers in every facet of the overwhelmingly agricultural Delta economy made seeking such transfers extremely unlikely. I was left with the conviction by summer's end that this approach was doomed to failure throughout the still largely segregated South. Indeed, within the next five years the federal government threw in the towel altogether on this futile gradualist, "voluntary" approach to school integration in the South.

This change in approach was precipitated by the Supreme Court's 1969 decision in *Alexander v. Board of Education of Holmes County*[45] three years after the events about which I am writing. Holmes County is also in Mississippi. By the late 1960s it too had failed to make any progress at school integration and a parent brought suit to compel compliance with *Brown* and other intervening cases such as *Green v. County School Board of New Kent County*.[46] Whatever "all deliberate speed" had meant to the nine justices in 1954, the court by 1969 would not countenance indefinite additional delay after 15 years of resistance. The new mandate was to "integrate immediately." I would not be in Mississippi to see how the new mandate played out there, but I followed its impact throughout the country in the upcoming decades.[47]

The second major project was to assist desperately poor African American tenant farmers in applying for welfare assistance. As far as I could determine, everyone to whom I was referred certainly qualified for such assistance, meager though it was. The catch here, as in so many other benefit programs, was that the white power structure had a vested interest in denying such benefits because obtaining them could lessen the economic dependency of their African American vassals on them. I recall especially two instances where this cruel reality struck forcefully home.

Visiting Clients in the Countryside and Encountering the Klan

The first instance was when I approached the Panola County welfare agent for an eligibility screening for a poor and struggling African American farm family. Somewhere in this lengthy process I discovered that the family were tenant farmers on a large (former) plantation owned and operated by the husband of the welfare agent. I soon saw in confronting a blizzard of technical obstacles raised by the welfare agent that she had zero interest in ameliorating the total financial dependency of my clients on their employer, the agent and her husband! The same harsh reality confronted the many other African American farm families similarly situated in the area. The only available recourse that I recall was a cumbersome and slow local county administrative appeal process where the employer controlled all the factual information bearing on an applicant's program eligibility as well as the outcome of the appeals process itself.

The second instance involved an African American couple who lived outside Batesville in a dirt floor shack owned by the white owner of the adjacent country store. One of my local contacts explained to me that my clients were dirt-poor and wholly dependent on the store owner for their income and housing, such as it was. Other than this information, I was given little more than their names and the location of the store. I was told that the couple would welcome assistance in obtaining any welfare benefits for which they might be eligible. When I asked how to locate the couple—I'll call them Mr. and Mrs. Jones—I was told that my contact was unsure and that I should ask for directions at the store.

This was monumentally bad advice, which I realized as soon as I climbed out of the Freedom Wagon and walked into the dimly lit and dusty store. When my eyes adjusted, I saw five or six white men playing a card game on top of a hogshead. Instead of making an excuse and leaving my mission for another day in view of the serious risk I saw my clients and I now faced, I stepped forward to ask where I could find the Joneses. A middle-aged man who I took to be the store owner told me to take the next right-hand dirt road and I would see the Jones' home behind a (barbed wire) fence. I thanked the man and left the store to climb back up into the Freedom Wagon. I was still determined—despite my dawning better judgment to the contrary—to try to see the Joneses that day. As I prepared to drive down the street, the store owner materialized beside the truck to ask whether I needed gas. I said, "No." He then asked if I was selling insurance and I again replied, "No." Finally, he said with pronounced hostility, "Then you must be one of those northern civil rights agitators." I replied truthfully that I was a law student working in the area that summer to advise residents about their rights. I do not recall his exact reply, but it was to the effect that no one in the area needed my advice on anything and that I should leave his property immediately.

I took him at his word under the circumstances but nevertheless drove down the road determined to warn the Joneses of the prospective peril my blundering approach had created for them. As soon as I had parked beside the fence gate, a man I took to be Mr. Jones appeared on the other side of the gate. I explained hastily to him who I was and what had just happened. I said that I'd consult with them at another time in Batesville[48] and added: "When they ask you what I wanted, you should say you don't know but you didn't ask anyone to come see you." I then saw the store owner and one of his fellow card players rapidly advancing toward me from Mr. Jones's side of the fence. I climbed back into the Freedom Wagon and left, a decision confirmed by angry advice to that effect from the two white men.

I immediately drove back to the Miles' farm nervously glancing in my rearview mirrors for any sign of pursuit. There was none. I parked the Freedom Wagon and went into the Miles' house. Seeing Mr. Miles in the living room, I told him what had just happened. He asked me who had sent me to see the Joneses, and I told him. He shook his head in bemusement and said, "Didn't he tell you that the store was the headquarters for the local Klan?" I replied, "No." He added that I had just walked into an informal gathering of the KKK and was very lucky that I had returned unscathed. I asked him if he had a pistol in the house. He said, "Yes," and brought out a suitably menacing-looking revolver. I asked him if I could keep it in my bedroom for a while, and he readily agreed. I don't know what I would have done had I needed to use that gun some night, but it gave me some security to sleep with it under my bed for the next several weeks.[49]

Joining the Nightly Integration Demonstration in Grenada and Carelessly Placing Myself at Risk

I will close by recounting an event that had nothing to do with anything my local contacts asked me to look into or advise about. On June 5 that summer, James Meredith, who had integrated the University of Mississippi when he enrolled in 1962, crossed into northern Mississippi on foot from Tennessee. His plan was to walk alone in a 220-mile March against Fear to the Mississippi Gulf Coast to encourage African American citizens to register to vote. Voter registration had been the major focus of the 1964 Freedom Summer campaign and while some progress had been made, the great majority of African American citizens in Mississippi were still unregistered by the summer of 1966. Meredith wanted to call attention to this gap and to encourage more African American citizens of Mississippi to register to vote. On June 6, as Meredith was resuming his solitary march near Hernando, Mississippi, he was shot three times from ambush by a white sniper and hospitalized. This was national news, and the civil rights movement came under pressure to take up the solitary march that Meredith had just begun. Under the banners of the SCLC, SNCC, CORE, and the Mississippi Freedom Democratic Party (MFDP), among others, the March against Fear quickly resumed down Highway 51. It passed through and briefly rallied in Grenada, Mississippi (a town of about 10,000 about 30 miles south of Batesville) before marching on.

In late June when I came to Batesville to take up my summer work there, the March against Fear reached the Mississippi capital in Jackson where there was a large rally on June 26. The march leadership then returned to Grenada to use it as a geographic locus to demonstrate for voter registration and more broadly for integration of the fully segregated Mississippi society that Grenada represented. The nightly rallies and town square marches that ensued were featured frequently on national evening news, with graphic videos of police beatings and hooded, armed Klansmen menacing the peaceful demonstrators notwithstanding the intervention of the local federal district court to enjoin interference with the marchers' First Amendment freedom to demonstrate.

I watched this drama unfold nightly on national television when I returned to the Miles' farmhouse after completing my daily activities in Panola County. As I did so, I became increasingly frustrated that I was playing no part in the Grenada demonstrations. I knew that such participation was not an expected part of my summer legal responsibilities—it might even have been frowned upon by my nominal supervisors at the Lawyers' Committee—but I still wanted badly to bear witness with the many others convening nightly in downtown Grenada. In the language of the twenty-first century—and the philosophy of the French writer Albert Camus, who had influenced me greatly at Wesleyan—I felt that my participation in the demonstrations was an existential moment for me. I told Mr. Miles and several other local contacts of my decision.

One evening in July I borrowed a venerable Chevy sedan from a Panola County MFDP contact and drove down US Highway 51 to Grenada to participate in the nightly demonstration. I parked my loaner Chevy outside the motel where I knew the march leadership stayed. I knew that the rally organizers met before the march each evening in the Bellflower Baptist church to be briefed by the FBI. I joined that briefing session on a typically muggy Mississippi night. Hosea Williams of SCLC was the lead spokesman for the marchers. There were several FBI agents present. They advised the group that there were going to be armed Klansmen present that night and the potential for violence was high. The agents strongly recommended that the march be called off that night. Hosea Williams briefly conferred with the others and firmly responded that the demonstration would go forward as scheduled.

Not long afterward, dozens of marchers lined up and headed for the town square. I joined in, though not without some trepidation in light of what the FBI had just reported and advised. I was well aware that on July 10 Oliver Rosengart (also a NYU law student, who had trained with me in Jackson), Henry Aronson, and an official of the Federal Community Relations Service had been fired on in Grenada by two white men using a submachine gun.[50] Luckily none of the three men was hit by the gunfire.

As we marched around the square, we were encircled by a mob of angry cursing white protesters. The only protection for the marchers from the mob were a number of Mississippi state highway patrolmen in riot gear. They were armed and looked like they would rather be elsewhere doing anything else. I do not recall seeing any weapons in the mob, but I am sure that there were some. Nevertheless, the demonstration concluded without any overt acts of violence. Relieved, I walked back to the church where we disbanded. I then walked on to the headquarters motel to retrieve my borrowed Chevy to drive back to Batesville on Highway 51. It was sometime around 9 p.m. and quite dark. By this time I largely discounted Henry Aronson's sound advice never to drive alone at night in rural Mississippi. I had even seen Henry that night at the march and learned that he was staying at the headquarters motel in Grenada.

Once I was on Highway 51 heading north, I was further lulled into a false sense of security by the lack of traffic and the languid nature of the countryside that summer night. When I was about 20 minutes into my drive, a marked Mississippi Highway Patrol car passed in the left lane at high speed. I gave it little attention until I passed over a rise and saw the car parked on the right shoulder with its red lights blinking. Before I could assimilate what was happening, a second patrol car suddenly appeared in my rearview mirror closing on me fast. Quickly, I was sandwiched between the two patrol vehicles and signaled to pull over between them. I did so with a growing sense of unease. I could see that there were two troopers in the front car and three in the rear car. Two troopers approached my car and asked for the registration and my license.[51] They asked who owned the car, and I replied with the first thought that came to my mind: "The MFDP." Of course, that was not the case, as I soon realized. It was owned by the MFDP contact who had loaned it to me. By this time the troopers had checked the license plates and registration. I could see that they were ill-humored after their night protecting demonstrators in Grenada they openly despised.

One of the troopers then said, "You were reckless driving. Swerving all over the highway. Didn't you realize that?" I replied futilely that I had not been swerving or recklessly driving. I was then ordered to leave my car and get into the back seat of the rear patrol vehicle. There was one trooper driving and two more sitting on either side of me in the back seat. Without a further word to me, both cars then sped up the highway toward Batesville. When we had driven about five minutes, we came to an official crossover that led to the southbound side of Highway 51. Both patrol cars took it, and we were soon heading back in the direction of Grenada. We came shortly to a marked exit, which they took. We were quickly swallowed up in the darkness of rural Mississippi. Meanwhile, the trooper to my right had a shotgun in his right hand and a shotgun shell in his left. He regularly tossed the shell up in the air and then caught it. His behavior was very effective in heightening my already fraught sense of anxiety about the coffer dams and swamps I was sure were all around us.[52]

Eventually, after what seemed an interminable drive through the unlighted countryside but was in fact likely no more than ten minutes, both cars came to a stop near a sign that read "I.W. Irby Justice of the Peace." We drove up a small rise and came to a stop outside what I took to be Irby's farmhouse. Shortly thereafter Irby came out in a nightshirt and asked what was going on. One of the troopers replied: "We stopped this feller reckless driving on the Interstate, Mr. Irby." Irby responded that he would convene "court," and we walked across the farmyard toward what I thought was a chicken coop but turned out to be Irby's court. We walked into the "court" which was sparsely furnished with a raised judge's bench in the center and a few chairs. Behind the bench on the wall was a Confederate flag and underneath it was emblazoned the words "Support Your Local Citizens Council." Irby immediately convened court and asked the lead trooper to state the charge. He repeated the reckless driving claim, which I immediately disputed. Irby then asked me how I pleaded. I said I wanted to consult an attorney before responding. After a long silence, Irby to my immense surprise and relief said: "Well, boys, the Supreme Court says he has a right to one call to an attorney."

Irby then led me back across the farmyard to his house and let me in the back door. He pointed to a rotary dial telephone. The only attorney I could think of to call was Henry Aronson back at the headquarters motel in Grenada. Fortunately, and to my immense relief again, I was able to reach the motel and was then put through to Henry. With Irby standing next to me, I rapidly explained my predicament to Henry. He told me to put Irby on the phone, which I did. I could only hear Irby's side of the conversation, which did not sound encouraging. Irby then put me back on the phone with Henry. Henry told me to plead guilty immediately and pay the fine, because "if you're held overnight in the county jail we might not find you there in the morning." I explained to Henry that all the money I had was a $20 traveler's check and $1 in cash. Henry then stated the obvious—that I had better hope the fine was not more than $20.

Irby and I went back to his courtroom, where he asked me for my plea. I replied "Guilty," and Irby immediately announced, "The fine is $20 and court costs are $1." After Irby agreed to accept my $20 traveler's check to pay the fine, he adjourned court and I was bundled back into the patrol car with the three troopers. I was driven back to my loaner Chevy parked in the breakdown lane of Highway 51. With a final warning "not to be out at night reckless driving again,"⁵³ the two patrol cars sped off northward toward Batesville and Panola County. When I had regained enough composure to drive, I drove off without incident in the same direction toward the relative security of the Miles' farmhouse.

Conclusion

In reflecting on these incidents now after the span of half a century, I again realize how lucky I was to have avoided the fate of Chaney, Schwerner, and Goodman in 1964 and of many others before and after that date. I also realize that my brief brushes with the Klan and the State Patrol were but short moments frozen in time compared with the infinite variety of bone-chilling experiences that our African American fellow citizens routinely encountered throughout the country then and now. Their raw courage and fortitude inspired me in 1966 and still does today.

I Don't Want to Die in Vietnam

Paul Harris

It was June 1968, and Martin Luther King and Bobby Kennedy had been assassinated, the US invasion of Vietnam had reached a turning point, police riots at the Democratic convention in Chicago were on the horizon, and I was in very unfamiliar territory. I was sweating and walking in the energy-draining heat of Albany, Georgia, after a pounding rainstorm. With me were a tall, curly-headed, mustached Jew named Richard Greenberg from New York University law school and a handsome, African American classmate of mine, Ed Wilson, from Berkeley law. Alongside us we heard a radio blasting from a 1964 Chevy Impala with a Confederate flag license plate. We could hear the DJ: "This is WALG, Johnny Reb radio. It's a beautiful morning. Let's go out and kill a commie." We hurried on and passed by two wide-eyed teenagers: "Are you a rock group from Atlanta?" they asked. "No, we are civil rights workers." They left confused.

We then crossed two unpaved, rain-soaked muddy sidewalks and streets that were part of the "colored" part of town and arrived at the imposing law office of legendary lawyer C. B. King. He was the only civil rights lawyer in all of southwest Georgia. Twenty-four years later a federal courthouse would be built in Albany and named after him, but in 1968 he was hated and feared by the racist power structure. The three of us were to be his summer interns.

Since I had a specialty in selective service law, one of the many cases I was assigned had to do with a "hardship discharge" claim for 20-year-old Douglas Johnson. His mother, Lula Mae Johnson, had a family of five children. She had been separated from her husband for five years and received no money from him. The oldest child, Douglas, worked in Albany, made $68 take-home pay per week. He lived with the family and used this money to support them. In June he had received his draft notice and never having heard of the selective service regulations on hardship deferments, not having access to a draft counselor, and not having a draft board that would inform him of his statutory (if not human) rights, he was put on a bus to the induction center.

Mrs. Johnson came to attorney King last week out of desperation. For the last month following her son's induction the family's total income had been less than $10. Her 15-year-old daughter picked butter beans and was paid $1.50 per day. Mrs. Johnson cut potatoes and was paid a few dollars minus a dollar for the transportation she had to pay to the man who took her back and forth to the fields. She also had three children under eight. She already had to pay $3.40 for two bus fares into Albany to see attorney King. Her grocery bill was overdue. Her nine-year-old son, who had been sick all his life, needed medical care but she already had doctors' bills. And of course, her children needed clothing, the apartment needed repairs, and Mrs. Johnson needed a few dollars to spend on one or two pleasantries instead of spending it all on rat poison, roach killer, wood for the stove, and bus transportation. She had attempted to apply for Aid to Families with Dependent Children over three years ago but was given an insulting runaround by the Lee County welfare office and never received the payments she deserved under the law. As Mrs. Johnson said, "Lee County is not a good place for people of my color."

Mrs. Johnson was telling me that she lived in "the old colored schoolhouse." I naively asked, "What color is it?" I had slipped into being a human, devoid of whiteness or blackness, devoid of political experience, but Mrs. Johnson's surprised look brought me back to Albany, Georgia. The "old colored schoolhouse" did not refer to the paint job outside—it referred to the people inside.

The next week Ed and I drove attorney King's car 150 miles to Mrs. Johnson's residence in the abandoned schoolhouse. We had seen her four times, and finally I had good news. I had taken four affidavits: one from a minister even though he had feared retaliation from the draft board, one from Douglas's previous employer at the pecan-processing plant promising him a job, one from a neighbor attesting to Mrs. Johnson's living conditions, and one from the family doctor at the clinic. I had put together a rock-solid hardship claim under the applicable selective service regulations. Meanwhile Douglas was in basic training at Ft. Dix. If the law meant anything to me, it meant getting her son back home where he belonged.

Three months later, after one of the most enlightening and rewarding experiences of my life in Georgia, I sat in my Berkeley apartment when the phone rang. It was Douglas calling from a few miles away at the Oakland army base, two days from being shipped out to kill Vietnamese. His local, all-white draft board had denied his hardship claim. We set up an escape plan. Douglas would have an off-base pass the next day. That morning he called, and we put our plan into action.

"Douglas, take a bus to downtown Oakland. Go to the movie show at the Paramount theater on Broadway. Sit in the side section on the right-hand side in the back of the theater."

"OK, I can be there in 45 minutes. I don't want to die in Vietnam."

"All right, I'll be there at 11:30. I will walk in carrying a briefcase. I'm 5′ 10″ about 150 pounds with dark, long hair and I'll be wearing an old blue and gold Cal jacket."

"A what jacket?"

"It's from the university here. Watch for the briefcase in my right hand. When you see me, get up and say, 'Is that you Paul?' Any questions?"

"No sir."

An hour later I drove down Broadway. At 11:30 I walked into the large movie house. I walked slowly down the right-hand aisle. I heard a voice saying, "Is that you Paul?"

I looked at a thin, very dark teenager. "Yes, are you Douglas?"

"Yes, sir."

We walked a block to Ed Wilson's car. I noticed that the boy's hands were shaking. He was dressed in regular civilian clothes: Levi's, brown T-shirt, and a flimsy worn-out jacket.

"You can relax, Douglas. No one is looking for you yet. You have until evening before anyone notices you are gone. We are taking you to the city of Richmond. It's a half hour from here. We are going directly to the Greyhound bus station. We will give you money to buy a ticket to Atlanta and enough to transfer to Albany. We will also give you $100 cash for the trip and your family. After you see your family, go to Albany, and call the lawyer on this piece of paper. His name is C. B. King."

"I know attorney King. Every colored person knows Mr. King. He's the only lawyer in all of southwest Georgia that will stand up for us. But I got no money for him."

"You don't need any money. He has agreed to take your case for free. He will help you fill out forms for a hardship release from the army, and he will surrender you and defend you. He says you will spend some time in jail at Ft. Dix for going AWOL. But then he believes he will win your discharge."

"Thank you, Mr. Paul and Mr. Ed. My mother will pray for you."

Ed and I wanted to talk to Douglas about the Vietnam War and imperialism and how it was tied up with the power of southern Dixiecrats in Congress. But instead, we talked about Douglas's family and how one tries to survive in Lee County, Georgia.

We waited in the small, fairly empty Greyhound station. Within the hour Douglas boarded the bus, safely on his perilous journey.

Douglas made it safely home, and he and his mother went to attorney King's office. With the hardship claim I had previously filed, my legal memo on how to proceed under the military regulations and C. B. King's eloquence and persistence, Douglas got 60 days in the brig and then was finally discharged.

One year later I received a letter that in part said the following: "Thank you for keeping Douglas out of Vietnam. . . . That's very nice you graduated from law school. I wish you the best of luck. Only one thing, you should be a lawyer in Georgia. We need lawyers like you down here. Best of luck, Lula Mae Johnson."

My Dad as a Role Model

Chevene King Jr.

My earliest memories of my father involved two settings. One is of him being at my grandfather's two grocery stores following his return home at the end of the day, when he would routinely walk to the opposite end of the block on which we lived, maybe stand outside the store just long enough to pick out of the cracker barrel the perfect apple, and then enter where he would encounter my grandfather at either the checkout counter or the meat at the rear of the store. Before reaching the meat section, he might stop at the soda cooler, where he would reach down into the cooler's water and grab a bottle of Nu-Grape soda, unbutton his suit coat, so that he could place his hand on his hip, and with his head aimed skyward, take that initial thirst-quenching gulp, something that a fellow from the neighborhood re-enacted for me not long ago, almost as though it was a ritual to those who witnessed him engage in that routine with great precision.

In the years that followed his passing, I would occasionally run into people who recalled the scenes, mainly because he was just that kind of figure within the community. Someone who was always impeccably dressed and manicured, whose booming voice carried and could be heard from one end of the block to the other, and whose choice of words and laughter distinguished him like no other. Once inside, and only after greeting Miss Opal, the young college-age lady located at the checkout counter, he would proceed to the rear of the store, seeking out my grandfather where the two would launch into detailed discussions, generally about recent news events that for them at least were the subject of local and national importance.

I could not have been more than seven or eight years old at that time. Judging from his attire, I had no clue as to what he did for a living. On each morning, he would leave the duplex that we lived in on S. Jefferson Street, dressed as though he was going to church and returning at the end of the day looking no different from when he left, with maybe his tie loosened or slightly undone.

In terms of where he worked, I could not tell you much about that either. I knew that it was an office building located near downtown on the second floor at the very rear of a dimly lit hallway and next door to the Ritz, which was the only movie theater located in town that did not require black patrons to sit in the balcony as a part of a segregated seating scheme.

My second most vivid recollection of who or what my father did for a living stemmed from an occasion when perhaps I was in the fifth grade, and we were celebrating Negro history month. The program involved several students dressing up as and portraying key figures, such as Booker T. Washington, Harriet Tubman, Mary McLeod Bethune, George Washington Carver, and Dr. Martin Luther King Jr. On that particular occasion, I was asked to be my father, attorney C. B. King. I do not recall whether I understood the reason why my father was chosen to be among that list of noted figures. Upon reflection, my guess is that by that time, my father had gained widespread recognition as a civil rights hero of sorts after becoming the victim of a bloody attack from a local sheriff. What I do recall from that point going forward is the constant refrain "When you grow up, are you going to be a lawyer, just like your father?"

Of the many characteristics that I believe were most noteworthy about my father, I recognized his generosity and ability to see well beyond society's superficial labels. I can recall an instance in which a Mr. Murray, who was a farmer and one of my dad's clients, offered to pay my father with produce from his farm because he was involved in a land dispute with neighboring white landowners but could not afford the fee my father charged. Consequently, on a couple of Saturday mornings my father would drive out to Mr. Murray's farm where we loaded up the trunk of my father's sedan with watermelons and cantaloupe to the point that we could not drive the car out of the field.

The significance of this memory and how I see it as being an illustration of how my father interacted with his clients came about when one of my younger brothers got stung by a wasp as we were playing around Mr. Murray's barn. Up to that point, I had judged this farmer to have been poor and uneducated. But as my father began to contemplate whether he should cut short his visit with this client, Mr. Murray had my father grab my brother's head as he pulled out of the recesses of his jaw a wad of chewing tobacco and thereafter place it over the area where my brother had been stung. Within a matter of a few seconds, my brother stopped crying and to my amazement claimed that he was no longer in pain. As we drove back into town, I can remember wondering if my standards for judging who was truly educated, as well as my understanding of real wealth, were at all correct.

Another of my father's attributes was his courage and street smarts. I can remember that there was one occasion in which he traveled to a courthouse outside Albany on a hot summer day and that after he had gotten back on the road he began to feel extreme heat under the driver's seat of his car. Ultimately, the heat became so intense that he pulled over into someone's yard to inspect the situation and learn that someone had poured battery acid on to his seat and that by that time it had begun to burn his pants and bottom side of his thighs. Some years after my dad's death, I ran into a gentleman who approached me as I was leaving a courthouse in a neighboring town. He asked who I was and upon being advised, recounted how he had met my father on one occasion. He said that he was a teenager at the time and who happened to have met my father while standing outside a courthouse. After introducing himself, my father asked him, "Young man, are you doing anything for the next couple of hours?" Responding that he was not, the then-teenager stated that my father paid him to watch his car while he was in the courthouse. The teenager indicated that he did not understand at the time of my father's request what was going on, but simply thought that it was such an honor to have helped a man he had only heard so many great things about from others.

Always Know More than One Way Out of Town

In another instance not long before my father died, he accompanied me to a town south of Albany near the Florida state line. As we were returning to Albany, he began to give me alternative, if not backroad, directions on where to turn. I asked him for his reasons, and he would only say that he had had an experience or two on certain roads that he wished to avoid. Because his pain medication appeared to be wearing off, I did not press him for details. Instead, I assumed that his reasons were not to be questioned, nor the product of mere intuition.

Approximately two years later, I was representing an Albany resident who had been arrested along with his girlfriend in Troy, Alabama, for the daytime theft of a jewelry store. The client's mother, who was in the final stages of her battle with cancer, requested that I do what I could for her son notwithstanding her inability to pay the attorney's fees. As a consequence, approximately a week or two before trial, I asked one of my younger brothers to accompany me to Troy to investigate the case and see my client. One of the things that we did was to visit the jewelry store as a means of determining how such a crime could have happened during store hours and in broad daylight. Accordingly, I had my brother act as though he was a potential customer, while I photographed his interaction with the salesperson. When the owner observed what we were doing, he called the police. And as we were leaving the premises, the police arrived and confronted us about our presence at the store. Upon advising the officer of our purpose, he stated that he was taking us to jail. When I told him that that was my next destination, he became puzzled. The officer led us to the jail where the sheriff was waiting. Upon introducing myself to the sheriff, he explained that I was breaking the law and threatened to contact the local judge and district attorney. I invited him to do so and proceeded to visit with my client.

As we began to leave the jail, the sheriff was noticeably absent. And as we began to make our way back to the highway that we had used coming into Troy, we noticed no fewer than four or more police cars positioned along the road and saw two pulling in behind us. At that point, I pulled into a gas station and upon explaining the situation to a black customer there at a nearby gas pump, asked if there was there a "back way" out of town. He thereafter obliged us and got us safely on our way.

Three days later, we returned for trial. He was acquitted of all charges. As we were returning to Albany, an off-duty policeman whom I had hired for extra protection asked me why we were using such a circuitous route back to Albany. My response was clear. "My father said to always know more than one way out of town."

Relax and Take Your Time

One of my father's greatest pastimes was the time he spent in his garden after work. In fact, whenever he would travel throughout the state and beyond, he would always take time to stop by roadside fruit stands and search out nurseries with wide variety of plant life, particularly those that were manned by growers whose knowledge of the plants' biological names matched or exceeded his own. Plants and poems were his passion.

After court, he was apt to stop at a fruit stand to grab a bag of peaches, scuppernongs, muscadines, or sometimes sugarcane on his way home. But when it came to his yard at the house, it was his heaven and a complete source of relaxation, his joy and pride. He enjoyed Japanese gardening the most. It appeared to me that because of the constant pruning and detailed attention that the Japanese approach to growing trees and shrubs requires, it was no different from what he did each morning when it came to manicuring his beard or maintaining his wardrobe.

This attention to detail was not lost to simply his love for gardening and fine clothes. Instead, it was but a mere extension of how he conducted himself in trial. Whenever he began a trial, judges and attorneys alike knew that they needed to be prepared for what was apt to be a lengthy process, one in which he was going to be painstakingly slow and detailed in practically every way, from the moment that jury selection began till the moment that the jury goes into deliberations.

My father's method of conducting cross-examination is by far the greatest lesson that I have ever received as an attorney. The first rule that I learned from his approach to cross-examination was to take your time in going into the facts elicited on direct examination or from testimony developed at a prior, proceeding with such detail that you develop a likelihood that the witness will make a misstep, get confused, or step into an area of testimony that they had not thought to prepare for. Secondly, look for opportunities to take advantage of the witness's or judge's hostility toward the cross-examiner. This typically comes across in the form of the witness's arrogance toward defense counsel or the judge's appearance of being biased when called upon to make his rulings on objections. In response, my father would avoid acting as though he had been deterred or angered by such behavior. The goal here is to strip the witness or the judge of their respectability so that the jury would become more concerned about the unfairness received by his client. And last, but not least, was his ability to very skillfully baffle the witness, opposing counsel, and the judge with his vocabulary. Even when the opposing witness was a well-prepared expert in law enforcement or forensic science, they were outmatched by his vast vocabulary, knowledge of history, and his own brand of Shakespearean delivery that ultimately caused the witness to appear as though they had no idea as to how best to respond. The bottom line is to simply relax, appear competent, and remain respectful in the face of adversity.

Muster Courage, Courage, and More Courage

Many have said that my father was a brave man because at one time he was the only black lawyer south of Atlanta. In fact, his mother tried to dissuade him from returning to Albany upon his graduation from Western Reserve University's law school in Cleveland, Ohio. Although he took and passed the Ohio State Bar exam before leaving for south Georgia in 1953, it was only as a safety maneuver if Georgia denied him a license to practice as opposed to him failing to pass the bar exam.

So where did my father's courage come from? He got it from his father, who got it from his father. According to family lore, my father's grandfather, Allen King, moved his family to Albany from Jackson County, Florida, after beating a white man within an inch of his life. Thereafter, my father's father, Clennon W. ("C. W.") King Sr., moved to Albany after working his way through Tuskegee Institute as a buggy boy for Booker T. Washington. As a staunch believer in Washington's approach to the liberation and empowerment of black people in America, my father's father sought to buy land wherever he could and opened several businesses including a local newspaper. He was one of the founding members of the local chapter of the NAACP as well as the founder of a voter's league that invited Dr. Martin Luther King Jr. to come to Albany following his success with the Montgomery bus boycott. With C. W. King's financial independence and determination to empower black residents, it meant that he was an individual who could neither be bought nor controlled. It was with this level of commitment, philosophy, and indomitable spirit that he raised his seven sons, all of whom were college-educated and several of whom assumed positions of community leadership throughout their lives.

How did my father sometimes illustrate or explain this aspect of his personality? One way would be to describe my father's response whenever asked by whites why did he go by "C. B." instead of his birth name of Chevene. With very little hesitancy, but coupled with some consideration as to who was asking, my father might attempt to enlighten the listener by explaining that because some white folks wanted to assign second-class status to black folks through addressing us by only our first name, he, like his father, would deprive them of that opportunity by using only the initials of his first and middle names. In other words, the initials C. B. did not denote juvenile status for inability. Ultimately, he would say with a slight grin, "It's your choice . . . C. B. could mean 'colored boy,' or it could mean 'contemptuous black.' What do you think?" And that, of course, was a subject matter never to be touched on again.

On one occasion I had the privilege of witnessing the contemptuous black in action. I might have been eight or nine years old when my father took me with him to court in Albany. From what I recall, the courtroom was a smoke-filled room that was dimly lit. Although our presence in the courtroom was very brief, whatever was discussed took place at the judge's bench and therefore outside my hearing range. But as we began to leave the courtroom, I recalled the judge yelling to my father from the bench, "Hey C. B., the sheriff says that you're a liar." In response, my father paused and turned around just long enough to say to the judge, "Well, you tell the sheriff that he's another."

Litigation Marked with Regret

In the last months of my father's life, he shared some of his reflections on cases he had been involved with. While proud of the victories, he also acknowledged that the filing of these school desegregation suits may not have been in the best interest of the black community and therefore something he began to regret.

What caused him to question the merits of this type of civil rights litigation in 1988 stemmed from what he said he had witnessed as unfavorable changes to Albany's black community since integration of the public schools. While it was understood by many within the legal community that the primary rationale and justification for integration was to find a way of ensuring the "equal" distribution of a school system's assets, expenditures, and other resources, attempting to dissolve the racial identity or composition of neighborhood schools did not bring about an improved quality of education and resulting outcomes for most black children. To understand what, how, and why my father was beginning to develop these concerns, you need only hear the conversations between my mother, Carol Roumaine Johnson King, and him.

My mother was a lifelong educator who met my father when he was attending law school in Cleveland, Ohio. After they got married and moved to Albany, my mother spent several years teaching in private and public schools before becoming the director of the Harambee Child Development Council, one of the first and most innovative Head Start programs in the country.

As someone who firmly understood that "it takes a village to raise a child," my mother was instrumental in sensitizing my father on matters such as how, at that time, black teachers had relationships with their students and their families that went well beyond the school grounds or the confines of school hours. To the extent that a student's family and school staff were in most instances already friends, neighbors, and relatives of one another, the school was a preexisting extension of a child's home, the absence of which many believe has greatly contributed to a less effective educational experience for black children.

In the end, I believe my father embraced my mother's concerns as to where the greater battle for the minds and future of the black community was to be fought. Was it in the courtroom or in the classroom? As she reminded my father on many occasions, "If I and my staff had had only a fraction of the money that family had paid you to get their child out of trouble, that child would never have been in that courtroom as a defendant."

My Memories of the Civil Rights Movement

Kenneth Cloke

First, some personal history. I was born into a family that was strongly opposed to racism and prejudice of all kinds. My parents had both been communists during the Depression; my father had fought in the Abraham Lincoln Brigade alongside Black volunteers during the Spanish Civil War; my mother had worked as a welder and riveter alongside African American women in the shipyards during World War II; and my brother and I had both had non-White childhood friends.

In 1959, I gave the valedictorian speech at my graduation from Reseda High School (a small nearly all-white school in the highly segregated San Fernando Valley where I had been student body president), which I called "The Family of Man," inspired by a book with the same name with photographs of people around the world. In my speech, I spoke publicly against prejudice, hatred, and racial injustice.

In 1960, as a student at UC Berkeley, I began working actively for civil rights, supporting fair housing and equal employment opportunity. In the spring of 1960, I picketed Woolworths department store in Berkeley on behalf of students sitting-in at their lunch counters in Greensboro, North Carolina. I joined the Student Nonviolent Coordinating Committee (SNCC) and worked closely with its president John Lewis when he came to Berkeley, and with many other southern civil rights leaders in supporting the movement. In 1961, I organized the San Fernando Valley Chapter of the Congress of Racial Equality (CORE), which for a short time was the largest CORE chapter in the country, and helped organize, recruit participants, and support the Freedom Rides.

I continued working as an organizer supporting SNCC, CORE, and similar organizations, publicizing and raising money to support southern sit-ins among supporters in the Bay Area. I authored numerous resolutions of support for victims of racial injustice and southern sit-ins as a member of student government and chairman of SLATE, a campus political party that frequently demonstrated and fought vigorously for racial equality.

On entering UC's Boalt law school, I became one of the principal organizers of the Law Students Civil Rights Research Council, helping set up a branch at Boalt to support law students in offering assistance to attorneys aiding the southern movement. I helped edit the *Civil Rights Handbook and Civil Liberties Docket*, worked on a number of high-profile civil rights lawsuits, and became active in the Ad Hoc Committee against Discrimination, where I picketed Mel's Drive Ins, the Sheraton Palace Hotel, and Cadillac Row in the San Francisco Bay Area. I was also an active participant in the Free Speech Movement (FSM) at Berkeley, largely led by veterans of the southern civil rights movement, and worked to support legal defense teams for people arrested in sit-ins.

In 1964, I went south as a civil rights worker and began organizing in Selma and Montgomery. I was then sent by SNCC to Greensboro, Alabama, where I was trapped with others in a church for several days, teargassed, surrounded by the KKK, attacked by local police with dogs, and chased by an angry white mob while the FBI sat comfortably doing nothing a few blocks away.

I then went to work in Albany, Georgia, as well as in Americus, "Bad Baker," and "Terrible Terrel" counties, primarily as a law clerk for the amazing, brilliant, unbelievably courageous civil rights attorney, C. B. King, in Albany, as well as working to support the Albany movement.

C. B. was one of the most articulate and funny people I have ever met. He was both kind and clever, sophisticated and humble, brilliant and folksy. When asked anything about "the South," he would often begin with these words: "When the mellifluous odor of honeysuckle and magnolia blossoms waft heavy on the evening zephyr" and then launch into a paean about the virtues of Southern White womanhood or any other topic. On the other hand, when asked how things were, he would likely answer, "White folks still winnin' boss."

Because of the pervasive threat of lynching, exclusionary segregation, rigid Jim Crow laws, and an unapologetic reign of terror that controlled everyday life for Black people throughout the South, C. B. understood quite well that one part of his role was to stand up, speak out, and risk being smarter than White people when others couldn't without losing their lives.

I remember C. B. in one case asking a police officer on cross-examination what his "ethnic identity" was. He hesitated, then answered, "I'm a police officer." C. B. wouldn't let it go, and went back over the same question several times, "I asked you, sir, what your ethnic identity was!," pronouncing each word slowly and correctly, completely humiliating him in front of an otherwise terrorized black audience seated 20 rows in the back, who giggled and cackled with glee at the courage of a Black man to stand up to the police, until the judge finally jumped in to rescue him.

Dennis Roberts, C. B.'s invaluable assistant, my close friend, and a fellow student at Boalt Law School [UC Berkeley School of Law], wrote to me later recalling a similar case of C. B. questioning a jury commissioner testifying in Fitzgerald, Georgia, asking him: "You mentioned Walter JONES in your earlier testimony. Kindly elucidate for the memorialization (the record) what was said here regarding the ethnic identity of Mr. JONES?" After a bit of silence, the commissioner said: "I do believe he's an undertaker."

On another occasion, C. B. was arguing a case in Baker County that dragged on until late at night. At one point his opposing counsel asked for a glass of water, which was brought to him. C. B. then asked for a glass of water, and one of the sheriff's deputies said, "Oh, I'll get it for him, Your

Honor." He went outside to what amounted to a horse trough and brought him a rusty bucket filled with dirty water and dipper, causing laughter all around, including from the judge.

What was inspiring was how C. B. handled it. He spoke calmly and with great dignity and resolve to the court reporter, and said, "I would like the record to reflect that what the deputy has brought me pursuant to my request for a glass of drinking water is a bucket filled with filthy water." He then took *at least* a half hour—which felt like six or seven hours—to describe in excruciating detail the "detritus" and "flotsam," rust, and filth they had handed him. They had no idea what he was talking about half the time, but they got the point. They had screwed up, he had caught them at it, and he was able to rub their noses in it in a way they were powerless to prevent. He was truly amazing.

The most memorable event during my time in the South also took place in the Baker County courthouse. SNCC, led by the extraordinary, brilliant organizer Charles Sherrod and about 20 local organizers, especially from the Miller family, had been arrested for trying to enroll African American kids in what was then an all-white school. On their behalf, we filed a "removal petition" in federal court, which automatically took jurisdiction away from the Baker County court. We appeared in court along with all the defendants and the local police to notify the judge. Judge Crow said, "I guess that's it. Court's dismissed."

At that point Sheriff L. Warren "Gator" Johnson stood up, pulled out his gun, and shouted, "Y'all sit down!" The judge and deputies who knew L. Warren's propensity for violence immediately sat down, followed by the rest of us. L. Warren proceeded to point his gun at us and then at the children who were present, all sitting there helpless, and proceeded to rant for maybe 20 interminable minutes, threatening to kill everyone present and declaring that "No [n-words] going to take over MY courtroom." His anger abated somewhat, he then ordered all of us to "get out of my courtroom," and as we were leaving, he proceeded to kick those he could reach, including children, in the pants, pointing his gun at them and threatening to shoot.

In that moment I experienced intense rage, and had it not been for the calm nonviolent presence of Charles Sherrod, I might have done something foolish. In that moment I also saw, with great clarity—as Martin Luther King Jr. beautifully described it—that "[r]eturning violence for violence multiplies violence, adding deeper darkness to a night already devoid of stars. Darkness cannot drive out darkness; only light can do that. Hate cannot drive out hate; only love can do that."

Another occasion etched in my memory happened when I was driving an "integrated car" in Baker County and we were pulled over by a police motorcycle driven by one of L. Warren Johnson's deputies who I believe was his cousin. I rolled down my window and in my best lawyerlike voice asked, "Excuse me, Officer, are we under arrest?" He pulled out his pistol, put it to my head, and said, "You motherfucking son of bitch, you keep your mouth shut!"

I realized in that moment that he could actually shoot us and get away with it, but was saved, I think, by the fact that there were too many of us in the car, I was White, and he knew I was associated with C. B. and might be a lawyer. So instead, he gave me a ticket for crossing a broken white line which he claimed was unbroken and yellow, assigned me $500 bail, and set a trial for the traffic ticket five months later when he thought I would be gone, and he knew I didn't stand a chance in front of the judge anyway.

I later learned that L. Warren and his deputies often used this trick with out-of-state drivers and raked off the money to supplement their income from the sale of moonshine liquor made with stills operated by the Johnson family. L. Warren often bragged that he had killed over 20 people in his life, including two White women and a Treasury Department agent investigating his stills.

What I Learned in the Civil Rights Movement

My experience in the civil rights movement, especially in the South, was probably the most consequential in my life, which has been filled with consequential experiences. Among other important life lessons, I learned these "top ten" among many—mostly from Black sharecroppers, church women, courageous children, and dedicated organizers—which *vastly* exceed everything I learned attending college in Berkeley:

1. Racism isn't really about race. It's about domination, humiliation, cruelty, arrogance, fear, guilt, theft, rape, and the use of power over and against others. It is about the bitter, destructive *consequences*—socially, economically, politically, ecologically, and psychologically—of living a lie that invents inferiority in an effort to justify the genocidal logic that supports hostile, inhuman behaviors.

2. All biases and prejudices follow the same playbook, and it makes little difference whether they are racist or misogynist, antisemitic, homophobic, xenophobic, colonialist, Islamophobic, ageist, or whatever, as beneath each particular hatred lies a common desire to raise oneself by standing on the necks and backs of others, "canceling" them, taking what is rightfully theirs, using stereotypes to deny their humanity and make them as ashamed and powerless as the people who engage in these follies actually feel themselves.

3. Within *days* of living in the Black community in the South, I went from seeing White people as "like me" to being frightened whenever I saw a White person, and feeling safe whenever I saw someone Black. I have never recovered from that feeling, even on returning to the North, and to this day feel uncomfortable in nondiverse, exclusively White, male, heterosexual environments.

4. The *lie* of racism and all other hatreds; the clear contradiction of basic moral, ethical, religious, and humanitarian principles; the cruelty, trauma, and infliction of emotional punishment—not only toward others (who are subconsciously recognized as equals) but also toward the kindest parts of *themselves*—all these require enormous energy to maintain and replenish, making them vulnerable to social solidarity, communities of resistance, and the simple courage and kindness of ordinary people.

5. While the law was obviously flawed, insufficient, and profoundly compromised by a gross imbalance of power, for those who had *no* power, it played a crucial role—saving lives, offering cover and protection, and opening opportunities for deeper change. Our presence as attorneys and law students significantly discouraged lynching, protected organizers and activists, and offered a legal rationale for dismantling American apartheid.

6. The law could not have played this role without the support of countless lawyers, organizers, and activists bringing, researching, funding, and publicizing lawsuits; raising money and securing media coverage exposing racism, especially in the North; and voting for candidates who they could *compel* to pass legislation, and at times, send troops to enforce it.

7. The law is a blunt instrument, designed, on the one hand, to discourage resort to violence, and, on the other, to coerce compliance. When it fails, it defers to power and the threat of violence, revealing an iron fist within the velvet glove. The law can punish lynching and declare the right to sit where one wants on a bus, but if we want to engage people in dialogue, learn how to live together, and change hearts and minds, a more subtle approach is necessary.

8. The compelling logic of the right to freedom, equality, justice, dignity, respect, and self-determination; of having one's own voice; of gaining power over one's own life, all of which were learned in the civil rights movement, continued to ripple rapidly outward, invigorating student protests and educational reform, movements for women's and gay liberation; opposition to the war in Vietnam; labor and poor people's campaigns; Chicano, Puerto Rican, Native American liberation; and support for environmental protection.

9. To bring about social change in the South, it was necessary to bring about legal change. To bring about legal change, it was necessary to create political change. To create political change, it was necessary to work for economic change, and vice versa, as each change required deeper ones, and in this way the prevailing *system* of bias, inequality, and domination was revealed.

10. I knew before traveling to the South that doing so meant risking my life. I also knew that *not* doing so meant being cowardly, complicit, and betraying my values. What I did *not* know was that taking that risk would be profoundly freeing; that dedicating my life to a just cause would be heart-opening, joyful, and a gateway to wisdom; or that I would be given *far* more in doing so from those I went to support than I could ever have given in exchange.

As always, there is much more to say and still more to do. We now know that it is possible for all the gains we made to be rolled back, for lessons to be forgotten, for prejudice and cruelty to return and raise their vicious heads. But the deepest lesson of all is that fundamental change is *possible*, and that the need to organize and support movements that make it happen never ends.

Notes

1 "The Reuter Transcript Report," March 10, 1993, available in LEXIS, Nexis Library.
2 Quoted by Yvonne Thomas, representing Zeta Phi Beta Sorority in her testimony in support of Clarence Thomas's nomination to the Supreme Court, September 19, 1991, available in LEXIS, Nexis Library.
3 I conducted 38 formal oral history interviews between 1992 and 1999. In 1988, when the council officially closed, its files remained in its offices and in the basement of the ACLU building on W. Forty-Third Street in New York City. Over time, files were damaged and destroyed. What survives is archived at the Seeley Mudd Library of Princeton University Libraries, which had provided generous support for the project. Interviewees were typically gracious in granting access to their private files. Additional documentation was discovered in small collections of council participants, foundation archives that funded the council, and law school archives of law student organizations. The San Francisco Foundation files in the Bancroft Archives at the University of California at Berkeley and the Carnegie Corporation Foundation files in the Rare Book and Manuscript Library at Columbia University provided additional documentation.
4 Manning Marable, *Race, Reform and Rebellion: The Second Reconstruction in Black America, 1945–1982* (Jackson: University of Mississippi Press, 1984), 69.
5 Arthur Kinoy, *Rights on Trial: The Odyssey of a People's Lawyer* (Cambridge: Harvard University Press, 1983). Len Holt, *An Act of Conscience* (Boston: Beacon Press, 1965). Interview with Luke Hiken, April 21, 1994. Interview with Dennis Roberts, April 19, 1994. Interview with William Robinson, February 24, 1994.
6 See, e.g., *Schware v. New Mexico*, 353 U.S. 532 (1957) and *Konigsberg v. California*, 353 U.S. 552 (1957).
7 The October 1940 issue of the *Lawyers Guild Review* reports, e.g., the NLG's decision to work more closely with the National Bar Association, a professional bar association founded by African American attorneys. Martin Popper, "With the Guild Committees," *Lawyers Guild Review* 1, no. 1 (October 1940): 24.
8 LDF was also charged with the responsibility for continuing the legal offensive, begun in 1935, to dismantle the separate but equal provisions of *Plessy v. Ferguson*, 163 U.S. 537 (1896), particularly as they applied to education. NAACP's well documented legal strategy to end school desegregation was a massive effort, conceived and coordinated by Marshall and others, which culminated in the success of *Brown v. Board of Education*, 347 U.S. 483 (1954). Note that in 1962, Len Holt, an African American attorney based in Virginia, independent of the NAACP filed an omnibus desegregation suit against officials of Danville, Virginia, in an effort to desegregate public facilities in that city. See generally Jack Greenberg, *Crusaders in the Courts* (New York: Basic Books, 1994; and Holt 1965).
9 See generally Sarah Hart Brown, "Subversive Southerners: Three Uncommon Lawyers and Social Policy in America and Europe 1945–1965" (PhD diss., Georgia State University, 1993). Thomas Hilbink, "Filling the Void: The Lawyers Constitutional Defense Committee and the 1964 Mississippi Freedom Summer" (Undergraduate

thesis, Columbia University, 1993). Samuel Walker, *In Defense of American Liberties: A History of the ACLU* (New York: Oxford University Press, 1990).

10 Ann Fagan Ginger and Eugene Tobin, eds, *The National Lawyers Guild: From Roosevelt through Reagan* (Philadelphia: Temple University Press, 1988), 92, 188–89. Len Holt, *The Summer That Didn't End: The Story of the Mississippi Civil Rights Project of 1964* (New York: Da Capo Press, 1992). Kinoy, *Rights on Trial*. Walker, *In Defense of American Liberties*. Holt, *Act of Conscience*.

11 Walker, *In Defense of American Liberties*. Hilbink, "Filling the Void."

12 The guild was never listed on Brownell's list of subversive organizations. The effort to redbait the guild because of its member's representation of labor organizers and other progressive causes lasted well into the 1970s. See Ginger and Tobin, *National Lawyers Guild*, chap. 9, 336.

13 Greenberg has written that he was "worried about giving anyone any slim reason to attribute anything we did to advancing the party line." In other words, Greenberg did not want to be associated with an organization that was presumably a "mouthpiece for the Communist party." He was concerned that affiliation with the guild would be yet one more reason for civil rights opponents to discredit the Inc. Fund. Greenberg, *Crusaders in the Courts*, 350–51.

Greenberg's concerns reflected mainstream, conservative opinion about the National Lawyers Guild that, during the 1950s, had resulted in attacks on the organization as well as on individual attorneys. Despite these threats, the guild steadfastly refused to condemn communism or to require its members to take a loyalty oath. Although some guild members were members of the Communist Party, the guild's policies and practices have always reflected a broad spectrum of progressive legal workers. See generally Claybourne Carson, *In Struggle: SNCC and the Black Awakening of the 1960s* (Cambridge: Harvard University Press, 1981). Ginger and Tobin, *National Lawyers Guild*. Victor Rabinowitz, *Unrepentant Leftist: A Lawyer's Memoir* (Chicago: University of Illinois Press, 1996). Walker, *In Defense of American Liberties*.

14 See generally Thomas L. Shaffer and Robert S. Redmount, *Lawyers, Law Students and People* (Colorado Springs: Shepard's, 1977). Robert Stevens, *Law School: Legal Education in America from the 1850s to the 1980s* (Chapel Hill: University of North Carolina Press, 1983).

15 Junious L. Allison, "The Evaluation of a Clinical Legal Education Program: A Proposal," *Vanderbilt Law Review* 27 (1974): 371–87.

16 Interview with Amanda Hawes, August 8, 1992. Interview with Carol Ruth Silver, April 21, 1994. Interview with Howard Slater, February 3, 1994.

17 Washington Civil Rights Program, Higgs proposal ca. 1963, Fingerhood Files, in author's possession. Interview with Steve Antler, April 27, 1994.

18 Slater interview. Roberts interview.

19 Antler interview. Slater interview. Roberts interview.

20 Jack Greenberg has claimed credit for introducing LSCRRC leaders to the Field and New World foundations. Greenberg, *Crusaders in the Courts*, 377.

21 See generally Herbert Haines, *Black Radicals and the Civil Rights Mainstream, 1954–1970* (Knoxville: University of Tennessee Press, 1988), chap. 2. It is interesting to note that in 1963, officials of the Kennedy administration arranged for the Taconic Foundation to make grants for voter registration projects to a consortium of major civil rights groups. Haines, *Black Radicals,* 125. LSCRRC was one of the beneficiaries of these funds.

22 Just before and during my tenure as program director of LSCRRC (1983–86), the Ford Foundation provided grants that were earmarked for internships at agencies that were funded by Ford. Similarly, grants from the EEOC and the Legal Services Corporation were earmarked for internships at only those offices funded by those agencies.

23 One of the most well-known LSCRRC fundraisers was the boat ride around Manhattan, held during the summer months. LSCRRC sold blocks of tickets to this boat ride to major New York City law firms which incorporated the ride into their activities for their summer associates. Pro Bono Publico dinners were also held in the late '70s and early '80s honoring major figures in the civil rights community such as Cyrus Vance. Interview with Wilhelm Joseph, August 22, 1994.

24 Greenberg, *Crusaders in the Courts.* Slater interview.

25 Roberts interview. Antler interview. Interview with Michael Starr, June 24, 1994. Interview with John Brittain, February 4, 1994.

26 Greenberg 1994, Slater interview.

27 LSCRRC's Articles of Incorporation embodied the founders' goals and extended their vision to include commitment to provide research in the service of civil rights. The articles stated, in relevant part, that the goals were:

> To engage in non-partisan research, study and analysis of the law with a view to eliminate prejudice and discrimination; to defend human and civil rights secured by law; and to make public the conclusions reached through such study.
>
> To provide a civil rights apprentice program where students may study with and assist members of the legal profession in the civil rights field on behalf of indigent, poor and distressed or underprivileged litigants in civil rights cases.
>
> To provide loans, grants, and scholarships to study and research in the field of civil rights.

28 These are the earliest enrollment figures available concerning the numbers of students of color in law schools. American Bar Association, Section on Legal Education and Admission to the Bar, *A Review of Legal Education in the United States, Fall 1995* (Chicago: ABA Press, 1996).

29 During the early 1960s, LSCRRC participants initiated a law library program intended to provide law books to poverty law offices or community organization offices in slum neighborhoods in the North. The program was short-lived since the law books that were donated were out-of-date; Antler interview. Al Katz, a 1964 white intern, currently teaching in Florida, and two other LSCRRC participants, Marilyn Kennedy and Nancy F. Johnson, developed a proposal for a secretarial program that

was intended to provide volunteer secretarial support to civil rights attorneys down south; Prospectus of Civil Rights Secretarial Program, ca. 1964–65, Fingerhood files, currently in author's possession. Interviewees do not remember this program, and available documentary evidence gives no indication as to whether the prospectus was discussed at any meeting or if the program was ever functional.

30 Memo from Steering Committee, 1965; Fingerhood files, currently in author's possession.

31 In 1957, the board of directors of the Henry Street Settlement House in New York City voted to support a delinquency prevention project that would provide comprehensive services to the Lower East Side community where juvenile delinquency was a severe problem. This project, Mobilization for Youth (MFY), was first funded in 1962 through President Kennedy's Committee on Juvenile Delinquency. Initially, the program offered a vast array of social services, including recreational programs and family aides, but did not provide any legal assistance. Finally, in 1963, at the suggestion of the Ford Foundation, MFY developed a plan for delivery of legal services that was initially funded by the Vera Foundation. The MFY Legal Unit's first director, Ed Sparer, argued that the unit's major objective should be strategic litigation "designed to change the institutional structures that created and sustained poverty," rather than direct legal services to individual clients on discrete issues. This vision of legal services delivery became the model for other legal services units developed throughout the United States in the 1960s. See generally Martha Davis, *Brutal Need: Lawyers and the Welfare Rights Movement, 1960–1973* (New Haven: Yale University Press, 1993).

32 As part of its mission to recruit southern African American law students to LSCRRC's programs, the organization raised funds for additional scholarships earmarked for these students. During the 1960s, those law students who worked during the summers of their law school career generally worked at nonlegal jobs or private law firms whose summer stipends were substantially higher than what LSCRRC offered. See generally Hugh Stevens and Robert Spearman, *A Step Toward Equal Justice: Programs to Increase Black Lawyers in the South: 1969–1973* (New York: Carnegie Corporation, 1974).

33 Wulf noted in his 1977 evaluation, that in 1976, the board of directors approved a policy of encouraging students to develop project proposals. According to Wulf's evidence, approximately one half of the 1977 summer interns were employed working on these special projects. Wulf also noted that the shift in policy had political consequences that he felt should be evaluated. Most notably, Wulf was concerned that there was the "danger that the needs of the client-community will be subordinated to the subject interests of the students"; Melvin L. Wulf, "An Evaluation of the Law Students Civil Rights Research Council," October 1977, pp. 10–11, archived at Bancroft Library, University of California at Berkeley. By 1983, however, when I was hired as LSCRRC's program director, the internship program reflected a definite balance in favor of placements in traditional legal services, civil rights, and community-based organizations.

34 The foreword to *Voices of Civil Rights Lawyers* by Marian Wright Edelman, whose life was also changed by her civil rights activism (an arrest for a sit-in in Atlanta led her to law school instead of the Foreign Services), provides a powerful overview of the social and personal impact of the movement.
35 Names and other identifying information have been changed to protect client confidentiality.
36 I learned subsequently that the company had complete freedom to hire foremen because they are salaried employees. The lines of progression were irrelevant.
37 Tuskegee is an HBCU, a historically black college or university.
38 Pub. L. 88–352, 78 Stat. 241.
39 Pub. L. 89–110, 79 Stat. 437.
40 Later to become widely known by her married name, Marian Wright Edelman, as a founder and longtime head of the Children's Defense Fund.
41 Aronson would later become a renowned advocate for the civil rights of American servicemen in Vietnam.
42 Martin Luther King Jr. spoke at Wesleyan three times while I was a student there, including once to the interdisciplinary College of Social Studies, in which I studied, as well as at my graduation ceremony in June 1964. Being in his immediate presence conferred a unique measure of inspiration.
43 Yet I have never eaten pig's brain in the ensuing 56 years.
44 347 U.S. 486 (1) 1954.
45 396 U.S. 19 (1969).
46 391 U.S. 430 (1968).
47 The issue of resistance to school integration in Boston, where I settled after law school, was nationally publicized.
48 I did later meet with them in Batesville to give them guidance on how to apply for benefits.
49 At some point I learned that the Miles' farmhouse had been fired at on at least one occasion in earlier years, which had led Mr. Miles to buy a gun or guns.
50 *New York Times,* July 10, 1966, p. 1, col. 7.
51 My license was issued by my home state of New Hampshire.
52 Two summers earlier, student volunteers James Chaney, Andrew Goodman, and Michael Schwerner had been stopped, arrested, beaten, and shot in Neshoba County. They were buried beneath a hastily constructed coffer dam in a rural area.
53 I did not need any further persuasion on that point.

2

Southern Legal Action Movement

SLAM: The Organizing Drive and the Summer Institute

Jim Rowan

We—Joseph Tieger, Carson Taylor, Alex Hurder, Dave Hough, and me—started law school in the fall of 1967 in what were heady times.[1] It did not take long before we discovered that even at Duke Law School there were kindred spirits. That fall, there were campus protests about the war and the treatment of campus workers. Draft resisters were in jeopardy and were counseling anyone who approached them about ways to avoid the military draft. At the center of all this activity was Joseph Tieger. He was a draft resister. He had been with Students for a Democratic Society and then SSOC—the Southern Student Organizing Committee. He had been working in the South and was the guide for other northerners—only Alex Hurder was a southerner—who flocked around him.

The ragtag bunch formed the Student Legal Action Movement to organize our nascent efforts. We wanted to do draft counseling and pored over each mailing that arrived from the Selective Service Law. We fought the university's efforts to maintain order with a pickets-and-protest policy. We worked to establish a legal aid program and a law school clinic. We worked with welfare organizers and the Malcolm X Liberation School. We played volleyball and ate communal dinners. In other words, we worked to support our own self-interests. We managed to survive the first year of law school. We put together the Durham Research Institute in the summer after our first year and went about doing advocacy of various sorts.

When we returned to school in the fall of 1968, and began to think about the future, we wanted to keep doing good work forever and thought that it could best be done where we were—in the South. We knew or dimly recognized how ill equipped we were and how much help we would need to succeed. We already knew every progressive lawyer within fifty miles.

Julius Chambers's firm—Chambers, Stein, Ferguson and Lanning—had an outpost in Chapel Hill staffed by Adam Stein, and he brought us news from the legal struggle for civil rights. Conrad Pearson was the black lawyer called on when there were arrests for protests and demonstrations. And we got connected to the National Lawyers Guild, the Civil Liberties Union, and LSCRRC and its summer internships.

We devoured news from the alternative press. The *North Carolina Anvil*. The *Kudzu*. The *Protean Radish*. The *Great Speckled Bird*. And the flow of newsletters from progressive organizations all over the South that poured into the SSOC house in Durham. We were talking to SCLC, SCEF and SNCC, the Black Panthers, and the Progressive Labor Party. We got it in our heads that we could do ourselves and the movement a favor if we gathered progressive lawyers and law students into a supportive network for mutual aid. We could educate one another. Employ one another. Encourage one another.

We went to the National Lawyers Guild with this half-formed idea. The guild had done in some cities and regions what we wanted to do in the South. They had hired some hardworking and inspiring organizers—smart recent graduates who were well connected—such as Bernardine Dohrn and Joan Anderson, who toured the South and organized student chapters. Early in the fall of 1968, we started to press our new allies in the guild for funding and support for the guild in the South. But we asked for support for an independent organization that would affiliate with the guild but not belong to it.

First, we had to find our constituents. We divided the southern states and pledged to visit all the law schools and meet all the students interested in movements for social change. We would also look for progressive faculty members and local lawyers and talk with them to see if they had unmet needs. We had some lists of contacts from our own work, what we had read in the alternative press, the names of cooperating attorneys of the NAACP, Inc. Fund, Civil Liberties Lawyers suggested by Reber Boult from Atlanta, and the National Lawyers Guild contacts from Ben Smith and the national chapter organizers. Alex Hurder did most of the travelling in March of 1969 from the SSOC headquarters in Nashville, but the rest of us did a state or two. Alex logged more than 2,200 miles in ten days and submitted a bill for $88 at 4 cents a mile not including the tire he had to buy. The net result of the collective efforts was a pretty solid list of 154 law students and 22 law professors and lawyers who formed the core of those invited to Tuscaloosa to plan the summer institute. Tuscaloosa was home to Jack Drake and other allies at the University of Alabama, and it was there that the plans for the first conference were hammered out.

The first summer institute was held at the Assembly Inn in Montreat, North Carolina, over an eight-day period (Sunday, August 24–Monday, September 1) divided into two four-day components. It started with a four-day introduction for law students on three topics: military law, political repression, and poverty law. The second four-day session included lawyers starting with political repression, and included presentations on prisons, omnibus litigation, employment discrimination, and ended with military law. For $65, people got a place to stay in the lodge, three meals a day, and the run of the place including swimming in the lake. There were campsites for $1.50/day and scholarships if money was tight.

Attendance records indicate the representation by state: Alabama (7), Louisiana (7), Mississippi (5), North Carolina (30), South Carolina (6), Tennessee (8), Texas (4), Florida (21), Georgia (11), Kentucky (6), Virginia (8), West Virginia (2), New York/New Jersey (19), Washington, DC (3), and California (2) for a claimed total of 150.

Sunday, August 24, began with a lecture on military law that ran from 7:30 to 10 p.m. and was led by Loni Levy, Victor Rabinowitz, and GI organizers from Ft. Bragg and Ft. Jackson. Loni Levy was the coordinator and authority at the NY Draft and Military Law Panel while Rabinowitz was the president of the NLG, and partner in Rabinowitz and Boudin—the standard bearer of progressive NYC law firms. When the conference reconvened the next morning, the introduction continued from 9:30 to 10 a.m. with added expertise from Laughlin McDonald and Peter Rindskopf.

On Tuesday, the conference turned to the role of movement lawyers with another powerhouse collection of lawyers: Mike Sayre from the southern office of the Center for Constitutional Rights; Adam Stein from Chambers, Stein; Carol Lefcourt from the law commune Lefcourt, Garfinkle; and Bill Allison from SCEF—the Southern Conference Education Fund.

By the third day, a SLAM resolution had been drafted setting out the purposes of the organization and after strenuous debate it passed on August 30 before the conference ended. The resolution dedicated SLAM to assist practitioners, defend movement lawyers, provide for innovative forms of practice, establish of a military law panel, support paraprofessionals, and form a speaker's bureau.

On Wednesday, Kent Spriggs had assembled leaders from legal services programs, and they introduced welfare (J. V. Henry, California Rural Legal Assistance), consumer (Blair Shick of Center for Consumer Law), housing (Joseph Segor from Rural Advocacy Project), and farm poor law (Kent Spriggs, North Mississippi Legal Services, and J. V. Henry, CRLA). The evening session ended with a presentation on organizing in the poor white community by Dick Landerman from ACT in Durham.

Some of the lawyers started showing up on Thursday, August 28, and the pace and intensity kicked up another notch with a morning session that featured Howard Fuller from Malcolm X Liberation School and Anne Braden of SCEF. Books have been written by and about each of these heroes of the civil rights movement. They were followed by Arthur Kinoy, who was consistently challenging and supporting progressive legal movements, and Bob Sedler, a law professor at Kentucky and counsel for *McSurley v. Ratliff* and *McSurley v. McClellan*. And that was just the morning. It may have been that day at lunch that the unruly crowd started a food fight in the dining room when the Highlander staff served grapes to the group who had been boycotting the fruit since the United Farm Workers action began.

Michael Tigar appeared after lunch, not as the expert on selective service but on the issue of fighting mass school expulsion, which was his new passion as he eased into his role as a USC law professor. The rest of the day was devoted to issues of criminal defense and police misconduct with Howard Moore from Atlanta's Southern Legal Assistance Project and George Daly of Charlotte, who was representing the Black Panthers.

Arthur Kinoy was back in the spotlight on Friday morning talking about affirmative injunctions and declaratory relief on a day that focused on political oppression. Ben Smith, from New Orleans, followed Kinoy and talked about the removal of cases from state to federal court. Ben was the face of the guild in the South as a long-standing union lawyer and member of the national leadership. Kinoy's law partner and nationally known trial lawyer Bill Kunstler took the floor in the afternoon to talk about conspiracy laws and the trial of the Chicago Seven and the Black Panthers—make that the Chicago Eight. The afternoon was rounded out with a panel on lawyer repression that included Howard Moore, Daniel Taylor (fighting the Kentucky Bar), and James Winfield from LSCRRC. After dinner, Philip Hirschkop, the legal director of the Virginia ACLU, talked about affirmative litigation of prison conditions.

Julius Chambers led off on Saturday with two hours on omnibus litigation to hold cities and federal agencies accountable for perpetuating apartheid. Chambers was acknowledged to be the most successful civil rights lawyer in the country and was to become the director of the NAACP Legal Defense and Education Fund. He was followed by Richard Sobol of the Washington Research Project on the evolving practice of employment discrimination cases. Participants got the choice to spend the afternoon either with Chambers talking more about omnibus litigation or Sobol on Title VII employment discrimination. The afternoon ended with a session on job placement and support of new practitioners. The evening ended with a panel of community organizers from Mississippi and West Virginia addressing the uses and abuses of litigation and warning about emasculatory movement lawyers who failed to politicize issues and acknowledge community wisdom.

Military law dominated the remainder of the conference and the need for and shape of a prospective military panel of lawyers became the focus of the participants. GI organizers and attorneys explained the range of problems that needed attention, described some of the work that was being done, and began to sketch plans for the future. The attorney presenters were among the most experienced civilian military lawyers in the country—Laughlin McDonald, Michael Kennedy, Peter Rindskopf, and Loni Levy.

The conference ended with a decision by the coordinating committee to establish a military panel to serve the needs of the organizing that was going on at bases throughout the South. It was acknowledged that funds would have to be raised and staff would have to be recruited and supported but the members of SLAM were convinced of the necessity and encouraged by the enthusiasm of the conference to launch an effort to make it happen. The remaining chapters of the Southern Legal Action Movement will have to await another day. Many of the people who attended the conference did practice in the South and some are at it to this day. This was the tale of how a few progressives organized for their own self-interest and did some good for themselves and for those who got caught up in their enthusiasm. It is also the story of the generosity of the movement advocates of the day—a characteristic that continues to endure and inspire activists eager to share their expertise and to welcome the next generation to the struggle for justice.

Southern Legal Action Movement

Jack Drake

In 1968 I received a telephone call from Jerome "Buddy" Tieger to ask whether I would be interested in helping start an organization of law students, lawyers, and legal workers who were opposed to the Vietnam War and supportive of equal rights under the law for all Americans. Buddy further said that the organization would be one made up by people who lived and worked in the American South. I said that I would be interested. Within a relatively short period of time Buddy and Ginny Ericson came from Durham, North Carolina, to Tuscaloosa to talk about the formation of what would be known as the Southern Legal Action Movement or SLAM. In 1968 I was a student at the University of Alabama Law School, from which I graduated in May 1969. Buddy and Ginny were law students at Duke.

Buddy and Ginny drove down to Tuscaloosa for a visit and conversations about how to proceed. We did a mailing to as many people as we could think of on our own and others we identified from organizations that shared names with us. We found the names of law students, for example, who were student members of the National Lawyers Guild or the ACLU. We held our first meeting on a weekend in Tuscaloosa in early 1969.

About 40 people came to that first meeting. Most of the attendees were from North Carolina, Alabama, Mississippi, and Georgia.

I was able to secure meeting rooms at the University of Alabama Law School where we held maybe three different meetings. While we were inside the building, the local FBI were outside writing down the tag numbers of cars parked in the school parking lot. The FBI also had information about who attended the meetings from some unknown informant. I know the FBI was surveilling us because I have obtained copies of most documents contained in my FBI file from those days, and that information is right there in black and white.

We also had at least one meal and a lengthy discussion after dinner at the home of Alberta and Jay Murphy. Alberta taught political science at the University of Alabama, while Jay was one of my professors at the law school. The Murphys had been pillars of Tuscaloosa's liberal white community for many years and had had the proverbial cross burned in their front yard. But the cross was not apocryphal. It was real, and it was burned. One of the things I remember from that meal and meeting are comments made by Alberta and her neighbor and friend Nancy Fowler. When planning the meeting I said to Alberta and Nancy something like: "All we need are some sandwiches," and they replied, "That would be too expensive. We will make a big casserole and have coleslaw or something like that." So Nancy cooked pork ribs layered between mounds of sauerkraut baked in an oven for an hour or two, served with mashed potatoes, salad, and hot bread. It was all wonderfully good.

If it sounds odd that I would remember food stories from that time, I will have to say that my interest in food mixed with political action and the law has continued to this day. Over a 40-plus-year career, I have tried many complicated lawsuits and criminal cases, many of which lasted for a week or more. In all those cases I was the lawyer who made sure that we had easy, regular access to good food. A colleague once questioned my plan to have food brought in during a trial and I told him that every great legal team needs at least one lawyer who can read and write and at least one who makes certain that all of the legal team gets fed.

At the meeting at the Murphy's we decided that we wanted an organization that would be information-sharing and educational and would provide both emotional and real support to members who were, or would be, doing difficult civil rights or antiwar activities. We also concluded that the way to begin was with a retreat kind of meeting with panel discussions about the law and as much reporting as we could get from lawyers who were actually involved day to day in law practices around the South. The retreat was held in Montreat, North Carolina, at the Montreat Conference Center in the fall of 1969. My recollection is that about 150 people attended that meeting. We had several panel discussions covering substantive matters of law and heard from well-known activist lawyers such as Bill Kunstler, Mike Tigar, and Arthur Kinoy. We also had some organizational sessions to continue our efforts to define what the organization was and what it would do. That defining effort resulted in the adoption of a "statement of principles" which I reviewed for the first time in 50+ years a few days ago. The statement seemed so very important at the time. In fact, there was almost a sense of urgency in writing it and getting it adopted by the Executive Committee. But whatever urgency drove its adoption is long gone from my memory. More importantly I think that whatever historical significance SLAM has will not be based on that statement but will rest on what its members did individually and together to bring legal and economic change to America.

However, the statement did include two areas of the law in which we thought our organization and our members should be involved. Those areas were military law and litigation challenging state lawyer licensure requirements including residency requirements. Both of those areas received prompt attention from the members. In less than one year after the Montreat meeting, members Jim Keenan and Margaret Burnham filed suit challenging the State of North Carolina's one-year residency requirement to take the North Carolina Bar examination. That lawsuit resulted in a declaration that the residency requirement was unconstitutional and the court decision led to similar lawsuits and similar results in other states. Likewise, military law quickly became a focus of activities both by SLAM and its members as is discussed below.

But it was the personal relationships and working alliances that came from SLAM that produced lasting, significant change. Through SLAM I met several lawyers who played an important role in my development as a lawyer and as a person. Reber Boult and I met at the very beginning of SLAM at the Tuscaloosa meeting. Reber, at that time, was a lawyer in the Southern Regional Office of the ACLU in Atlanta. We continued that new friendship at the subsequent meeting in Montreat and another much smaller meeting at Reber's home in Atlanta in October 1969. So when I was contacted in early 1970 about a hate campaign conducted by state and local officials against the Lost Found Nation of Islam's efforts to own and operate a cattle farm in St. Clair County, Alabama, I called Reber to alert him to say that some of us needed to respond to this illegal activity.

Reber and I agreed to meet in Atlanta and draw up a lawsuit. Reber already knew about the problem because Orzell Billingsley, Chuck Morgan's longtime friend and colleague, had been arrested as a part of the hate campaign. The trumped-up charge against Orzell was that he acted as an agent for an unregistered foreign corporation by filing for recordation the deed by which the Nation bought the St. Clair County property. The arrest was typical of the kind of harassment Black lawyers routinely experienced in Alabama and the rest of the South in the 1960s and 1970s. Reber also asked SLAM member Jim Keenan, then in New Orleans but also one of the Duke Law School graduates who founded SLAM, to join us as co-counsel. Jim Keenan later became the first director of SLAM and many years later served as a US magistrate judge in California.

The factual allegations we laid out in the complaint described a coordinated campaign to drive the Nation out of St. Clair County and to prevent it from establishing a large cattle farm on the land it had purchased. Local white people, after they discovered the land purchase, held meetings and invited both local and state officials who assured the outraged locals that no stone would be left unturned to keep the Nation of Islam from operating a farm in that area. Among the actions taken against the Nation was a lawsuit filed in the local circuit court to enjoin the operation of the farm because it was a nuisance. One witness testified in deposition that the farm was a nuisance because cows moo and make other sounds.

Reber, Jim, and I stayed up all night to draft a lawsuit to be filed in the federal court in the Middle District of Alabama. The complaint alleged that a state statute and a resolution of the Alabama legislature were both unconstitutional in that they violated First Amendment rights of speech and association. The state statute required a host of organizations including the Communist Party USA and the Nation (as well as "Black Muslims") to register with the Alabama secretary of state and to make numerous disclosures including the names of its members. The resolution in question set up the Alabama Legislative Commission to preserve the peace, which spied on and collected information about individuals and organizations thought to be dangerous. The Alabama Peace Commission was similar to those set up by other states in the face of school desegregation and the civil rights movement of the 1960s. Both the statute and the resolution were typical of the kinds of off-the-wall, unhinged efforts to stop public school integration and to stop marches and demonstrations in various cities in the South.

Since I had to go back home to Alabama anyway, it became my job to carry the complaint and related papers to Montgomery for filing. Reber told me that I would be met at the airport by a lawyer named George Dean, who would also be in the case with us. When I got off the plane, I walked into the small airport building and a man came up to me and said, "Sweet boy, let me help you," as George took the briefcase I was carrying out of my hands. I learned that George often called younger men "Sweet Boy" and that he had numerous other eccentricities with which I became comfortable over the next seven or eight years as we worked together on many lawsuits. George Dean developed the factual record we needed by taking depositions of various witnesses including local St. Clair County officials who had attempted by every possible means to drive the Nation out of their county. I attended the depositions and learned from George both what a deposition was and how one was taken.

The case was submitted to a three-judge court as required at that time for all cases attacking the constitutionality of state statutes. The resulting ruling declared both the State Statute and the Legislative Resolution unconstitutional. *Wallace v. Brewer,* 315 F. Supp. 431(M.D. Al 1970). The ruling was a significant step in erasing unconstitutional efforts to suppress the free speech and association rights of African Americans living in Alabama.

Had it not been for SLAM and its various meetings, I may never have met Reber Boult, Jim Keenan, or George Dean. Between 1970 and 1978 I was involved in numerous lawsuits with the three of them or some combination of the three. George, Ralph Knowles, and I represented roughly 200 University of Alabama students who were arrested in May 1970 after protesting the murder of students at Kent State University. That representation went on for more than two years and resulted in at least a dozen separate trials in Tuscaloosa Municipal court. Because George and I had worked on both *Wallace v. Brewer* and the student trials, George decided to bring me into a lawsuit styled *Wyatt v. Stickney* that resulted in the most significant decisions in mental health law in American history. The first decision in *Wyatt* came in 1970 but the major ruling was a set of comprehensive standards that, in effect, defined constitutionally acceptable minimums of adequate treatment for institutionalized mental health patients and was issued in 1972. The Wyatt case went on for another 30 years, but my participation lasted only about eight years.

Reber Boult, Jim Keenan, and I also worked together on what we loosely called in SLAM, military law projects. When SLAM was formed the war in Vietnam was at its height. Many soldiers in the US military opposed the war, as did millions of Americans who were civilians. SLAM established as part of its mission and purpose an effort to provide legal services to American military personnel who were disciplined or prosecuted for antiwar activities and beliefs. One thing I did to make myself available for such representation was to contact people in Alabama who were organizing antiwar efforts among active-duty military personnel. Those organizers were generally located near military posts or bases. One Alabama army post at that time was named Ft. McClellan and was located just outside Anniston, Alabama. Ft. McClellan was a small army post where enlisted men and women were sent for their basic training. The women soldiers at that time had not been incorporated into the same units as men but were in the Women's Army Corps (WAC).

Among the male enlisted men was a small number of African Americans who felt that they were being discriminated against by the army. One day they decided to conduct a protest march on base and in uniform. That of course did not set well with the commanders at the post. The commanders deployed as many military police as they could muster and a confrontation quickly developed. Many of the African American soldiers ran into the Post PX, a kind of general retail store. Some merchandise was thrown to the floor and a lot of pushing and shoving went on. A military police officer claimed to have been threatened, and then struck with a fist. Many African American soldiers were chased down and arrested. Of those arrested most were placed in pretrial confinement, a practice normally reserved for persons charged with the most serious of offenses. The army then conducted an investigation as a result of which felony charges were brought against one soldier thought to be the ringleader of the march and what the army called "the riot." The local antiwar organizers with whom I had a relationship called me to represent the soldier charged with the felony offenses. I then contacted Reber and Jim. The three of us handled the court-martial from beginning to end.

In 1972 when this court-martial took place the Uniform Code of Military Justice had only been recently amended with sea changes implemented. The most important change was to provide for a type of jury trial where in the past there had been a decision made by an officer, generally a command officer. Under the prior system there had been no judge but rather a "law officer" who would tell the decision-maker what the law was and was not. Under the revised system, there was a judge who was in charge of the proceedings in much the same way as one would find in a state court. Under the new system the jury was called "the court," but for simplicity purposes I will call it the jury.

We pored through the new code, known as the UCMJ, looking for every avenue we could find to provide our client with a chance to win his case. We thought we had a strong factual basis to show that the military police had arrested the wrong man. But for that argument to prevail, we also decided that we had to have a young jury and a jury that had at least one African American member. We were extremely aggressive in jury selection. We asked for, and were given, the right to extensive voir dire of the prospective jury members. The voir dire of any criminal proceeding comes as the case is beginning and involves questions posed to the panel of prospective jurors. In the voir dire of the jury, we were able to get two different Lt. Colonels to say that they would always believe the testimony of an officer over that of an enlisted man. Our judge, himself a full colonel, granted our challenges against all the older white officers. We ended up with a jury chaired by an African American captain who was probably no older than 30. After a three-day trial we won a complete acquittal for our client, not guilty on all charges. That was a great victory for us. However, there were other court-martials I tried at Ft. McClellan and which we lost. Other proceedings resulted in a plea deal to save our clients from any kind of confinement. In all I believe that I handled 12 or maybe more court-martials at Ft. McClellan.

I also represented the civilians who lived in the Anniston area and worked with soldiers on the post by helping those soldiers in any way possible and by publishing a newsletter that contained information about the rights of soldiers who opposed the Vietnam War. As one might anticipate, the civilians themselves experienced some difficulty with local police. One day the antiwar organizers were handing out leaflets on a street and were arrested for disorderly conduct. In perhaps 1972 I appeared in the Anniston city court to represent the two people so charged. When I walked into the small courtroom, I saw a man who turned out to be the judge seated at a traditional kind of judicial bench. But what caught my attention more was a man dressed in green work clothes sitting up on the bench to the judge's left. The green clothed man had a huge ring of keys on one side of a belt.

I could not figure out why that man was sitting up on the bench until they called the first case. The defendant came forward and when the complaining witness also walked up to the front, the two of them, both women, got into a fight. I mean a hitting-and-grabbing-and-cussing fight. The man dressed in green jumped down from his perch, grabbed one woman at a time and threw each woman into a room off the courtroom and locked the door. The judge then called my case. I said to myself, "Now, whatever, do not piss off that guy in green."

When the judge announced my case, he called out the name of the arresting officer and then swore him in as a witness. The judge proceeded to ask the police officer questions. I blurted out an objection or maybe it was just a question. The judge looked at me and said: "Well Mr. Drake, in this court we do not have a prosecutor. I ask the questions of the city's witnesses and present the city's case. Then I make a decision. My questions of course do not unduly influence my decision." I decided that since I was about to lose, I would simply go through the motions and appeal the guilty verdict. That is what I did and a few months later got the cases dismissed. I thought for about five seconds about suing the City of Anniston for the unconstitutional way it ran its court. But I decided that I had more important things to do and just stayed away from that court.

SLAM lasted for only five years or so. As I look back, we might wonder why it did not survive beyond those years. As one would suspect about any organization, there are multiple reasons. But I think one was the driver for all others: most of the leaders in SLAM were young recent law school graduates. As they became enmeshed in practicing law, the demands of ordinary life began to interfere with their idealism and their available time. People began to have children, buy homes, expand their law offices, or work on those academic chores that would bring tenure and promotion. Some people abandoned the law altogether to pursue artistic ventures or became entrepreneurs. In short SLAM succumbed to all the activities brought by changes in the ordinary lives we all lead. We should not forget the central message of Walker Percy in all his novels: discovering the secrets of the universe is difficult but not nearly as hard as living an ordinary life. SLAM had an enormous impact on my life. But it went away as things do.

Note

1 Memory and conversation only go so far. Much of the contents of this summary came from a file Joseph Tieger assembled and shared with Professor Greg Michel, a historian at the University of Texas, San Antonio, who catalogued and stored the material and sent it to us when Kent Spriggs requested it.

3

North Mississippi Rural Legal Services

Bonds, Bridges, and Defining Moments

WILHELM H. JOSEPH

When one's career has been the beneficiary of an extraordinary abundance of opportunities, goodwill, and support, it is particularly challenging to reflect on and extricate from the resulting abundance of endeavors and challenges those aspects significantly impactful beyond a merely personal and narrow sense of relevance. This dilemma is justly complicated by a corresponding inner commandment that demands an appropriate response. Hopefully, this attempt to confront the aforementioned challenge will produce some highlights of experiences and insights that would complement the rich body of contributions that Kent Spriggs has elicited from a team of outstanding civil rights lawyers from the 1960s and '70s.

In a nutshell, this brief essay will share some of the factors and circumstances (more truthfully, the people and the relationships) that shepherded me into a career in law with a lifelong focus on civil and human rights, domestically and internationally.

Choosing to Go to College in the United States

In the fall of 1965, I arrived in the region of Mississippi known as the Delta. I turned 21 years old in June of that year and with two other companions had traveled from the Caribbean twin-island country of Trinidad and Tobago to pursue a college education at Mississippi Valley State University (then Mississippi Valley State College) in the town of Itta Bena, Mississippi. This tiny town is located between Greenville (to the west) and Greenwood (to the east) in the poorest section of Mississippi. Anyone with a cursory knowledge of Mississippi would know that my colleagues and I had, in fact, landed in the belly of the beast. The perennial question posed to me has been, "Why did you go to MVSU?" The uncomplicated answer is that the institution, an HBCU, offered me a full-benefits, athletic (track-and-field) scholarship that I appreciated then and since.

What I left in Trinidad was an early background of poverty, though even then there were things to be hopeful for. Two major background factors suggested a better future could be constructed. First, I had gained entry (via national examinations) to, and graduated from, a highly prestigious high school in Trinidad and Tobago—Queen's Royal College. QRC, as it has been known, was established by the British colonial powers in 1870, and up until I graduated in 1963, its principal was actually appointed directly by the sovereign leader in the United Kingdom, that is, the reigning king or queen at that particular point in time. The second contributing factor to a path that could lead me out of poverty was my appointment at the age of 19 to a position within the civil service of Trinidad and Tobago. Against this backdrop, it was natural for me to believe firmly that a third step, the attainment of a university-level education, would be a capstone event in the climb toward a better standard of living than I had experienced during my early years. Attending MVSU on a full scholarship was much more than a case of "any port in a storm." It was a life-enhancing opportunity.

Why Did I Become a Civil Rights Lawyer?

The journey from college to a career in civil and human rights has been shaped by many key events. Here are a few:

> In 1965, on my arrival in the Mississippi Delta, despite the enactment of the Civil Rights Act of 1964 and the US Supreme Court's decision in *Brown v. Board,* apartheid in all its nefarious forms was alive and thriving in the state. Unchecked police brutality, segregation in schools at all levels, blatant discrimination by various arms of the state, and a range of other indignities were being practiced and preserved, with African Americans as the victims. The very existence of black lives, except for the regular portrayals of blacks as criminals and lowlifes, was not acknowledged in the local press or other platforms of the media.

> US escalation in the Vietnam War was being sustained by an increased number of Black draftees and regular enrollees into the military services. Furthermore, many of these servicemen and -women were returning to the United States and the South in particular with strong feelings about having served the country and defended its way

of life. Yet on their return they were not being afforded the respect and rights of full citizenship. Many of these veterans were entering the colleges and universities with the financial support provided by the GI Bill, and they were participating significantly in the civil rights marches and protests in the streets and institutions of higher learning. The consciousness they exhibited was infectious and this emboldened others with whom they came into contact. Student protests became the order of the day. Such activity was occurring in universities all over the country including Berkeley in California, Cornell and Columbia in New York, Central State in Ohio, Duke in North Carolina, and, not surprisingly, Mississippi Valley State University, Jackson State, and Delta State, in Mississippi. The principal demands of these university-centered movements were cessation of America's participation in the Vietnam War, improvement in education, jobs, health, housing, and so on for Black and Brown Americans and an end to the existence of Jim Crow law and its vestiges.

The year 1968 was particularly significant in the movement for civil and human rights in the United States. Major relevant events included the assassinations of Reverend Dr. Martin Luther King Jr. and Robert Kennedy; the escalation of US involvement in the Vietnam War; and the events surrounding the convention of the National Democratic Party in Chicago.

In 1969, the year of my graduation from MVLS, while I was serving as president of the student union, the student body mounted a massive protest of the school's conditions, its relationship with its students, and its role or lack thereof in the wider community. One response of the school's administration in collaboration with the state's education and government apparatus was to attack a peaceful demonstration of students and expel several hundred student protesters from the university. Additionally, several student government officers and protest leaders were singled out for arrest and carted off to the notorious Parchman Farm state penitentiary. Not surprisingly, my name was first announced as one of the 16 students selected for arrest and incarceration. Miraculously, I escaped arrest only because I had been away on a personal matter. It was against this background that I was confronted by a choice: either accept an internship to be trained as an executive (my college-level major was business administration) with a leading top-100 American corporation or attend law school (at the University of Mississippi, or Ole Miss as it is more popularly called) to embark on a quest for legal justice. In the mode of a well-known civil rights movement–related tenet, I did "what the spirit say do" and joined the law school in 1969. I graduated in the summer of 1972.

As it turned out, the higher authorities in Mississippi, acting through the Mississippi Sovereignty Commission, had been closely monitoring my movements and activities at MCLS and elsewhere. When the commission received news of my admission to law school at Ole Miss, they engaged in a concerted effort to prevent my attendance. An excerpt from the minutes of the Sovereignty Commission's August 1969 meeting says in part:

> The August meeting of the Commission was held on August 15, 1969. The main topic of discussion was the latest news pertaining to the fact that Wilhelm Joseph, the very controversial President of the student body at Mississippi Valley State, a foreign student from the British West Indies, had been enrolled in the Law School at the University of Mississippi. Mr. Tutor had already discussed this with Colonel Stewart, the Director of Student Affairs at the University and learned that steps had been made to prevent Joseph's being enrolled but without any degree of success.

After graduating from MVSU, I attended law school at Ole Miss. Upon graduation from law school in the spring of 1969, I initiated a lifelong career in public interest law, first with the Law Students Civil Rights Research Council (LSCRRC), an organization with legislators in New York City and branch offices in San Francisco, Chicago, and Atlanta. This organization was established to identify and recruit students from underrepresented communities such as African Americans, Latinos, women, and others, and establish supportive programs to ensure their completion of law training. After two years as a national director of LSCRRC, I returned to Mississippi in 1974 to serve initially as a staff attorney and later as the executive director of North Mississippi Rural Legal Services in Oxford, Mississippi, which also is the hometown of the University of Mississippi.

During law school and beyond, to maintain focus and purpose, I have often reverted to remembering the words with which civil rights leader Fannie Lou Hamer repeatedly confronted me during one of our up-close-

and-personal mentoring/engagement sessions at her home in Ruleville, Mississippi. During my tenure as student-government president at MVSU, Mrs. Hamer listened attentively to the litany of grievances and complaints I listed regarding the conditions at MVLS and the institution's relationship to the state apparatus and the wider community. Then she looked me squarely in the eye, with a penetrating stare yet with an encouraging demeanor, kept asking me, "Ok, so now what are you going to do? What are you going to do?" Mrs. Hamer was a patient listener who had a low tolerance for talk without action. (I recently saw a poster that reminded me of Mrs. Hamer. The caption advised, "If you want someone to talk about something, ask a man. If you want someone to do something, ask a woman.")

The Civil Justice Gap in America: A Continuing Concern

The Constitution of the United States has never guaranteed the right to counsel to an indigent person seeking legal redress in a civil case. None of the constitutions of the fifty states does so either. Consequently, indigent individuals with a need to seek justice in a civil dispute find themselves in a very uneven playing field. Such persons may include the following:

- an elderly or disabled person whose public assistance benefits have unlawfully and summarily been denied

- an indigent family who is facing an eviction

- a child who is unlawfully expelled from school

- a poor consumer who has been the victim of a fraud

This lack of a guarantee to the assistance of competent counsel in proceedings that are noncriminal in nature is commonly described as the "justice gap." A well-documented study has concluded that only 20 percent of indigent people who need the assistance of counsel in a civil case of significant consequence actually obtain such assistance. While this situation reflects the existing, national status quo, one can only imagine what the situation was in the state of Mississippi and other southern states. In Mississippi the combination of parochial attitudes, blatant anti-Black racism, and scarce resources ensured that access to justice in civil cases was overwhelmingly unattainable by poor, particularly Black, residents of the state.

This is the backdrop for the founding, in 1968, of North Mississippi Rural Legal Services (NMRLS), with funds provided by the federal government of the United States.

My own affiliation with NMRLS began as a client in the spring of 1969, when I was a college senior at Mississippi Valley State University. NMRLS attorneys, together with Armand Derfner from the Lawyers Constitutional Defense Committee, successfully challenged, in federal court my unlawful, summary expulsion from the university. Later, in the summer of the same year, just before my impending enrollment at the University of Mississippi School of Law, NMRLS attorneys, this time led by Jim Lewis, again represented me in a criminal matter when I faced bogus charges in a rural town in the Mississippi Delta.

I graduated from the law school at Ole Miss in June 1972 and immediately headed to New York City to assume my duties as national director of the Law Students Civil Rights Research Council. At the end of a two-year stint with LSCRRC, I returned to Oxford, Mississippi, in the fall of 1974 to serve, initially as a staff attorney, and subsequently as the executive director of NMRLS.

At that point, NMRLS was headquartered in Oxford and operated out of an additional three branch offices—in Holly Springs, West Point, and Greenwood. In August 1974, President Richard Nixon, in one of his last official acts as president, signed legislation that created the federally funded yet independent Legal Services Corporation (LSC). Within two years of its founding, in the early period of the Jimmy Carter administration, the LSC was put in a position to redistribute a significant increase in federal funding to local legal services programs. The approach to this funding initiative was then called "equalization." The goal was to "equalize" the level of federal funding "per poor person" throughout the 50 states. At that juncture, Mississippi was a woefully underfunded state, and as such, was in line to receive a substantial infusion of equalization funds from the LSC. This increase in resources enabled NMRLS to expand its staffing and to substantially increase local community access to its services by opening new branch offices in Tupelo, Lexington, Greenville, Batesville, Grenada, and Cleveland. In addition, the program was able to acquire dedicated space in Oxford for its central administrative operations, thereby enabling the existing, local service office in Oxford to expand its capacity to accommodate more attorneys and other support personnel.

This expansion in service capacity facilitated the hiring of a new cadre of courageous, committed young attorneys, many of whom were Black, and including several native sons and daughters of Mississippi. Illustrative were Solomon Osborne, Alvin Chambliss, Willie Perkins, Isaiah Madison, Lewis Myers, Jesse Pennington, Deborah Jackson, Beverly Druitt, Leonard

McClellan, Sentwale Aiyetoro, and Ben Cole (the current executive director). Some of these new outstanding attorneys, like recently deceased Catherine Kilgore of Batesville, were white. During this era, these new attorneys and their clients enjoyed the luxury of having the support and assistance of an equally outstanding force of paralegals and community advocates/activists including June Johnson, Margaret Kibbe, Mary Gordon, Henry Boyd, Annie Burt, Dorothy Walls, and others. Just as critical to the growth, development, and strength of NMRLS was its core team of professionals, such as public relations specialist and editor Joseph Delany, program development and training expert John Buffington, and chief financial officer Joyce Davidson.

The major, perennial challenge that local legal services face has been the lack of sufficient financial resources to augment the paltry amount of support that the US Congress provides via the Legal Services Corporation. A few states—Maryland, Washington, and New York come to mind—through the efforts of private and public parties, have substantially supplemented the financial and other resources of their local legal services programs. At the same time, the state of Mississippi, not surprisingly, historically and presently remains unresponsive toward taking measures to narrow the ever-present civil justice gap.

For the first time, the low-income residents of the 38 counties that made up the jurisdiction of NMRLS could interact with attorneys who looked like them. This development represented a sea change in the relations between the regular black and poor population, on one hand, and the local and state powers that be, on the other. Black citizens were more willing to step forward as plaintiffs in numerous civil cases that challenged racial discrimination in government and private hiring practices; racially motivated, police misconduct; inhumane jail and prison conditions; unlawful, local government denials and terminations of federally funded, subsistence-level economic benefits; and exclusion of Blacks from juries. During this era, several white attorneys involved in private practice in Mississippi, mainly in the capital city, Jackson, were joining the efforts of lawyers from NMRLS and the other legal services programs in the state to protect and advance the civil and human rights of low-income Mississippians.

Thus, we are not where we were, but we are not where we need to be.

From the Law School to the Community: The Early Years of North Mississippi Rural Legal Services, 1966–70

Michael B. Trister

Thank you very much.[1] It is a pleasure to be back in Oxford after all these years, especially for an occasion as significant as this one. Believe me, there were many times when no one would have believed that NMRLS would ever celebrate a fifth anniversary, let alone a fiftieth—certainly not the members of the Mississippi Bar and political establishment who fought so hard to make us go away, and not even those of us who worked in the program during its early years.

I am going to talk about how North Mississippi Rural Legal Services (NMRLS) came to be and how and why it evolved in its first few years, particularly how the program came to leave the university's sponsorship, and the federal case and investigations that followed. The events I will describe all took place during the years 1966 through 1970.

The OEO Grant to the School of Law

The legal services program, then known as Lafayette County Legal Services, was established in 1966 as one of the earliest legal programs funded as part of the War on Poverty by the Office of Economic Opportunity (OEO). The program was the brainchild of Joshua Morse, who had become the dean of the University of Mississippi School of Law a few years earlier and saw the program as one way to add badly needed financial resources to support the school's academic growth. Structurally, the program was administered as part of the university through the school of law.

When I, along with several of my Yale Law School classmates from the class of 1966, joined the law school faculty that fall, the program was operating as a hybrid of what we would later come to call a judicare program, using private attorneys from the Oxford Bar who were paid to represent indigent clients, and a clinical program, using law students to assist those lawyers. Aaron Condon had been hired as the first executive director of the program, a job he performed while also serving on the faculty. There were no staff attorneys or paralegals, only two social workers, Sally Thames, the wife of a law student, and Diane Zimberoff, the wife of a graduate student, who worked out of a small office just off the square in Oxford.

Since the program was slow in getting started and had few cases in its early months, in the summer of 1966 program funds were used to pay stipends to a group of students from the school of law who were given clerkships in legal services programs throughout the United States. Samuel M. Davis, who later became dean of the School of Law, has written in the *Mississippi Law Journal* that his experience that summer "opened my eyes to the world beyond my provincial upbringing."[2] Upon his return, Davis became one of the first law students to participate in the clinical element of the program.

Staffing Up, Expansion to Marshall County, and Controversial Lawsuits

Because the program was part of the university, there was no board of directors or other body to evaluate whether it was meeting the needs of the local community. Under pressure from OEO, Dean Morse agreed to appoint an advisory committee made up primarily of faculty to oversee the program's activities.

In the summer of 1967, Luther McDougal, a native Mississippian who had been on the advisory committee, agreed to take over as executive director, and under an agreement with Dean Morse, I started to work for the program, while continuing to teach part-time at the school of law. Part of my responsibility included teaching a seminar on poverty law for the law students who participated in the clinical program. In addition, the social workers and I started what we called a community worker program, modeled on the pioneering work of the Dixwell Legal Rights Association in New Haven, which hired and trained local citizens to act as advocates for their neighbors in matters involving the public assistance and other government programs. Annie Burt, Mary Gordon, and Lena Wiley were part of the first group of community workers in Lafayette County.

Fall 1967 also saw the opening of a new office on the square across from the courthouse in Holly Springs, under the name Marshall County Legal Services, initially staffed by Stanley Taylor, who had grown up in Crosby, Mississippi, graduated from Tulane Law School, and was part of the first Reginald Heber Smith Fellowship class funded by OEO through the University of Pennsylvania. John Maxey, from New Albany, Mississippi, became the second staff attorney in the Holly Springs office after he graduated from the school of law in January 1968. Henry Boyd directed the community workers who were hired when that program expanded to Marshall County.

Marshall County was chosen as the location for the new office because of its large, indigent population and the presence of a Head Start program at Rust College that provided us with ready access into the client community. There also was a growing grassroots movement, then, I believe, called Marshall County Citizens for Progress, that was beginning to raise a range of social issues as part of an effort to elect Black candidates who for the first time ran for a number of countywide offices in 1967.

One of the important issues raised during this campaign was the announcement by the Marshall County board of supervisors that the county was going to discontinue the federal food stamp program for low-income families at the beginning of 1968. I particularly remember a Citizens for Progress meeting in late November 1967, chaired by Alfred "Skip" Robinson, who had run unsuccessfully for county sheriff. Skip asked me during the meeting what the group could do to force the supervisors to change their decision concerning the food stamp program. I replied that the organization could start a petition drive to have the question placed on the ballot at the next regular election, though, in truth, at that time I was not even sure if such a procedure existed under Mississippi law. The subsequent petition campaign provided an opportunity for the Citizens for Progress group to continue their organizing efforts in the Black community and ultimately led to a favorable decision of the Mississippi Supreme Court, *Gill v. Woods*,[3] after the board of supervisors refused to order an election in response to the submission of the appropriate number of signed petitions.

In the summer of 1968, Bill Joyner and Robert Kelly became the first staff attorneys in the Oxford office, after their graduation from the school of law, and they later opened a satellite office in Batesville. The use of staff attorneys to provide program services was not well received by the private bar in Lafayette and Marshall counties, since they had accepted the program when it was established, albeit grudgingly, primarily because of the fees they could receive from the program for handling cases.

More controversial in terms of the future of the program were two federal actions filed by the program's staff attorneys during early 1968. The first was a school desegregation case filed in federal court by John Maxey and Stan Taylor on behalf of Black parents in Holly Springs and Marshall County.[4] Since there was no Mississippi state agency with authority over local school districts that could be sued in a single, statewide desegregation action, as in other southern states such as Georgia and Alabama, the more than 150 school districts in Mississippi each had to be sued separately by the Department of Justice or the civil rights attorneys in Jackson. Neither of these had the resources to sue every district, leaving places such as Marshall County and many other counties in the northern part of the state without desegregated schools more than ten years after *Brown v. Board of Education*.[5]

The second case brought by the program involved a constitutional, right-to-travel challenge to the state's one-year residence requirement before indigent families could become eligible for what was then known as the AFDC—Aid to Families with Dependent Children—welfare program. Similar challenges had been brought by legal services programs in other states, usually in places where there was a concern on the part of the state that families would move to the state to receive higher welfare benefits. No one, for certain, was moving to Mississippi to receive welfare benefits, which were then the lowest in the nation, but our community workers had a client who had returned to be with her family in Mississippi after living for a period of time out of state, and so we filed a federal case on her behalf. The case was successful, and our position was ultimately upheld by the US Supreme Court in one of its first welfare rights cases, *Shapiro v. Thompson*.[6]

Political Pressure; Moving to Mary Holmes College

The program's original grant expired in January 1968, but it was extended while an application for renewal was being considered. In February, OEO sent a letter of intent to renew the grant at approximately $300,000 through March 31, 1969. However, the paperwork for the renewal was never completed. Instead, during the spring of 1968, while the program's application for renewal was pending, Dean Morse came under intense pressure resulting from the two federal lawsuits as well as the alleged involvement of program attorneys and other staff in civil rights activities in Marshall County. In April, the Mississippi Senate Committee on Universities and Colleges, chaired by William E. Corr of Panola County, held a hearing in Jackson at which Dean Morse, Porter Fortune, the recently appointed university chancellor, and Dr. E. R. Jobe, executive secretary of the Board of Trustees of Institutions of Higher Learning, were called to testify about our activities. A report prepared later by the American Association of University Professors, based on a transcript of the hearing, later found that "much of the questioning was designed to discredit the Legal Services project so as to induce the university to stop sponsoring it."[7] Threats were made to move the school of law to Jackson, and to enact a prohibition on any state employee suing an agency of the state; and a state audit of the law school's finances was ordered.

As it became clear that the university would likely discontinue its involvement with the legal services program, Luther McDougal and I approached Mary Holmes Junior College in West Point about becoming the program's sponsor. Having another institution of higher education as the sponsor was absolutely critical because under the Economic Opportunity Act community action and legal services projects sponsored by colleges and universities were exempt from the statutory provision allowing the governor to veto any such project carried out within a state. To avoid a governor's veto, Mary Holmes was already sponsoring the Child Development Group of Mississippi (CDGM), a Head Start program that had come under attack by Mississippi senators John Stennis and James O. Eastland, and the college agreed to take us in when, at the end of May 1968, Chancellor Fortune instructed Dean Morse not to apply for a renewal of the program.

Our ability to keep the program alive through Mary Holmes College caught the politicians off guard after they learned that our proposal would be funded by OEO. The acting director of the southeastern regional office of the legal services program in 1968, a professor from Emory Law School who had just assumed his position, subsequently wrote a file memorandum titled "My Summer in Mississippi," in which he described the numerous calls made by the offices of Governor John Bell Williams, Senator Stennis, and other officials demanding that Mary Holmes not be funded. The Mississippi State Bar Association, which had until then showed no interest whatever in meeting the legal needs of the poor, put together a competing proposal for a statewide judicare program that it claimed would provide more and better service to the client community. But this was rejected by OEO, and we were refunded effective July 1, 1968, under the new name of North Mississippi Rural Legal Services to reflect our plans of growing into more counties.

Suing the University

Having failed in their attempts to defund or replace the program, the governor and his collaborators in the legislature and state bar had one last quiver in their bow. Relying on a 1966 policy adopted by the Board of Trustees of Institutions of Higher Learning, which authorized members of the university faculty to engage in outside employment provided that, inter alia, "it does not bring discredit to the institution and that it does not bring the employee into antagonism with his colleagues, community, or the State of Mississippi," the university advised Luther McDougal, George Strickler, another faculty member who was working with the program, and me that, while we could return to the faculty on a full-time basis, we could no longer work part-time for the legal services program while remaining on the faculty.

Luther McDougal agreed to return to the faculty, on the condition that he could remain as chair of the NMRLS board on a volunteer basis, where he was joined by John Robin Bradley, another faculty member. George Strickler and I, however, refused to accept the university's terms and were instructed to leave our law school offices and university housing on short notice. On July 30, 1968, we filed a civil rights action in federal court challenging our forced dismissal as unconstitutional, represented by attorneys from the Lawyers Constitutional Defense Committee. The case—known as *Trister v. University of Mississippi* only because I won a coin flip with George to determine whose name would come first in the complaint—was tried before Hon. Orma Smith, a very recent appointee to the Northern District bench, in late August. At the conclusion of the trial, Judge Smith issued an opinion finding that our rights had not been violated because there was evidence that our continuing to work for NMRLS would have an adverse impact on the quality of instruction received by law students.[8]

Other developments that ultimately proved significant took place while our appeal was pending in the Fifth Circuit. During his testimony before the Mississippi Senate Committee in April, Dean Morse had unsuccessfully warned that any legislative interference aimed at defunding the legal services program could have adverse consequences for the school's accreditation. Responding to our complaints, the American Association of Law Schools (AALS), one of two national law school accrediting bodies, at its annual meeting in December 1968 voted to open an investigation into the circumstances surrounding our departure from the school of law and the defunding of the legal services program.

An AALS investigating committee made up of the deans of the University of Virginia School of Law and the University of Georgia School of Law visited the university in May 1969. While the committee initially equivocated on whether our constitutional rights had been violated, that position became moot when the Fifth Circuit on October 9, 1969, reversed the district court's ruling in a split (2–1) decision rejecting the idea that our work for NMRLS would interfere with our teaching and finding that "the only reason for making a decision adverse to appellants was that they wished to continue to represent clients who tended to be unpopular. This is a distinction that cannot be constitutionally upheld."[9]

Subsequent to the Fifth Circuit decision, the Committee on Academic

Freedom and Tenure of the AALS issued a report finding that the association's rules had been violated, and the full membership of the association voted at its 1969 annual meeting to accept the committee's recommendation that the school's accreditation should be suspended following a hearing in which the school of law would be allowed to contest this decision.

Before this hearing took place, Dean William Bunkley, who had replaced Dean Morse when he left in 1969 to become the dean at Florida State Law School, offered George Strickler and me the opportunity to teach a course at the school of law, which I accepted in the spring semester of 1970. I believe A.C. Wharton, who later became mayor of Memphis, Tennessee, was enrolled in that class on employment discrimination law.

Expansion to West Point and Greenwood

In 1969, funds were provided to open additional NMRLS offices in West Point and Greenwood. West Point was staffed by Jesse Pennington, who had just graduated from Howard Law, and Tom Royals and Tom Mayfield, who had worked for NMRLS as students in the school of law. Greenwood was staffed by Alix Sanders, who returned to his hometown immediately after his own graduation.

During this period, under the direction of Kent Spriggs, NMRLS expanded its school desegregation docket with suits against a large number of school districts in the northern part of the state, including in Oxford, and we began filing employment discrimination cases on behalf of Black citizens who were turned away from employment at factories in the area. While we are here today mostly to remember the lawyers and other employees of NMRLS over the years, these cases remind us that it was the clients who served as plaintiffs who took the biggest risks and without whom no cases would have been brought.

One of the plaintiffs I remember the best was Jewell Madlock of Sardis, who, after Title VII of the Civil Rights Act of 1964 took effect, piled a number of her friends into her car and went from segregated plant to segregated plant trying to apply for jobs. After they were turned down without being allowed to even submit applications, she filed a number of complaints with the Equal Employment Opportunity Commission that later became the basis for Title VII lawsuits brought by the Jackson office of the Lawyers Committee for Civil Rights, NMRLS, and the EEOC itself. These cases eventually opened up jobs for our clients at US Industries in Batesville, Sardis Luggage, and Chromcraft Corporation, among others.

It was also in this period that NMRLS represented a group of students from Mississippi Valley State College who had been arrested when they protested conditions on campus. Wilhelm Joseph who was a student leader and later became executive director of NMRLS was involved in these protests.

Another major event involved the protests by Black students at the university during a concert by a group known as Up with People. And it was during this same year that at the insistence of the Mississippi State Bar Association NMRLS attorney John Brittain was arrested for practicing law without a license.

Finally, I would like to mention another case that further illustrates the role of NMRLS in trying to ensure that Mississippi's programs for poor people complied with federal requirements. When the Medicaid program to provide health care to low-income people was enacted in 1965, states initially had the option of whether to participate. Even though most of the funding for the program was provided by the federal government, the Mississippi legislature refused to establish the program until 1969, when it became mandatory under federal law. However, the legislature limited eligibility only to those welfare recipients whom it believed it had no choice but to include. Thus, in the case of Aid to Families with Dependent Children, the state provided health benefits for the dependent children but refused to provide them for the children's mothers, grandmothers, and other caretakers. With the assistance of Rims Barber, an organizer for the Delta Ministry who was one of the state's strongest advocates for the poor, we brought a class action in federal court in 1969 alleging that the exclusion of the caretaker relatives violated the Social Security Act, and in 1971 Judge Orma Smith ruled that we were correct.[10] The state later reported that more than 27,000 poor adults were added to the program as a result of the suit, a victory worth millions of dollars in medical care each year.

Conclusion

Dean Joshua Morse and the faculty of the school of law deserve lasting credit for their courage and vision in bringing the legal services program to the school of law only four years after the university itself had to be desegregated by federal authority acting with the support of federal troops. Morse and the faculty were also far ahead of their time in recognizing the value of clinical legal education. In the years since that first OEO grant to the school of law, clinics today have become a recognized and important component of the academic programs at virtually every law school.

However, I believe the separation of NMRLS from the University of

Mississippi School of Law was inevitable, given the state's political climate in the 1960s and the university's own recent history. With the benefit of hindsight, no organization devoted aggressively to seeking change to the racially charged social and economic policies still prevalent in Mississippi at that time could expect to thrive if it was subject to the control of the state legislature, the governor, and other public officials and institutions.

In moving to Mary Holmes College, NMRLS took an important step toward not only continuing the program's ability to serve the tremendous legal needs of the poorest people within the nation's poorest state, but also in making clear that the services provided could not be shackled by interference from even the most powerful political forces within the state. This fight for independence continued well beyond these early years.

Holmes County, Legal Services, Summer 1970

Kent Hull

In the late summer of 2022, my memories of interning with North Mississippi Rural Legal Services (NMRLS) in the summer of 1970 connected with more recent legal and political events. Two events came directly from Mississippi.

First was the decision in *Harness v. Watson* by the full (en banc) US Court of Appeals for the Fifth Circuit. Over the dissent of seven circuit judges speaking through three opinions, a majority of ten other circuit judges held that Article 12, Section 241 of the Mississippi Constitution of 1890 disenfranchising persons convicted of enumerated crimes—which the plaintiffs contended had been considered "black crimes," "chosen for the specific purpose of disfranchising African Americans," and "selected to suppress" Black voters—had *not* been "motivated by discriminatory intent."[11]

The second Mississippi event was the failure of Jackson's municipal water system, which left that city's residents without drinkable or usable water. A class action complaint filed in federal district court states that of the city's 150,000 residents, 82.5 percent are Black, with 24 percent living in poverty.[12]

A third event, announced by my former mayor, Secretary of Transportation Pete Buttigieg, was that, "a long-delayed plan to dismantle Interstate 375, a 1-mile depressed freeway in Detroit that was built by demolishing Black neighborhoods 60 years ago [will] remove a racially divisive roadway [and] transform the stretch in Detroit into a street-level boulevard, reconnecting neighborhoods and adding amenities, such as bike lanes [in] predominantly African American neighborhoods, [which had been] razed as part of the 1950s creation of an interstate highway system, displacing 100,000 Black residents and erecting a decades-long barrier between the downtown and communities to the east"[13]

Among the lawyers appearing in the *Harness* case was Armand Derfner, whom I met more than a half century ago in Jackson at the Lawyers Constitutional Defense Committee. Pete Buttigieg's recognition of the destructive effects of earlier highway construction reminded me of a 1970 case in the Greenwood office of NMRLS that challenged a city's failure to provide municipal services—like street repair—in the Black parts of town comparable to services provided in white neighborhoods.

NMRLS is headquartered in Oxford, home to a renowned resident, Nobel Laureate for Literature William Faulkner. Faulkner's famous statement in *Requiem for a Nun*—"The past is never dead. It's not even past."—has been confirmed in my recollections of Mississippi.

The threat to Black voters in Mississippi was neither "dead" nor "even past" when I worked in Holmes County. As the 1960s decade ended, civil rights lawyers continued litigating against discrimination in voting, education, and government services, but began to bring cases involving predatory lending, habitability of rented property, administration of public benefits, and environmental justice. Race had been, and remained, central to litigation, but cases soon addressed economic and social problems—underlying structural issues—that burdened not only people of color, but all those living in "the other America."

My personal work with NMRLS was a minor part of larger efforts, and I write instead about the place, the people, and what we tried to accomplish. That those aspirations remain unfulfilled would not surprise the residents of Holmes County whom I knew and with whom I was privileged to work.

The Place

I had worked the previous summer of 1969 in Holmes County with a project from the University of Illinois anthropology department (and the university's medical school in Chicago), which provided training in health and medical services to residents in the Black community who, in turn, taught and assisted others. Urban anthropologists were also studying the community structures among Black residents and their emigration from Holmes County to Cook County, Illinois. I had completed my first year in the University of Illinois College of Law and, with zero legal experience, arrived as an all-purpose gopher.

The county seat, Lexington, 60 miles north of Jackson, sat in foothills on the eastern edge of the Delta, in a county with 800 farms owned by Black families who cultivated their fields independently, not as tenants or sharecroppers. Robert G. Clark, a popular high school teacher and coach from one of those families, had just won election to the Mississippi state house of representatives, the first Black legislator in that body since Reconstruction.

In the late nineteenth century populist attempts to unite poor farmers and workers—Black and white—could not overcome the power of racism, and the two groups remained segregated throughout the rural South. New Deal reforms in the Great Depression brought change, but the Agriculture Adjustment Act reinforced the power of white planters to deny benefits to tenants and sharecroppers. The more innovative Resettlement Administration, transformed into the Farm Security Administration, "floated the radical idea of extending money directly to would-be landowners or relocating tenants in model communities where they received housing and industrial employment," wrote the historian William P. Hustwit, who found that Holmes County "hemorrhaged population from 39,710 in 1940 to just over 27,000 in 1960."[14]

The county's landowning Black farmers were leaders in the struggle for voting and civil rights, especially around the Mileston community. Two extraordinary people I met in 1969, Henry and Sue Lorenzi (later Sue Lorenzi Sojourner), had arrived from California in 1964 and stayed five years as community workers. They helped the Mississippi Freedom Democratic Party elect Robert Clark. Eddie W. Logan, who arrived in the county in 1962 as a high school teacher, and whom I knew as director of the Holmes County Health Research Project, has written of the importance of Black extended families in bringing about changes to Holmes County.[15]

I had little experience with the county's white population. Among them was a woman I did not but should have met: the publisher of the *Lexington Advertiser*, Hazel Brannon Smith, who had arrived from Alabama City, Alabama, in 1936 committed to segregation. She supported a biracial religious group in the county, Providence Co-operative Farm, established in 1939 with a credit union, consumer cooperative, clinic, and adult education center, an endeavor that ended in 1955 because of terrorism from whites.

By 1964 Smith supported integration and that year won the first Pulitzer Prize for editorial writing. Martin Luther King Jr. had been her houseguest in Tchula, a town near Lexington.

Certainly, I never had any encounters like those portrayed in the movie *Mississippi Burning*, I'm sure in part because I have cerebral palsy and walked with crutches then. An evident disability undoubtedly works to diminish any threat to observers, at least physical ones.

The Legal Work—Then

In 1969, in *Alexander v. Holmes County Board of Education*, litigated by the NAACP Legal Defense and Education Fund, the Supreme Court had issued a decision that, Prof. Hustwit wrote, "marked the apogee of the Court's impatience with southern loitering on school desegregation." After first requiring school integration "with all deliberate speed," but then seeing much delay in implementation, the court announced "the obligation of every school district . . . to terminate dual school systems at once and to operate now and hereafter only unitary schools."[16]

By 1970 the administration of President Richard Nixon, elected with a southern strategy of opposing integration, delayed implementing the *Alexander* ruling, though forces within the US Department of Health, Education and Welfare—the principal source of federal funds supporting public schools and led by Secretary Robert Lynch—favored effective enforcement of the new policy. Implementation would fall to lawyers litigating individual cases and the federal judges hearing those cases.

One prominent lawyer was the late Michael Trister, brought to the University of Mississippi law school faculty upon graduation from Yale Law School in 1966 by a new dean, and who, with the permission of his dean, cooperated with NMRLS as a litigator and clinical teacher. A panel of the US Court of Appeals for the Fifth Circuit described what Trister, his fellow professor George M. Strickler Jr., and NMRLS encountered: "During the spring of 1968 it became apparent that the Legal Services Program was not looked upon favorably by some political and civic groups, and the program was discussed and testimony relative to it received at State legislative committee hearings."[17]

The university directed that Trister and Strickler could not remain on the faculty if they continued to work with NMRLS, but it did allow other professors to teach and pursue more traditional legal practices. The Fifth Circuit wrote, "It appears clear that the only reason for making a decision adverse to [Trister and Strickler] was that they wished to continue to represent clients who tended to be unpopular," a distinction that treated them in a "significantly different manner from" other law professors and denied them equal protection of the law. The court ordered their reinstatement to the faculty. Representing Trister and Strickler were Armand Derfner, with his colleague James A. Lewis of the Jackson office of the Lawyers Constitutional Defense Committee, and Richard B. Sobol of LCDC's New Orleans office.[18]

The Fifth Circuit, journalist Jack Bass has written, was "the institutional equivalent of the civil rights movement itself."[19] Four judges—Richard T. Rives from Alabama, Elbert W. Tuttle and John R. Brown from Texas, and John Minor Wisdom from Louisiana—consistently ruled in favor of civil rights plaintiffs. Rives had been nominated by President Harry S. Truman, but Tuttle, Brown, and Wisdom were Dwight Eisenhower nominees.

Wisdom—for whom the Fifth Circuit courthouse in New Orleans is today named—had been a business lawyer and opponent of the Huey Long organization, teaching estate planning at Tulane Law School and residing in the Garden District of New Orleans. Those credentials—including his leadership in Eisenhower's campaign for the 1952 Republican presidential nomination—were not ordinarily associated with civil rights advocates.

Jack Bass summarized Wisdom's achievements on the court:

> As the scholar and driving intellectual force on the old Fifth Circuit Court of Appeals, Judge Wisdom transformed the law of school desegregation, and he developed the constitutional rationale for affirmative action. He wrote trail-blazing opinions involving voting rights, jury selection, and employment discrimination. He helped develop the structural injunction as a new force in the American legal system, used to restructure an ongoing social institution. It was applied to school systems, prisons, and mental health hospitals—and to reapportion state legislatures.[20]

Adjoining Holmes County to the southwest was Yazoo County, with its courthouse and most prominent lawyer, John C. Satterfield, in Yazoo City. Satterfield frequently represented school boards resisting integration, but his law practice had not prevented the American Bar Association from electing him president in 1961. During his term—despite the prominence of civil rights issues—Satterfield's priority was stopping "unauthorized practice" of law by realtors, labor union advocates in workers compensation hearings, and other professionals who threatened to divert business from lawyers.

The ABA, however, moved beyond Satterfield when, at President John F. Kennedy's request, it established and funded the Committee for Civil Rights Under Law (known as the President's Committee), which today continues significant litigation. In the committee's Jackson office, I met Frank Parker, a voting rights litigator, and the managing attorney, Lawrence "Lare" Aschenbrenner, an Oregon lawyer who later litigated Native American cases. They allowed me to use their very good law library.

The Legal Work—Later and Future

As I completed my internship, changes, in law and in politics, were imminent. NMRLS would be institutionalized into the Legal Services Corporation. Michael Harrington's 1962 book, *The Other America,* together with Dwight Macdonald's 1963 review, "Our Invisible Poor," in the *New Yorker,* had influenced Kennedy's creation of the Office of Economic Opportunity. After *Gideon v. Wainwright* established the right to appointed counsel for indigent defendants charged with felonies, Attorney General Robert F. Kennedy, speaking at a Law Day event on May 1, 1964, at the University of Chicago Law School, acknowledged the corresponding need in civil cases:

> Lawyers must bear the responsibility for permitting the growth and continuance of two systems of law—one for the rich, one for the poor. Without a lawyer of what use is the administrative review procedure set up under various welfare programs? Without a lawyer of what use is the right to a partial refund for the payments made on a repossessed car? ...
>
> The tenants of slums, and public housing projects, the purchasers from disreputable finance companies, the minority group member who is discriminated against—all these may have legal rights which if *we* are candid—remain in the limbo of the law.[21]

Edgar and Jean Cahn, future co-deans of Antioch Law School, had envisioned neighborhood poverty law offices that would "require both fiscal independence and the approval of the bar."[22] They recognized that the "law's capacity to create issues, to bring controversies into focus, tends to make neighborhood legal services too controversial" if sponsoring organizations "must retain the support, or at least the sufferance, of the major institutions in a city."[23]

The Cahn marital partners had identified a central dilemma for legal services. Local programs required government funding, but their lawyers required professional independence to represent clients, both in class action cases against Medicaid, public housing, and social security, and in cases suing or defending against local power elites—landlords renting substandard properties, debt collectors repossessing cars, banks denying credit or charging usurious interest.

In December 1970, California governor Ronald Reagan attempted to stop federal funding of California Rural Legal Services, which had won cases representing farmworkers from Mexico and poor children denied free lunches at schools. CRLA's cooperation with the United Farm Workers met opposition from Reagan, from the growers hiring the workers, and from some local governments supporting the growers. A lengthy federal investigation, with public hearings, absolved CRLA of impropriety.[24]

President Richard Nixon proposed eliminating legal services, then shifted to a plan creating the Legal Services Corporation. The new LSC legislation restricted activities of local programs and of the national backup centers that provided assistance on housing, consumer protection, welfare policy, education rights, and other complex issues. Ronald Reagan became president, but failing to end LSC, reduced funding.[25]

The great paradox was the administration of President Bill Clinton, Yale Law School graduate and spouse of another Yale Law graduate (and future presidential candidate) who had volunteered at New Haven Legal Services. Congressional Republicans advancing a "contract with America" almost ended LSC. Only with support from Republicans such as Senator Warren Rudman of New Hampshire did the Clinton administration preserve a weakened LSC, now prohibited from bringing class actions or requesting attorney fee awards in litigation. President Barack Obama's administration eventually stabilized funding with legislation that also removed the attorney fee prohibition.

Throughout these controversies local programs—sometimes with the help of private law firms—won cases that reformed the law affecting poor people. In *Goldberg v. Kelly,* the Supreme Court held that public aid benefits could not be terminated before recipients had the opportunity for an evidentiary administrative hearing at which they could contest the agency's decision. In *Javins v. First National Realty Co.,* the US Court of Appeals for the District of Columbia Circuit held that leases carried an implied warranty of habitability standards for rental property. That principle, later accepted by the Mississippi Supreme Court, strengthened impoverished tenants in disputes with landlords. Much later the independent Black farmers of Holmes County benefited from litigation challenging racial discrimination in the US Department of Agriculture support programs.[26]

Leaving

As my internship ended, the political—and the legal—soon became personal, in C. Wright Mills's phrase. I returned to Illinois, where I had been an unsuccessful and unhappy law student. Law itself—its history, the logic or illogic of its reasoning and the ambiguities of legal practice—interested me. Law school, by contrast, with its uniform culture, standardized curricula resisting change, and oblique teaching methods, discouraged me.

That I would spend almost four decades as a law teacher—in classrooms or in clinical settings—would have surprised, amused, and probably shocked my law professors. Two forces determined my work.

One was the redirection of legal education from classes of mostly white men taught by faculties of mostly white men to diverse student classes with diverse faculties. Those students and teachers brought new curricula and better teaching skills while applying different testing methods.

Second was the emergence of a disability rights movement. I left Holmes County in August 1970; by November Illinois voters had approved a new state constitution with a Bill of Rights section stating, "All persons with a physical or mental handicap shall be free from discrimination in the sale or rental of property and shall be free from discrimination unrelated to ability in the hiring and promotion practices of any employer." In the next two years students with intellectual disabilities won federal cases in Pennsylvania and the District of Columbia requiring public schools to provide appropriate education, even for students with the most severe disabilities. Passage of the 1975 Education for All Handicapped Children Act, later rewritten as the Individuals with Disabilities Act (IDEA), extended those policies throughout the nation.

Section 504 of the Rehabilitation Act of 1973 prohibited discrimination against otherwise qualified handicapped individuals in programs and activities receiving federal financial assistance and eventually had sweeping effects. Michigan's Handicappers Civil Rights Act of 1976, a state law prohibiting discrimination in employment, housing, public accommodation, public services, and education[27], anticipated the federal Americans with Disabilities Act of 1990.

I would spend five decades litigating disability rights cases (as well as housing, public benefits, and consumer cases). The notion that people with disabilities should assert legal "rights" was, to me, novel, even in 1970. For my own disability, it was an era and culture following what I still consider the courageous example of Franklin D. Roosevelt: accepting the physical limitations one could not change and avoiding discussing the subject, except for occasional self-deprecating humor.

I may have thought that the urgency of racial crises and the Vietnam War displaced secondary personal concerns about the mysteries of living with a disability. If so, I was wrong in not seeing that those concerns pointed to injustice and implied a broader responsibility to fight discrimination.

The Fifth Circuit judges who decided *Harness v. Watson* in 2022 in a courthouse named for John Minor Wisdom demonstrate the challenges yet remaining for advocates on many fronts. I benefited very much from observing the work of very good lawyers at NMRLS and elsewhere in Mississippi. May all of them and their fellow workers keep on keeping on.

Notes

1. This is the manuscript of a presentation on April 22, 2016, by Michael B. Trister, the first executive director of North Mississippi Rural Legal Services, at NMRLS's fiftieth anniversary celebration's Historic Litigation Conference, and is published posthumously. The video of the presentation is available on the NMRLS YouTube channel, https://www.youtube.com/watch?v=9vfTVXakcmA.
2. Samuel M. Davis, "A Tribute to My Dean, Joshua M. Morse, III," *Mississippi Law Journal* 82, no. 7 (2013): 1217–20.
3. 226 So. 2d 912 (Miss. 1969).
4. Anthony v. Marshall County Board of Education, 409 F.2d 1287 (5th Cir. 1969).
5. 347 U.S. 483 (1954).
6. 394 U.S. 618 (1969). The NMRLS case was *Jackson v. Winstead*. It never went to trial.
7. "Academic Freedom and Tenure: University of Mississippi," *AAUP Bulletin* 56 (1970): 75.
8. Judge Smith's opinion is unpublished.
9. Trister v. University of Mississippi, 420 F.2d 499, 504 (1969).
10. Triplett v. Cobb, 331 F. Supp. 652 (N.D. Miss. 1971).
11. Harness v. Watson, 47 F.4th 296 (5th Cir. 2022), cert. pet. filed Nov. 02, 2022 (No. 22–412); the plaintiff-appellants' opening brief to the Fifth Circuit, which characterizes the 1890 provision as "chosen" and "selected" to disenfranchise Black voters, is at 2019 WL 7039797.
12. The case is *Sterling v. City of Jackson,* No. 3:22-cv-00531-KHJ-MTP (S.D. Miss.), filed September 16, 2022.

13 "Grant to help Mich. with plan to tear down divisive highway," WLNR 29889090, *Chicago Tribune,* September 20, 2022.
14 William P. Hustwit, *Integration Now: Alexander v. Holmes and the End of Jim Crow Education* (Chapel Hill: University of North Carolina Press, 2019), 24.
15 Eddie W. Logan and Dennis A. Frate, "The Struggle for Black Community Development in Holmes County, Mississippi: Internal Efforts, External Support, and the Role of Science," in *The Extended Family in Black Societies,* ed. Frate et al. (The Hague, the Netherlands: Moulton, 1978), 3–20.
16 Hustwit, *Integration Now,* 138n6; Alexander v. Holmes Cnty. Bd. of Ed., 396 U.S. 19, 20 (1969).
17 Trister v. Univ. of Miss., 420 F.2d 499, 500 (5th Cir. 1969).
18 *Id.,* at 504; a district judge sitting by designation on the panel dissented.
19 "John Minor Wisdom and the Impact of Law," Mississippi Law Journal 69 (1999): 25, 26.
20 *Id.,* at 29.
21 Gideon v. Wainwright, 372 U.S. 335 (1963); excerpts of Kennedy's speech are reprinted in Edgar S. Cahn and Jean C. Cahn, "The War on Poverty: A Civilian Perspective," 73 *Yale Law Journal* (1964): 1317, 1336–37n27.
22 Cahn and Cahn, "War on Poverty," 1349n14.
23 *Id.*
24 Taylor Cozzens, "Ronald Reagan v. CRLA: Politics, Power, and Poverty Law," *California Legal History* 15 (2020): 175–206.
25 Alan W. Houseman, "Rationing Justice: Access to Justice and the 40th Anniversary of the Legal Services Corporation," *Georgetown Journal on Poverty Law and Policy* 22 (2015): 469.
26 Goldberg v. Kelly, 397 U.S. 254 (1970); Javins v. First National Realty Corporation, 428 F.2d 1071 (D.C. Cir. 1970), cert. denied, 400 U.S. 925; O'Cain v. Harvey Freeman & Sons, 603 S0.2d 824, 831 (Miss. 1991) (implied warranty of habitability); In re Black Farmers Discrimination Litig., 856 F. Supp. 2d 1 (D.D.C. 2011), as amended (Nov. 10, 2011).
27 Illinois Constitution, Art. 1, § 19; Pennsylvania Ass'n, Retard. Child. v. Commonwealth of Pa., 334 F. Supp. 1257 (E.D. Pa. 1971); Mills v. Board of Education of District of Columbia, 348 F. Supp. 866 (D.D.C. 1972); IDEA, 20 U.S.C. § 1401, et seq.; Section 504 is codified at 29 U.S.C. § 794; the Michigan law was No. 220 1976 Mich. Pub. Acts 583 (codified as amended at Mich. Comp. Laws Ann. §§ 37.1101–.1607 [West 1985]).

4

Trying Cases

Louie Baeza and the Fork in the Road

David Kern

Early in 1994, I established a law office near downtown El Paso, Texas, in a stately old three-story mansion once owned by one of El Paso's richest families, the Ainsas. Although some still referred to the mansion as the "Ainsa House," by the time I moved in a famous El Paso trial lawyer, Malcolm McGregor, had owned it for many years, and each of the oversized bedrooms upstairs, the den downstairs, and the separate carriage house in the yard were in use as lawyers' offices. The upstairs bedroom in the northwest corner became my office in the "law mansion," and I furnished it with a big oak desk, a brown leather desk chair, a couple of upholstered guest chairs, and a black leather sofa long enough to catch a nap if the occasion arose. I had an Indian rug partially covering the oak floors, and instead of law books I opted for shelves filled with old Indian pots.

Malcolm's words when I rented the office have stayed with me to this day. He said, "Show up on time, work hard for your clients, be fair and honest, and good things will happen." Simple words of sage advice that proved to be true. Malcolm's been gone a long time, but there are still a lot of lawyers in El Paso, including me, who will tell you he was more than a landlord to the attorneys who officed at his law mansion. He was a father figure and a mentor to us.

The lawyers in the mansion had various specialties. Some practiced plaintiffs' personal injury or criminal defense law. Another was a formidable family law specialist. I was the one and only employment lawyer in the building. By then, I'd been board certified in labor and employment law by the Texas Board of Legal Specialization for a couple years and was busily plying my trade representing workers in various types of wrongful termination and retaliation cases—rough seas to sail on the waters of a staunchly business-oriented, employment-at-will state like Texas. But I was making a go of it.

The palatial and opulent front lobby of the building had begun life as the living room of the mansion and looked the part. The front porch faced eastward and had huge colonial pillars at the corners and at the top of the steps. The beautiful entry doors were windowed with leaded glass. The floors inside the lobby were tiled with huge white marble slabs. The 20-foot ceiling was ornamented with crown molding painted gold. A huge crystal chandelier occupied the center of the room, and the lowest crystal hung about eight feet above the floor. To the left of the front door, the southern wall was mostly filled by a prodigious fireplace with a large and beautiful dark oak mantel and surround. To the right of that at the back of the room, double glass doors led into a large wood-paneled dining room with a 16-foot Queen Anne style dining table and about a dozen matching chairs. To the right of the dining room a majestic Tara-like stairway swept up and westward to the balconies on the second floor where the upstairs offices were. A large and very old Persian rug covered the center of the marble floor, and around it elegant and colorful period furniture that looked original to the house adorned the room. In stark contrast to the rest of the lobby, a very simple and small wooden desk that looked like it could have been purchased in a garage sale occupied the northwest corner of the room and behind it sat the receptionist.

It was our receptionist's primary job to answer phones and route calls to appropriate lines in the mansion. But she also did all the initial screening for potential new clients who either called or walked in, and due to the prominent location of the law mansion and the reputations of those who officed there, we had a considerable number of walk-ins each week. She balanced and handled her multiple tasks with infallible accuracy while projecting an air of friendly professionalism to all who called or dropped by. She made her work look as simple and easy as going to the grocery store to buy some milk and eggs, but we all knew it was a lot more difficult than that and we were grateful for her help.

One early summer's day in 1994, as the first hints of warm breezes to come were in the air, I was shuffling through paperwork in my office when the receptionist buzzed my line to tell me someone with an employment problem had come into the lobby downstairs. I rose from my desk and walked through the hall to the balcony at the top of the stairs. From there, I saw in the lobby below a tall and serious looking Hispanic man with a large cardboard box of documents sitting on a dark purple chaise longue looking like an extra who had accidentally wandered into the filming of a scene from *Gone with the Wind*.

I studied him from the balcony for a moment and took in my first impression of the man. He had carefully combed dark hair, was wearing a very clean and neatly ironed white short-sleeved shirt, and had on nicely pressed khaki dress slacks. Both of his neatly laced and well-shined brown dress shoes were firmly on the floor. I had the impression that he was not wearing his normal attire and had dressed up for the occasion. He was sitting up very straight with an air of urgency that conveyed to me that our soon-to-occur meeting was of great importance to him.

Naturally, I was curious to find out what we were meeting about as I headed down the stairs.

He looked up and met my eyes, then stood and smiled and extended his hand.

"Are you Mr. Kern?" he asked as we shook hands.

"Yes, I am, nice to meet you, and you are . . . ?"

"Louie Baeza," he responded, then continued, "You're the employment lawyer here, right?"

"Yep, that's me," I confirmed as I showed him into the dining room, which the lawyers in the mansion used as a conference room.

We sat next to each other, and Louie set his box of documents beside him on the long dining room table.

I eyed the box warily and thought to myself: "Surely he doesn't expect me to go through all those documents with him in our 30-minute free consultation."

Then, to my surprise, he began vetting me.

"How long have you been an employment lawyer?" he asked.

"About ten years," I said.

"And what did you do to become an employment lawyer?"

I thought I was supposed to be asking the questions, but I went along with it.

"Well . . . I practiced labor and employment law with a big firm in Washington, DC, for about five years right out of law school. Then I was with a firm in Dallas doing both employment law and personal injury. A couple years ago I got board certified in labor and employment law. You have to pass a pretty tough exam to get board certified in Texas, and they won't even let you take the exam without at least five years' experience in the specialty and recommendations from lawyers and judges."

I paused, thinking that would satisfy Louie, but he persisted.

"How many employment cases have you handled?" he asked.

Louie had walked into my office without an appointment for a free consultation—which I was giving him—and he was interviewing me like I had gone to *his* office to apply for a job. I was beginning to get mildly annoyed, but I let it slide and answered: "I don't have an exact count, but hundreds."

Then, before he could ask another question, I launched into my initial consult routine and told him I only had about 30 minutes to meet with him and it would help us get through the meeting in that limited timeframe if he let me ask the questions and provided short answers without volunteering too much additional information.

Louie nodded and agreed to the ground rules, and I started in on my usual screening questions:

"Where do you or did you work?" I asked.

"I'm a paramedic for the City of El Paso." He answered and stopped.

"You're currently employed by the City of El Paso?" I confirmed.

"Yes."

"Are you Hispanic?"

"Yes, I am," he said proudly.

"How old are you?"

"I'm 41."

"Do you have any disabilities that affect you at work?"

"No."

"Is the City planning to terminate you?"

"No."

"Have they demoted you?"

"No."

"Are they threatening to do so?"

"No."

I liked the way he was carefully following my instructions and providing short answers without volunteering extra information—something potential clients often struggled to do. Hopefully, that was a good indication he'd be easy to work with if he had any viable causes of action—which I hadn't uncovered yet—worth pursuing.

"Did you get a bad evaluation?" I continued.

"No."

"Did they pass over you for a promotion?"

"No."

"Are you experiencing any kind of harassment at work?"
"No."
"Is the City retaliating against you for something you did that they didn't like?"
"No."
"Is the City mishandling an injury you had at work?"
"No."
"Is the City accusing you of doing *anything* wrong?"
"No."

I paused for a breath. I was starting to feel like a contestant on the *What's My Line?* TV show I watched as a child. Then I asked the wrap-up question:

"Is the City discriminating or retaliating against you in *any* other way because you're Hispanic or because you're 41?"

"No," Louie answered.

I was beginning to feel that the meeting was a waste of time. Louie didn't seem to have any of the typical employment problems that could trigger legal liability, yet here he was all dressed up in front of me with a big box of mystery documents.

"I'm a little confused" I said. "If you aren't having any problems at work, then what brings you here?"

"I don't think they are paying us right," he said.

"Who is 'us'?" I asked.

"All the paramedics who work for the City of El Paso."

Even though I was board certified in labor and employment law and had been practicing for about ten years, I had never handled a pay case and knew very little about the Fair Labor Standards Act. As it turned out, however, I was about to be educated on that by Louie Baeza.

I didn't have a good follow-up question, but I continued:

"That's interesting," I said. "Why do you think El Paso isn't paying its paramedics correctly?"

At this question, Louie smiled broadly and reached for the box of documents he brought with him. It was immediately clear that this was the question he had come prepared to answer.

The first document he showed me was a copy of a Fair Labor Standards Act (FLSA) regulation that said firefighters were only entitled to receive overtime pay after working more than 53 hours in a week. I'd never seen the regulation before, but the copy was well worn and Louie had already highlighted the pertinent language. He began reading it to me.

When he finished reading the regulation, he summed it up by saying, "We get paid like firefighters, but we don't do the same work that firefighters do."

I had no idea where he was going, but I played along. "Why do you think that's important?" I asked.

Once again, Louie was ready. He reached back into the box and took out a copy of a case that, like the regulation he showed me earlier, was dog-eared and had sentences highlighted.

I looked over his shoulder and read the case name "Alex v. City of Chicago," but for a brief moment I misread it and thought I saw "Alice v. City of Chicago," probably because I was starting to feel like I had gone down the rabbit hole into Wonderland and was meeting with the Mad Hatter.

"Is that case from Chicago?" I asked.

"Yes, it is," he said.

"What does a case from Illinois have to do with us here in Texas?" I wondered out loud.

Louie confidently answered: "These paramedics in Chicago were paid just like we get paid in El Paso," he said.

I still wasn't sure where he was going, but I asked him to continue.

Then Louie began reading select passages from *Alex v. City of Chicago*, which I saw over his shoulder had recently been decided by the Seventh Circuit Court of Appeals in July 1994.[1] I had never read the case, never heard anything about it, and still had no clue where Louie was going with all this. But our meeting was getting interesting if nothing else.

Louie read from the first page of the opinion: "current and former paramedic employees of the Fire Department of the City of Chicago [claim] they are entitled to overtime pay for hours worked in excess of 40 hours per week, in accordance with section 7(a) of the Fair Labor Standards Act, 29 U.S.C. § 207(a)(1)." But, "the City asserts nonliability under section 7(k) of the Act which established a limited exemption from the overtime provision for employees in 'fire protection activities,' 29 U.S.C. § 207(k)."

At that time, Sections 7(a) and 7(k) of the FLSA meant very little to me, but I was getting curious where this was going.

"Go on," I said.

Louie read several more highlighted passages from the *Alex* opinion about the similarities and differences between Chicago's firefighters and paramedics. I gleaned that Chicago's paramedics and firefighters worked a similar schedule, but the paramedics had different training, certifications, and responsibilities than the firefighters. The firefighters were trained to put out fires and rescue fire victims, but the paramedics were not allowed to enter burning buildings or smoky areas and could be disciplined for engaging in firefighting activities. Firefighters were trained in special rescue techniques and use of specialized rescue equipment like hydraulic jacks, cutting torches, saws, and ropes, but paramedics did not have that training or equipment. Paramedics also had to stay a safe distance away from a fire and couldn't treat fire victims until firefighters first safely evacuated them.

Louie then came to a concluding sentence that sounded important to me: "the City of Chicago has treated fire department paramedics as subject to the §7(k) fire protection exemption by only paying them overtime compensation for hours worked in excess of . . . 53 hours per week [but] Chicago Fire Department paramedics do not fall within the scope of §7(k) and are fully entitled to overtime compensation for hours worked in excess of 40 hours per week."

The light bulb was beginning to illuminate. "How does the City of El Paso pay you?" I asked.

"Just like the paramedics in Chicago got paid," Louie answered.

"How about the other paramedics who work for the City of El Paso?" I asked.

"We all get paid the same," he said.

By now we were already a couple hours into what was supposed to be a 30-minute initial consultation and I needed to get back to the stack of work on my desk and so I asked: "Can you bottom line this for me?"

Louie then jumped several pages ahead in *Alex* and pointed to highlighted text on the page: "Here's the most important part," he said. "It says we're not exempt under Section 7k unless we were trained in rescuing fire, crime, and accident victims."

"Didn't you get some training in rescue techniques?" I asked.

"Nope!" was the quick and surprising response.

"Hold on," I said, "Isn't going to accident scenes most of what you do?"

"It is," said Louie, "but it says here [pointing to a line in the *Alex* opinion] that 'rescue refers to actions taken to free a victim from imminent danger or harm by the most expeditious means.' To rescue people, we have to be trained to remove fire victims from burning buildings and operate special equipment like the jaws of life and we're not trained in that, or any other rescue activities. Firefighters do all the rescue work. Our work is strictly medical."

The light bulb was burning brightly now. "Then you don't fall under the exemption," I said.

"That's right!" Louie exclaimed. "We're just like the EMTs in Chicago."

"And since you're not exempt, you should be paid overtime after working 40 hours in a week."

"Right!"

"Got it," I said, as the voice in my head added: "About time, dummy!"

"Do you get paid any overtime now?" I asked.

"Only after we work 53 hours in a week."

"But you get paid straight pay for those 53 hours?"

"Yes, we do."

"So, you're talking about not getting paid the difference between the straight pay you received and the overtime you should have received for the 13 hours between 40 and 53 for every week you worked more than 40 hours."

"Exactly," said Louie.

"And the same goes for every other paramedic who works for the City of El Paso."

"That's it!" Louie said with a broad smile.

Louie seemed pleased, but I wasn't sure whether to feel lucky about what I had just learned or a little foolish for not already knowing about it. In truth, I felt a mixture of both.

Louie Baeza, a paramedic for the City of El Paso, had just spent a few hours educating me—a board-certified labor and employment lawyer with a decade of experience—about a complicated niche area within employment law that I knew almost nothing about and he knew everything important about. He came to our meeting extraordinarily well prepared. As a paramedic with no legal training, Louie had independently studied the legal and factual issues in a very complex area of employment law and with a combination of dogged persistence and high intelligence he had connected the liability dots on the complicated elements of a cause of action for the City's nonpayment of overtime to its paramedics. The research, analysis, and explanations Louie shared with me were as well-thought out and comprehensive as those of a highly skilled attorney. And like a gifted college professor, he patiently explained it all to me with a clarity that made it easy to understand. To say I was impressed would be a gross understatement.

"What do you think," he asked, "do we have a case?"

I paused to take in the moment before carefully answering, "It's definitely worth exploring further." "Is it just you who wants to pursue this, or are other EMTs interested as well?"

"A group of us want the City to pay us the back pay they owe us," he said, "and they sent me to find a lawyer who could help us."

"You found him," I said.

We talked a bit more and I learned some personal things about Louie. He was married to Edna, and they had three children, Jay, Selena, and Matthew. Louie had served in the Marine Corps for five years and spent two of those years in Vietnam. In addition to being a senior paramedic with El Paso Emergency Medical Services he was a member of the El Paso mountain rescue team and a flight medical team. His eyes lit up when he talked about his wife, kids, and beloved Harley Davidson motorcycle. Despite the serious vetting he gave me at the start of our meeting, it turned out he was a very friendly and charismatic guy with a great sense of humor. My first impression that he had dressed up specially for the occasion of our meeting proved to be true. By the time he left my office he had freely admitted—with a booming laugh that bounced off the walls and rattled the windows—that he was usually in jeans and a T-shirt when he wasn't wearing his EMT uniform.

Louie left his box of documents with me—a treasure trove of valuable research—and went on his way. Within a few days I met with him and a core group of about a dozen El Paso paramedics who, as Louie had promised, already were committed to pursuing the case. Soon thereafter Louie organized several educational meetings for paramedics interested in learning more about the case. We tag-teamed in those meetings, with me first explaining their legal rights to overtime pay (a topic I had educated myself on considerably since my first meeting with Louie) and with Louie and the other core plaintiffs then answering questions about how participating in the case would affect them at work, which supervisors were likely to be difficult about it, and so forth. After those meetings almost all El Paso's paramedics decided to join the case and within a couple months we filed the lawsuit, *Baeza et al. v. The City of El Paso*, along with the FLSA consent forms of close to 100 paramedics in federal district court in El Paso before Judge Harry Lee Hudspeth. There were a few holdouts—the usual crew of inveterate brownnosers, people up for promotions, and so on—but with Louie's help we achieved close to a 100 percent opt-in rate and ended up with a very cohesive class of plaintiffs.

The City of El Paso at first tried to defend the lawsuit using the city attorney's office, but soon realized they needed outside help and brought in one of the big defense firms in town. That turned out to be a blessing in disguise because the defense lawyer, who was board certified in labor and employment law, understood the case. Not long afterward, the City asked to mediate with federal magistrate Janet Reusch and we agreed. We were then only about eight months into the lawsuit, and by the end of the mediation the City offered to settle for $800,000, or about $80,000 a plaintiff,[2] which was by far the biggest settlement of my career to that point. The City was emphatic that it needed 100 percent participation by all the plaintiffs in the settlement, and I didn't think that would be a problem. I was feeling like the blind hog that found the golden acorn, but there was a little more drama to come before the deal could be consummated.

My fee agreements in wage/hour class and collective actions have for decades contained class management provisions that create plaintiffs' steering committees, empower them to make important decisions on behalf of the class, establish formulae for fair pro rata division of settlement proceeds among class members, and so on. But in 1994, I had signed up my very first FLSA collective action as a complete novitiate. Consequently, I had not included *any* class or collective action management provisions in the attorney-client agreements signed by all the opt-ins in *Baeza et al. v. The City of El Paso*. The potential consequences of that omission, one never repeated since, became apparent when I met with the plaintiffs to review the settlement offer.

I coordinated with Louie and other core plaintiffs, and we picked a good time to schedule a group meeting when most of them and many of the other plaintiffs were off duty. During the meeting, I planned to discuss the settlement offer, recommend it, and hopefully secure approval. Louie and all the core plaintiffs already were on board with the settlement, and I didn't anticipate any problem getting it approved by the larger group. I had run the numbers in advance and prepared approval forms for each plaintiff to sign, agreeing to the settlement and their approximate recovery. I rented a hall that would accommodate about 100 people and felt well prepared for the meeting. All seemed to be going well.

Many of the plaintiffs, including Louie, were motorcycle riders, something that seemed to be a part of the paramedic culture in El Paso. Knowing that, I wasn't surprised when Louie and many others rode their Harleys to the settlement meeting and showed up in their motorcycle clothes and motorcycle boots. When I got up to address the group to explain the settlement offer and looked out on the room, I felt for a moment like I was addressing a motorcycle club.

I explained the virtues of the settlement and the formula for dividing net proceeds based on the number of weeks each plaintiff earned unpaid overtime during the FLSA window of recovery. After I did so, there were a few questions from the group and then the great majority of the plaintiffs, about 80 percent, readily agreed to the settlement and signed off on their individual approval forms. A smaller group of about ten plaintiffs signed off on the settlement after they received some additional assurances from Louie and other core plaintiffs. A still smaller group required more in-depth explanations and Louie and I met with each of them individually, answered their questions, and secured their approval. At the end of that process and about an hour into the meeting only one remaining holdout still refused to sign his approval form. Because the City required 100 percent participation in the settlement, this was a significant concern.

In talking to him, I realized the holdout was looking at it all wrong. He viewed himself as similar to the owner of the last house on a city block being cleared to expand a highway. The way he figured it, the longer he held out the more money he'd get. In the world of highway projects that may be true at times, but the analogy wasn't working here because if the holdout got more than his fair share that would need to be disclosed to the plaintiffs who had already agreed to the settlement based on the distribution formulae. Making an exception for the holdout would not only be unfair to the other plaintiffs who had already agreed, it also would risk them reneging on their agreements and blowing up the entire settlement.

I tried to reason with the man, but that proved difficult because there was nothing logical about his reason for refusing to agree to the settlement. He didn't express any qualms about settling the case, or question the formula for dividing the proceeds, or even challenge the fairness of his own net recovery. He simply wanted more money and was convinced that the longer he held out the more money he would get. His motivation was as old as the human race and has been an ugly part of human nature since the first humans made it out of the caves—good old-fashioned greed. And the more I tried to talk him into looking at it from a more altruistic "one for all, all for one" perspective, the more stubborn and difficult he became. Finally, I ran out of words and was reduced to simply watching helplessly as the settlement slipped away, like a swamped yacht going under the waves.

That's when Louie came to the rescue and said, "Let us talk to him privately." I wanted to ask how that would help, but before I could say another word, Louie and a group of core plaintiffs had surrounded the man. Since everyone in the core group was in their motorcycle gear and the holdout had come directly from work in his EMT uniform, it was a stunning sight watching them hustle him out the door to the parking lot. From where I stood, it looked like a motorcycle gang abducting a paramedic to take him to a hideout to give medical care to a wounded club member.

For some reason, probably out of sheer exasperation, the thought flitted through my mind like a mantra, "take the holdout to the hideout . . . holdout to the hideout . . . holdout to the hideout," but I didn't have long to think about it because they were back inside the meeting room in about three minutes. I never asked what was said outside in the parking lot, but when they came back in the stubborn and obnoxious holdout was indeed hiding out and in his place was a pale and mild-mannered look-alike.

Louie had one hand gently resting on the man's shoulder as he said to me in a very steady voice, "We're all set now . . . it was just a misunderstanding . . . he's agreed to the settlement."

I looked at the man and asked, "Is that true? Have you agreed?"

He nodded affirmatively.

Then Louie said to him gently, but firmly, "You need to answer out loud." And he quickly said, "Yes, I've agreed."

"And you are voluntarily agreeing based on everything we talked about earlier, correct?"

"Right," he said sheepishly. Then he signed his approval form and quietly left the meeting hall.

These days, we often hire specialized settlement administrators to handle settlement distributions as simple business transactions. But I handled the distribution of my first FLSA collective action settlement personally. The money went in my trust account, and we drew up checks for each of the plaintiffs and asked them to come into the office to pick them up and sign an acknowledgment of receipt. I personally met with every one of them (including the holdout), shook their hands, thanked them for their service to the City of El Paso, told them to let me know if they had any problems with the City going forward, and handed them their checks. Some of them still call or email me nearly 25 years later to ask for advice about legal problems they're having.

For Louie and me the case marked the beginning of important career transitions.

I finished up my wrongful termination cases and have spent the next 25 years doing civil rights work of a different kind—wage and hour class and collective actions on behalf of workers not paid what they were legally entitled to receive for their labor. It's very gratifying work that has been good to me and made it relatively easy to smile back at the face in the mirror as I have aged.

Louie left his paramedic job with the City of El Paso and spent the next 20 years as a union organizer with the International Union of Operating Engineers. It came as no surprise to anyone who knew him that he was better than superb at that job and helped a very long list of workers to have better pay, benefits, and working conditions. He retired from IUOE in 2016.

Louie was more than a client. He became a good friend, and we were in touch many times over the years. After he retired, he enjoyed a few years hitting the open road on his Harley, but then regrettably developed serious heart problems, perhaps due to exposure to Agent Orange in Vietnam.[3] He left this world at the age of 67 on September 18, 2020, and is laid to rest at Ft. Bliss National Cemetery in El Paso.

Most of all, I miss hearing his laugh.

Louie Baeza, February 8, 1953–September 18, 2020

A Sometimes Strange and Unusual Career

Gerry Hebert

I started practicing law in 1973 and began my legal career as a trial attorney in the Civil Rights Division of the US Department of Justice. In the first six years of my DOJ career, I worked on school desegregation cases, mostly in the Deep South. In 1979, I transferred to the Voting Section at the suggestion of Drew Days, who then was assistant attorney general of the Civil Rights Division.

One of my first voting rights cases was a case brought against Dallas County, Alabama. Selma, Alabama, considered the birthplace of the 1965 Voting Rights Act, is in the heart of Dallas County. The case, *United States v. Dallas County Commission*, had been filed by the United States in 1978 and challenged the at-large method of electing the all-white Dallas County Commission. At that time, Dallas County's voting-age population was around 48 percent black and 52 percent white. Black voters had been unable to elect a candidate to the county commission due to the presence of extreme racially polarized voting. Opposing counsel included Cartledge Blackwell and McLean Pitts. The case was before Judge Brevard Hand in the Selma Division of the US district court for the Southern District of Alabama.

I had heard stories about Judge Hand when I was in the Education Section doing school desegregation cases. He had a reputation of being against civil rights and had been openly hostile to DOJ and private attorneys during court proceedings in school desegregation cases. The Dallas County case was still in discovery when I was assigned to it with other attorneys in the Voting Section. Because they lacked substantial trial experience and I had extensive litigation and trial experience from my six years working on school desegregation cases, I served as the lead attorney and managed the litigation.

Each Judge Is Different; Some Are Even Strange

The Selma federal courtroom is unusual in the way it was set up, and that's important for this story. The judge's bench was against one wall at the front of the courtroom and overlooked two tables for counsel. What made it strange to me was that the plaintiffs' table was in the front and defense counsel sat at a table directly behind plaintiffs' counsel table. From the perspective of sitting at counsel table and facing the judge, there were large windows on the left and a jury box against the wall to the right of the counsel table. As will become obvious shortly, the location of these large windows on the left plays a role in this account. Judge Hand had some unusual habits during court proceedings. He often left the bench and wandered around, sometimes sitting in the jury box and sometimes sitting in the windowsills. On one occasion, he left the bench, walked to the door leading out to the hall, opened it and stood in the doorway with one foot in the courtroom and one foot in the hall while he smoked a cigarette! I asked courtroom personnel at recess what that was all about, and she said that the judge felt with one foot in the hall he wasn't actually smoking in the courtroom. Of course, that Judge Hand did this during the trial as testimony was ongoing was distracting to me as I asked my questions of my witness, and perhaps that was Judge Hand's purpose.

For reasons not relevant here, Judge Hand took a liking to me, often engaging in small talk off the record during pretrial court hearings. I think perhaps he liked me because I treated him with respect and honor on the first day of the trial when I said, "Judge, I've never had the privilege of appearing before you, and this is my first time trying a case before you and my first time in this courtroom. Is it permissible for me to have my dozens of boxes of exhibits in the jury box?" He was pleased I was humble and showed him such respect. He asked me to repeat what I just said, which I did. He then added that's the first time any Justice Department attorney had shown him such respect, and he quickly gave me permission to store my dozen or so exhibit boxes in the jury box (this was a bench trial before the judge, so there was no jury).

Judges Sometimes May Cross-Examine Your Witnesses; Sometimes They Get Answers They Don't Like If They Don't Support the Judge's Likely Ruling

There were many highlights to the trial that lasted intermittently, for a few months. For one, I called as a witness at trial a civil rights hero in Selma, Ms. Marie Foster. I had interviewed Ms. Foster many times before trial and was proud to sit with her in her living room, where Dr. King had sat tearfully watching then President Lyndon Johnson call on Congress to enact the Voting Rights Act. As I look back on my career, the opportunities to meet true heroes of the civil rights movement like Ms. Foster are without a doubt among the highlights. Ms. Foster had been working on voting rights matters since the 1950s, teaching blacks how to pass the state's racially discriminatory literacy test. Ms. Foster also was one of the creators of the Dallas County Voters League, a group of black citizens who demanded improvements in the voter registration process. She was on the Edmund Pettus Bridge with John Lewis on that fateful Bloody Sunday in 1965, beaten by Alabama state troopers, which ultimately led to the Voting Rights Act being enacted in August of that year. I called Ms. Foster as a witness because she could provide details of the recent history of racially discriminatory voting practices in Dallas County. At that time, there was one place would-be voters could get registered: the Dallas County courthouse. It was only open several days a month (never the same days each month), and its hours were quite limited (closed during lunch). The Dallas County Registration Board was all white, and Ms. Foster detailed how difficult it was for black citizens to get registered (and this contributed to their inability to elect black candidates to the Dallas County Commission). I could tell Judge Hand was buying none of this, but Ms. Foster continued to provide compelling testimony. She then told the judge that many blacks who wanted to become registered still felt fear of going to the courthouse (where former Dallas County sheriff Jim Clark in 1965 had beaten voting rights activists trying to get registered to vote). Ms. Foster said that it was her experience that many elderly blacks living in rural parts of Dallas County felt that the local courthouse was a symbol of voter suppression and remained "a stigma" for the black community of Dallas County. Judge Hand couldn't contain himself once he heard this testimony. He said to Ms. Foster, "Come on, are you telling me that blacks in Dallas County are afraid to go to the county courthouse?" She said, "Yes." He then said to her, "Don't you blacks get your welfare checks at the county courthouse, and you don't have any fear doing that?" Ms. Foster, employed as a dental hygienist, replied to the judge that she did not receive public assistance but the welfare office in Dallas County was not in the county courthouse and that it was in another part of Selma close to the segregated black community. But Judge Hand was undeterred. He then said to Ms. Foster, "You blacks don't have any trouble going to the county courthouse to pay your fees for license plates, do you?" Her reply was this: "Judge, it is true we do pay license plate fees at the county courthouse, but here's the difference. They didn't beat us up at the courthouse for paying taxes, Judge." Judge Hand, stymied by the truth and wisdom of Ms. Fosters's answers, was so visibly upset that he adjourned the trial for the day, even though it was just midafternoon.

In a Bench Trial, Rules of Evidence Can Be Applied Fast and Loose or Sometimes Not at All

As the trial continued, and we at DOJ had presented all of our evidence on behalf of the United States, it was the defendants' turn to present evidence. They called to the witness stand a member of the Dallas County Commission. One of the things we had shown at trial when we put on our evidence was that the all-white Dallas County Commission had been unresponsive to the particularized needs of the black community, and in fact had given only white residents privileges on county services, particularly road improvements, fire protection, and drainage ditches. As I mentioned earlier, Cartledge Blackwell was one of the defense attorneys, and he asked his own witness a question that went like this: "Isn't it true, Commissioner, that the Dallas County Commission has been and continues to be responsive to the special needs of the black community in the areas of road services, housing, health issues, education, and all public services?" I objected on the grounds it was a leading question. Judge Hand looked down at me with disdain and snarled, "Overruled, Counsel." The commissioner then said, "Yes," in response to Blackwell's question. What followed was another blatant leading question with defense counsel basically formulating details and asking the witness to agree to it. I again objected, stood, and said, "Defense counsel is basically testifying and asking his witness to affirm his testimony." Judge Hand again got a mean look on his face and snarled again, "Overruled,

Counsel." When it happened a third time, I again stood up to object to a leading question, which was so long and detailed it took Mr. Blackwell a few minutes to finish it. I said, "Judge, Mr. Blackwell is apparently unable to ask a nonleading question of his own witness and to save time, may I have a running leading question objection to all his questioning"? Judge Hand responded to me as follows: "Whatever turns you on, Counsel." I said, "I'll take that as a 'Yes' if that was agreeable to the court." Judge Hand said: "If that's what turns you on, Counsel."

In a Trial, Be Prepared for the Unexpected, Even the Bizarre

What happened next in the trial involves those windows I mentioned earlier that lined the entire courtroom and were on my left ten feet or so away from me as I sat at counsel table. As I was leaned over writing trial notes of Mr. Blackwell's ongoing testimony, suddenly a darkness fell over me and my table. Since it had been a sunny day, I assumed dark clouds had rolled into Selma and we were in for a rainstorm. I looked up from my yellow writing pad to see the dark clouds, but instead I saw Judge Hand standing right next to me, so close to me his black robes darkened the light from the nearby windows. He then put his hand on my head and ran his fingers through my hair, saying, "You know, Gerry, I just love jerking your chain." Meanwhile, the entire time this was going on, Mr. Blackwell continued his testimony through leading question after leading question. I can't explain why I wasn't so shocked and flustered by this incident that I was speechless. To the contrary, I immediately replied, "Yes, that's apparent and you seem to really enjoy it, Judge. You know from your time as a lawyer before being a judge that he's leading his own witness." Judge nodded and smiled and then picked up my yellow writing pad of detailed notes, he said, "Wow, these are even better than the trial transcript, so detailed." He then said: "Maybe you could lend them to me after trial when I write my opinion?" I smiled and said, "No way, Judge. I just love jerking your chain." He laughed and walked back to the bench.

This incident is without a doubt the most bizarre thing ever to happen in any of my cases over the course of fifty years. Yet, it strangely illustrates how as legal counsel you can establish a rapport even with a judge who is openly hostile to your case. Years later, after a trip to the court of appeals reversing his ruling against the United States, Judge Hand ordered a redistricting plan for Dallas County that I had submitted for DOJ. It was such a momentous occasion that the leaders of the black community in Selma were in the courtroom that day and openly wept when he said that while he disagreed with and didn't understand the theory of vote dilution, he would nonetheless order a new plan into effect, and that plan eventually elected several black members to the Dallas County Commission, the first in modern history.

Some Judges Don't Understand Statistical Evidence or Even Basic Math

The Dallas County trial also provided me with another incredible incident, this one involving my cross-examination of defendants' expert witness, Dr. James Voyles. This particular incident may explain why Judge Hand earned a nickname among those of us handling civil rights cases in his court. You've no doubt heard of the famous judge, Judge Learned Hand. Well, our Judge Hand earned the nickname the Unlearned Hand, and you'll see why in a few minutes.

One issue in voting rights litigation requires plaintiffs to prove that voting patterns are racially polarized. The inquiry into racially polarized voting, also sometimes referred to as racial bloc voting, typically entails the use of complex statistical analysis. Traditionally, courts have relied upon two main statistical methods to examine the question of polarization: homogeneous precinct analysis and bivariate ecological regression analysis. In recent years, some courts have begun to adopt a third method: ecological inference. Each of these methods are used to present evidence about the voting patterns of black voters and white voters. Each of these methods allows expert witnesses, using aggregate data, to draw certain conclusions about voting preferences of groups of voters—specifically, how members of particular racial or ethnic groups cast their ballots. Because the secret ballot prevents the tabulation of electoral data at the individual level, voting behavior typically must be inferred from precinct-level electoral data using these two methods.

Dr. Voyles testified that he had employed the statistical test of bivariate ecological regression analysis. Bivariate ecological regression analysis attempts to estimate the relationships between the racial composition of voting precincts and the total votes cast for each candidate in those precincts. So if the percentage of the vote for a black candidate in a precinct goes up as the percent of black voters increases in that precinct, there's a correlation. This correlation is given a score called an R-Square. Dr. Voyles testified on direct examination that to have racially polarized voting, the R-Square grade had to be .7 or above. Now I knew he had testified in three cases prior, so in my cross-examination I asked if he always had used .7 as the watermark for determining racially polarized voting and he answered in the affirmative. I knew this wasn't true and then proceeded to use his trial testimony from the three prior cases to impeach him.

My own expert, Dr. Allan J. Lichtman, had advised me that such a threshold of .7 was ridiculously high and he was unaware of any other expert who shared such a view. What Dr. Voyles didn't know was that not only had I read his prior testimony, but I had copies of his trial testimony in three prior cases and he had testified that .5, not .7, was the threshold for determining racially polarized voting. To make matters worse, his R-Squared calculations in the Dallas County case were all above .5 but below .7. So, as a result of his changing the threshold from .5 to .7 to determine if voting was polarized, he was able to claim that voting wasn't polarized. I then took him through his testimony in three prior cases where he had testified that .5 was the threshold. I felt not only did I prove him to be untruthful, but also that if he had employed his standard approach in the Dallas County case as he had in the prior three cases, he would have found racially polarized voting in Dallas County.

It was at that point that Judge Hand tried to bail out Dr. Voyles. Judge Hand said, "Mr. Hebert, .5 or .7, what's the difference? If that's the best you got, then your case is pretty weak." I said that Voyles's testimony that he always employed a standard of .7 was untrue and that I proved it was. But Judge Hand was unmoved. Again, he said, ".5 or .7, what's the difference?" I said, "Judge, he increased his threshold for determining racially polarized voting by 40 percent." Judge Hand asked, how do you get 40 percent? I said, "The difference between .5 and .7 was .2, and that .2 over .5 is a 40 percent increase." I couldn't believe that here I was having to educate a federal judge on elementary school math. Judge Hand asked, "What's that, the new math?" I replied, "No, Judge, it's fifth-grade math!" Not exactly the most respectful answer I could have given, but it was true and I was really ticked off because I couldn't believe this judge was essentially going to let Dr. Voyles get away with what I felt was perjury! When Judge Unlearned Hand eventually ruled against the United States, it wasn't based on my flippant response or the issue of whether voting was racially polarized. The judge eventually ruled that black voters are unable to elect candidates to the Dallas County Commission because they are apathetic. On appeal, the Eleventh Circuit reversed his decision.

Know as Much as You Can about the Judge without Stalking Them, Especially What Is Most Likely to Be Personally Meaningful to Them and Affect Their Ruling

A few years later, two colleagues of mine in the Department of Justice tangled with Judge Hand in a different voting rights case, United States v. Marengo County, AL. Like the Dallas County suit, the Marengo County case was another vote dilution case in which the United States alleged that the at-large method of electing the Marengo County Commission and the Marengo County School Board diluted the voting strength of black voters in violation of the Voting Rights Act. At one point in the trial, my DOJ colleagues, attorneys Paul Hancock and Sheila Delaney, called as a witness a schoolteacher. If I recall correctly, the teacher was called to the stand to provide testimony on the unresponsiveness of the Marengo County School Board to the particularized needs of black faculty and students. On cross-examination by Mr. Blackwell, he asked an objectionable question that not only called for hearsay but went outside the scope of the direct examination. He asked the teacher if she had heard that some teachers said that if they cooperated in the DOJ's lawsuit they would be fired. But despite objections, Judge Hand told her to answer the questions. She said she had heard this but lacked any personal knowledge herself. Judge Hand asked her for the names of any teachers she might know who felt they would be fired if they cooperated with DOJ. She demurred, saying she lacked personal knowledge, but Judge Hand persisted, asking her for the names of teachers she might have heard felt this way. Again, she demurred explaining she didn't have any personal knowledge of which teachers or staff felt this way, and again Judge Hand compelled her to name names. She then named a handful of teachers or staff members who she thought possibly might feel this way, but added she didn't really know. Judge Hand then did something I can only describe as an abuse of his authority. He told the courtroom marshal to have subpoenas issued for each teacher or staff member named and told the marshal to serve them on these teachers and staff that night.

The next morning, when DOJ attorneys Hancock and Delaney arrived at the courthouse where their office was on the second floor adjacent to the courtroom, there on a bench seated outside the courtroom were the teachers and staff who had been served with subpoenas issued under Judge Hand's authority. These persons recognized the DOJ attorneys and, obviously appearing upset and distressed by being called late the previous night, to the federal courthouse in Selma fifty miles away, asked the DOJ attorneys what this was all about. Hancock and Delaney briefly chatted with the black teachers and staff and tried to allay their fears.

When the trial convened, Judge Hand called each of the teachers or staff members to the stand and interrogated them, as did Mr. Blackwell. Blackwell in particular had seen or heard that these witnesses had spoken to the DOJ attorneys briefly and told Judge Hand that Hancock and Delaney had "tampered with the court's witnesses" (of course, they had done no such thing). Judge Hand blew up, however, and raised his voice saying that he had not given them permission to talk to "the court's witnesses." Shortly thereafter, Judge Hand sent a letter to the Department of Justice stating that he no longer would permit Mr. Hancock or Ms. Delaney to appear in the Southern District of Alabama, accusing them of vague ethics violations. Upon receipt of Judge Hand's letter, a thorough review of this incident was undertaken by the DOJ Ethics Office, which found no evidence of ethics violations and that the two attorneys' conduct had been ethical and professional in every respect. A letter was prepared at DOJ addressed to Judge Hand informing him of the Ethics Office review and its finding. Judge Hand, upon receipt of the letter, didn't rescind his ruling barring the two attorneys from appearing in his court. He wrote back to the Department of Justice that since he was chief judge of the Southern District of Alabama, he could take action disciplining attorneys for misconduct and he had done so in this case.

Meanwhile, Judge Hand had ruled in favor of Marengo County and the case was on appeal to the Eleventh Circuit. The Eleventh Circuit reversed Judge Hand and remanded the case to Judge Hand for further proceedings. DOJ wrote to Judge Hand stating that there had been no conduct that warranted any discipline, that the attorney general has authority to decide which attorneys will represent the United States, and on remand Hancock and Delaney would still be handling the case. Judge Hand again responded that they would not be permitted to appear. The Department of Justice then decided to file a motion with Judge Hand in the Marengo County case explaining why he lacked authority in this instance to bar these attorneys (given they had done nothing wrong, unethical, or unprofessional), and that the attorney general possessed authority to name these attorneys to represent the United States of America. A hearing was set on the motion for the federal court in Selma. Around this time, I had been in Mobile, Alabama, for several weeks and I received a call asking me to go to Selma on the day of the hearing, which I agreed to do. I should add that Paul

Hancock was my DOJ supervisor, and I considered him to be one of DOJ's finest attorneys. I had worked with Ms. Delaney as well, and she, too, was a fine attorney. The Department of Justice sent Mr. Brian Landsberg to argue the motion in Selma, which I saw essentially as a motion to readmit Mr. Hancock and Ms. Delaney into the Marengo case. Brian Landsberg was a veteran and brilliant Civil Rights Division career attorney who had held several important supervisory positions and did so with distinction. He was rightfully held in high esteem by attorneys throughout the Civil Rights Division. I drove to Selma the night before the hearing and had dinner with Mr. Landsberg. He explained the arguments he would make the next morning along with the points and legal authorities that solidly backed up his arguments. I told him that the arguments that he would be advancing on behalf of the United States should easily carry the day, but not to be surprised if Judge Hand acted like he didn't care about those arguments or what court cases said and would likely deny the motion.

The next morning, the hearing started. Hancock and Delaney had come to the hearing, but to avoid a confrontation inside the courtroom in the event Judge Hand ordered them to leave the courtroom, Mr. Hancock and Ms. Delaney stayed outside the courtroom in the US attorney's office down the hall. I sat in the audience. Since the United States was the moving party, Mr. Landsberg was the first to speak. A gifted oral advocate who had argued many cases, including one voting rights case in the US Supreme Court, Mr. Landsberg brilliantly presented the arguments in support of the government's motion. Judge Hand seemed disinterested. I don't recall him asking any questions, and then it was Mr. Blackwell's turn. All I can recall of Mr. Blackwell's argument was that he said despite the arguments made by the United States, the two attorneys had tampered with the court's witnesses without court permission. This inflamed the judge all over again. But then the hearing took an odd turn.

Judge Hand said from the bench, "Is that Gerry Hebert sitting out there?" I stood and gave him a nod and waved. He asked what I was doing there. I said I was there to watch the hearing. He then said, "Gerry, you need a haircut, your hair is way too long." I explained to him that I had been in Mobile for several weeks. He then responded, "We have barbers in Mobile." I told him I was aware of that but I didn't want a Southern haircut or a mullet. He laughed and then said that he had cut hair decades earlier when he was in the Navy. He said he would be happy to cut my hair in his chambers after the hearing. I said, "Judge, with all due respect, I'm a little uncomfortable turning my back on you when you have a pair of scissors in your hands." He laughed again and said, "You're one funny Yankee lawyer."

He then asked me what I thought of this matter that was now before the court. I then said something I knew would be important to him. I said "I saw you at the Methodist church in Mobile last Sunday." He said, "I didn't see you." I said, "I was sitting near my friend Larry Menefee." Judge Hand then said, "I saw him. He had his arm around his girlfriend in church and I don't think that's proper or right." I then said that the message from the pastor that day was about forgiveness and I knew he surely understood how empowering forgiveness can be. I said, "Mr. Hancock and Ms. Delaney are sorry this whole thing had happened." Note that I didn't say that the two DOJ lawyers were sorry for anything they had done. I was careful to say that they were sorry this entire incident had led to all this. He asked where are they; I said down the hall in the US attorney's office. He said, "Go, get them." I knew at that moment he was going to rule favorably for the United States because he was not calling them into the courtroom to say that they weren't allowed in his courtroom. After all, he wanted them there, I thought. I was right. When we returned, Judge Hand said that he was in a forgiving mood and they could handle any further proceedings. I knew Judge Hand really well. I had even stopped by his chambers in Mobile on my honeymoon and introduced him to my wife, a woman from Georgia. When he met her, he was enthralled with her, telling me he was "so happy I had married a southern belle." I think that's another reason Judge Hand liked me; he liked my choice of a spouse, especially where she had been born and raised! When I returned to DC, and got to my office, there was an envelope on my chair from the Civil Rights Division's deputy assistant attorney general James P. Turner. The note read, "Thanks for all you did recently in Selma. I understand you had Judge Hand eating out of yours." It meant a lot to me when I read those words.

Judges Hostile to Civil Rights Can Sometimes Be Personally Hostile to Lawyers Handling Such Cases

Judge Hand was just one of several southern judges I interacted with who were hostile to civil rights and voting rights. I was arguing a school desegregation case in Gulfport, Mississippi, in the mid-1970s before US district judge Daniel Russell, who was notoriously slow to rule and always heard other non–civil rights cases in the morning and made civil rights lawyers wait until the afternoon to have their hearing. After the lunch break, I returned to the courthouse and went to get a drink at the water fountain. There, getting a drink and leaning over with his hand on the wall was federal judge Harold Cox. I knew Judge Cox to be a segregationist and openly hostile to civil rights attorneys. I wasn't about to interact with him if I could help it. I didn't have a watch on, and I was concerned not to be late for court, so as Judge Cox leaned on the wall and was drinking from the water fountain, I tried discreetly to read the time on his watch. Apparently, I wasn't discreet enough. He saw me trying to read the time on his watch and put his hand over the watch and said to me, "Get your own time." This was puzzling, as I thought no one really owns the time of day, even if it's on your watch. Oh, well. But I think he might have known who I was and why I was there.

Some Federal Judges Are Extremely Competent and Even-Handed, and Know and Enforce All the Rules

I had interactions with terrific trial judges in the DC federal court in two voting rights cases in the early 1980s. One case was *Busbee v. Smith* and the other was *City of Port Arthur, Texas v. United States*.

The *Busbee v. Smith* case is important for history, as it eventually led to the creation of a majority-black congressional district in the Atlanta metropolitan area that then went on to elect the late Congressman John Lewis, a civil rights hero who served for decades with such excellence in Congress until his passing in 2020. I played a background and minor role in the case *Busbee v. Smith* (basically helping to prepare a few trial witnesses).

In *Busbee v. Smith*, Georgia sought Voting Rights Act approval (known as preclearance) of their congressional redistricting plan and sue the US attorney general before a three-judge court in the District of Columbia to seek approval. In the case, the ACLU filed a motion to intervene as a defendant, on the side of the US attorney general, which opposed preclearance of Georgia's plan because it was enacted with racially discriminatory purpose. The ACLU's voting rights project's lead attorney was Laughlin McDonald, who served as co-counsel with Frank Parker of the Lawyers' Committee for Civil Rights under Law, who represented the defendant-intervenors (voters) in the case.

Preparing a Nervous or Reluctant Witness Can Require "Outside the Box" Thinking

The voters the ACLU represented and who were serving as defendant-intervenors included Georgia state senator Julian Bond. Bond had been elected to the Georgia state House of Representatives in the mid-1960s, but Georgia representatives refused to seat him because he had criticized the United States over its involvement in the Vietnam War. Bond sued in federal court but lost. On direct appeal to the US Supreme Court, Bond won a 9 to 0 victory in the case *Bond v. Floyd,* which held that Bond's First Amendments rights had been violated by the Georgia House and the court ordered him seated. He served in the Georgia House until the mid-1970s when he was elected to the Georgia Senate. He was in the Georgia state senate in 1981 advocating for the creation of a majority-black congressional district in the Atlanta region. But the Georgia legislature refused to do so when the legislature enacted the congressional redistricting plan that was at issue in *Busbee v. Smith.*

Cases like *Busbee v. Smith,* in which a state is seeking preclearance of a new redistricting plan, are required to be heard by a three-judge federal court under the Voting rights Act. One judge is from the DC Court of Appeals and two district court judges in DC are the other two members of the court. The *Busbee v. Smith* panel consisted of Circuit Judge Harry Edwards and district judges Aubrey Robinson and June Green.

Georgia was represented in the courtroom by then Georgia attorney general Michael Bowers. When the trial was under way, Frank Parker and Laughlin asked me if I could help prepare Julian Bond for his trial testimony. I admired both men and was pleased to assist. At the hotel, on the day of his testimony, Julian Bond appeared more nervous than I expected him to be. After all, he was a leading Georgia civil rights activist and was used to public speaking. But he had never testified at a trial where he would be under oath and cross-examined. We painstakingly prepared him, reviewing the questions that McDonald or Parker would ask and tried to prepare him for the likely cross-examination questions Attorney General Bowers or one of the other Georgia lawyers might ask him. After a while he seemed less nervous but still hesitant. As we walked to the courthouse, I assured him that both McDonald and Parker, his lawyers, were among the very best voting rights lawyers in the country. I also told him I had handled lots of civil rights cases, that I felt he was ready, and that he would do really well.

As we got to the courtroom, we stood outside and looked through the porthole windows where the trial was ongoing. The doors were big swinging doors with little windows that you look through. We could see another witness was on the witness stand. I said to Julian Bond, I would bang the door before he entered and everyone would turn to see what the noise was and I would slowly open the door for him to walk in. He asked me why. I said, the rule has been invoked, which means witnesses can't be in the courtroom until it's their turn to testify. He said then why am I going in? I said, because you are a party to the case and the rule doesn't apply. I said, "AG Bowers is going to object to you being in the courtroom but I or one of the judges will remind Bowers you are a party and you'll be allowed." He shrugged but reluctantly agreed to my little scheme. I banged the door and in strolled Julian Bond. On cue, AG Bower stood and objected: "We have a witness in the courtroom, Judge." Judge Aubrey Robinson quickly said, "Mr. Bond is a party to this suit, Mr. Bowers." Bowers replied, "Sorry, Judge, my mistake, objection withdrawn." Julian sat in the courtroom audience, and I sat next to him. He leaned over and said, "Thanks to you, I'm not nervous anymore. You really know your way around and if you think I'm ready, then I'm ready." Julian testified brilliantly and in cross-examination, answered each question with precision and they never laid a glove on him. At the end of the trial day, Julian and I spoke and he noted that first they wouldn't seat him in the Georgia House and now they tried to deny him a seat in the courtroom. I've repeated this story many times over the years, and I often add that when Julian strolled into the courtroom I seem to recall trumpets playing and angels singing. Julian had a regal look about him, that's for sure.

In Cross-Examining Expert Witnesses, Review in Advance Everything They Have Written or Said on the Topic at Hand

It seems that some of my best moments in the courtroom have come during the cross-examination of expert witnesses during a trial. One case from the early 1980s, *City of Port Arthur Texas v. United States*, 517 F. Supp. 987 (D.D.C. 1981), gave me the opportunity to cross-examine two expert witnesses, Dr. Susan MacManus and Dr. Joseph Zimmerman. Here's what the case was about.

The City of Port Arthur, Texas, sought Voting Rights Act approval (known as preclearance) of annexations and the consolidation of adjacent predominantly white political subdivisions. The City proposed two different methods of electing the nine member City Council in the expanded City. First, an 8–0–1 plan in which eight members would be elected at large from residency districts (8), zero single-member districts (0), and the mayor elected at large (1). Hence the label 8–0–1. Second, a 4–4–1 election plan. The 4–4–1 plan provided for a nine-member council including a mayor who continued to be elected at large. Four council members would be elected from single-member districts (4). These same districts would also serve as residency districts for the four remaining members who would be elected on an at-large basis by the City (4). The mayor would continue to be elected at large (1). To obtain preclearance approval of the annexation and consolidations, the City had to prove that either of these election schemes fairly reflected minority voting strength in the enlarged City (if the annexations and consolidations were approved).

Because voting in Port Arthur was racially polarized, and blacks constituted over 40 percent of the City's voting-age population, DOJ took the position that neither of the two methods of election fairly reflected minority voting strength. Indeed, under the 8-0-1 plan, no black preferred candidates could get elected, and under the 4-4-1 plan black voters would be able to elect only two candidates of their choice in the enlarged City. So whether and to what extent voting patterns in past elections in Port Arthur exhibited racially polarized voting patterns was an important issue in the case.

I got to cross-examine two of the City's expert witnesses, Dr. Susan MacManus (University of South Florida) and Dr. Joseph Zimmerman (State University of New York). Judge Charles Richey presided at the trial before the three-judge court. In district court cases involving three-judge courts, it is not unusual for one judge to be the managing judge and oversee the trial, even though all three judges sit on the bench together during court proceedings. The other two judges were Circuit Judge J. Skelly Wright and District Judge John Lewis Smith Jr.

MacManus testified first and, like James Voyles had done in the Dallas County, Alabama, case discussed above, changed her threshold for determining whether voting in Port Arthur was racially polarized. As the three-judge court would later write in their opinion: "The testimony of Dr. MacManus, however, fails to withstand scrutiny. While she insisted on direct examination that any polarization score below 90 was not indicative of significant racially polarized voting, Dr. MacManus admitted on cross-examination that she had used a threshold polarization score of 75 to determine 'highly significant' polarization in a study relating to the City of Houston. MacManus Dep. II, 53–59. According to her own figures, eleven of twelve black versus white contests between 1969 and 1977 evidenced 'highly significant' polarization if the threshold is fixed at 75." It makes the task of cross-examining an expert so much easier when experts are inconsistent in their approach to analyzing the data.

Then came the City's other expert who, like Susan MacManus, did the same thing and changed his method of analyzing the data. Of course, I had transcripts of his prior testimony from other cases and after I asked him if it was true that in previous cases he had a different mode of analysis, he did something that experts should never do: he was downright rude to me, his opposing counsel. I had seen and experienced experts being evasive in their answers, and I had developed my cross-examination skills to the point where I could pin experts down, but I did it respectfully. So I had Zimmerman's testimony from prior cases marked as exhibits and asked him to turn to a particular page. Instead of complying, he shot back at me saying, "You have the transcript, read it yourself." Judge Richey then spoke next. He said to Dr. Zimmerman, "Surely you don't talk to one of your students like that in the classroom, do you?" Zimmerman's reply was "as a matter of fact I do." That seemed to infuriate Judge Richey. Judge Richey then raised his voice a little and said to Zimmerman, "Well, this is a courtroom not a classroom." Judge Richey then educated Zimmerman on the courtroom hierarchy. He started and said we are the three judges and we are at the top. Then comes Mr. Hebert and your own lawyer who are officers of the court. Then comes the US marshal, then the court reporter. Then he said, "We haven't gotten to you yet. Understand?" My cross-examination continued and Zimmerman folded like a cheap suit, admitting the existence of severe racial voting patterns. In the three-judge court's decision, the only mentions of Zimmerman's analysis are two footnotes where the court cites his testimony for these two statements: "the election results reflected severely polarized racial bloc voting" (517 F. Supp. at 996); and "Plaintiff does not dispute the fact that most of the elections . . . have been characterized by severe racial polarization" (517 F. Supp. at 1006–7).

The Corum Claim: A New Remedy

John Gresham

In January 1992 the North Carolina Supreme Court ruled that a professor at Appalachian State University had a direct cause of action against the provost of the university under the Declaration of Rights contained in the North Carolina Constitution and that this cause of action was not subject to the defense of sovereign immunity. The Declaration of Rights includes among its protections freedom of speech and equal protection of due process. The Declaration first adopted in 1776 preceded the federal constitution.

The genesis of the private right of action was a short article in the *North Carolina Bar Journal* that invited civil right lawyers to consider bringing a claim under the North Carolina Constitution to safeguard the rights of North Carolina citizens. Justice Exum, writing in the *State Bar Quarterly*, suggests that it is time to "dust off the constitution" because we give our Constitution a liberal interpretation in favor of its citizens with respect to those provisions that were designated to safeguard the liberty and security of the citizens in regard to both persons and property. When I read Justice Exum's admonitions, I tucked it away and hoped that a client would walk through the door with a case that the Supreme Court might turn Justice Exum's invitation into a decision that would provide the safeguards of the Declaration of Rights.

The Client Arrives

Al Corum arrived in my office in 1987 and was steadfast in his determination to see the case through. As years passed, Al was not only the client I had hoped for but also someone who became a good friend. When he passed in 2018, I spoke at his funeral about the unique man who took on the university system, for his unusual route to becoming a university professor prepared him to be the plaintiff in the case that created what is known by attorneys and judges as a "Corum claim."

Born into poverty with a Native American father and an Anglo mother, Al escaped the mills because he was a high school pitching star and signed a professional baseball contract. Three years later he left baseball, enlisted in the US Navy and served in battle during the Korean Conflict. A decorated veteran, he used the GI Bill to go to what was then Appalachian State Teachers College. After receiving an F+ on his first test, he proceeded to serve as class president and graduate with honors. He then received a master's and doctorate from the University of Miami, and ten years after departing he returned to his alma mater where he became the Dean of Learning Resources and a tenured professor.

The Demise of the Appalachian Collection

The issue of concern that led to Al Corum's case was the demise of the Appalachian Collection. The collection was the widely used and appreciated integrated collection of traditional library materials and a wide array of cultural artifacts. Given the location of the university in the southern Appalachian Mountains, the collection, in addition to the library materials, included books written about the traditions of the southern Appalachian Mountain people and their ancestors and their traditions together with unique cultural artifacts, antique furniture, old manuscripts, poems, songs, and musical instruments. Many of the items had been donated with the understanding that the university would preserve and maintain their gifts.

Dr. Harvey Durham, a vice chancellor, was in charge of learning resources. In 1984 as new buildings were coming online, Durham assured Al that the collection would remain intact when it moved from the library where it had been housed. However, Durham had surreptitiously decided to split up the collection at different sites around the university. While out of town he sent his subordinate to advise Dr. Corum of the decision to split the collection. When Dr. Corum said he would delay the move until he could speak with Dr. Durham, the vice chancellor ignored the call. Without speaking to Corum, Durham returned to campus the next day. Since he did not have the power to fire Dr. Corum because he held tenure, he stripped him of his deanship and placed Corum, a full professor, at a desk in the basement of the library at a reduced salary. His life experiences led Al to battle for nine years over his demotion for voicing his opposition to the dissolution of the Appalachian Collection.

The Litigation

After Dr. Corum had exhausted his institutional remedies, the matter moved to the Superior Court in which the complaint named a number of university defendants. The defendants filed a motion for summary judgment asserting that Corum had failed to exhaust his remedies in the university system. When that motion failed, the defendants filed a second summary judgment on substantive grounds asserting neither claim was valid under existing law and then appealed from the denial of that motion.

The Court of Appeals reversed the denial of summary judgment on this action on the Section 1983 claim except the injunctive relief against Durham and two other defendants. On the state constitutional claim the Court of Appeals found that all claims against defendants in their official capacity should be denied but that Corum could proceed against Dr. Durham and John Thomas, the chancellor at Appalachian State, in their individual capacities for violation of Corum's state constitutional rights.

Based on a dissent in the Court of Appeals, the Supreme Court heard argument and entered its opinion on January 3, 2002. The Supreme Court decision recognized that the fate of the Appalachian Collection was a matter of public concern, that Dr. Corum had a right to speak out about the dismemberment of the collection, and that Dr. Durham had deceived Dr. Corum about the plan to split the collection until it was too late to halt the process. Based upon the findings the court found there was a valid Section 1983 claim against Durham in both his official and personal capacity, but dismissed the remaining defendants.

Turning to the claim under the Declaration of Rights, the Court discussed a number of decisions dating back to 1805 and then quoted Justice Exum's article in the *State Bar Quarterly* to determine that any person who did not have an adequate state remedy against a state entity has a direct claim of action under the state constitution against a state actor in his official capacity for injunctive and monetary relief. This private right of action is not subject to the doctrine of sovereign immunity.

The Result

When the case was called for trial, the judge, James Long, who had been one of the initial proponents of mediation in the state, called counsel to his chambers and began a mediation that resulted in a settlement as the jury, which had been seated, waited impatiently. After considering the possible outcomes from a jury verdict, Al accepted the offer by the university. The offer included two years of paid leave at a substantially increased salary to prepare for a position in the Department of Leadership and Higher Education, as well as Al's out-of-pocket attorney fees. Al enjoyed his return to a satisfying position until his retirement in 1997.

The Legacy of *Corum*

While cases following *Corum* have dealt with findings of violations of freedom of speech and due process, the Supreme Court has recently used *Corum* on two major issues many North Carolinians cared about.

In February 2022 the court on *Moore v. Harper* cited *Corum* over 14 times in striking down a partisan gerrymander under the equal protection, free speech, and freedom of assembly claims of the Declaration of Rights, and in *Hoke County Board of Education v. North Carolina* the Supreme Court cited *Corum* to mandate increased funding for public schools under Article 15 of the Declaration of Rights that states that people have a right to the privilege of education and it is the duty of the state to guard and maintain that right. This case that has been litigated for years will result in hundreds of millions of dollars for public schools in North Carolina.

Little did Al Corum know what his fight would bring when he asked me as we were headed to the Supreme Court to tell him about the precedents for his state law claim and I smiled and said, Al, there aren't any. I'm sure he would be smiling today about the decisions his case has spawned.

From Wall Street to Occupy Wall Street: A Journey

Alan Levine

I was barely a year out of law school[4] in mid-1963 when I began working at a small Wall Street law firm, Stroock & Stroock & Lavan, located at 61 Broadway in lower Manhattan.[5] A six-minute walk up Broadway would take me to what later became Zuccotti Park. Fifty years later—I was then representing the NYC Chapter of the National Lawyers Guild—I was at the northeast corner of the park handing an order to a police commander signed by New York State Supreme Court justice Lucy Billings requiring that the NYC police cease the eviction of Occupy Wall Street protesters who had occupied the park for the past several weeks. There are many waypoints in that 50-year journey from 61 Broadway to the northeast corner of Zuccotti Park, but one in particular—a several-month period beginning during the Freedom Summer of 1964 and continuing into 1965 when I lived and worked in Alabama, Mississippi, and Louisiana—was personally, professionally, and politically life-changing. These reflections tell the story of those months in the Deep South and how they shaped that journey.

My Decision to Go South

By the spring of 1964, I had been at Stroock several months doing dull corporate work. But boredom was not the only problem. There was more than a little discomfort, too. For weeks, newspapers and television had been describing protests in Birmingham, Alabama, that sought to dismantle segregation and secure the right to vote. There were haunting pictures of police on horseback clubbing peaceful protesters and children being knocked to the ground by powerful water hoses and large dogs. I had a law school education that I could have used to do something useful, and instead I was drafting corporate bylaws.

One night after watching these images on the evening news, I visited a college friend to talk about what was happening in Birmingham. I had grown up in a Jewish family during and after the Holocaust and, in terms that resonated most powerfully with my own lived experience, I expressed my increasing unease: "We are standing by, doing nothing, while dogs and water cannons are used on people who simply want to vote! We're being good Germans." I meant me.

By coincidence, a few weeks later, someone in the firm with whom I had shared my misgivings left a letter on my desk signed by Father Robert Drinan, then the dean of the Boston College Law School, later a distinguished member of Congress. He was writing on behalf of a newly created organization, the Lawyers Constitutional Defense Committee,[6] which had been formed to provide legal assistance in the South during what was being called the Freedom Summer of 1964. Organizers of the Freedom Summer, principally the Student Nonviolent Coordinating Committee (SNCC), had recruited approximately 1,000 northern students to go south to work with local civil rights workers. Drinan was asking lawyers to volunteer for two-week stints in the southern states where civil rights workers would be active. The letter announced a training session at Columbia Law School some weeks later.

I decided to sign up as a volunteer and, a few weeks later, joined other lawyers at Columbia where we were given a sense of what was in store for us that summer. We learned about SNCC's plans to assist large numbers of Black people to register to vote and to establish "freedom schools" in Black communities throughout Mississippi, and we learned about the threats of "massive resistance" from white Mississippians. The possibility of mass arrests and violence, we were told, was real, and lawyers might be no less likely to be targeted than the activists. We learned about the kinds of legal issues that volunteers would be dealing with and were taught how to remove criminal cases from state court to federal court under a post–Civil War civil rights statute that turned out to be one of the most effective things lawyers in the South did that summer.

But no one talked about something that would turn out to be vitally important—that is, the difference between representing individual clients and working with a political movement. Our clients would encounter legal problems—usually criminal prosecutions—that arose from activity that had been undertaken for political goals. The political and community organizers of the civil rights movement had a stake in how lawyers addressed those legal problems. They, after all, were the ones who would endure the burdens of racist violence and discrimination after the lawyers had left. Their right to engage in legal decision-making that would affect their lives was self-evident.

Lawyers, however, were not used to tailoring their legal advice to the wishes of political activists. It turned out to be a sometimes-fraught issue. Lawyers sometimes negotiated deals in criminal cases that might have been acceptable in other circumstances but not in the political environment of Mississippi in the summer of 1964.

There was a *New York Times* reporter at the Columbia training session and, the next morning, a story appeared describing the formation of LCDC and the training session. Some of my colleagues at Stroock knew that I had volunteered to join the LCDC effort in the South, and when I arrived at work the next day there was a message to come to the office of the firm's managing partner. When I entered his office, I saw that the *Times* was sitting on his desk opened to the story about the Columbia gathering. "I hear you'll be going south during your vacation this summer." He then asked about the *Times*'s reference to threats of violence and the risk of getting arrested, looked at me, sympathetically I thought, and said that if I got arrested—the thought flashed across my mind that he was going to give me his home telephone number—"Don't mention that you work for Stroock."

Permit me a quick flash forward to understand the part that the managing partner's remark played in my political and personal journey. It's the early fall and after two months in the South—I had extended my two-week volunteer stint with additional vacation time and a one-month leave from Stroock—I had returned to the firm. Another young partner who had been a mentor and confidant stopped by my office to ask about my experiences. I told him with great passion about what I had done and what I had seen and how profoundly the experience had affected me. He listened without interruption, congratulated me, and added: "I hope you've gotten that out of your system." Although it felt like a kick in the stomach, it took me only a few seconds to catch my breath and reply, "Actually, I think I've gotten Stroock out of my system." I quit a couple of weeks later and, after doing volunteer work for the New York Civil Liberties Union, returned to the South for another six months.

Voter Registration, the MFDP, and the Betrayal of Atlantic City

While I came to Mississippi having seen pictures of dogs and fire hoses and cattle prods being deployed against protesters marching peacefully for the right to vote, nothing prepared me for the pervasive hostility and palpable threat of violence that characterized the white community that summer. Gun-toting sheriffs, barking angry orders at protesters and clubbing them with nightsticks, made it clear that the threat was not to be taken lightly.

On the other hand, nothing prepared me for the extraordinary courage and determination that I witnessed in Black communities throughout Mississippi that summer. What Black citizens from every walk of life did to secure their rights in the face of physical violence and economic reprisal is a story of popular resistance that became an inspiration for social and political movements throughout the remainder of the twentieth century and into the present. In my interactions with those movements over the years, I often saw the influence of the Mississippi Freedom Summer.

The focus of the summer's activities was voting. Two related campaigns were undertaken. The first was to increase the number of officially registered voters. In 1964, Black people represented approximately 40 percent of the state's voting-age population. Yet, by virtue of a combination of white violence and intimidation, hostile election clerks, and a series of state-enacted voter restrictions, only some 28,500 Black people were registered to vote, as opposed to approximately 500,000 whites.[7] Over the summer, with the support and encouragement of Freedom Summer activists, some 17,000 Black men and women attempted to register to vote. Despite the presence of the national media, and promised support from the federal government, election officials, with almost unlimited discretion to decide who would and would not get to register, backed up by the continuing threat of white violence, ensured that only some 1,600 succeeded.

While those registration efforts were proceeding, local Mississippi activists, with the assistance of civil rights workers, formed the Mississippi Freedom Democratic Party as an alternative to the regular Mississippi Democratic Party. Their campaign extended to every county in the state, meetings were widely advertised in both Black and white communities, and they attracted the participation of thousands of Mississippi Black people throughout the state who, for the first time in their lives, were able to debate public policy and consider the merits of delegates to represent them.[8] In barely six weeks, an astonishing 80,000 men and women were registered to vote in the party. Impressed as I was with the MFDP's organizing in communities throughout the state, it was something else—the events that occurred that August at the National Democratic Convention in Atlantic City, where the FDP presented its credentials and challenged those of the regular Mississippi delegation—that most lastingly impacted me.

The justice of the FDP challenge could not have been clearer. The Mississippi Democratic Party was openly segregationist, committed to the exclusion of Black people from the political process, and unwilling to commit its support to the national party's presumptive nominee, Lyndon Johnson, because he was considered pro–civil rights. The MFDP, by contrast, had invited all Mississippians, Black and white, to participate in their nomination process and had pledged its loyalty to the national Democratic nominee and to the party's platform.

The case to seat a loyal party delegation with a commitment to civil rights, as opposed to a disloyal delegation with a record of hostility to civil rights, was unassailable.

By the time the MFDP delegates arrived in Atlantic City, they had attracted widespread support from many state delegations. It was also clear, however, that party leaders—including some of the leading Democratic liberals of the time—were working in the background against the MFDP, worried that a refusal to seat the "regular" Mississippi delegation might alienate Democratic supporters in the South. The party's Credentials Committee would recommend to the convention which Mississippi delegation to seat. It fell to Vice-Chair Fannie Lou Hamer, a former sharecropper who had lost her job and had been mercilessly beaten and left permanently injured as a result of her voting rights work, to make the FDP's case to the committee. As SNCC leader John Lewis subsequently wrote, "It was Fannie Lou's testimony that everyone had been waiting for."[9] She proceeded to describe "the violent violations of her basic rights as a human being and as an American citizen." Lewis went on:

> With tears welling in her eyes—with tears filling the eyes of almost everyone watching—she asked, in the unrehearsed, down-to-earth, plain language of an everyday American, the question we all wanted answered: "If the Freedom party is not seated now, I question America. Is this America, the land of the free and the home of the brave, where we have to sleep with our telephones off the hooks because our

lives be threatened daily, because we want to live as decent human beings, in America?"[10]

Watching on television, President Johnson understood the impact of Hamer's words and hastily called a press conference in the middle of her speech. TV cameras turned from Hamer to the president. Then the arm-twisting and threats began. Members of the Credentials Committee and of state delegations who had signaled their support for the FDP were promised political favors or threatened with political retaliation. In the end, most of the FDP's support evaporated. A so-called compromise—the "Mississippi regulars" would be seated as full-voting delegates and the FDP would be given two nonvoting seats; in other words, they'd be invited in as spectators—was offered to the FDP and flatly rejected.

The betrayal of the FDP's cause by some of the politicians most identified with civil rights had a profound impact on the organizers of the Freedom Summer. One of them, Cleveland Sellers, put it this way: "After Atlantic City, our struggle was no longer for civil rights but for liberation."

My own drift away from liberalism toward a more radical politics began with Atlantic City and was reinforced by many events of the 1960s and thereafter: the war in Vietnam, US policy that was openly hostile to popular resistance movements around the world, aggressive militarism, the illiberal economy, criminal justice, and anti-immigrant policies of successive Democratic administrations. And so much more. All those events I consider to be part of my political radicalization. But it was Atlantic City, where self-professed liberals turned their backs on a cause that was so obviously just, both legally and morally, that was shape-shifting. My view of the world was forever changed.

Arrests at a Segregated Library, a Judge, and Two US Marshals

Then there was the judge who reminded me that, notwithstanding the failings of political liberalism, there were sympathetic liberals in the South who acted to do what was right in response to the Freedom Summer's demand for justice. I was in an LCDC office in New Orleans one late afternoon when we received a call that a small group of Black children had been arrested for refusing to leave a segregated library after they were told they could not borrow any books. They had been jailed in a town some 30 miles north of New Orleans in a region known to be particularly hostile to civil rights activities and we were worried about them spending a night in jail.

We immediately began to prepare a petition for removal to file in federal court, but it was getting close to the time when the courthouse would close and we needed more information about the arrests to complete the papers. We called the courthouse and were put through to the chambers of Judge Herbert Christenberry, who had previously ruled in favor of civil rights claims. We told the judge's clerk about the arrests and said that we wanted to file a removal petition. However, we told him that the papers could not be completed until after normal business hours. He consulted with the judge and told us that the judge would be willing to meet us in his private chambers in the courthouse and that we should call when the papers were completed.

It was early evening before we were done, at which point we called the clerk and arranged to meet at the courthouse. When we arrived, the clerk took the papers to Judge Christenberry, and after a short time we were shown into the judge's chambers. He had obviously read our papers because he seemed incredulous. This was a man who surely knew the many injustices committed in the name of segregation. But still he seemed taken aback. Maybe it was the utter pettiness of it. "Do you really mean that they were arrested just because they insisted on the right to borrow library books?"

He signed our papers without hesitation. But then there was the matter of serving the sheriff with the papers and getting him to release the children from jail. Given the hostility of the sheriff and the local community, the judge asked the two US marshals, who were in chambers with us, to serve the papers and get the children. However, one of the marshals, who knew the area where they were being held, worried that, when they showed up at the jail to take the children, the sheriff would spread the word of what was happening and that local Klan members might interfere. So there followed a scene unlike any I have seen in any federal courthouse: A federal judge and two US marshals sitting around a table with a hand-drawn map of a town's streets plotting out the route the marshals would take to get in and out of town without being detected by hostile whites. A plan was hatched, and the judge gave instructions that he be called, regardless of the hour, as soon as the children were safely in the marshals' hands. I received a call late that night from the judge's clerk that the children were in the marshals' custody and on their way to a rendezvous with their parents.

What had impelled a judge and two federal marshals—white men from Louisiana—to do what they did? Maybe it was simply a feeling that, after all the violence and hatred and indignities of segregation, it was time finally to say, "Enough." Or maybe it was the recognition that something out of the ordinary was demanded of them, knowing that a group of children had had the courage to say that they would not be denied the right to read books because of the color of their skin. One can never know. What is undeniably true, however, is that the lives of people such as the judge and the marshals were irrevocably changed by what these children did and by similar acts of courage that occurred repeatedly throughout the South that summer, acts that conveyed in simple, unambiguous terms that Black people would refuse to accept anything less than full equality.

Epilogue

I have told the stories of Atlantic City and Judge Christenberry because each, in its own way, had a personal significance for me and helped shape my career as a civil rights lawyer. But more than anything, what stays with me are the memories of a summer spent among people who struggled together, marched together, sang together, and let the world know that they were determined to bring justice to a place in which racism had ruled. It was some of that hope and spirit that I observed among the occupiers of Zuccotti Park. Which is why I happened to be at the park's northeast corner some 50 years later serving a police commander with a restraining order.

Notes

1. Alex, et al., v. City of Chicago, 29 F.3d 1235 (7th Cir. 1994). https://scholar.google.com/scholar_case?case=15857319175241362989&hl=en&as_sdt=6&as_vis=1&oi=scholarr
2. In Texas, as elsewhere, settlements with governmental entities are public record and are not confidential.
3. For more information on the health effects of Agent Orange, see the U.S. Department of Veteran Affairs article: https://www.publichealth.va.gov/exposures/agentorange/conditions/ischemicheartdisease.asp
4. This essay is dedicated to the memory of Henry Schwarzschild, the executive secretary of the Lawyers Constitutional Defense Committee, under whose auspices I went south in the summer of 1964. He brought to all LCDCs volunteer lawyers the inspiration of his lifelong commitment to justice.
5. In 1963 Stroock & Stroock & Lavan consisted of fewer than 30 lawyers. Today, practicing under the name Stroock, the firm has offices in four cities employing hundreds of lawyers.

6   What I did not know at the time was that part of the impetus for the creation of LCDC came from the refusal of some of its founders to cooperate with lawyers from the National Lawyers Guild because of its leftist politics, even though the guild was already planning to send lawyers to the South that summer. The history of the LCDC was described in a senior history thesis submitted by Thomas Hilbink, "Filling the Void: The Lawyers Constitutional Defense Committee and the Freedom Summer of 1964" (Undergraduate thesis, Columbia University, 1993).
7   These statistics were contained in a brief submitted on behalf of the MFDP to the Credentials Committee of the National Democratic Party. https://www.crmvet.org/docs/6408_mfdp_brief.pdf
8   A good description of the MFDP's activities that summer is available in the history compiled by the civil rights activists themselves: "Mississippi Freedom Democratic Party (MFDP) Founded (April)" in "Civil Rights Movement History 1964 Jan–June," Civil Rights Movement Archive, https://www.crmvet.org/tim/timhis64.htm#1964mfdp
9   *Id.*, at 7.
10 *Id.*

5

Movement Figures

Lawyers Constitutional Defense Committee, 1964–66

BRUCE ROGOW

I have hundreds of stories to tell about life, love, law, and lawlessness in Mississippi, and I have told many to students, congregants, friends, acquaintances. I think sharing the stories adds a flavor, an urgency, to history, and I hope to convey a small sense of the time by introducing the reader to some of the people who made Mississippi memorable and some of the places that I will never forget.

What Was It Like to Know Henry Schwarzschild, Charles Morgan Jr., Alvin Bronstein, and R. Jess Brown?

Henry Schwarzschild

Henry was the headmaster of the Lawyers Constitutional Defense Committee (LCDC). In 1964 he created LCDC within the framework of the ACLU. He came to the United States from Germany when he was 13, an eastern European Jewish immigrant. He was an activist, energetic, smart, wiry, intense, sensitive and with a great sense of humor.

I had met Fannie Lou Hamer, who was the head of the Mississippi Freedom Democratic Party, in the summer of 1964 at the Democratic Convention in Atlantic City. I had been admitted to the Florida Bar in June 1964. Ms. Hamer said, "We need you in Mississippi. Lawyers are coming." She told me to see George Crockett, a National Lawyers Guild director.

I looked him up—a Jacksonville native—but he lived in Detroit. He was a successful lawyer and political figure. I drove to Detroit and met him, told him I wanted to go to Mississippi, and he told me that the National Lawyers Guild was viewed as a subversive organization in Florida and that if I wanted to practice in Florida, I should go to New York and see Henry Schwarzschild, who was putting together a lawyers' group under the auspices of the ACLU.

I was 24 years old and had no real conception of how important a person Crockett was. He became a congressman in 1986, perhaps the only congressman who had headed the judiciary committee and who had served four months in prison for contempt for his 1949–50 defense of Communist Party members. Over and over again, as you will see below, I met people who were way above my pay grade in every respect.

I drove to New York. Henry and I hit it off. He offered me $250 a month and the room of my choice in a "Lawyer's Freedom House" that LCDC planned to rent. My only debt was a $75 a month car payment. Two fifty, no rent to pay, was fine.

Henry told me that a 37-year-old lawyer named Al Bronstein would head the office and I would be his associate. This was late October 1964, but Al had not yet made his arrangements for our office and housing, so I was told I should go to Atlanta and work with Chuck Morgan, who had opened an ACLU office in Atlanta.

I drove to Atlanta.

"Chuck" Morgan

My first impression of Chuck Morgan was that he was "large." Large in girth, large in humor, large in commitment to civil liberties, very large in legal knowledge, legal strategy, and large in kindness to me. He found me an apartment and sent me to work on a research project, and when I asked where the law books were, he laughed and said, "Go over to the US Court of Appeals courthouse on Forsyth Street and ask to see Judge Tuttle. I called him and he said you can use his library."

I look back at how naive I was. I had no idea that Elbert P. Tuttle was the chief judge of the US Court of Appeals for the Fifth Circuit; that he was the most important, or at least one of the most important judges of the civil rights movement; that Jack Bass's book *Unlikely Heroes* would chronicle how he and other members of his court made civil rights laws and the Constitution "work" in the states of the Fifth Circuit (Texas, Louisiana, Mississippi, Florida, Georgia, and Alabama). In 1938 lawyer Tuttle had argued and won *Johnson v. Zerbst,* the foundational "knowing, intelligent and competent waiver" case. One of my favorite appellate moments was when I was arguing a waiver case in the 1970s in Atlanta and Tuttle and Brown were on the panel, Brown asked me, "Do you know who argued *Johnson v. Zerbst?*" and I smiled and said, "Yes"—only that one word. Tuttle beamed. The assistant US attorney asked me afterward, "What was that all about?"

Judge Tuttle, and his staff, treated me as if I was a part of his office. His respect for Chuck Morgan was the reason. Chuck had been an Alabama lawyer, always interested in civil rights litigation. The Birmingham church bombing in 1963 and the killing of four young girls radicalized him. He had argued *Reynolds v. Sims* in the Supreme Court, reapportioning the Alabama legislature, and had had enough of Alabama, so he was in Atlanta with the ACLU.

Chuck was gregarious, patient with me, and while unrelenting in his commitment to civil liberties, he clothed his arguments in a gracious manner. A lesson learned.

Later, his Vietnam War Supreme Court cases for Julian Bond and Muhammad Ali continued his commitment to civil rights. I left Chuck in January 1965. Just having been in his presence for two months, listening to his stories, watching him work, prepared me for the lawyer stage of LCDC in Jackson.

Alvin Bronstein

Al Bronstein was very different from Chuck Morgan and Henry Schwarzschild. Henry was not a lawyer; he was an organizer, an intellectual, an "energizer bunny" kind of person, and a smoker. He had kept me informed about Al and efforts to get the office started, but not much about Al himself. As I drove from Atlanta to Jackson on a cold early January morning, I did not know what to expect.

I had the address of the office—605 N. Farish Street. I parked in front and walked up a flight of wooden stairs. The building was a wooden frame building, perhaps 25 years old. At the top of the stairs was a door to the right. I opened it and saw Al standing at a desk. I don't recall if Julie (who later became Julie Bronstein) was there, but I saw Al—short, maybe 5' 8", solid build, shirtsleeves rolled up, electric heater in the room keeping him warm. A smile of sorts, a little impatient. It was late morning. He asked if I was hungry, and I said no, and he said if I needed to eat, the place to eat is Stevens Kitchen, right across Farish Street from the office. Farish Street was the main business street in the Black community.

Al did not waste any time putting me to work. He told me that there was a young man in jail that we needed to get out on recognizance bond and that I needed to go over to the police station and get him out. Al told me that it was a matter of getting the paperwork signed and at the police station they would tell me where to go to get it done.

Of course, I did not even know where the police station was. Al gave me directions.

I went to the booking desk at the jail and said I was there to get the recognizance bond for my client, and the first response was "it is lunchtime and the papers won't be available until after lunch." When I asked when lunch was over, the response was "whenever the clerk gets back."

That was the start of a dance that lasted until just about dark on that early January day. When I got the necessary paper, I was directed to one office after the other to get the proper signatures. It dawned on me that there was a method to the Jackson Police Department's release rigamarole: frustrate this young man and maybe he will give up and leave us alone.

That insight had a direct effect on my life as a lawyer. I accepted every diversion, every delay, every demand to see another official, with a smile and a gracious "Thank you." The lesson has never left me: be patient, be calm, be optimistic. Do not be angry.

When release finally occurred, I drove the appreciative young man to our office. Al called his mother. When they left, Al told me "I think you are going to be good." He was not an easy boss.

Al Bronstein's family was from Eastern Europe. He and Henry had an interesting relationship. Al's practice before he came to Mississippi was a "make a living" practice. I think that while he certainly was committed to civil rights, the LCDC position was an opportunity to leave New York and a divorce and start anew. He was a practical man. Henry was a philosophical fellow. I still have copies of correspondence from Henry to Herbert Marcuse, a German American philosopher. Al had no time for that; he was a nuts-and-bolts guy. Get lawyer volunteers down to Mississippi, put them to work getting folks out of jail, file affirmative litigation protecting demonstrations, keep the SNCC (Student Nonviolent Coordinating Committee) volunteers safe.

In the first months of 1965 he built, and Henry backed, a cadre of young lawyers in their twenties who lived, seriatim, in our house on Lewis Street. Alan Levine, Bill Kopit, Malcolm Farmer. Then some more experienced lawyers: Armand Derfner, Dick Sobol, Don Jelinek. And then legions of one- or two-week volunteers from all around the country: Bobby Kaplan and Tim Green from Ohio, a Saltonstall, and Mark De Wolfe Howe from

Boston, for example. Across Farish Street, Henry Aronson and Marian Wright Edelman were the NAACP Legal Defense and Education Fund lawyers.

And then there was Anthony Amsterdam, the most brilliant of all—Tony could dictate complaints and motions/memoranda for injunctive relief, with citations, off the top of his head. Mel Wulf, the ACLU general counsel, and Carl Rachlin, the Congress of Racial Equality general counsel, were visitors to Al's LCDC law firm. Al was not the "senior counsel," he was the glue that made LCDC a force for change in Mississippi, Alabama, and Louisiana.

What was it like to be surrounded by these people? Life-changing. And among them was one special man with whom I had a daily special relationship.

R. Jess Brown

To file a pleading in the Southern District federal court in Jackson, a Mississippi lawyer had to sign the pleading. None of the LCDC lawyers was admitted to the Mississippi Bar. No white lawyer in Mississippi would sign our pleadings.

In the Northern District, Judge Claude F. Clayton, an honorable man, allowed us to sign pleadings. The Southern District was ruled by William Harold Cox. He had been college roommates with Senator James Eastland, one of the leading segregationist leaders of the 1950s and '60s. He would refer to black lawyers only by their first name.

R. Jess Brown agreed to be our "signator." I think Henry and Al worked out some financial renumeration with R. Jess, but that was not my business. My business was to draft pleadings, edit pleadings, find R. Jess, and have him affix his signature.

But R. Jess Brown was not a "figurehead." He was civil rights lawyer royalty. To be sure, two other Black lawyers in Jackson—Carsie A. Hall and Jack H. Young Sr.—had, like R. Jess Brown, a long history of challenging segregation, but to me, R. Jess was special in so many ways.

He was born in Kansas. In 1965 he was 53 years old. He passed the Mississippi Bar in 1953. He had been a teacher in Jackson and was fired after he sued the school board seeking equal pay for "colored" teachers. So he went to Texas Southern Law School and became a Mississippi lawyer.

Brown had defended Mack Parker, who had been accused of raping a white woman in Pearl River County in February 1959. Three days before trial, Parker was taken from his cell, beaten, shot, and then dumped in the Pearl River. The original plan had been to castrate him and hang him from the bridge over the river. R. Jess Brown had seen a lot.

He was a slight man; maybe he weighed 125 pounds. He had a wispy mustache. He always wore a suit jacket and tie, sometimes a bowtie. He was tired. His hair was tending to gray. Climbing the stairs to our office was a bit of an effort.

My desk was in the front room, facing Farish Street. (I think Al put me there because if someone tossed a bomb up into the window from the street, he, whose office was in the back of the building, would be spared. Julie and the other volunteers were in the middle office.) From my window I could see R. Jess walking up Farish. He was enormously interested in the pleadings; reading them made him smile. He would sign, and then we would talk.

Sometimes he was hard to find. I did not know much about his family, but he never complained about anything. Once in a while he was hard to find, though, which led to me having to (with his permission) sign "R. Jess Brown." I was good at forging his signature.

What It Was Like "Outside" in Bolivar County; Selma, Alabama; and Tallulah, Louisiana

Bolivar County

We received calls about demonstrators in Bolivar County, Mississippi, being arrested, and Cleveland, the county seat, was my first foray out of Jackson. Cleveland is about two hours north of Jackson, in the Delta.

Two Bolivar County towns there were special to me. The first was Mound Bayou, which was founded in 1887 by former slaves and was (is) a Black-governed community in the heart of the Delta. Today it is one of the largest all-Black towns in the United States, a town that provides safety, health care, and voting opportunities that were not easy (or possible) to come by in the Delta.

The other town was Shaw, Mississippi. Bess and Dan Seligman were owners of the largest plantation in Shaw. Dan Seligman controlled the town's lawyer—Ancil Cox—and much of my litigation with Cox revolved around Shaw ordinances that were designed to curtail demonstrations in Shaw and in Bolivar County. I had not met Dan Seligman, but the fact that his was a Jewish family of plantation owners intrigued me—what were they doing in the Delta, in a town where they lived since 1940?

The picketing demonstrations in Bolivar County were always peaceful, and the county attorney, John White Valentine, and the sheriff, Charlie Capps, were always accommodating. Valentine was/is a gentleman. Sheriff Capps would call me in Jackson and say, "Bruce, I've got 75 in the jail. Get them out of here."

And the vehicle for doing that was the filing of a petition for removal in federal court under 28 U.S.C. 1443(1), alleging that the arrestees had been denied or could not enforce their constitutional rights in Mississippi courts. We would turn out removal petitions on a Gestetner mimeograph machine, typing hundreds of names on a blue stencil and rolling them out en masse along with motions for release on recognizance. The motions were, at least in Bolivar County, always agreed to by Sheriff Capps and County Attorney Valentine. Having a good relationship with the local officials was easy with them; not so with others.

The removal gambit, which kept folks out of jail and on the streets and sidewalks, ended in June 1966 when the Supreme Court in *City of Greenwood (Mississippi) v. Peacock,* 384 U.S. 808 (1966), held that §1443(1) did *not* create a right to remove state criminal cases to federal court on the allegation that the state courts would not enforce federal rights. So now we had thousands of cases that were destined to go back to state courts.

My last months of 1966 in Mississippi were spent cajoling local district attorneys to drop the state charges. They did, not because of my relationship with some of them but because they did not want the burden of prosecuting those cases. But "removal" had served its purpose.

Charlie Capps, "my" sheriff, was instrumental in the post-*Peacock* effort. Capps, who had been a political, economic, and social force in Cleveland for years, became sheriff in 1964 and quickly became president of the Mississippi Sheriff's Association, where he used his "clout" to encourage other sheriffs to forgo charges when I called upon them to do so. There must have been more than a thousand "cases" that evaporated.

Another lesson—relationships with county attorneys and sheriffs can be more productive when one is collegial.

But I was never collegial with Dan Seligman. I never met him until 20 years later. My uncle, who had retired to Palm Beach, invited me to a cocktail party at his apartment. A short balding man approached me and asked, "Bruce?" I replied, "Yes," and he said, "I'm Dan Seligman." I was stunned. He explained that his children had convinced him that he was "on the wrong side." He had sold all but 200 acres of his thousands of acres and had retired to Palm Beach. He met my uncle and recognized the last name—

Rogow—and asked Louie if he had a son. Louie said, "No," a nephew, and Dan told him the story of my suing him over and over. My nemesis had become my uncle's best friend.

Dan Seligman died in 1990 in Palm Beach. His wife, Bess, died in 2001 in Boca Raton. Both are buried in the Greenville, Mississippi, Jewish cemetery.

Selma

Al must have thought I was doing a good job because he told me to drive over to Selma, Alabama, for the 1965 march over the Edmund Pettus Bridge. I arrived a couple of days early, having arranged for a motel room a few days after the "Bloody Sunday" march, knowing that the sequel would be a major event.

I am not sure what was expected of me other than to work with other lawyers who would be there to get people out of jail. That seemed to be my "specialty."

The night before the march, the gathering was at the Brown Chapel AME church in Selma. Hundreds of people had come: religious leaders, the civil rights leaders, young people, Black and White, all gathered at the church. On the church chancel were Dr. King, Hosea Williams, other SCLC (Southern Christian Leadership Conference) leaders, as well as Stokely Carmichael, John Lewis, James Forman, and other SNCC (Student Nonviolent Coordinating Committee) members.

It was very crowded on the "stage," and Henry Schwarzschild was there, standing behind the leadership, and, as I saw it, straining to be in the picture. That amused me. He knew this was momentous stuff, and he wanted to be in the picture. I was sitting in a pew, close enough to be overwhelmed by the spectacle. This was the first time I had seen such a scene, and the speaking, the singing, the crying, the shouting, and the laughing filled the church for hours.

Finally, folks were told to get their rest, they would need their energy for the march. The pews of the church were to be the sleeping place for many, and two Episcopal ministers who I knew from Philadelphia were preparing their pew "beds." I told them I had two beds in my motel room, but they said no—they were witnesses for Christ and would sleep in the church. I told them where I was going to be in case they changed their minds.

Around midnight three Episcopal ministers knocked on the door of my motel room. We slept two to a bed, and they were well rested for the march in the morning.

I watched from the sidewalk on the bridge as folks lined up, with my yellow pad in hand and seeing how people were jostling to try to be in the front with Dr. King and others. I told my last night's bed mates to stay back a little, it is safer. They wanted to be as close to the front as possible. The Alabama Highway Patrol looked ominous. There was a prayer; there was movement, and the hundreds of marchers crossed the bridge and started their six-day hike. I followed on the side, a bit separate from the body of marchers, for a mile or so, and seeing that peace was prevailing, walked back to the motel.

I packed my bag to go see Zelma Wyche in Tallulah, Louisiana, where peace was not prevailing. Zelma wanted to watch the arrival in Montgomery with me.

Zelma Wyche and the KKK

Al, before Selma, had received a call from a minister in Tallulah, Louisiana, about the arrest of 50 people who were picketing in town. He told me to drive over, meet the families at the church, and get the folks out of jail. Tallulah was about 35 miles west of Vicksburg, Mississippi, across the Mississippi River. This was in February 1965.

I got to Tallulah in the late afternoon and was greeted by a large group of people and the civil rights leader of Tallulah, Zelma Wyche. He was gregarious, upbeat, confident, and he had a paper bag in one hand as he shook my hand with the other. Zelma said, "First, we sing and pray, then we take this bag of money to the sheriff's office." The bag had $5,000 in cash—in ones, fives, tens. I was surprised because in Mississippi there was rarely cash available for bond. Property was sometimes pledged, or a removal petition secured releases, but Tallulah had a different economic vibe. It was a strong Black community. Zelma was the town barber, with a nice shop in the center of town.

The folks at church seemed in no special hurry to head to the sheriff's office, so we sang, prayed, and had a light church supper before heading to town in a convoy of trucks, some driven by men who were large, strong, and fit. That was my introduction to the Deacons for Defense and Justice. The Deacons started in Bogalusa, Louisiana; Tallulah's chapter was made up of men who had played football, some at Louisiana and Mississippi historically black colleges like Alcorn A&M and Grambling State University. The Deacons for Defense and Justice were the antidote to the Ku Klux Klan. They were impressive men.

I had learned that the sheriff's name was Bruce something or other. When Zelma and I were deposited at the sheriff's office, we walked in with the paper bag and I introduced myself (he knew Zelma), thinking that "Bruce to Bruce" might soften the encounter. Not so.

I said I would like to post the bond for the 50 arrestees, and he said, coldly: "$5,000, a hundred a head." I said fine—here is $5,000. He seemed a little surprised and said, "Stand here and watch me count it." He spread the bills on the table and first put them in piles: ones, fives, and tens, and maybe there were one or two twenties, but small bills were the bulk.

That exercise seemed to take a long time. The "piling" was very precise. Each George Washington was placed face up, as was Abraham Lincoln and Alexander Hamilton. Maybe there was an Andrew Jackson or two, but ultimately, the bills were organized, and then each pile was counted with the sheriff listing how many of each denomination, and then the total of each list was carefully added. He said: "$5,000, now you can go get 'em."

How long did it take? Twenty minutes, a half hour? I don't know, but when we walked out the door to cross the dark street to the jail, we had to walk through a phalanx of silent, hooded KKK costumes.

But as Zelma and I walked that plank, we could look up at the second-floor jail windows and my clients could see us and were singing, in beautiful crystalline voices, on that cold February night:

Oh, freedom, oh freedom
Oh freedom over me.
And before I'll be a slave,
I'll be buried in my grave,
And go home to my Lord and be Free.

The jail door opened, Zelma and I were hugged. No attention was paid to the Klansmen, who dispersed as the arrestees came out. Everyone piled into the trucks, and we headed back to the church to sing and pray some more. There was food, too.

Around 11 p.m., I said I had to drive back to Jackson because I had to be in court in the morning. Zelma and the Deacons for Defense and Justice insisted I wait until the morning. When I resisted, they said, OK, but we will follow you in our trucks and when you get to the bridge to Vicksburg, we will block any traffic heading east to give you a 20-minute headstart. And so, I left Tallulah in the protection of the Deacons for Defense and Justice and safely got back to Jackson.

* * *

My connection to Zelma was strong. When I left Selma and he called and insisted I come to Tallulah to watch the end of the march with him at his barbershop, I did not hesitate. We watched, hugged, and cried.

Zelma went on to be the police chief in 1969 and then the mayor of Tallulah in 1986. In 1988 Jacquelyn, my wife, and I, went to the Marriot Hotel in Boca Raton for an event of some sort. As we walked into the lobby, I saw a notice announcing a convention of Black mayors. I knew of Zelma's election, and I asked the woman at the Black mayor's registration desk if Mayor Wyche was attending. She said yes, and that the meeting was just breaking and if I went through "that door," I could go in now.

I did, and as I opened the door of that meeting room and stepped in, Zelma Wyche jumped from his seat in the back of the room and shouted "Bruce!" We embraced. The times, they had changed.

Zelma died in 1999. He is buried in Tallulah. A street is named after him there.

* * *

There is a lot more to tell of course. My Mississippi time had threats, car chases, an arrest, laughter, love affairs, and learning. It formed the foundation for my legal career. The vignettes I have set forth above about the people who helped shape me are a reminder to me that they helped form my foundation as a person. I hope they have given you a few moments of reflection.

The Civil Rights Movement Comes to an End: The 1966 Meredith Mississippi March against Fear

Melvyn R. Leventhal

The march from Selma to Montgomery, in early March 1965, followed the script for protest demonstrations to the letter and was hugely successful.[1] First, the movement's leadership and the Black community were united around a single objective—obtaining new voting rights legislation. Then the nation was horrified by the sight of police on horseback violently attacking and tear-gassing march participants on Selma's Edmund Pettus Bridge, captured by TV cameras and broadcast to every part of the world. The federal government weighed in when the legendary Judge Frank M. Johnson Jr. held that the march could proceed to Montgomery and President Lyndon Johnson delivered a nationally televised address in which he declared that "we shall overcome." The 54-mile march ended with a massive rally in Montgomery, a signature speech by Dr. King, and the enactment of the Voting Rights Act of 1965.

One year later, it all fell apart. The leaders of the June 1966 Meredith March against Fear bickered over objectives and strategies, Mississippi's governor reined in police brutality, President Johnson turned his back on the Meredith march, and the movement ran out of money with donations reduced to a trickle. This essay explains why and how all of this happened and is offered as a cautionary tale for human rights advocates of today.

Background

James Meredith, who started the 1966 march, was best known for integrating the University of Mississippi in 1962. But after he graduated from Ole Miss in 1963 he retreated to a more private life. He traveled, studied, and lectured in Africa and Europe and then returned to New York with his wife and child, to enroll in Columbia Law School.

On the first two days of June 1966, Meredith attended a White House conference of civil rights activists. At the end of the conference, he announced that he would lead a march from Memphis to Jackson to "encourage Negroes to register to vote." Meredith saw a need to breathe life into the newly enacted Voting Rights Act: as of 1965, of the 450,000 Black Mississippians eligible to vote only 30,000 were registered. He also said that he would walk the length of Mississippi's Highway 51, from Memphis to Jackson, to conquer the fear that Black people felt when they traveled in Mississippi. Although he urged others to join him, he wanted only small groups of men and not major civil rights organizations. No one, however, appeared to give the walk a second thought. So there was Meredith, on Sunday, June 5, 1966, with four of his buddies setting out from the lobby of the Peabody Hotel in Memphis with backpacks and walking sticks and with pretty much no one paying attention.

On June 6, when Meredith with a larger group reached Hernando, Mississippi—just south of the Tennessee-Mississippi border—Meredith was shot and wounded by a sniper. The nation's civil rights leaders believed that the shooting required an immediate and strong response: Dr.

Martin Luther King Jr. of the Southern Christian Leadership Conference (SCLC), Stokely Carmichael, the chairman of the Student Nonviolent Coordinating Committee (SNCC, pronounced "SNICK") and Floyd McKissick, the national director of the Congress of Racial Equality (CORE), converged on Meredith's hospital bed in Memphis to express outrage at the shooting and to announce that they would continue Meredith's walk, transforming it into a demonstration of national importance. The model, they said, would be the Selma march of 1965: they would lead a column of marchers down the highway, arrangements would be made for food and portable toilets, and large tents would be pitched at a new location each night. This was not what Meredith had envisioned, but he was no longer in control.

I Join the March

"Hey, Mel, you finished with finals?" It was Marian Wright [Edelman]—then head of the NAACP Legal Defense and Education Fund's office (LDF) in Jackson, Mississippi, where I had worked as a law student during the summer of 1965. Marian was phoning me in early June 1966 from a hotel room in Memphis. I was sitting in my dorm at NYU Law School. "Listen, Mel," she continued, "Martin's ready to do some more marching. De Lawd says he's walking from Memphis to Jackson. Need you to catch the next plane to Memphis; need you to march with him." [To insiders, in private, Dr. King was "Martin" or "Doc" or "De Lawd." And any directive from him was often affectionately punctuated with "praise be De Lawd."]

"Marian," I answered, "Dr. King will say he needs a real lawyer; he won't settle for a law student." "Well, he'll have to," she answered, "because I can't find a lawyer willing to walk 200 miles of Mississippi Highway in 90° heat. I'm offering you because you're as close as I can get to a lawyer and besides, Colored folk take to you."

I caught the next flight to Memphis and met Marian at her hotel. We then drove to the Black-owned Lorraine Motel, where Dr. King was staying and where he would be assassinated two years later. During the Jim Crow era, there were few motels owned by or even open to Black people and those that existed were often only marginally acceptable, products of segregation and discrimination. The Lorraine, however, had the feel and look of one of the many new and well-kept, modular two-story roadside Holiday Inns being built along the newly constructed interstate highway system throughout the South. The Lorraine and the Centenary Baptist church in Memphis would serve as Dr. King's and the march's headquarters.

Dr. King greeted us near the motel's entrance with smiling eyes that lit up his entire face. "Come here girl, give me a hug," he said to Marian, squashing all 100 pounds of her in his arms. The public knew Dr. King's bearing as always deliberative and his speaking voice as controlled, rhythmic, and somber, always at the pulpit, in performance. But now he was with a friend—relaxed and unguarded. I felt privileged to be with him and Marian at such a moment.

The three of us walked to the motel's restaurant where we settled into breakfast with a few members of his staff at a large table. Dr. King was all business. He said that he would use this march to revive interest in the movement and to educate the Nation about the virulent and entrenched racism in Mississippi. He said that while Mississippi was the "hardest nut to crack" it was time the state got his attention. He envisioned voter registration drives and rallies in towns located off the main route of the march. He added that the march would also be used to desegregate public accommodations and raise Black consciousness. And he was thinking of concluding it with a demonstration on the steps of the capitol in Jackson. "It will be bigger, much bigger, than the Selma to Montgomery march, and I assume you'll march with us."

"Well, Martin," Marian answered, "I've got my own White folk to deal with and little staff and time to do it all. Mel here will stand in for me." She added that I would keep her and Henry Aronson, her colleague at LDF's Jackson office, up to date with telephone calls. Dr. King and his staff were disappointed, but they had no choice. Marian's final instructions to me were "don't get yourself arrested; we'll need you to get people out of jail, not keep them company in jail."

Marian did meet with me when the march reached Greenwood, and Henry spent almost all of his time in Grenada, a beehive of movement activity during the march. I kept in touch with them using pay phones on the route or a phone available in the home of a local civil rights worker. I participated in the walk for about 100 of the 200 miles and slept in tents on about ten occasions. I also spent several days at the Centenary Baptist church in Memphis, working with SCLC staff on public relations and arranging for food, portable toilets, and tents. My clearest memories of the walk are of the state police and the curious, sometimes threatening onlookers—both a constant presence; also, that I was always looking for the water truck and fighting dehydration. Travel to and from the march site was easy: cars were always coming and going at random times with the drivers inviting march participants looking for a ride to "hey, jump in."

Governor Paul Johnson Defuses the March

Contrary to King's hopes and expectations, the Meredith march was a failure for a host of reasons. First, Mississippi finally adopted an effective strategy for defusing the march: don't brutally attack demonstrators, instead protect their First Amendment right to peaceful protest.

As King had explained a year earlier, in the context of the Selma to Montgomery march:

> The goal of the demonstrations in Selma, as elsewhere, is to dramatize the existence of injustice and to bring about the presence of justice by methods of nonviolence. Long years of experience indicate to us that Negroes can achieve this goal when four things occur:
>
> 1. Nonviolent demonstrators go into the streets to exercise their constitutional rights.
> 2. Racists [often led by a local sheriff] resist by unleashing violence against them.
> 3. Americans of conscience in the name of decency demand federal intervention and legislation.
> 4. The administration [President Lyndon Johnson's] initiates measures of immediate intervention and remedial legislation.

This strategy had worked in Selma. Alabama's racism, callousness, and police brutality—orchestrated by the sadistic and violent Selma-Dallas county sheriff Jim Clark—shocked and prodded the nation, Congress, and the president into enacting the Voting Rights Act of 1965.

However, a year later, Mississippi's governor Paul Johnson adopted a strategy of nonconfrontation and acquiescence and worked hard to keep Mississippi's virulent and entrenched racism in check. At the outset, he said that Meredith's attacker, Aubrey Norvell, would be charged with "assault with intent to murder." Then both houses of the Mississippi legislature adopted resolutions deploring the "unfortunate and criminal shooting" of Meredith. In fact, in November 1966, Norvell pled guilty to "assault and battery with intent to kill" and received a five-year sentence with three years suspended and parole eligibility after 18 months. He was released from Parchman Penitentiary in June 1968.

Most important, Governor Johnson promised protection so that the "demonstrators get all the marching they want." There was not much to fear, he said, since Mississippi had many "such marches down here all the time." A state trooper added, "They can march for as long as they want." The Mississippi Highway Patrol inspected cars along the march route for firearms—finding and confiscating some. Mississippi Highway Department workers mowed the grass along the highway's shoulders to facilitate our walk. Roy Reed of the *New York Times*—my favorite reporter covering civil rights—wrote that even the KKK distributed leaflets in Batesville urging nonviolence. State highway patrolmen also met with town officials before the marchers arrived to brief them on steps that had been taken by other towns to avoid racial incidents. Dr. King was clearly aware of and frustrated by this new approach, describing it as a "more sophisticated form of resistance."

When the march reached the town of Grenada, still another chapter was added to the book on how to defuse a civil rights demonstration. Grenada officials agreed to nighttime voter registration and to the appointment of four Black registrars. Also, Grenada had three bathrooms in its courthouse: one reserved for the use of both male and female Black people, a second for the use of "White men" and a third for the use of "White ladies." The three signs "COLORED," "WHITE MEN," and "WHITE LADIES" were taken down during the march. In addition, Grenada permitted demonstrations at the Confederate monument on the courthouse lawn—ordinarily a sure way to provoke a violent confrontation with the local police and White supremacists. But while tensions ran high, the police mostly restrained both themselves and the angry White onlookers during the three weeks the march demonstrators were in town.

Of course, after the march left town, Grenada closed its registration books, discharged the Black registrars, restored the three signs to the courthouse bathrooms, and refused requests that it eliminate segregated seating in the local movie theater—all of which were unlawful under the Civil Rights Act of 1964.

Incidents of Police Misconduct

To be sure, there were serious tests of Governor Johnson's strategy. For example, in Philadelphia, the town in Neshoba County, Mississippi, most feared by civil rights workers, Dr. King attempted to hold a rally to commemorate the death of the three civil rights workers—Michael Schwerner, Andrew Goodman, and James Chaney—murdered by the county sheriff, Lawrence Raney and his deputy, Cecil Price, and Klansmen, exactly two years earlier. I was in Jackson when this rally was held, but, according to newspaper reports, Deputy Price barred Dr. King and the other protesters from the courthouse lawn while an angry and aggressive mob of several hundred Whites encircled the group. Dr. King and the demonstrators, fearing for their lives, retreated toward the Black community and were attacked by the mob. The local police intervened and stopped the assault but only after the demonstrators had begun to defend themselves. King was badly shaken by the confrontation, saying that at this moment "I had yielded to the real possibility of the inevitability of death." He vowed to return to Philadelphia, with a larger group of protesters, "before the week was out."

During the second follow-up rally, which I did attend, Governor Johnson gave us his new strategy full blast. The mayor of Philadelphia actually stood on the speakers' platform alongside Floyd McKissick of CORE and used a megaphone to warn the large group of threatening Whites standing around the periphery that he would not tolerate any misconduct. He then handed the megaphone to McKissick. In this manner the mayor of what was generally regarded as the most racist and violence-prone town in Mississippi, acted as the emcee for the head of the Congress of Racial Equality and for a national civil rights demonstration. Although the angry Whites shouted racial slurs, this time they were roped off and kept in check by the local police. Speeches were made by the civil rights leaders without any serious disruptions.

The most violent confrontation between the police and march participants occurred on June 23, 1966, in Canton, Mississippi—just 25 miles north of Jackson. The leaders of the march had decided to camp that night on the site of Canton's McNeal Elementary School for Negroes. At first the demonstrators had been allowed by the police to enter the school grounds and this was celebrated as a victory. But then the superintendent of schools, backed by the town's police chief, read aloud to the march's leadership and the demonstrators his decision and order that the school could be used only for school-sponsored events. The demonstrators were then threatened with arrest if they did not leave the site at once. Dr. King, his deputy Andrew Young, Stokely Carmichael, and Floyd McKissick decided to disobey that order and to ignore the threat of arrests. They said that the Black elementary school was an example of Mississippi's segregation and that they had a right to use the school grounds.

But by then about fifty Mississippi state highway patrolmen had arrived in their patrol cars and were lying in wait near the school. The march's leaders, realizing that they were about to be attacked, urged the demonstrators to sit down and lock arms. The patrolmen then charged on to the school grounds firing tear-gas canisters—far more than what was required to disperse the demonstrators—with several canisters aimed at and hitting the march leaders. The patrolmen then moved through the group wearing gas masks, forcefully swinging their rifle butts, and seriously injuring the demonstrators. Within a half hour from the start of the attack, the group of about 1,000 people—angry, exhausted, eyes and throats burning, many seriously injured—settled in for the night in the auditorium or on the grounds of a Catholic school while others fled to their homes.

The leadership's insistence on setting up camp on the grounds of the elementary school had backfired. It was made to appear, at least in the forum of public opinion, and at the White House and the Department of Justice, that the tear-gassing had been provoked by the unreasonable demands and lawlessness of the demonstrators. It was argued that while Mississippi had proved itself reasonable—it had offered three alternative campsites—the demonstrators, in refusing to leave the school grounds when ordered to do so, had acted unreasonably and unlawfully.

Thus, the march leaders were perceived as losing the moral high ground. They had violated a controlling principle. The movement, Dr. King had said, "must exercise extreme caution so that our program is not conducted in a manner that might be considered provocative or an invitation to violence." Governor Johnson had seen an opening and pounced with a vicious show of force that was not condemned by the nation or the president.

Thus, Governor Johnson's tactic of defusing the protests was largely effective as it played out over the three weeks—from when Meredith was shot on June 6, 1966, through the conclusion of the rally in front of the capitol on June 26, 1966.

March Leaders Disagree on Objectives

The Selma march of 1965 had a clearly articulated single objective: obtaining for Black people the right to vote, the unfulfilled promise of the Fifteenth Amendment. And the Selma march had only one recognized leader—Dr. King. In contrast, there were a number of presumptive leaders of the Meredith march—the ones most visible and outspoken during the march—and they spent a great deal of time arguing about objectives among themselves and in the media. Dr. King said the march would provide an impetus for the enactment of President Johnson's proposed Civil Rights Act of 1966 that would protect civil rights workers and bar discrimination in housing and on federal juries. At other times Dr. King spoke of a "freedom budget," federal voting registrars, and laws requiring employment of Black persons as law enforcement officials in state and local governments. But then there was Carmichael arguing that achieving political power by arousing "Black consciousness" should be the goal. McKissick fell somewhere in between, though much closer to Carmichael. And, as noted above, Meredith stated that his goal was to register voters and to help Black people overcome the fear they experienced when they traveled in Mississippi.

In addition to the above disagreements, the leaders of the Meredith march were questioning whether their stated objectives were responsive to the compelling and immediate needs of the nation's Black communities. To be sure, the new civil rights laws of 1964 and 1965, and the movement's many court victories, improved the lives of the Black middle and privileged classes. However, these successes generally did not reach the poor communities of urban America—which were disproportionately Black.

March Leaders Disagree on Strategies

The earlier generation of leaders—Dr. King of SCLC, Roy Wilkins of the NAACP, Whitney Young of the Urban League, John Lewis of SNCC, and James Farmer of CORE—had aired and debated their differences. But these leaders were all consensus builders. They sought to uproot racism from all aspects of American life, and they believed that this goal could be achieved only (a) through a coalition of people from diverse backgrounds, (b) with support from the president, Congress, and the nation, and (c) relying on nonviolent resistance.

However, in May 1966, Stokely Carmichael had replaced John Lewis as chairman of SNCC. Carmichael, aged 24, a graduate of the exclusive Bronx High School of Science in New York and of Howard University, had played a significant role in organizing the Lowndes County [Alabama] Freedom Organization—better known as the Black Panther Party—a political organization created in 1965 to run Black candidates for county offices. Carmichael, and the so-called militants, believed that achieving political power and "Black consciousness" were strategically critical and could be pursued and achieved, to a large extent, without the support of White America. As best I could tell, however, Carmichael's principal objective was to bully his way into the national spotlight created by Dr. King and the Meredith march and to use that spotlight to make the goal of racial integration, the strategy of "nonviolent resistance" as well as King himself look anachronistic and ineffectual.

Also present at the march was Floyd McKissick, who had replaced James Farmer as national director of CORE in March 1966. Farmer had been a groundbreaker: he had conducted sit-ins to desegregate restaurants in Chicago as early as the 1940s and also had organized and sponsored the 1961 Freedom Riders who put their lives on the line desegregating bus terminals in the Deep South. In contrast, Floyd McKissick walked the tightrope between courting White supporters and national political figures while he also joined Carmichael in supporting a more "militant" and hostile narrative and in undermining King's leadership. Clearly, the old guard was being pushed out by the more "militant" new one.

March Leaders Criticize President Johnson

Early in the march, Carmichael circulated a "Manifesto" that was so critical of President Johnson and his proposed new civil rights legislation that Whitney Young of the Urban League and Roy Wilkins of the NAACP refused to sign it. And while Dr. King also did not sign the manifesto, he failed to voice opposition to it, perhaps because he didn't want to break ranks with SNCC and Carmichael. This silence contributed to alienating our most important ally and advocate, President Johnson, who had muscled through the Congress the Civil Rights Act of 1964 and the Voting Rights Act of 1965. Johnson had also introduced the new Civil Rights Act of 1966, worked hard to gain considerable support for the measure, but then, after the Meredith march, allowed the bill to die in the Senate.

Moreover, after being roundly attacked in the "Manifesto," President Johnson turned his back on the Meredith march. Although the Justice Department would file suit against Philadelphia officials for failing to adequately protect protesters from the White mob, President Johnson refused King's request for federal support. Even after march participants were teargassed in Canton, the president refused to intervene. Instead, he said that he had been assured by Governor Paul Johnson that the demonstrators would be protected and that was good enough for him. To me it was obvious: the president was furious with and felt betrayed and unappreciated by Dr. King and the movement and he was letting us know it would cost us dearly.

White Participation in the March and "Black Power"

White civil rights workers—including me—had been welcomed, fed, housed, and embraced like family members by courageous local Black families throughout the South. An important and never questioned stanza in the movement song, "We Shall Overcome," was "Black and White Together." In fact, two of the three civil rights workers murdered in Philadelphia and celebrated by Dr. King during the Meredith march, Schwerner and Goodman, were White, as was Viola Liuzzo, who had been murdered by the KKK for her participation in the Selma march of 1965. These events were still fresh in Dr. King's and the movement's mind.

Nevertheless, White workers often faced snide and hostile remarks from Black workers who thought White people should accept subservient status or not be in the movement at all. They argued that our presence interfered with efforts to provide and develop Black role models and leaders. We were regularly urged to get out of the way and to turn our attentions to organizing poor White people.

However, while the issue had for years been the subject of all-night arguments among civil rights workers, it had never before been debated by the movement's leadership in the national media. And this debate worked to alienate—indeed frighten away—many of our supporters. It was a setback for the movement when Carmichael, during the Meredith march, openly stated that White people were not welcome. McKissick appeared somewhat more reasonable to me by arguing that White people should be encouraged to participate but that Black people had to be in charge. James Meredith confused everyone when he said that only Black *men* should be allowed on the march. Dr. King welcomed and expressed appreciation for the participation of White people. Indeed, a year after the Meredith march he dedicated his final book, *Where Do We Go from Here: Chaos or Community?* to "the committed supporters of the civil rights movement, Negro and [W]hite, whose steadfastness amid confusions and setbacks gives assurance that brotherhood will be the condition of man, not the dream of man." But Dr. King was not able to control or contain the idea and the march's leadership was viewed by the public as racist.

This debate among the leaders spilled over into a national debate on the use of the slogan "Black Power." At early rallies in towns located along the march route, SNCC workers began using the phrase as a rallying cry. At a meeting in Greenwood, Marian Wright and I listened and watched Willie Ricks, a longtime SNCC worker, jump onto the roof of a car and chant, "What do you want?" prompting the collective response of onlookers, "Black Power." Carmichael then shouted, on cue, "I'm tired of getting arrested; I'm tired of White people handcuffing me and harassing me and beating me up. What we need is Black Power." Marian expressed shock and distress, making it clear that she believed this slogan would prompt a backlash and a setback for the Movement; I agreed.

Yazoo City Meeting

The fragmentation of the leadership over the role of White people and over the use of the "Black Power" slogan came to a head during a meeting of march leaders held in Yazoo City, a town located 50 miles north of Jackson. I had told Dr. King, just before the start of that meeting, that the rally he planned for Jackson was barred by a state law that prohibited demonstrations on the steps of the capitol. Dr. King then asked me to attend the meeting to explain the statute.

We met in the living room of the local Catholic parish house. Dr. King sat in an overstuffed chair and presided while everyone else sat around him in a semicircle on either the floor or on other chairs or couches. Dr. King began the meeting by telling the group that "Mel's here because the lawyers have identified a problem we need to address." He then asked me to explain the antidemonstration statute. Before I could open my mouth, George Raymond, head of the CORE chapter of nearby Canton, Mississippi, shouted, "We don't need to hear from no White man about anything, so he should just get the hell out of here."

Dr. King, foreclosing all debate over my participation, stated quickly and firmly that "the man's here because we need him, so please let him talk." In another setting, I would have preferred him to say that "we're all in this together," but Dr. King had understandably concluded that this was not the time or place for another all-night debate over race. I then summarized the statute and its potential impact on the march. The group's response was that Governor Johnson would not interfere with the rally since this would lead to police brutality, mass arrests, and bad press for him and Mississippi—precisely what this march needed and precisely what the governor had worked hard to avoid.

However, Dr. King disagreed. He viewed the law as a possible obstacle to the successful conclusion of the march, and he was in no mood for arrests or even for further discussion. He stood up and said he would immediately telephone Governor Johnson to obtain assurances that the law would not be enforced and to be certain that there "would be no surprises" when the march reached Jackson. Dr. King then went into the bedroom of the parish house to make the phone call. Ten minutes later he returned to the living room and announced that he had spoken to the governor and had obtained assurances that the antidemonstration law would not be enforced. He then asked me to leave.

Dr. King was to devote a long chapter to "Black Power" in his abovementioned book *Where Do We Go From Here.* . . . Therein he states that "for five long hours [during the Yazoo City meeting] I pleaded with the group to abandon the Black Power slogan." Although Dr. King agreed that the movement needed slogans, he argued that "Black consciousness" or "Black equality" were preferable. According to Dr. King, he told SNCC and CORE leaders that the words "Black" and "power" together gave the impression that we were talking about Black domination rather than Black equality and he noted the "implication of violence that the press had already attached to the phrase." At the meeting, SNCC and CORE leaders argued forcefully against Dr. King's position. McKissick of CORE insisted that "Black Power" meant only that Blacks must assume all leadership positions; that "race pride" but not "Black nationalism" was the objective. Despite their differences the leaders agreed, at the Yazoo City meeting, that they would not chant "Black Power" for the remaining few days of the march.

But it was too late. The media and the public were to debate the implications of the phrase "Black Power" for more than a year after the Meredith march. And the phrase was to be used by many to justify and explain the so-called White backlash against further advances in civil rights. Stokely Carmichael and SNCC had caused the march and the movement profound and irreparable injury: the phrase had injected *fear* into the White community from which the movement would not recover.

Perhaps the best evidence of this backlash was the dramatic decline in financial support for the movement. At the Centenary Baptist church march headquarters in Memphis, I watched and listened to Hosea Williams, a member of Dr. King's inner circle, on the phone with AT&T. He was begging—trying to find a way to persuade—the company into waiving the $2,000 deposit required for the comprehensive services the march needed. After he hung up the phone, Hosea turned to me and said, "Yeah, Mel, the movement's broke."

The March Lacked Grassroots Support

As the economist John Kenneth Galbraith observed in *The Affluent Society,* "[i]f the individual's wants are to be urgent they must be original with himself. They cannot be urgent if they must be contrived for him." This principle was the bedrock of civil rights advances: goals were achieved when they sprang from and reflected the community's deeply and urgently felt needs. Black leaders were unable to contrive objectives for the community.

Dr. King's 1955 Montgomery bus boycott, protesting segregation and discrimination on city buses, had best illustrated this point. There, the object of the protest struck a chord that so resonated within the community that the boycott was virtually 100 percent effective—only a handful of Black people rode the buses during the year the boycott was in effect. The Selma march also enjoyed such grassroots support: many widely attended demonstrations demanding "the vote" had taken place in Selma before the march and securing voting rights was the indisputable sole purpose of the march. Moreover, the number of participants in the Selma march increased gradually from several hundred, when demonstrations began, to 3,000 at the time the march proceeded across the Edmund Pettus Bridge. At its end, 25,000 people attended a rally held at the capitol in Montgomery, giving a thundering ovation to Dr. King's exhilarating speech predicting the coming of a "society at peace with itself, a society that can live with its conscience."

In contrast, the Meredith march failed to gain grassroots support because there were too many leaders and too many disagreements among the leaders, and no clearly identified single objective that captivated, and that was experienced by the community, as a deeply felt and immediate need. As far as the one concrete objective of the march—registering voters—only about 4,000 Black Mississippians registered during the march—less than 1 percent of the estimated 450,000 eligible—with 1,200 of the 4,000 registering in Grenada.

Moreover, the Meredith march was much too long—in terms of distance (200 miles) and time (three weeks)—to be sustainable emotionally, logistically, or financially. Contrast the Selma march of 54 miles and five days, which itself tested the upper limits of what was realistic.

On June 26, 1966, the final day of the march, about 5,000 people, led by Dr. King, walked to the capitol from Tougaloo College, a private Black school located eight miles north of Jackson. A rally was then held on the grounds of the capitol, with about 10,000 people in attendance. However, the majority of people who assembled at the capitol that Sunday afternoon resided in Jackson and nearby communities. They came not to join in the march but rather to be present, to experience the rally as a unique community event and to see and hear Dr. King speak.

Moreover, there was a palpable lack of energy in the crowd and among the speakers at the rally. Almost everyone seemed detached from the march—most people were curious onlookers rather than participants. Dr. King was not able to muster enthusiasm, in either himself or his audience, and I don't recall a single moment of eloquence or of spontaneous applause. When the rally ended, participants left the capitol subdued, heads down, much like a group leaving a funeral.

After the Meredith march, the movement's focus shifted to urban areas, particularly in the North, where Dr. King said, "Progress for the Negro . . . has been relatively insignificant, particularly in terms of the Negro masses. What little progress had been made . . . applied primarily to the middle-class Negro." He also had said in 1965 that "America today [not just in the South] is an extremely sick nation" and "the truth is that deep prejudices and discrimination exist in hidden and subtle and covert disguises." After the Meredith march, Dr. King as well as other civil rights leaders, tackled discrimination in jobs, schools, and housing in northern cities. The intersection of race and poverty became the focus. "On a longer-range basis," Dr. King said, "the physical ghetto itself must be eliminated."

But the civil rights movement's northern programs fell victim to the same forces that undermined the Meredith march: specifically, a breakdown of the interracial coalition, divided leadership, an often hostile nation and president, insufficient grassroots support, and more sophisticated strategies used by state and local officials against mass protest demonstrations. And then the assassination of Dr. King on April 4, 1968, left little doubt: the civil rights movement of the twentieth century had for these reasons and in this manner, come to an end.

Why I Went South and What I Did There

CHARLES STEPHEN "STEVE" RALSTON

Growing Up

In order that the reader might understand why I chose a career that meant that I would go down south instead of going into academia, which was the reason I decided to go to law school, a brief look at my background and politics might help. With one important exception, I had no connections, through family or otherwise, with the South. I was born in San Francisco in 1937, a fourth-generation Californian, and went to public schools, including UC Berkeley undergraduate and law school. My ethnicity and culture were thoroughly western European (nothing to be proud of as I realized later in life), with my cultural pantheon inhabited by Shakespeare, Beethoven, and later, George Balanchine.

The one exception was that my family lived in Galveston, Texas, for one year while my father taught at the University of Texas medical school. I was seven years old and, unrealized by myself until long afterward, attended second grade in a segregated school. None of us liked Texas, and we were happy to return to San Francisco in the summer of 1945.

However, I did have one important and lasting experience while living in Galveston. We lived in a middle-class neighborhood in an OK house. I used to take our dog for a walk occasionally down about four blocks and then took a left along that street. There was a dramatic contrast between where my family lived and the street I was now on. It was lined with much poorer houses than ours, many of them almost tumbledown shacks. In warm weather people sat on their porches and often waved to me as I went by.

They were Black. It hit me, at age seven, that something was wrong, but I didn't know what. Why were these folks living in such conditions, in old houses and with old clothes? What I saw and the questions it raised stuck with me, and I didn't realize until later in life—at 15 or 16—that the reasons were directly related to the color of their skins and to their "race," and that the differences between them and us "whites" was no accident.

My family did vary from most in America, in that politically we were pretty far to the left. Although FDR was almost God in our house (no other god was recognized), we had a more socialist background. I watched the Army-McCarthy hearings on television and loved seeing the archenemy disgraced. However, we were also wary of talking to the neighbors about our political views given the climate of the '50s.

UC Berkeley Undergraduate and Law School

Off I went to UC Berkeley in 1955, at the same time as the student movement was beginning. I did not really participate in that movement, however, but the civil rights movement—particularly the sit-ins and the Freedom Rides—definitely caught my attention. My family's leftist preoccupations did not include the issue of race in America with regard to African Americans, Indigenous peoples, Latinx, and others. To the contrary, they held all-too-White American views of minorities in general. I am not conscious of ever sharing their views, but certainly by the time I was in about sixth grade I was seriously questioning and rejecting them because they made no sense to me.

By the time I was in law school I was thoroughly radicalized on a number of issues, and I and similarly minded folks were talking about the need for a "new left"—uncapitalized—and strangely discovered that some who considered themselves on the right had similar views as to some of the issues. The common thread was the rejection of the overbureaucratic, so-called superpower nation-state, including not only the Soviet Union but, in many respects, the USA.

In my last year of law school, I was inclined to postpone going into teaching at law school. Instead, I wanted to get into representing people in the civil rights movement and thereby doing some good as well as gaining practical experience that could make me a better law professor. As it turned out, actually being involved in the movement as a lawyer led me to abandon academia permanently. A number of my classmates went into the Civil Rights Division of the Department of Justice, and I applied there also.

However, I was faced with the very likely prospect of being drafted—I had gotten deferments all the way through law school, but was still only 25, so I was at the top of the draft list. Since I had no interest in the judge advocate general or winding up somewhere in Southeast Asia, I joined a US Army Reserve medical unit for six months of active duty (which, incidentally, got me back to Texas, this time in San Antonio, a wonderful city, for training as a medic).

To Alabama as NAACP Legal Defense Fund Lawyer

When I got out, I spent a year at Columbia Law School, as an associate teaching first-year students legal research and writing. I again applied to the DOJ, but then learned about the NAACP Legal Defense and Education Fund, Inc., and what it was doing with regard to the civil rights movement and the issues of segregation and discrimination. Since I was not inclined to work for the government (see above), I applied to the Legal Defense and Education Fund and began working there in September 1964.

There were 12 lawyers at LDF when I started. The civil rights movement was at its height and was focusing on voting rights in particular since the Civil Rights Act of 1964 had just been enacted and had, to a large extent, dealt with the problem of segregation and discrimination in public facilities and places of accommodation such as restaurants, hotels, movie theaters, gas stations, and so on. LDF was heavily involved in representing voting rights cases involving both demonstrations and barriers to equal voting rights.

However, LDF was still involved in school desegregation cases all over the South and my first assignment that took me south involved the Montgomery, Alabama, school case where I was sent to aid Fred Gray Jr., one of the towering figures among Black lawyers in the South. He was having difficulty getting the school board attorney to give satisfactory responses to discovery requests, so he scheduled a conference with Judge Frank Johnson of the US District Court for the Middle District of Alabama.

Fred, the school board lawyer, and I went to Judge Johnson's chambers, and I had my first experience meeting and observing a federal judge. The experience almost ruined me in a way, since the judge was all that I thought a judge should be: courteous to both sides, reserved, and firm and determined but fair. I thought that he represented what federal judges in general would be like, but later I had experiences with a number of federal judges who sadly did not meet my expectations. I learned from Fred that Judge Johnson came from a county in northern Alabama that had tried to secede from Alabama when Alabama tried to secede from the United States. He was a Republican, appointed by President Eisenhower, but a Lincoln Republican. In fact, almost all the great judges in the South who did so much to dismantle the system of segregation were Republicans before the GOP shifted right following the passage of the Civil Rights and Voting Rights Act, and absorbed former southern Democrats who fought to uphold segregation and discrimination, for example, Strom Thurmond.

The conference before Judge Johnson was short. Fred Gray described the difficulties he was having with discovery. Judge Johnson peered at the school board attorney (don't remember his name, but let's call him Smith) over his glasses and said, calmly, "Well, I don't suppose we're going to have any more trouble with discovery, are we, Mr. Smith." Mr. Smith, who was literally shaking in his boots (or shoes), stammered out, "No sir, Your Honor." And the conference was over and the problem at least temporarily solved.

To handle the many demonstrations and other issues raised by the civil rights movement, the LDF staff was divided into teams for various states. I was assigned to Alabama and Georgia, and spent much of my time in my first years at LDF in those states. Selma, Alabama, had become the biggest hot spot in that state, and along with other staff attorneys, Norman Amaker and Charles ("Chuck") Jones, I went down to work with LDF–cooperating attorneys Peter Hall, Oscar Adams, and Demetrius Newton.

LDF had become the legal arm of the civil rights movement and worked, in conjunction with local lawyers, to provide legal advice and defense to the variety of groups that made up the movement. LDF's role was not to tell members of the movement what they could, could not, should, or should not do. If we were consulted our role was to give our best opinion as to the possible legal consequences if a planned action was carried out, but it was up to the movement to make the ultimate decision of what they would do. We would provide legal backup, which to a large extent meant going into the local federal court and seeking injunctive relief.

In Selma, the demonstrators took action that was almost always protected by the First Amendment. However, neither Sheriff Jim Clark nor the local state court judges cared about the federal constitution or laws, and met demonstrations with mass arrests. At that time we were able to remove the state court prosecutions to federal court using an obscure and rarely used provision of the old civil rights acts. Under the guidance of Tony Amsterdam, a brilliant law professor (in my opinion, one of the few actual geniuses around), lower federal courts permitted the removals. We then asked the federal court to order the release of the demonstrators, and they were able to go back and demonstrate by the next day.

We filed many removal petitions, which involved doing a lot of work quickly. We had forms into which we plugged the names of the demonstrators along with other pertinent information. However, we had no computers, copying machines, faxes, and so on (all to be invented or made available much later). We had to rely on mimeograph machines to make the necessary copies, a slow and messy process. Unfortunately, the use of civil rights removal eventually got to the US Supreme Court, and it severely limited the use of removal, a bad mistake that was based on the illusion of some of the justices that state courts could be trusted to enforce federal laws and the Constitution.

I spent many days in Selma, and had a variety of interesting experiences, including Chuck Jones introducing me to Stokely Carmichael (later Kwame Ture), whom we ran into on the main street of Selma early one evening.

Another Alabama experience (outside Selma) involved Greenville, in Greene County. Oscar Adams, whose office was in Birmingham, called LDF one day and told me that he needed help as quickly as possible. Demonstrators in a small city in Greene County had been arrested and mistreated by the local sheriff, and Oscar had been contacted for legal assistance. I checked with Jack Greenberg, and he OK'd me going immediately to Birmingham to meet up with Oscar. I put papers and pleadings together and caught a late plane that arrived in Birmingham at around midnight. Oscar met me, and as I got into the passenger seat of his car he said, "It's in the glove compartment." I asked, "What is?" and he replied, "The gun." So there I was riding shotgun as we drove into the dark night—and I mean dark as only a country night can be. Me, who joined the US Army Medical Corps since, as a nonofficial conscientious objector, I hated guns and had no intention of ever shooting anyone.

We got to Greenville without incident, spent the rest of the night getting our legal papers together, and filed them in the nearest federal court the next day. We asked for an immediate hearing for a preliminary injunction to stop more arrests and interference with the demonstrators. After we had put on our witnesses, the other side put on the sheriff to justify his actions. Oscar cross-examined the sheriff and gave him no quarter, but questioned everything he had done and exposed both his ignorance and his arrogance.

The courtroom was filled with our clients, mostly local folks who were fed up with not being able even to register to vote. The judge gave us the preliminary injunction, and I learned a lot from the experience. The sheriff, typical of counties in southern states, was the most powerful official in the county. He had never before been subjected to any questioning of his power and authority to do anything he liked by anyone, let alone an African American lawyer in front of a room full of Black citizens whom he had been free to harass, injure, and bully as the mood took him. The impact on the Black citizens who were there was palpable. I realized that what we were able to do went beyond providing legal representation and advice to the movement, as important as those things were, but that we as lawyers were able to advance the movement's goals by giving long-oppressed people some measure of hope that things could change and thereby encouraging them to go forward with their efforts to bring about such change.

The biggest event coming out of Selma that I took part in was the case that allowed the Selma to Montgomery March to take place in the spring of 1965.[2] On March 15, to become known as "Bloody Sunday," a number of other LDF lawyers and I were hanging out at one of our apartments. The television was on, and someone called the rest of us in to watch the broadcast on CBS News. When we saw state troopers and Sheriff Clark's posse tear-gassing and beating the peaceful demonstrators we knew that we had to take action. We called Jack Greenberg and received various assignments. Norman Amaker and I went to the LDF office as did Norman's secretary, and we drafted a complaint, a motion for a temporary restraining order, and a preliminary injunction. We also asked for an immediate hearing. During our phone call with Jack, we realized that Gov. George Wallace had made a big mistake by sending out the state troopers to Selma. This allowed us to file the suit in the Middle District of Alabama before Judge Johnson, and not in the Southern District, where all the other cases involving Selma had to be filed. Judge Thomas, the judge there, while not one of the bad federal judges, had been hesitant to take firm action against the city and county authorities, while there was no doubt that Judge Johnson would not hesitate to act.

Norman flew down to Montgomery early Monday morning and filed our papers. Judge Johnson denied our motions, but sua sponte issued a temporary restraining order against the demonstrators prohibiting any further attempt to march pending the court's order. He set a full hearing on our motions for Thursday of that week, just three days away. I flew down to Montgomery on Tuesday, I believe, to help with the preparation for the hearing.

I stayed at the hearing only a couple of days, since I was not taking an active part. However, a number of exchanges during the hearing were instructive (and at times entertaining). One of our first witnesses was an African American man (let's call him George). The local lawyer for the defendant, Mr. Pitt, started out his cross by saying "Now, George . . ." Every lawyer at plaintiffs' table leaped to their feet to object—they didn't need to. Judge Johnson (who, as was his custom, did not wear a robe) looked down at Mr. Pitt and said, "Mr. Pitt, in *this* courtroom all witnesses are treated with respect!" Later in the day, our witness was an African American woman. Mr. Pitt rose to cross-examine, paused, and then turned to the lawyer for Gov. Wallace, and asked in a whisper that could be heard throughout the room, "What do I call a n——r woman?"

One incident illustrated why a lawyer should never ask an open-ended question at trial, particularly when he didn't know what the answer might be. Hosea Williams, our lead plaintiff, was on the stand. Williams was one of Dr. King's chief lieutenants and had appeared often in court. The elder Pitt's son (whom we had dubbed "Junior Pitt") got up on cross and asked, "Now Mr. Williams, you testified that there were incidents of police brutality. Just what did you mean by that?" Williams spent the next half hour or more describing in great detail the beatings, tear-gassing, and riding down with horses, and more, and there was nothing the defense could do to stop him. I now realized why more than one professor at my law school had warned against asking such a question on cross, and I never forgot the lesson.

Work in Georgia with C. B. King

In addition to Alabama, I spent a great deal of time in Georgia, particularly in rural Georgia with another one of our cooperating attorneys, C. B. King, who in many ways became my mentor. C. B., as we all called him, was a great man and a great lawyer whose office was in Albany, Georgia.[3] The regard he was held in is shown by the naming of the C. B. King Federal Courthouse in Albany in 2000. I worked with C. B. in a variety of cases, including federal habeas corpus (before the Supreme Court and then Congress gutted the application of the writ to state cases), civil jury discrimination litigation, voting rights, school desegregation, and federal welfare law litigation.

The first appellate case I argued was a voting rights/segregation case that C. B. had brought when an African American woman ran for justice of the peace in one of the small Georgia counties.[4] When she went to the polling places, she found that there were three polling booths—for white men, white women, and colored. She refused to use the "colored" booth and attempted to vote in the white women booth. She was, of course arrested, and C. B. brought an action in federal court to enjoin the prosecution, to prohibit future segregation, and to require that a new election be held. The district court judge granted the first two requests, but denied the third based on law traditionally applied in election challenge cases, that is, the plaintiff had to show that the result of the election would have been different if the challenged practice had not been used.

We appealed to the Fifth Circuit (then the best federal court of appeals to bring civil rights cases) and argued that traditional election law was beside the point. Ms. Bell was entitled to have an election without blatant racial prejudice, since it was impossible to know whether the results would have been different in an election free of such an obvious violation of federal law. The panel of the Fifth Circuit was a good one, but it gave me a very hard time during the argument, asking one difficult question after another. After the argument, C. B. and I were upset. C. B. felt that the court just didn't understand.

Three weeks later, the court issued its unanimous opinion, authored by Judge Brown, who had asked the hardest questions. It ruled for us and remanded the case, ordering that another election be held without the racism that had infected the first. I learned from that experience not to try to predict the outcome of an appeal based on the oral argument or anything else, but to wait for the actual result. It was then clear to me that the judges had been inclined to rule for us, but wanted some issues that might be in the way clarified and handled.

Another case I worked with C. B. on was the Dougherty County school desegregation case, which was before Judge J. Robert Eliot, who was hostile to any kind of civil rights case. (Judge Eliot does not have a courthouse in the Middle District named after him!) As we entered the courtroom, we could feel the dislike C. B. and Judge Eliot had for each other. During his direct testimony, a witness (let's call him Mr. Smith) for the school board consistently referred to Black people as "nigra." When C. B. got up to cross-examine he asked, "Mr. Smith, can you say 'knee'?" Mr. Smith said, "'Knee.'" "Mr. Smith, can you say 'grow'?" Mr. Smith said, "'Grow.'" "Mr. Smith, can you put those two words together?" Mr. Smith could and did.

Judge Eliot was not amused.

One more anecdote about C. B. illustrated his determination to speak truth to power whatever the circumstances. LDF held a conference soon after the Civil Rights Act was passed. One of the chief concerns was how Title VI (which prohibited recipients of federal funds from discriminating on the basis of race) was going to be enforced by the Johnson administration. A number of federal officials were invited to the conference to discuss this and other issues.

It turned out that the plan was to enforce Title VI by relying on attestations from local school officials that they were not engaged in any discriminatory practices. The civil rights lawyers at the conference, particularly African American lawyers who had spent years dealing with recalcitrant school officials, were not pleased, to put it mildly. They were generally amazed and appalled, and a rather heated discussion ensued during which various federal officials tried to justify their plan of nonaction. Finally, C. B. King stood up and said, in his magnificent, deep-bass voice, "The question is, in the words of the old union song, 'Which side are you on, boys, which side are you on!'"

In 1968–70, I was sent by the LDF to open an office in San Francisco, where we had received a grant to be able to litigate cases in the West. I was only too happy to return to my hometown for a while, though Jack had made me sign in blood a promise to come back to New York after a couple of years. When I returned to our main office, I was put in charge of our newly established subsidiary, the National Office for the Rights of the Indigent (NORI), whose purpose was to litigate issues that particularly impacted low-income people and which, therefore, disproportionately affected African Americans and other minorities. I was able to return to Georgia and work some more with C. B. until his untimely death from cancer in 1988.

LDF Takes on the Federal Government

In 1972, I became involved in employment discrimination cases against federal government agencies. Title VII of the Civil Rights Act of 1964 was amended in 1972 to cover federal government agencies. I discovered, because of a walk-in client who was a federal employee of the US Army in New York, that the administrative process set up by the US Civil Service Commission to enforce Title VII was almost totally useless. I was thoroughly upset over the federal government's cavalier attitude about discrimination within itself, while at the same time going after state and local governments and private industry. As Jack Greenberg put it, "Steve Ralston and Bill Lee [a fellow LDF lawyer], . . . treated the issue as a personal vendetta."[5]

At first, the fight against the Feds did not take me south, since Bill Lann Lee and I were busy litigating a variety of procedural issues in the federal appellate courts all the way to the Supreme Court. Our opponent was the Civil Division of the Department of Justice, which apparently did not know or did not care that many of the positions they took opposing Title VII were contrary to the positions taken by the Civil Rights Division or the federal EEOC when the government was enforcing Title VII. After we had won virtually all the procedural issues, we were able to litigate the merits of the cases, and I returned to the South, specifically Texas, Georgia, and Florida, to litigate cases against the US Postal Service, the National Labor Relations Board, the US Marine Corps, NASA, and others. In these cases I worked closely with local cooperating attorneys and with my LDF colleague, Gail Wright.

Why I Was Glad to Leave the South Behind

I left LDF in 2002, after 38 years as a staff attorney with various titles and as a consultant in 2001–2. I have not returned to the South since, except in 2015, when I was invited back to Selma for the fiftieth anniversary of the Selma to Montgomery March, as one of the few surviving lawyers from the team that brought the case back in 1965. I was happy to see again Fred Gray, still going strong, and his partner, Solomon Seay, who, sadly, passed on a short time later. Selma looked just about the same, though the old white guard was gone. President Obama was there, as was John Lewis, Michelle Obama, and their daughters, and President George W. Bush, who had signed the last re-enactment of the Voting Rights Act. I joined the march led by the president and others to the crest of the Edmund Pettus Bridge on the way to Montgomery. I got to have my picture taken with President and Mrs. Obama, and to see other former LDF colleagues and friends.

I must confess that I have ambivalent feelings about my trips to the South. I met and worked with many wonderful people, some of whom became friends and colleagues. However, I did not like the vast majority of the so-called white people I dealt with. There were exceptions, of course: the white attorneys who took on the system of segregation and discrimination, a number of courageous federal judges who carried out their sworn duties to enforce federal law, regardless of the consequences to themselves personally, and other whites who joined the fight in various ways.

Being from California, I was used to meeting and welcoming newcomers from all over the United States and the world. That was part of the heritage of the state, and its progressiveness reflects that heritage. In the South, on the other hand, white residents often showed their hostility toward anyone who was from "outside" unless perhaps they came from some other southern state. That was obviously part of their heritage, and I found the fabled "southern hospitality" limited to those who looked and thought like themselves. This attitude was something of a shock to me—I thought of the United States as being one nation, and not a bunch of parochial enclaves, and the idea that any American would be considered an "outsider" I found appalling.

I got the impression that some whites found me hard to figure out. They could understand (but not like) a lawyer who was Black, or Jewish (whom they liked even less), but I was neither. I was as white as they were, even had blue eyes, but was fighting against their "southern heritage." I could have told them that one of my great-grandfathers fought for the United States during the War of the Southern Rebellion, but that probably would not have endeared me to them. I could have said that I was one of those naive folks who sincerely believed in the promises of the Declaration of Independence and the Constitution, but also believed that there was much to be done to make those promises realities for many, if not most, of our people. But they probably would have dismissed me (or worse) as just being one of those leftist/socialist/commie traitors to the *true* America that was in danger of being destroyed by me and my fellow conspirators.

Be that as it may, I am glad that I will pass my last few years in the great state of California, while hoping that the South will at last join the United States of America in spirit as well as in law.

When Lawyers Could Win Civil Rights Suits in Alabama

James Blacksher

In the introduction to their indispensable history of race and the Supreme Court, Vernon Burton and Armand Derfner warn the reader that, contrary to popular belief, the Supreme Court's "race and civil rights... accomplishments date from a short period in history, from the 1930s to the early 1970s. Before that time, the Supreme Court spent much of its history ignoring or suppressing those rights, and in the half century since the early 1970s the Court's record on civil rights has retreated far more than it has advanced."[6] I was fortunate to begin practicing law in 1971, at the tail end of that relatively short window of time when the federal judiciary was leading a progressive movement toward equal rights for racial minorities and women. The heroic battles in the 1950s and 1960s pursued the clear-cut objective of ending de jure racial segregation, and they had succeeded. My generation of civil rights lawyers faced the more complicated issues of applying the promise of equal rights to factually messy, real-world circumstances.

We could depend on the readiness of the federal judges who came out of that era to enforce the Equal Protection Clause, the Civil Rights Act, and the Voting Rights Act. They were giants in American history, and what follows are some stories of my encounters with them. They include Frank Johnson, Virgil Pittman, Winston Arnow, and Harold Murphy. Their example was followed by Alabama's first two African American federal judges, U. W. Clemon and Myron Thompson. This essay will attempt to show how being before these particular judges made possible whatever litigation success my colleagues and I enjoyed. The Supreme Court and most of the lower federal courts have become much more hostile to civil rights and voting rights, and many of my generation's victories are being rolled back today. After a short review of my personal background, I will organize what follows in three sections, one focused on my early work in employment discrimination and K–12 school desegregation, a second on voting rights, and a third on the Alabama higher education desegregation case.

My Background

Judges Johnson, Pittman, Arnow, and Murphy all served in the armed forces during World War II. They were part of the Greatest Generation, and much has been written about how the defeat of European fascism and the brave service of Black soldiers (even before President Truman ordered desegregation of the armed forces in 1948) led many White veterans to support Black veterans' demands for an end to Jim Crow. It is no coincidence that I came to this work through the military, too.

I left active duty in the Navy in January 1968 to go to law school and get involved in the movement. But I had not always opposed racial segregation. The Naval Reserve Officers' Training Corps scholarship I received sent me to the University of Utah in 1958, where in 1961 I helped defeat a request by the student government association to sell $1 "freedom buttons" to support the Freedom Riders in Alabama. "Y'all are just meddling," I said. Years later, when I told this story to Lani Guinier, she asked what caused me to change stripes? I could not give her a clear answer then, and the best answer I can give now is to say one had to live through the turbulent 1960s to understand how there was no avoiding taking sides, and I finally decided to get on the right (or left?) side of history.

I was born in Mobile in 1940. My Southern Baptist father was from Brewton, and my Roman Catholic mother was from Mobile. Their "mixed" marriage in 1939 caused a small scandal, but Daddy signed the pledge and I was raised Catholic. My ancestors on both sides of the family included slaveholders, and I grew up a southerner in the culture of de jure White supremacy. We moved to Oak Ridge, Tennessee, during the war, where my father worked in one of the Atomic Energy Commission plants. On the elementary school playground, in that cosmopolitan community brought together by the Manhattan Project, I lined up with the Rebels to oppose the Yankee kids. My parents were segregationists, but they demanded that their children treat Black people with respect—so long as they stayed in their place. Daddy supported Big Jim Folsom for Alabama governor, but he voted for Strom Thurmond and the Dixiecrats in 1948.

We moved to Paducah, Kentucky, in 1951 when a new AEC plant opened there, and my brothers and I were enrolled in Catholic schools. White Catholic schools, that is. Holy Family was the Black Catholic school in Paducah. Then things started changing after *Brown v. Board* in 1954. The small Catholic high school I attended, St. Mary's Academy, was run by the Sisters of Charity of Nazareth, Kentucky, and they enrolled the first Black students in 1957. My high school mates recently told me that not all the nuns were in favor of integrating the Catholic schools, but the priests insisted. Mother was president of the PTA, and desegregation made her uncomfortable, but she gave it her support. I'm told the first three Black students only lasted a year or two at St. Mary's, and I don't know when permanent racial integration returned. Dad died in 1960, and Mother moved back to Mobile, but I was already at college in Salt Lake City. And even though I didn't like Utah students "meddling" in Alabama, I was being pulled into the civil rights movement by the election of the first Catholic president. I could vote for JFK in 1960, a decade before the Twenty-Sixth Amendment was ratified, because Kentucky then was one of the few states that allowed 18-year-olds to vote.

Graduation and off to the Navy in 1962: nuclear power school and submarine school 1962–63; USS *Woodrow Wilson* (SSBN 624) 1963–65; and USS *Ray* (SSN 653) 1966–68. When Mary Lucia Carter married me in Charleston in 1965, she probably expected a career Navy life. But cruising around under the Mediterranean Sea reading Faulkner novels and following civil rights developments back in my home state already had me halfway out the door.

While I was riding around under the ocean, Judge Frank Johnson was beginning to dismantle de jure racial segregation in Alabama. In lawsuits brought by Fred Gray, Solomon Seay, and Charles Langford, assisted by the NAACP Legal Defense and Education Fund, Johnson ended the Montgomery bus boycott by ordering the buses desegregated, then he proceeded to order desegregation of the city's parks, airport terminal, and recreational facilities. He led the three-judge US district courts that ordered desegregation of most of Alabama's public schools, struck down the poll tax and the Tuskegee gerrymander, and required the malapportioned Alabama legislature to equalize districts. The latter case became *Reynolds v. Sims* (1964), which established the constitutional principle of one person, one vote. The list goes on. At least four biographies of Judge Johnson have been published, and an entire issue of the *Yale Law Journal* was devoted to him after his death in 1999.

My first encounter with Judge Johnson was in law school. I was one of several law students who did some volunteer work for plaintiffs' counsel George Dean in the landmark lawsuit known as *Wyatt v. Stickney*, in which

Judge Johnson issued detailed orders setting constitutional standards for conditions in Alabama's mental hospitals. By 1972 George Dean had been joined by Jack Drake, Ralph Knowles, and my classmate Ed Still. Later, after I began practicing in Mobile, Judge Johnson appointed me a member of his oversight committee for Searcy Hospital in Mount Vernon. *Wyatt* led to reforms throughout the nation in the care and treatment of persons with mental illness or disabilities. But my experience on Judge Johnson's oversight committee showed me how difficult comprehensive institutional reform can be. There is ongoing debate over whether the turn away from institutionalization has created new problems for mentally ill persons in prisons and among the homeless.

After graduating from law school in January 1971, I was fortunate to get hired as a law clerk by US district judge Frank McFadden in Birmingham. He kept two law clerks, and I worked first with John Falkenberry then with Lynwood Smith. Judge McFadden also had been an officer in the Navy, and he grew up in Oxford, Mississippi, home of William Faulkner. In Faulknerian terms, Frank McFadden was far more Compson than he was Sutpen. He was fun to work for. And challenging.

Judge Johnson's three-judge *Lee v. Macon* court had farmed out to the Northern and Southern Districts all the K–12 school desegregation cases that had been consolidated after Governor George Wallace overplayed his hand and exposed state officials to federal court jurisdiction by telling local school boards to ignore desegregation orders. Chief Judge Seybourn Lynne in Birmingham was a great judge, respected by all us lawyers. But he was a segregationist. He dissented in the Montgomery bus case, *Browder v. Gayle,* and was reversed several times by the Fifth Circuit for failing to enforce the Supreme Court's school desegregation mandates. Eventually, Judge Lynne declined to sit on any school desegregation cases. That shifted more of them to Judge McFadden's docket, where Solomon Seay, U. W. Clemon, the NAACP Legal Defense and Education Fund, and Justice Department lawyers representing Black schoolchildren received a better, if still lukewarm, response. I admired the way Sol and U. W. faced down school board lawyers who were indignantly defending massive resistance.

Judge McFadden agreed to release me before serving a full year if I cleared his motion docket. And write the first draft of the three-judge court opinion for him and Judge Rives in *Frontiero v. Laird* (1972), which held that requiring a female Air Force officer to prove her husband was a dependent, while a male officer's wife was presumed to be a dependent, did not violate the Fifth Amendment. Judge Johnson dissented, and the Supreme

Court agreed with him in *Frontiero v. Richardson* (1973), the case that put Ruth Bader Ginsburg on the map. Only Justice Rehnquist dissented, "for the reasons stated by Judge Rives in his opinion for the District Court." I could say that I actually agreed with Judge Johnson and was only performing the duty of a junior naval officer, but that won't wash.

In December 1971, when my clerkship ended, I joined Vernon Z. Crawford's law firm in Mobile. Vernon was a cooperating attorney with the NAACP Legal Defense and Education Fund, and A. J. Cooper Jr., who had joined Vernon in 1969, recruited me to take over the firm's LDF docket. "Jay" Cooper was busy building a career in politics, and he was elected the first Black mayor of Prichard in 1972.

Vernon Crawford was in the merchant marines during World War II and was one of the many Black veterans who challenged Jim Crow after the war. He got a bachelor's degree in 1951 from Alabama State College (now Alabama State University), the HBCU in Montgomery. The University of Alabama Law School did not admit Black students, so Vernon commuted to Brooklyn Law School, where he graduated in 1955. I never asked Vernon if he got any of the out-of-state tuition assistance Alabama provided to Fred Gray and other African Americans who wanted to attend law school; I was told he supported his young family by working as a maître d' at the Mobile Country Club. Vernon opened his law office in 1956. He became the second Black lawyer in Mobile, after Clarence Moses, since Reconstruction. Frankie Fields Smith, who arrived in 1967, was the third Black lawyer and first Black female lawyer in Mobile. After Jay Cooper, David Coar was the next Black lawyer in Mobile. He joined Vernon the same year I did in 1971. David grew up in Birmingham and had a JD from Loyola of Chicago and an LLM from Harvard Law School. He left Mobile two years later and ended up back in Chicago, where he taught at DePaul Law School and became a US district judge in 1994.

Cain Kennedy joined us shortly thereafter. Cain grew up in Prichard and had retired from a long career in the Navy. He got his law degree from George Washington University in 1971. He was elected to one of the majority-Black House seats Judge Johnson's court had ordered implemented in 1974. In 1979 Governor Fob James appointed him to become the first Black circuit court judge in Alabama since Selma's Roddy Thomas during Reconstruction. Cain retired in 1998 and died prematurely in 2005.

Michael Figures came home to Mobile to join Vernon's firm in 1975. Michael was one of the first four Black students, along with Booker Forte Jr., Ronald Jackson, and John England Jr., to be admitted to the University of

Alabama School of Law. Michael was a lawyer with a mission. His greatest interest was in restoring the land lost by Black farmers during Jim Crow and saving the small farms they still owned. But after a few years, Michael, too, left Vernon's firm and ran for public office. He was elected in 1978 to one of the three majority-Black Senate seats in Judge Johnson's court-ordered plan, where he soon became president pro tem and one of the most influential members of the legislature. Michael was a founder, along with Hank Sanders and Richard Arrington, of the Alabama New South Coalition, which competed with the Alabama Democratic Conference (ADC), the Black caucus of the Alabama Democratic Party, endorsing candidates in state and local elections. The impact Michael had on Mobile's mayor-council government through the Zoghby-Figures Act, which I discuss later, continues to this day. Michael Figures died suddenly of a brain aneurysm in 1996, leaving us much too soon.

In addition to me, Vernon Crawford also gave a start to five other White lawyers, Greg Stein, Larry Menefee, Clint Brown, Wanda Cochran, and Caryl Privett. We were all scattered in different directions by 1978. Vernon Crawford had a debilitating stroke in 1985, after he had qualified as a candidate in the first city council elections held under the Zoghby-Figures Act. He died in 1986. Today he is remembered as the dean of Mobile's Black lawyers, and the Mobile chapter of the National Bar Association is named in his honor.

Employment Discrimination and K–12 School Desegregation

The year 1971 was an auspicious year for me to begin a civil rights practice in Mobile. The Supreme Court had just handed down both *Griggs v. Duke Power Co.* and *Birdie Mae Davis v. Board of School Comm'rs of Mobile County*, one of four companion cases decided with *Swann v. Charlotte-Mecklenburg Bd. of Education*. For me, the first five years was a blur of employment discrimination and school desegregation cases. LDF had a growing Mobile caseload for me to jump into.

Most of our employment discrimination cases landed on Judge Brevard Hand's docket. He had been a vocal opponent of desegregation and had just been appointed to the bench by President Nixon in September 1971. Vernon had given Brevard an upcheck with the Senate judiciary committee; it was a matter of not striking the king if you can't kill him, Vernon told me. My first trial before Judge Hand, in *Stevenson v. International Paper Co.*, was tense. I returned his hostility with some unwise hostility of my own. Kent Spriggs, whom LDF sent to help me try *Watkins v. Scott Paper*

Co., recalls the hostile atmosphere in Judge Hand's courtroom. But eventually our relationship became more cordial, even though I could depend on him to rule against my clients. At that time, we could depend on the Fifth Circuit Court of Appeals to reverse Judge Hand.

The Fifth Circuit judges who Jack Bass would celebrate in his 1981 book, *Unlikely Heroes,* were there vigorously enforcing the Fourteenth Amendment and Title VII of the 1964 Civil Rights Act. Our favorite Fifth Circuit decision was *Watkins,* in which Judge John Minor Wisdom struck down what we (not Judge Wisdom) called Scott Paper Company's "dumbest White man rule," because it required Black workers with no high school diploma to have at least as much grade-school education as the least educated White employee in the formerly segregated line of progression. That label makes me flinch today, because those White employees were not dumb, and we were being disrespectful. But it was even more disrespectful of the company to require their employees to say how many grades in school they had completed.

With LDF at my side, I had help from some of the best lawyers in the nation: Bill Robinson, Mike Baller, Sylvia Drew, Mel Leventhal, Peter Sherwood, Steve Ralston, Barry Goldstein, and Ted Shaw, to name a few. We successfully challenged racially segregated job positions and departments not only at International Paper and Scott Paper, but at Container Corporation, Union Carbide, Courtaulds, Alabama Power's Barry Steam Plant, the US Army Corps of Engineers, and the Mobile Police Department. In that postmovement climate, companies were prepared to enter consent decrees, and opposing counsel usually were cooperative, even supportive. I recall in particular Frank McRight, Brock Gordon, and Paul Brock.

There was much stiffer resistance in our school desegregation cases. *Birdie Mae Davis* had begun in 1963 through the efforts of John LeFlore and the Nonpartisan Voters League. John LeFlore has not gotten the attention he deserves in the history of civil rights. He was a Black postal worker who started Alabama's first chapter of the NAACP in 1925 and immediately began haranguing Charles Hamilton Houston and Thurgood Marshall to get more actively involved in his crusade against racial discrimination in Alabama. Over the next fifty years John LeFlore deluged the national NAACP and the federal government with complaints about racial discrimination in public accommodations and transportation, employment, education, law enforcement, and voting. He was responsible, for example, for the cases I later got involved in attacking segregated lines of progression in Mobile's big paper mill complex.

Mr. LeFlore's outrage over getting evicted from a segregated streetcar in 1925 was what got him started, and the less discriminatory seating plan he negotiated in the 1950s with Mobile's bus company was the model the Montgomery Improvement Association started with, leading to the 1955 Montgomery bus boycott. When Alabama outlawed the NAACP in 1956, John LeFlore and his close colleague Wiley Bolden migrated to the Nonpartisan Voters League, another grassroots organization in Mobile, where they continued their fight for civil rights and voting rights. The Nonpartisan Voters League recruited Vivian Malone to be one of the two students who in 1962 faced Governor George Wallace when he stood in the door of Foster auditorium at the University of Alabama. They recruited Birdie Mae Davis, Dorothy Davis, and Henry Hobdy to be plaintiffs in the lawsuit challenging racial segregation in Mobile public schools, and they recruited the NAACP Legal Defense and Education Fund to represent the students.

Jay Cooper had joined Vernon Crawford as local counsel in *Birdie Mae Davis* when it returned from the Supreme Court in 1971. Jay had been present when the desegregation plan approved by Judge Dan Thomas in 1971 was allegedly mediated by Fifth Circuit judge Griffin Bell over cocktails at the Piedmont Driving Club in Atlanta. Shortly after I arrived in December 1971, Jay handed the *Birdie Mae* files to me. Constance Baker Motley, Derrick Bell, and Norman Amaker were the LDF lawyers who had represented the plaintiffs during the 1960s. By 1971 they had been replaced by Norman Chachkin, who would be my mentor and colleague for the duration of my time as local counsel in *Birdie Mae Davis*.

Derrick Bell succeeded in getting Birdie Mae, Dorothy, and Henry admitted to Murphy High School, the largest White high school in the Mobile County system. But *Green v. New Kent County* (1968) held that *Brown v. Board* required more than freedom of choice. *Green* required local school boards to "fashion steps which promise realistically to convert promptly to a system without a 'white' school and a 'Negro' school, but just schools." In *Birdie Mae Davis* the Supreme Court said such a "unitary system" required sending White students to the Black schools, as well as Black students to the White schools. Redrawing attendance zones, pairing White and Black schools, and—most controversially—busing between White and Black neighborhoods, even if that meant in Mobile's case, crossing the interstate beltway, were all tools the Supreme Court said the school board had to consider. That ended up putting most of the burden of desegregation on Black students, who were bused to the formerly all-White schools. The parents of White students assigned to the Black schools almost uniformly refused to comply. We spent 17 years in a futile effort to eliminate "racially identifiable" Black schools. It is painful for me to review the excellent chronicle of proceedings in *Birdie Mae Davis* contained in the 2009 Auburn master's thesis of Brian Andrew Duke, titled "The Strange Career of *Birdie Mae Davis*," which is available online. Court-ordered school desegregation in Mobile succeeded in only limited respects.

The problem, of course, was—and is—the culture of White supremacy, the official policy of Alabama's 1901 Constitution, which we White Alabamians were raised in and continue to live in. A 2020 retrospective of *Birdie Mae Davis* published in the online newspaper *Lagniappe* quotes Black teacher Lee Taylor, who was the first principal of Council Elementary Magnet School:

> "Right now, today, you could take the most liberal-minded person dedicated to putting aside race, but when it comes to their kids, if their White child could come to a community school they may be able to love and adore, but they would be in the minority—many of them just can't do it," she said. "I don't know if you want to put that in the paper, but it's the truth. With the *Birdie Mae Davis* case, we did not integrate. We desegregated. It's technical but there's an important difference."

An important difference indeed.

Nevertheless, as local counsel for the *Birdie Mae Davis* plaintiffs, I supported the efforts of LDF and DOJ to enforce the Supreme Court's command to eliminate all racially identifiable schools, even after it was evident that White parents would not send their children to the Black schools. Judge Hand made it plain that he would not aggressively enforce racial attendance zone assignments, with or without busing, and I doubt he could have succeeded if he had tried to do so. But Judge Hand's refusal to get directly involved left it up to lawyers for plaintiffs, DOJ, and the school board to engage in ongoing settlement negotiations over zone changes and new school locations. Finally, after LDF brought desegregation expert Bob Dentler down from Boston to propose another massive busing plan, the school board and DOJ turned to magnet schools as a way to end the litigation. We agreed to a plan built around magnet programs for six Black schools and capital improvements for the remaining neighborhood Black schools. Judge Hand approved the "Mobile Plan" in 1988, the year my family and I moved to Birmingham. If the board fully complied with the plan, after five years the system would be declared unitary and the case would be dismissed.

My partner Greg Stein was left with the task of monitoring enforcement of the terminal decree, which had to be extended another five years before Judge Hand dismissed the case in 1997. Nobody was happy with the way *Birdie Mae Davis* turned out. The prevailing sentiment in the Black community was disappointment and anger that the case had not done enough to provide equal educational opportunity for Mobile's Black students. The Black community leaders who had consulted with us over the life of the litigation took a lot of heat and opposed dismissal. Poor Greg was accused of being a sellout, becoming the target of anger that should have been directed at me. Even Hazel Fournier, the Black central office administrator who drafted the magnet programs, now an elected member of the board, opposed dismissal of the case. Whether federal court-ordered school desegregation was a success in Mobile or anywhere else in the nation is the subject of bitter scholarly debate.

Voting Rights

John LeFlore came to Vernon's office in 1975 and asked us to bring a lawsuit challenging the at-large election of Mobile's city commission. Mr. LeFlore had been working for decades to get Black citizens registered to vote, often in collaboration with former state senator and city commissioner Joe Langan, another White World War II veteran who supported the cause of equal rights for Black Americans. When Senator Langan failed to stop the legislature from passing the Boswell Amendment, which established the infamous "read and understand the Constitution" test for voter registration, John LeFlore helped recruit plaintiffs for *Davis v. Schnell,* the federal lawsuit that struck down the Boswell Amendment in 1949.

I had very little knowledge of voting rights law. But my classmate and friend Ed Still in Birmingham, who did have some election law experience, agreed to join us, as did LDF. In addition to Mr. LeFlore, the plaintiffs included Wiley Bolden Sr. and twelve other members of the Nonpartisan Voters League. Their names are listed on a historical marker recently erected outside the federal courthouse in Mobile.

The *Bolden* complaint initially was assigned to Judge Hand's docket, and if it had stayed there the history of voting rights in the United States would have developed very differently. But the case was won when Commissioner Bob Doyle hired Charlie Arendall to defend the city. Judge Hand had a standing order that in the first years after taking the bench he would recuse himself in any case in which his former Hand Arendall firm appeared as counsel if any party requested it. I remember asking Vernon and Mr. LeFlore what to do, and they didn't hesitate: we asked Judge Hand to recuse himself, and the case was assigned to Judge Virgil Pittman.

Virgil Pittman had grown up in Depression-era Coffee County, worked his way through undergraduate and law school at the University of Alabama, served in the Navy during World War II, and entered private practice in Gadsden, where he was elected circuit judge. On the recommendation of Congressman Albert Rains, President Lyndon Johnson nominated Judge Pittman for a joint appointment to the Middle and Southern Districts of Alabama, and he was confirmed in 1966. He brought his New Deal bona fides permanently to Mobile when Judge Dan Thomas retired in 1970.

The difference Judge Pittman made is hard to overstate. Where Judge Hand opposed desegregation before taking the bench and took a more or less hands-off approach in *Birdie Mae Davis,* Judge Pittman ordered more aggressive desegregation of the Mobile Police Department in 1971. When Judge Pittman ordered single-member districts in his 1976 *Bolden* opinion he specifically cited the example of *Birdie Mae Davis* for "[t]he futility of piecemeal efforts to correct racially discriminatory problems here."

But the importance of Judge Pittman as the finder of facts was most evident in his native-born understanding of the continuing importance of history in Alabama political culture. Even in his 1976 opinion, in which at that time history was only one of several factors to be considered in the constitutional analysis prescribed by the Fifth Circuit's en banc decision in *Zimmer v. McKeithen,* he laid responsibility for the dilution of Black voting strength squarely at the foot of "[p]ast discriminatory customs and laws that were enacted for the sole and intentional purpose of extinguishing or minimizing black political power." In his 1982 opinion on remand from the Supreme Court, in which proof of purposeful discrimination was the controlling issue, Judge Pittman found that in turn-of-twentieth-century Alabama "good government, reform efficiency and the like became 'code-words' and euphemisms for anti-black sentiments." Proof of discriminatory intent behind adoption of a commission form of government in 1911 could be inferred, he wrote, from "[t]he inflammatory and subtle remarks made in a culture saturated with racial prejudice and fear."

I find it hard to imagine that Judge Hand would have made such findings of racial intent when they were based not on explicitly racist reasons but on the White supremacist context in which "apparent innocent words" were uttered to justify the statute in question. What, I ask myself, caused Judge Hand to be defensive of Alabama's official policy of White supremacy, a policy embedded in its 1901 Constitution? He was an honorable man, sincere in his beliefs. So I recall the testimony of Mills Thornton, the dean of Alabama historians, given a few years later in the higher education desegregation case, *Knight v. Alabama*. Mills said that White supremacists during Reconstruction believed they were fighting "to preserve civilization in the republic . . . they understand themselves to be fighting to preserve the essence of the republic."[7] That existential fear is apparent today in the threats to White rule, not just in radical "replacement theories," but in judicial efforts to elide the history Judge Pittman wrote about and to limit the ability of Black and Brown people to rely on that history to demand equal access to the political process. The Supreme Court now says "the presumption of legislative good faith [is] not changed by a finding of past discrimination."[8] And the Eleventh Circuit says "*Arlington Heights*'s historical background factor should be focused . . . on the specific sequence of events leading up to the challenged decision rather than providing an unlimited lookback to past discrimination."[9] At the same time the Supreme Court is striking down Fourteenth Amendment rights that it says are not "deeply rooted in this Nation's history and tradition" (*Dobbs v. Jackson Women's Health Organization* [2022]), it is discounting as irrelevant the White supremacy that has the deepest roots of all.[10] Apparently, as Professor Thornton said, for some justices, White supremacy remains the essence of the American republic.

So, we were fortunate to have *Bolden* assigned to Judge Pittman during a time when the federal judiciary were still attempting to eradicate the vestiges of America's original sin. In the first *Bolden* trial, which led to Judge Pittman's ruling in plaintiffs' favor on October 28, 1976, Larry, Ed, Greg, and I called only two expert witnesses, statistician Cort Schlichting from Spring Hill College in Mobile, and political scientist Charlie Cottrell from St. Mary's University in San Antonio. They addressed the *Zimmer* factors proving that the election at large of three Mobile city commissioners violated the Constitution. Judge Pittman rejected the City's argument that *Washington v. Davis*, decided on June 7, 1976, required our plaintiffs to prove that the at-large system was racially motivated.

LDF's Eric Schnapper helped us with the Fifth Circuit brief, and Drew Days, then assistant attorney general for civil rights, oversaw an amicus brief supporting us. I presented the argument in the Supreme Court on March 19, 1979. But, because Justice Powell was absent due to illness, I had to appear for reargument on October 29, 1979, a sure sign of trouble. Armand Derfner, Frank Parker, and Norman Chachkin all advised me to cite *White v. Regester* as often as possible and avoid getting engaged in a policy debate about whether proof of purposeful discrimination was necessary in the context of voting rights. That strategy didn't work, and Justice Powell joined the plurality opinion saying we must prove that Mobile's election system was racially motivated.

I vividly recall how all the blood drained from my face when, on April 22, 1980, Larry and Greg came into my office with the news we had lost in the Supreme Court. And I remember how a feeling of despair lasted for weeks, even after the Fifth Circuit remanded the case to Judge Pittman for further proceedings. Then Gerry Hebert, who had joined as counsel for the United States, told us he (or was it his co-counsel Ellen Webber?) had found a news article that might be a smoking gun. So, we gathered an all-star team of historians and political scientists. I remember sitting at home on our screened porch with co-counsel, political sociologist Chandler Davidson and historians Morgan Kousser, Peyton McCrary, and Jerrell Shofner planning the evidence we wanted to introduce in the remand trial. I enjoyed their debate about the relative value of empirical data versus narrative history for making the most convincing case that the at-large Mobile election system was intentionally designed to minimize Black voting strength. Of course, we presented both, and they complemented each other.

Abigail Thernstrom also joined our front-porch discussions on at least one occasion. Abigail supported our goal of Black empowerment, but she opposed majority-Black districts as a remedy, a position she pursued in the congressional debates over amending the Voting Rights Act. After trial she asked permission to interview our plaintiffs, but I declined on the advice of Armand Derfner, who together with Lani Guinier was leading the Leadership Conference on Civil Rights' effort to amend Section 2. Abigail understandably took offense at that snub, which I regret. Her opposition to drawing districts based on race had some merit in the theoretical sense, but our evidence made a compelling case that, at that moment in the history of the United States, entrenched racial polarization could be combated in no other way.

Judge Pittman's opinion finding the purposeful discrimination the Supreme Court had demanded was handed down on April 15, 1982, two and a half months before President Reagan signed the 1982 Voting Rights Act Amendments on June 29, 1982. Those VRA amendments eliminated the need to prove intentional discrimination in order to establish a violation of Section 2.

Judge Pittman's in-depth analysis of the history of Mobile's election methods was one of the first of its kind in federal jurisprudence. His discussion started with events in 1814, when Alabama was still a part of Mississippi Territory, and advanced through the eras from 1814 to 1866, from 1867 to 1874, from 1879 to 1909, and from 1911 to the time of trial. Relying primarily on the testimony of professors McCrary and Kousser, he considered the whole scope of this history to be relevant, part of a unified narrative that built on each change in the past. In other words, Judge Pittman approached his judicial task by accepting the methodology employed by professional historians. In doing so, he opened our eyes to the racism underlying most of the laws and events in Alabama history. In the following years we would build on Judge Pittman's *Bolden* opinion to prove statutory and constitutional violations in the state's local election laws and vestiges of racial segregation in Alabama's system of higher education. I have always thought that in *Bolden* the Supreme Court actually threw us into the briar patch.

Our historical approach to proving that Mobile's election method was purposefully discriminatory had gotten a test drive in Florida. Shortly after Judge Pittman found Mobile's at-large election system unconstitutional in October 1976, Larry and I were contacted by Henry and Charlia Mae McMillan, two prominent Black educators, who asked us to challenge the at-large election of members of the Pensacola City Council and the Escambia County Commission and Board of Education. With Ed Still and Kent Spriggs, on March 18, 1977, we filed *McMillan v. Escambia County* and *Jenkins v. City of Pensacola*. It was our good fortune that the cases landed on the docket of Judge Winston Arnow.

Judge Arnow was another one of those politically conservative southerners who came back from World War II a firm believer in the Constitution and federal law. He grew up in and around Gainesville, Florida, where he practiced law before President Lyndon Johnson appointed him to the federal bench in Pensacola in 1967. He firmly enforced Supreme Court mandates in the Escambia County school desegregation case; as soon as *Green v. New Kent County* came down he ruled in 1969 that the board must do more than provide freedom of choice.

When I entered Judge Arnow's courtroom in 1977 I was unaware of Escambia County's recent history of racial unrest, and I pretty much remained unaware of what was going on outside my litigation bubble. Most of what

I'm saying here comes from reading historian Michael J. Butler's *Beyond Integration: The Black Freedom Struggle in Escambia County, Florida, 1960–1980* (2016). Butler describes in detail the race riots, street marches, police violence, and prosecution of Black activists in Pensacola during the years leading up to 1977. Judge Arnow was right in the middle of it. Butler says "Judge Winston Arnow proved [to be] the only white official who used his power on behalf of racial justice in Northwest Florida" during that time.[11] Most of the racial turmoil involved white resistance to school desegregation, in particular Judge Arnow's order that Escambia County High School change its nickname "Rebels" and drop its display of the Confederate battle flag. The Fifth Circuit didn't support his initial 1973 "Rebels" injunction at first, and the issue dragged on until 1976, when the school board finally settled on the nickname "Raiders."

His handling of the EHS mascot controversy provides important insight about Judge Arnow's personal and judicial character. During the hearing addressing the Black students' complaint, Judge Arnow revealed that he personally saw nothing offensive about the "Rebels" nickname. In an exchange with Black student Belinda Jackson, he expressed his view that the Civil War was not about slavery and he wondered why "a pretty song" like Dixie offended Blacks. To which Ms. Jackson replied, "Because, being black, we were the slaves." Judge Arnow put aside the personal view of history he was raised in and enforced the constitutional mandate to eliminate vestiges of de jure segregation root and branch. He enjoined the Confederate icons because they "have become and are symbols of white racism in general and offensive to a substantial number of black students at this school."

But, according to Butler, Judge Arnow's decisions striking down the at-large election systems had the greatest and most enduring impact on Black empowerment in Escambia County and Pensacola. Advancing the cause of racial equality moved from the streets to the federal judiciary. That made Judge Arnow the target of White rage, and he was vilified in the Pensacola press much the same way Judge Pittman was vilified in Mobile. Henry McMillan, Elmer Jenkins, and the group of plaintiffs they led received backlash from the other direction; they were all members of the upper middle class in the Black community, and they were accused of abandoning the many Black activists who had been putting their bodies on the line marching for justice. Whether greater inclusion in the political process has improved the well-being of ordinary Black citizens of Escambia County is a question still being asked today.

Judge Arnow's findings of intentional discrimination turned out to be crucial. Before we went to trial in May 1978, the Fifth Circuit, on March 29, 1978, held in *Nevett v. Sides* that voting rights plaintiffs needed to prove intentional discrimination. *Nevett* was a challenge to at-large elections in Fairfield, Alabama, and Ed was one of the plaintiffs' lawyers, along with Birmingham lawyer Bill Dawson and ACLU lawyers Laughlin McDonald and Neil Bradley. The Fifth Circuit's *Nevett* opinion softened the blow by concluding that its *Zimmer* standards for vote dilution cases could establish the requisite racial intent. Nevertheless, in Judge Arnow's courtroom we called as an expert witness Dr. Jerrell Shofner, professor of history at what was then called Florida Tech and is now called the University of Central Florida. Jerrell, a native of Grapevine, Texas, was a great storyteller, and he held Judge Arnow's attention as he reviewed the historical events that revealed the role race played in the adoption of at-large election methods for all three local governing bodies.

But the coup de grâce was delivered by the sitting governor of Florida, Reubin Askew. In 1978 Askew was finishing his last term as a "New South" governor. But as a freshman state legislator for Escambia County in 1958 he had sponsored the bill that shifted the election of Pensacola City Council members from districts to at-large elections. When we approached him about this, he volunteered to come testify. As the Fifth Circuit noted in its 1981 decision, Askew denied any personal racial motives for introducing the bill, and he professed to have been unaware of the desire of incumbent council members to avoid a "salt and pepper council." Now Governor Askew expressed his support of single-member districts, testimony that gave Judge Arnow important political cover for his intent findings—if he needed any.

All three governing bodies appealed Judge Arnow's judgment finding their at-large election schemes unconstitutional. He suspended implementation of his remedy orders pending the appeals, and the Fifth Circuit withheld its decision to learn the outcome of *City of Mobile v. Bolden* in the Supreme Court. After the Supreme Court ruled in 1980, in a 1981 opinion written by Judge Phyllis Kravitch, the Fifth Circuit affirmed Judge Arnow's findings of discriminatory intent in the Pensacola and Escambia School Board cases, but it reversed his conclusion of racial motives behind the Escambia County Commission at-large elections. However, in 1982 the Fifth Circuit granted our request for rehearing and affirmed the intent findings against the County Commission, based on the Supreme Court's intervening decision in *Rogers v. Lodge*. By this time the City and school board had conceded and had adopted single-member district plans, but the county commission appealed again. Finally, in March 1984 the Supreme Court declined to address the constitutional issue of purposeful discrimination and remanded to the Fifth Circuit for a determination of whether the 1982 Voting Rights Amendments now provided a statutory basis for affirming Judge Arnow's judgment. In December 1984 the Fifth Circuit held that Judge Arnow's findings satisfied the new Section 2 results test, and the judgment against the county commission was affirmed.

But here is an aside that I personally find relevant. Judge Kravitch's 1981 opinion contains this sentence: "Thus, the commissioners asserted 'good government' reasons for perpetuation of the at-large system." In the original slip opinion, the sentence had read: "Thus, the commissioners asserted 'goodgovermint' reasons for perpetuation of the at-large system," and it dropped a footnote quoting a passage I had put in our appellees' brief from Flannery O'Connor's short story titled "The Barber." A "fat man" was heckling a college professor about why he wanted the barbershop customers to vote for a progressive political candidate: "see can you tell us without sayin' goodgovermint." O'Connor was a native of Milledgeville, Georgia, and Judge Kravitch a native of Savannah. I don't know, of course, but I suspect someone called her original language to the attention of former Mississippi governor Coleman, who was on the Fifth Circuit panel, and he objected. Anyway, I was disappointed that my literary gambit failed. But as I look back on the matter, I can't be certain what Flannery O'Connor meant by "goodgovermint."[12] She is recognized today as having been a segregationist, and her work is full of racist remarks. She was unapologetic about it. In a 1959 letter to a friend, O'Connor explained why she did not want James Baldwin to visit her in Georgia. "It would cause the greatest trouble and disturbance and disunion. In New York it would be nice to meet him; here it would not. I observe the traditions of the society I feed on—it's only fair." What this great White southern writer born in 1925 was saying is similar to what a great White southern jurist born in 1911, Winston Arnow, was saying to Black students in the high school mascot hearing. Both were candidly acknowledging the White supremacist culture that had shaped them, as a necessary predicate to writing and doing what was morally right.

Three months before his *Frontiero* dissent, Judge Johnson and another three-judge district court had ordered the first single-member districts for the Alabama House and Senate, delaying their implementation until the 1974 elections. *Sims v. Amos* (1972) was the last of the *Sims* line of cases that began in 1962, when Judge Johnson and the three-judge district court held that the legislature's failure to reapportion since 1901 violated the Equal Protection Clause and the Alabama Constitution. *Sims v. Frink* (1962). The district court's decision was affirmed by the Supreme Court in the landmark case of *Reynolds v. Sims* (1964), which announced the constitutional principle of one person, one vote. Chief Justice Warren later would say that *Reynolds* was the most important decision of his career. On remand, Judge Johnson emphasized that the provisions in the Alabama Constitution requiring legislative districts to be composed of whole counties should continue to be enforced to the extent practicable while complying with the federal constitutional requirement of substantial population equality. Providing each county separate representation, the court said, served two purposes: "First, to prevent gerrymandering, and, second, to insure compact geographic districts with legislators attuned to local problems." (*Sims v. Baggett* [1965]). The importance of whole counties would dominate legislative and congressional redistricting in Alabama for the next half century up to the present, where the plaintiffs in *Singleton v. Allen* are alleging that the congressional redistricting plan enacted by the legislature on remand from *Allen v. Milligan*, 599 U.S. 1 (2023), unconstitutionally divides Jefferson County along racial lines.

My involvement with redistricting the Alabama legislature began after the 1980 census. Judge Johnson, who had been elevated to the Court of Appeals by President Carter, was still there leading another three-judge district court. Fred Gray, Sol Seay, Ed Still, Larry Menefee, and I represented members of ADC, led by Dr. Joe L. Reed. Joe's influence with Peter Rodino, chair of the House judiciary committee, and Senator Howell Heflin helped get Myron Thompson appointed to fill the district court vacancy left by Judge Johnson. Myron and Judge Truman Hobbs joined Judge Johnson on the three-judge court in *Burton v. Hobbie* (1982).

This was the first Alabama redistricting case to address the impact of the Voting Rights Act on statewide redistricting. The Reagan Department of Justice objected under Section 5 of the Voting Rights Act to the House and Senate districts enacted by the legislature in 1981. The three-judge court, over Judge Thompson's dissent, ordered a slightly modified version of a new plan enacted in January 1982 to be used on an interim basis in the 1982 elections, even though it had not yet received Section 5 preclearance. After DOJ objected to the 1982 plan, Joe Reed negotiated a settlement with the chairs of the legislature's reapportionment committee, Representative Rick Manley and Senator Lister Hill Proctor, which the legislature enacted in early 1983. The Reagan Justice Department precleared the negotiated plan, previewing the Republican Party strategy of supporting majority-Black districts to undermine White Democrats. Joe Reed flew to DC for a press conference with William Bradford Reynolds to commemorate DOJ's support of Blacks' voting rights. This was a year after the famous compromise negotiated by Senator Bob Dole led to passage of the 1982 amendments to the Voting Rights Act.

Most important about the *Burton* opinions was the dialogue between Judge Johnson and Judge Thompson over how to reconcile the Fourteenth Amendment's goal of race-neutrality with the race-conscious command of the Voting Rights Act to provide Black voters an equal opportunity to elect candidates of their choice. This is a fundamental question still confronting the Supreme Court today. In *Burton*, Judge Johnson leaned more toward race-neutrality. He agreed with our contention on behalf of the Black plaintiff voters that the plans enacted in 1981 and 1982 unnecessarily violated the whole-county provisions of the Alabama Constitution in ways that suggested racial gerrymandering, and that reducing the number of counties split would increase the number of districts in which Black voters could elect candidates of their choice—what today we call "opportunity" districts. But Judge Johnson objected to the plaintiffs' proposed plans on the ground that pairing too many White incumbents in the same districts discriminated against Whites. Judge Thompson responded by pointing out that increasing the number of majority-Black districts, as required by the Voting Rights Act, would necessarily create conflicts between White incumbents. But both judges agreed that whole counties should be the starting point for balancing the goal of race-neutrality with the race-conscious goal of providing minority voters equal opportunity to elect their representatives. The unanimous 1983 *Burton* opinion said the 1983 enacted plan was "exemplary," reducing the number of split counties from 30 to 13. It increased the number of majority-Black House districts from 12 to 17 but left the number of majority-Black Senate districts at three. Writing for the court, Judge Johnson said, "Enactment of Act No. 83–154 marks the first time in Alabama's history that its legislature has provided an apportionment plan that is fair to all the people of Alabama."

That may have been Judge Johnson's last word on the subject. But fairness to Alabama's Black voters in statewide redistricting would have to be re-examined in litigation after the 1990, 2000, 2010, and 2020 censuses. That is a complicated story that goes beyond Judge Johnson's retirement in 1991 and his death in 1999.

Meanwhile, historical proof of intentional discrimination and the results standard of the 1982 amendments to Section 2 of the Voting Rights Act came together on the docket of Judge Myron Thompson to produce the most consequential political progress for Black Alabamians in state history. Myron was appointed to the Middle District bench in 1980, the Voting Rights Act was amended in 1982, he issued his first decision in *Dillard v. Crenshaw County* on May 28, 1986, and the Supreme Court handed down *Thornburgh v. Gingles* on June 30, 1986.

Larry Menefee, Ed Still, and I had included in the *Dillard* complaint claims against nine county commission at-large election systems based on both the Constitution and the amended Voting Rights Act. But, heeding the Supreme Court's 1984 instructions in *Escambia County v. McMillan,* we asked Judge Thompson to address the statutory VRA claims first, rather than the Fourteenth and Fifteenth Amendment claims. Nevertheless, because Section 2 violations now could be established either by proof of discriminatory intent or discriminatory results, we based our preliminary injunction on evidence that Alabama laws applicable to all local at-large elections were intentionally crafted to dilute Black voting strength and thus violated the VRA. We got University of South Alabama professor Peyton McCrary to lay out the historical evidence, and Judge Thompson found it compelling.

Myron Thompson was the second African American to become a federal judge in Alabama, U. W. Clemon being the first. Myron was born in 1947 in Tuskegee, and, like Fred Gray, he grew up determined to strike down as many vestiges of Jim Crow as possible. So after Myron graduated from Yale Law School in 1972 he came back home to Alabama to practice law. In his first *Dillard* opinion Judge Thompson was readily "convinced" that general laws passed in the 1950s and 1960s enhancing the racial vote dilution caused by at-large voting were "completely intentional." Like Judges Arnow and Pittman, he emphasized the long historical context in which these statutes were enacted, saying "any remaining doubt that the systems were racially inspired is dispelled by further evidence that the systems were created in the midst of the state's unrelenting historical agenda, spanning from the late 1800s to the 1980s, to keep its black citizens economically, socially, and politically downtrodden, from the cradle to the grave." Contrast that with the majority opinion in *Harness v. Watson,* the en banc Fifth Circuit's August 2022 decision rejecting a claim that the criminal disfranchisement provision in Mississippi's Constitution was racially motivated:

"the overall social and political climate in Mississippi in the 1950s and 1960s fails to carry plaintiffs' burden to prove that the 1968 amendment intentionally discriminated against black voters." The dissenting opinion of African American judge James E. Graves Jr. objects to this blinkered view of historical context by surveying the sordid details of racial discrimination in Mississippi from Reconstruction to the present. This comparison is one example of how the federal judiciary's willingness to enforce the voting rights of racial minorities has regressed in the last quarter century. Whether history is being read in Judge Graves's dissenting opinion in *Harness* or in Judge Thompson's opinion for the court in *Dillard* makes a huge difference in the lives of thousands of Black citizens.

The May 28, 1986, *Dillard* preliminary injunction invited the six defendant county commissions that had not already settled to propose nondiscriminatory election methods and postponed further remedy proceedings pending a full hearing on the merits. Then *Thornburgh v. Gingles* was handed down a month later, and announcement of the *Gingles* standard for proving discriminatory results vastly accelerated and expanded the proceedings. *Dillard* became a statewide defendant class action challenging at-large elections in ten county commissions, 30 county school boards, and 148 municipal councils. LDF sent Lani Guinier and Pam Karlan to assist us. Jerome Gray and I have published a detailed account of those two-decade long proceedings in the 2016 edition of the *Cumberland Law Journal*.[13]

The now familiar three-factor *Gingles* preconditions for proving a "results" violation of Section 2 of the VRA were lifted almost verbatim from a 1982 *Hastings Law Journal* article Larry and I had written.[14] Larry has described in *Voices of Civil Rights Lawyers* (2017) the conference we attended with lawyers, historians, and political scientists at the Biltmore Hotel in Atlanta shortly after the Supreme Court decided *City of Mobile v. Bolden*. We agreed to work on a law review article as part of the effort to develop a response to *Bolden* and to amend the VRA. Our 1982 *Hastings* article proposed a manageable judicial standard for determining when an at-large or multimember-district system violated the Fourteenth and Fifteenth Amendments. It was a definition of at-large vote dilution I had proposed when I appeared in a congressional subcommittee hearing on amending the Voting Rights Act in July 1981. In a way, it provided me the chance to publish the argument I wish I had made in the Supreme Court. Of course, it was closing the barn door after the horse had got out. So we were surprised when Justice Brennan in *Gingles* adopted our constitutional standard for use in claims brought under the results test in amended Section 2 VRA.

That unexpected development made it much easier to challenge at-large election systems regardless of whether they were racially motivated, and Judge Thompson wasted no time enforcing the amended Voting Rights Act. He appointed Dave Boyd and Susan Russ (now Magistrate Judge Susan Russ Walker) to coordinate the responses of all the local governing bodies to the settlement we worked out with then Alabama attorney general Don Siegelman's office. With such strong signals coming from the 1982 Congress and the 1986 Supreme Court, most of the local governments decided not to contest liability and entered into settlement negotiations with ADC state field director Jerome Gray and local ADC leaders to produce remedial election systems. Most of the consent decrees required changing to single-member districts. But, thanks to the special interest of Ed and Jerome in alternative voting schemes, over a dozen consent decrees imposed cumulative voting or limited voting rules on the existing at-large systems.

We knew in *Dillard* we had a unique opportunity to make hay while the sun was shining. We understood that before long the powerful advocates of states' rights and opponents of the VRA would mount a counterattack. And, of course, they did. As I write this essay in 2022, the state of Alabama in *Milligan v. Merrill* is asking the Supreme Court to declare the *Gingles* standard unconstitutional. And with the current far-right court they might succeed. But, with the help of Assistant Attorney General Jack Park, all the *Dillard* cases were successfully closed by 2009, and the legacy of Black political access to local governments that Judge Thompson left us still survives today.

In another voting rights lawsuit I participated in, Judge Thompson required the state to appoint Black citizens as poll officials, *Harris v. Siegelman* (1988). As a member of three-judge district courts, he later bailed out our plaintiff Black voters in legislative redistricting cases after the 1990 and 2000 censuses, when the Supreme Court agreed with his dissents and reversed the adverse judgments below (*Sinkfield v. Kelley* [2000]; *Alabama Legislative Black Caucus v. Alabama* 2015]). Judge Thompson's civil rights docket in cases I was not involved in has extended beyond voting rights to protect the rights of state employees, the mentally ill, prisoners, and, until the Supreme Court struck down *Roe v. Wade*, the reproductive rights of women.

Desegregating Higher Education in Alabama

The Alabama higher education desegregation case would demand at least half my time for over 25 years, which is why I moved my complaining family to Birmingham in 1988. It began a week after the US Department of Education notified Alabama that it must adopt a plan for desegregating its four-year universities to comply with Title VI of the 1964 Civil Rights Act. Donald Watkins, Larry Menefee, and I filed the complaint in *Knight v. James* in Montgomery on January 15, 1981, on behalf of students and faculty at historically Black Alabama State University. John F. Knight Jr., the lead plaintiff, was an ASU administrator and had just been elected to the Montgomery County Commission. Donald Watkins was the son of ASU's president Levi Watkins, and Dr. Watkins directed us to ask the federal court to order a merger with ASU, under the direction of ASU's board of trustees, of the branches Auburn and Troy State had opened in Montgomery. He was following the lead of the merger of historically Black Tennessee State University and historically White University of Tennessee–Nashville, ordered in *Rita Sanders Geier v. University of Tennessee*. But the merged Nashville universities were placed under the control of Tennessee's statewide board of regents. But Joe Reed, a member of ASU's board, like many of us, doubted that the powerful White political and financial interests in Montgomery would ever submit to control of Auburn University at Montgomery and TSUM by ASU's majority-Black board of trustees. Joe said he feared "Confederates" would end up controlling ASU.

Knight v. James was assigned to Judge Truman Hobbs, and in May 1981 he granted the state's request for a stay of litigation proceedings during the pendency of negotiations with the US Department of Energy over an acceptable administrative Title VI desegregation plan. When those negotiations failed, DOE referred the case to DOJ, which in 1983 filed *United States v. Alabama* in Birmingham as a statewide higher ed desegregation case. That omnibus lawsuit landed on Judge U. W. Clemon's docket, and we wasted no time asking him to allow the *Knight v. James* plaintiffs to intervene. Judge Clemon granted our motion and later allowed a group of alumni, students, and faculty of Alabama A&M University in Huntsville, led by Alease Sims, to intervene as plaintiffs, too.

It is hard to overstate the shock to White Alabamians caused by finding a Black federal judge in charge of desegregating the state's colleges and universities. Particularly when that Black judge was U. W. Clemon, who, before taking the bench, had been one of the most well-known and outspoken civil rights lawyers in Alabama. U. W. was one of nine children born of former Mississippi sharecroppers who had moved to Fairfield to work in the steel mills. He attended segregated public schools and graduated from Miles College, a private HBCU in Fairfield, where he participated in the 1962–63 student sit-ins and graduated as valedictorian in 1965. He earned a law degree from Columbia in 1968 and interned for a year with the NAACP Legal Defense and Education Fund before coming back to Birmingham to join Oscar Adams Jr. and Jim Baker. Adams, Baker & Clemon was the preeminent Black law firm in Alabama when I clerked for Judge McFadden.

U. W. Clemon and J. Richmond Pearson became the first Black state senators since Reconstruction when in 1974 they won two of the single-member districts created in Jefferson County by Judge Frank Johnson's 1972 *Sims v. Amos* decree. U. W. was nominated by President Carter in 1980 for one of three vacancies in the Northern District, and Fred Gray was nominated to fill the seat vacated by Judge Johnson in the Middle District. U. W. and Fred were opposed by the Democratic establishment at both the state and national levels, and both were deemed unqualified by the ABA, citing alleged financial issues. The controversy over their nominations made national news. In the end, thanks to support from Black political leaders, particularly Richard Arrington, who had just been elected the first Black mayor of Birmingham, U. W. was confirmed. But Fred eventually withdrew, and, thanks mainly to Joe Reed's influence, the Middle District seat was filled by Myron Thompson.

So the idea that this former Black student militant and civil rights lawyer could sit in judgment on the constitutionality of the state's most prestigious institutions appeared to Alabama's guardians of White supremacy as an unbearable insult. Only two months after the United States filed its complaint in July 1983, Auburn University and the State Superintendent of Education filed motions demanding that Judge Clemon recuse himself. The purported bases for recusal were Judge Clemon's prior representation of some K–12 plaintiffs in the *Lee v. Macon* statewide school desegregation case and the fact that his minor children were potentially members of the plaintiff class of Black college students. Judge Clemon denied the motions as procedurally insufficient, but on appeal the Eleventh Circuit reversed and remanded with instructions that the recusal motions be assigned to another judge. Senior district court judge Hobart Grooms then granted the recusal motions, citing Judge Clemon's representation of Black plaintiffs in *Lee v. Macon*. A public backlash centered on Judge Grooms's own involvement with the issues in the case, so he vacated his judgment and recused himself. The recusal motion then was assigned to Senior Circuit judge David Dyer, who held a hearing and concluded there was no basis for disqualifying Judge Clemon. We thought that ended the matter, and the case proceeded to trial in July 1985.

But after Judge Clemon rendered a decision finding vestiges of de jure segregation in Alabama's system of higher education and ordered the state to propose a remedial plan, the defendants appealed and renewed their recusal arguments. The Eleventh Circuit immediately issued a stay, and in October 1987 it disqualified Judge Clemon and remanded the entire desegregation case for a new trial before a new judge. The circuit panel rejected the argument that Judge Clemon's minor children required recusal. "To disqualify Judge Clemon on the basis of his children's membership in the plaintiff class . . . would come dangerously close to holding that minority judges must disqualify themselves from all major civil rights actions." What the appellate opinion should have said, but did not say, is that the allegation displayed an unspoken belief that the rights of Black Americans must ultimately be decided by White Americans. "Similarly," said the Court of Appeals, "the views expressed by Judge Clemon as a political figure and member of the Alabama State Senate do not mandate disqualification." Nevertheless, it held disqualification was warranted because Senator Clemon had sat on committees that confirmed members of the state universities' boards of trustees, had opposed appointing a majority-White membership for the ASU board, and had sponsored capital funding bills for Alabama A&M University (AAMU). In other words, too much advocacy for the interests of Black Alabamians as a member of the state legislature. If that was not enough, the Eleventh Circuit panel added that Judge Clemon had extrajudicial knowledge of facts in the higher education case, because in *Lee v. Macon* he had "presented testimony about the long, continuous history of racially discriminatory employment practices suffered by black high school principals in Alabama." In other words, the state of Alabama was entitled to a judge who had never seen evidence of the state's long history of racial discrimination in public school employment.

Whatever. It was clear that White state and federal governments were not going to allow Judge U. W. Clemon to decide how to desegregate Alabama's universities. On remand, several White district court judges were assigned to preside over the case, and each either recused himself or was disqualified by the Court of Appeals because of ties to one or more of the defendant historically White universities, ties that were even closer than the grounds relied on to remove Judge Clemon. Finally, the chief judge of the Eleventh Circuit appointed a judge from another state, the Honorable Harold L. Murphy, US district judge for the Northern District of Georgia.

The legacy Judge Clemon left was much more than the already voluminous evidentiary record Judge Murphy would begin with. He left us the enduring memory of White supremacy being called to account before a fearless and determined Black judge. In particular, we remember July 1, 1985, the day George Corley Wallace, then serving his last term as governor, was brought into Judge Clemon's courtroom in a wheelchair to answer for his infamous stand in the schoolhouse door. Ken Wallis, then Wallace's legal adviser, pushed the wheelchair and stood by him on the stand, repeating questions into an ear trumpet Wallace held to his head. The legal team representing the Black plaintiffs, ASU, and AAMU had designated me to begin examining Wallace, on some theory that questions from a White lawyer would have better effect. But I was not then an experienced trial lawyer (nor did I ever become good at it), and Wallace was much too clever for me. He claimed not to hear me well nor to be able to see a long list of published news articles I wanted to ask him about. Wallace would respond to my questions by saying "I don't quite get you. Come over here and talk to me." At which point Judge Clemon had to jump in: "Well, Mr. Blacksher, that poses a problem. Ken [Wallis], would you repeat the question to the governor? Remain at the podium, Mr. Blacksher." Needless to say, my efforts to cross-examine him fell pretty flat. Joe Whatley, representing AAMU, took over and finished our examination of Governor Wallace. It could all be summarized by this Wallace statement: "I was for segregation. I am not now. I haven't been for a long, long time." His admissions, however, provided support for our evidence that Alabama's universities, like its K–12 schools, had been racially segregated by law. But it was the historic spectacle in a packed courtroom provided by the encounter between Governor George Wallace and Judge U. W. Clemon that mattered the most.

The plaintiffs—and defendants—could not have asked for a better judge than Harold L. Murphy to direct the massive institutional changes in *Knight v. Alabama* litigation that would last from 1989, when Judge Murphy accepted the assignment, to 2006, when he finally dismissed the lawsuit. Like Judge Clemon, he had been a state legislator, but a generation earlier he was completing ten years in the Georgia Assembly when, by court order, Charlayne Hunter and Hamilton Holmes desegregated the University of Georgia in January 1961. Judge Murphy came from a well-known family of politicians. His second cousin and law school classmate, Tom Murphy, was the powerful Speaker of the Assembly for 40 years, a yellow-dog Democrat who kept the Republican Party at bay until 2002. Judge Murphy was nominated by President Carter and confirmed in 1977 for a seat in the Northern District of Georgia.

Harold Murphy was renowned in Georgia as a judge lawyers liked to practice before. Unlike judges Johnson, Arnow, and Clemon, who sometimes could be brusque and impatient with lawyers, Judge Murphy would let the lawyers put their case in the way they wanted to do. His demeanor demanded calm and civility in the courtroom. He treated witnesses, lawyers, and observers with such respect it deterred us lawyers from engaging in verbal combat with one another or with a witness. But when we crossed the line, he could bring us up short without raising his voice. My most shameful moment was when I let some Black faculty members cajole me into asking one of their colleagues who had been called by defendants if she felt like a "house Negro." Judge Murphy jumped right down my throat, this time raising his voice, and made me apologize. He made sure I understood how boorish I had been. In other words, his courtroom became an attack-free haven, a blessing for a trial that would last six months.

Judge Murphy was the only judge sitting in the Rome, Georgia, federal courthouse when Chief Judge Roney asked him to take over what was now called *Knight v. Alabama*. The Eleventh Circuit's 1987 decision had dismissed without prejudice the Title VI claims of the United States and Knight intervenors for lack of program specificity (this was before Congress overruled *Grove City College v. Bell*), temporarily leaving only the Knight intervenors and their Fourteenth Amendment claims to be retried before a new judge. We were designated lead plaintiffs, but we did not have the financial resources to prosecute the case. Fortunately, when the Eleventh Circuit in 1984 held that the HBCUs could not realign as plaintiffs, Judge Clemon had designated ASU and AAMU as "Allied Defendants" with the Knight-Sims intervenors, which provided much needed funding for expert witnesses, depositions, and other trial expenses. Larry Menefee had withdrawn as co-counsel, and Donald Watkins soon moved on as well. But Leslie Proll had joined me, and Demetrius Newton appeared as co-counsel for the Sims intervenors. More importantly, we could continue to rely on counsel for the Allied Defendants, namely, Sol Seay, Fred Gray, Terry Davis, and Armand Derfner for ASU, and Joe Whatley, Kenneth Thomas, Tyrone Means, and John Falkenberry for AAMU, to do a lot of the heavy lifting.

Judge Clemon's 1985 opinion had held that "the racial identifiability of the students, faculty, staff, and governing boards are probative" of whether vestiges of Alabama's dual system of higher education remain. He found that the historical underfunding of the two state HBCUs and the opening of branches of White universities that duplicated the educational programs at ASU and AAMU had impeded their ability to attract White students. But Judge Clemon's decision left hanging the unspoken question whether those two historically Black schools would have to be closed if reforming these discriminatory practices still left their student bodies nearly all Black. Alabama's culture of White supremacy was responsible for both the constitutional violation and the unfairness of the remedy: the HBCUs's nearly all-Black student bodies and the stigma White students would bear for crossing the color line to attend them. Just as the racial identifiability standard had resulted in K–12 school desegregation plans closing Black neighborhood schools, it posed an existential threat to the survival of historically Black state universities. This was the dilemma facing public HBCUs across the nation. Even some Black commentators were arguing that the only solution was to close those Black state universities that could not be turned into majority-White institutions.

But, as important as Black elementary and secondary schools were for Black Alabamians, ASU and AAMU played even greater roles in their lives, whether or not they had attended them. When slavery ended, the freedmen understood that their hopes of true equality depended on education, and with the help of northern missionaries they immediately established their own schools. The predecessors of ASU and AAMU posed the greatest challenge to White supremacy, which depended on keeping Black citizens in a subordinate social, political, and economic status. The history of how these HBCUs pushed back against White control and continually increased access to higher levels of education for Black students is one of the most heroic sagas in Alabama and American history. The distinct pedagogical and campus traditions they created grounded Black culture in the larger community. They challenged the claim of White supremacy to define what constitutes the "mainstream." In fact, in terms of how the United States is viewed around the world, the HBCUs and their history of struggle against oppression are among the most important components of American "exceptionalism." The restricted autonomy they were able to wrest from White control empowered their Black students and faculty to sit in against and stand up to Jim Crow and launch the civil rights movement. The closure of

ASU and AAMU would not have removed vestiges of de jure segregation. To the contrary, it would have been a victory for White supremacy, not for racial equality.

So we were fortunate that Judge Murphy allowed us to start trial in *Knight v. Alabama* with six days of testimony by two historians, Dr. J. Mills Thornton, "probably the preeminent living authority on the social and political history of Alabama," and Dr. James D. Anderson, born and raised in Greene County and an expert "on the history of American education in the South with an emphasis on the education of blacks." Judge Murphy understood the importance of this history evidence. "This Court must address the intensely factual questions about whether vestiges of historical racial discrimination persist in Alabama's system of public higher education. These questions cannot be answered accurately without a clear exposition and understanding of exactly what those historical policies of discrimination were—their specific forms and content, how they were intended to disadvantage black people and what effects they actually had." There would still be months of testimony by other witnesses to go, but I have often said that after professors Thornton and Anderson had laid the history foundation, proving plaintiffs' case was a downhill trip. With the assistance of his law clerk, Carlos González, Judge Murphy's December 30, 1991, opinion would devote 88 pages in F. Supp. to history evidence. And, citing *Swann v. Charlotte-Mecklenburg Board of Education,* he emphasized that in remedying vestiges of segregation, "Racially identifiable institutions are not offensive to the Constitution unless the state's policies and practices purposely maintain their racial identity for discriminatory reasons."

The findings of fact Judge Murphy made about the history of Black education in Alabama clearly influenced his legal conclusions about the required remedial standards. Then pending in the Supreme Court was the Fifth Circuit's ruling in the Mississippi higher education desegregation case, *Ayers v. Allain,* that once the state had discontinued its racially restrictive admissions practices and was implementing race-neutral policies it need not eradicate vestiges of other past discriminatory policies. Judge Murphy's reading of controlling Supreme Court desegregation precedents in the K–12 context led him to disagree with the *Ayers* majority and side with the partial dissent of Judge Patrick Higginbotham,[15] who would have required the trial court to "focus on the causal relationship between the *de jure* system and the present practices." For Judge Murphy, this meant the state had a constitutional duty to look for the "historical traces" of past segregation policies and change them.

As pleased as we were with most of Judge Murphy's findings of fact and conclusions of law, we were disappointed in his failure to order relief with respect to the limited missions of the HBCUs, the land grant issues, and the lack of African American content in the historically White universities' curricula. So the Knight plaintiffs filed a notice of appeal. Our appeal got a big boost six months later, in June 1992, when the Supreme Court rendered its decision in the Mississippi case, now styled *United States v. Fordice*. Justice White's majority opinion not only adopted the reference to historical traces in Judge Murphy's formulation of the relevant legal standard, it enhanced it: "even after a State dismantles its segregative admissions policy, there may still be state action that is traceable to the State's prior de jure segregation and that continues to foster segregation. . . . If policies traceable to the de jure system are still in force and have discriminatory effects, those policies, too, must be reformed to the extent practicable and consistent with sound educational practices." The Constitution might not require closure of Mississippi's HBCUs, the court said, if eliminating duplication of their programs by the historically White institutions succeeded in attracting White students. And we were pleasantly surprised that Justice Clarence Thomas added this reassurance in his concurring opinion, saying that because the *Fordice* standard "does not compel the elimination of all observed racial imbalance, it portends neither the destruction of historically black colleges nor the severing of those institutions from their distinctive histories and traditions."

The Eleventh Circuit handed down its decision in the *Knight* appeal in February 1994. It praised "Judge Murphy's management of this complex piece of institutional reform litigation," and congratulated him for anticipating, "without the benefit of Supreme Court guidance," the *Fordice* legal standard. But, because of his "wholly understandable failure to anticipate the *Fordice* standard in all its detail," it remanded the case for reconsideration of the issues raised by the Knight plaintiffs. Because Judge Murphy had found that the limited missions of ASU and AAMU were traceable to de jure segregation, he was instructed to take the next steps required by the *Fordice* standard and determine whether their continuing segregative effects practicably could be reformed. And his conclusion that there were no vestiges of racial discrimination in the much smaller agricultural extension and research programs assigned to AAMU, the Black land grant university, compared with similar programs at Auburn, the White land grant university, was inconsistent with his history findings of fact. Judge Murphy had found that Alabama's allocation of all 1862 Morrill Act funds to Auburn was racially discriminatory,[16] but he held this caused no current segregative effects because Auburn would have won those land grant funds even if there had been no discrimination. The Eleventh Circuit held that *Fordice* foreclosed the causation factor if the current policy favoring Auburn was traceable to its original racial purpose.

On remand, Judge Murphy presided over six more weeks of trial, and on August 1, 1995, he issued a new opinion and an additional remedial decree. But, as the opinion recites, "[s]everal months prior to the start of the remand proceedings the Court took the extraordinary step of appointing five neutral expert witnesses." They were Dr. Robert M. Anderson Jr., who headed the cooperative extension service at Iowa State University; Lt. Gen. Julius Becton, former president of Prairie View A&M University, the 1890 Morrill Act institution in Texas; Dr. Harold L. Enarson, president emeritus of the Ohio State University; Dr. Robben Flemming, president emeritus of the University of Michigan; and Dr. Bryce Jordan, president emeritus of Pennsylvania State University. "The Court charged the neutral experts to conduct a detailed review of the issues presented on remand and to separately recommend to the Court, what in their individual judgments, were the most educationally sound remedies to address the issues remanded by the Circuit."

Judge Murphy had already, in September 1993, appointed Carlos González special monitor of his 1991 remedial decree, and Carlos would play an indispensable role coordinating the work of the court's experts, all of whom, except for Dr. Anderson,[17] would be appointed members of the oversight committee established in the 1995 remedial decree. These neutral experts not only helped Judge Murphy formulate the pragmatic reforms set out in his decree, under the guidance of Carlos González, they greatly enhanced the likelihood that the court-ordered institutional reforms would actually work. In my opinion, this was the unique genius of Judge Murphy's decree. The active management provided by the special monitor and oversight committee over the next decade to a large extent forced the lawyers to step back and allow all the critical details of implementation to be worked out in a more negotiated and less adversarial way with officials of the state and all the defendant universities. The oversight committee gave Judge Murphy an unprecedented level of hands-on control over implementation and modification of his complicated reforms. Carlos in particular was responsible for keeping the remedial process on course, we all agreed. (He would afterward take his considerable arbitration skills to Tennessee, where he mediated final settlement of the *Geier* case.) John

Knight, the lead plaintiff, during much of this time was chair of the House finance and appropriations committee, which facilitated negotiations with the governor and state finance director.

It is impossible to do justice to the detailed opinion and decree Judge Murphy issued in 1995. When it came out, I had to create an outline of all the remedial provisions. Here are a few highlights:

Judge Murphy ordered the creation of endowment trust funds for ASU and AAMU. The state had to contribute $1 million annually to each HBCU for 15 years and match additional amounts ASU and AAMU were able to raise on their own. Neither HBCU previously had a significant endowment fund. Judge Murphy came up with this remedy on his own; none of the parties had proposed it. Today, 17 years later, ASU has over $100 million in its endowment trust, and AAMU has $50 million. The decree permanently prohibits invasion of the trust corpus; 25 percent of the income must be reinvested, but 75 percent of the income can be used for scholarships, endowed faculty chairs, and similar educational purposes. But it should not be overlooked that the huge point Judge Murphy made by these endowment trusts was that the state of Alabama could not close its HBCUs; it had to invest in them.

The decree contained a number of provisions aimed at helping ASU and AAMU attract more White students: controversial scholarships that only White students could apply for (which had to survive a constitutional challenge), and various restrictions on the ability of the historically White two-year and four-year institutions to duplicate programs at the HBCUs.

New programs were ordered for the HBCUs: allied health sciences, PhD programs, and a master's in accountancy at ASU; mechanical and electrical engineering programs and a master's of science education at AAMU.

Additional capital funding and operating funds were required for ASU and AAMU in amounts to be worked out by the oversight committee based on facilities and faculty needed to support the new court-ordered programs.

The most controversial part of the 1995 Remedial Decree was an order that the Agricultural Research and Extension services at Auburn and AAMU be combined in a unified system. Judge Murphy prescribed the organizational arrangements in great detail (presumably with the advice of Dr. Robert Anderson), and they are too complicated for me to summarize here. Their purpose was to provide the Agricultural Research Station and Extension Service at AAMU with access to all the resources in Auburn's much bigger programs. But even though AAMU was to retain control over its own research and extension faculty, the lines of authority seemed to make AAMU subordinate to Auburn's officials, at least to some degree. For example, the director of the Unified Agricultural Cooperative Extension System is appointed by Auburn's president "with the counsel and advice of the President of Alabama A&M University." AAMU was given the associate director for Urban Affairs and New Nontraditional Programs, and she or he is appointed by the Unified System Director "with the advice and consent" of AAMU's president and chief academic officer. The decree required both AAMU's and Auburn's extension programs to work out of one consolidated office in each county, and with Auburn's operating budget ten times the size of AAMU's, the latter's programs tend to get submerged. Extension faculty at AAMU were given the option of holding faculty rank at either AAMU or Auburn. Because over the years AAMU has been unable to keep up with Auburn's salary increases, AAMU has lost a third of its extension faculty to Auburn University. Those are only two examples of the bureaucratic confusion that came with unification. It is not surprising that no other state has chosen to unify its 1862 and 1890 agricultural research and extension services.

The *Knight-Sims* case was finally dismissed by Judge Murphy in 2006. He concluded he had done as much as practicable to eradicate vestiges of Alabama's dual system of higher education. An in-depth study of the lawsuit and the results of Judge Murphy's remedial decrees ought to be the subject of a PhD dissertation. I can only say this much now:

Enrollment figures reported to the US Department of Education in 2020 show that 90 percent of the 4,640 undergraduate and graduate students at ASU were Black or African American. Of the 6,560 undergraduate and graduate students enrolled at AAMU, 86 percent were Black or African American. Enrollments at the historically White universities ranged from 43 percent Black or African American of 5,212 students at Auburn's Montgomery campus to 5 percent Black or African American of 30,737 students at Auburn's main campus. At the University of Alabama at Huntsville, 9 percent of the 11,312 students were Black or African American. At the University of Alabama's main campus in Tuscaloosa, 11 percent of its 42,096 students were Black or African American.

ASU publications have thanked Judge Murphy for its endowment trust fund and its new programs. Its many master's degree programs and its PhD programs in educational leadership and microbiology are housed in the Harold Lloyd Murphy Graduate School in Montgomery. John Knight has recognized what really matters: "Of all the victories, all the gains that ASU and Alabama A&M made through *Knight v. Alabama,* the one that is most important . . . is recognition that historically black institutions have the right to exist . . . where you maintain the heritage, the name, all that you've stood for all those years, but not for the purpose of being segregated."

In 2002, while *Knight v. Alabama* was winding down, Chief Justice Roy Moore and the Alabama Supreme Court dismissed the decades-long education equity funding case in state court. Whereupon we asked Judge Murphy to rule that the property tax restrictions in the Alabama Constitution, particularly the amendments Governor Wallace pushed through the legislature in 1972 and 1978, were vestiges of de jure segregation subject to remedy in the *Knight* case. This was a bridge too far for Judge Murphy. He granted us an evidentiary hearing and issued an opinion in 2004 agreeing that the challenged state constitutional provisions were racially motivated. But he held that because property tax revenues go primarily to K–12 schools, their relationship to higher education desegregation was too tenuous. We appealed, but the Eleventh Circuit affirmed.

Thereupon Larry, Ed, Bobby Seagall, and I, with support from the Alabama Education Association, filed a new lawsuit on behalf of Black and White K–12 students in Sumter and Lawrence counties. *Lynch v. Alabama* was assigned to my old friend Lynwood Smith, who was now a US district court judge in Huntsville. We invested thousands of hours and thousands of dollars preparing and trying the *Lynch* case, but we lost. Judge Smith issued a book-length opinion in 2011 that is too long to be published in the *West Federal Supplement.* It contains one of the most detailed accounts of racial discrimination in education and taxation ever published anywhere in Alabama, not just in a judicial opinion. But he denied all relief. He acknowledged the clear racial purpose behind the millage caps first placed in the Alabama Constitution in 1875, when Conservative Democrats "redeemed" the state from Black rule and imposed caps aimed at protecting white landowners in the Black Belt. But he held the millage caps did not violate the Fourteenth Amendment because today they equally disadvantage all students, Black and White, when the figures are examined statewide. And he found that the amendments enacted in the 1970s that took farm and timber land almost entirely out the tax base of schools in the Black Belt counties, which whites were fleeing following court-ordered desegregation, were motivated by greed not racial discrimination. The Eleventh Circuit affirmed in 2014, expressing sympathy for our plaintiff schoolchildren:

> In deciding this difficult appeal, we are cognizant of Alabama's deep and troubled history of racial discrimination, and given the evidence at trial, we share in the district court's concern regarding Alabama's public education system:
>
> Alabama continues to be plagued by an inadequately funded public school system—one that hinders the upward mobility of her citizens, black and white alike, especially in rural counties. . . . [As a result,] [t]he children of the rural poor, whether black or white, are left to struggle as best as they can in underfunded, dilapidated schools.
>
> Courts, however, are not always able to provide relief, no matter how noble the cause.

Eric Schnapper graciously crafted a last-ditch petition for writ of certiorari that the Supreme Court speedily denied.

A better trial lawyer than I am would have forced the legislator witnesses who passed the 1970s amendments to admit that Alabama's culture of White supremacy made it impossible for them to deny relief to White landowners in the Black Belt, who had just taken their children out of what became all-Black public schools. That may or may not have made a difference in the outcome. A better chance was missed decades earlier when we did not target school revenue laws as vestiges of the dual system in the *Lee v. Macon* cases. There is no precedent for what we were asking Judge Murphy and Judge Smith to do: strike down tax laws because they were racially motivated and force a state to raise taxes on its citizens. That is what White Alabamians as far back as Reconstruction have called "socialism," taxing White wealth to pay for education and social services that benefit Blacks. Moreover, we were challenging not just Alabama values but American values. I remind myself that when Thomas Jefferson wrote "Life, Liberty and the pursuit of Happiness" in the Declaration of Independence he was plagiarizing John Locke's "life, liberty, and property." In the United States there apparently is no constitutional right more sacred than property, the pursuit of which was the main driver behind our revolt from British rule.

So I end where I started, with Burton's and Derfner's assertion that we have been able to practice law during a window of time C. Vann Woodward called the Second Reconstruction. Today we must litigate in what must be called the Second Redemption. As they say, what goes 'round comes 'round, so maybe there will be a third Reconstruction.

Notes

1. I wrote this essay shortly after the Meredith march ended, based almost entirely on my personal recollections of specific events and on my opinions of that moment in history. I then revised it slightly in 2022. For an excellent and comprehensive study of the march, see Aram Goudsouzian, *Down to the Crossroads: Civil Rights, Black Power, and the Meredith March against Fear* (New York: Farrar, Straus and Giroux, 2014).
2. Williams v. Wallace, 240 F. Supp. 100 (M.D. Ala. 1965).
3. For a fine overview of Dr. King's life and career, see Mary Lawson, "C. B. King," *New Georgia Encyclopedia*, last modified Mar 28, 2021. https://www.georgiaencyclopedia.org/articles/history-archaeology/c-b-king-1923-1988/
4. Bell v. Southwell, 376 F.2d 659 (5th Cir. 1967).
5. Jack Greenberg, *Crusaders in the Courts* (New York: Harper Collins, 1994), 426.
6. Orville Vernon Burton and Armand Derfner, *Justice Deferred: Race and the Supreme Court* (Cambridge: Harvard University Press, 2021), 1.
7. In Senate hearings on the nomination of Jeff Sessions for a federal judgeship in Mobile, he was alleged to have repeated a remark by Judge Hand that I was a "disgrace to my race." If Judge Hand did say that, I believe he probably had a smile on his face. But even as a joke, this familiar insult has a significant subtext, namely, that the United States is a White republic and it deserves loyalty from members of its national tribe.
8. Abbott v. Perez, 138 S.Ct. 305, 2324 (2018).
9. *League of Women Voters of Florida, Inc. v. Florida Secretary of State*, 32 F.4th 1363, 1373 (11th Cir. 2022) (cleaned up).
10. A Supreme Court amici brief filed in July 2022 in support of the Black plaintiffs in *Milligan v. Merrill*, on behalf of U. W. Clemon, Fred D. Gray, Henry Sanders, and the Legislative Black Caucus, cites a recent scholarly study of Alabama showing "that the concentration of enslaved persons in a given county in 1860 predicts negative racial and race-related political attitudes of white citizens living in those counties today." See Avidit Acharya, Matthew Blackwell, and Maya Sen, *Deep Roots: How Slavery Still Shapes Southern Politics* (Princeton: Princeton University Press, 2018), 60–62. They conclude that "the contemporary correlation is in significant part explained by historical path dependence."
11. J. Michael Butler, *Beyond Integration: The Black Freedom Struggle in Escambia County, Florida, 1960–1980* (Chapel Hill: University of North Carolina Press, 2016), 115.
12. My son, Manny Blacksher, who specializes in literary criticism, points out that "govermint" appears several times in Finley Peter Dunne's famous *Mr. Dooley's Philosophy*. https://www.gutenberg.org/files/7976/7976-h/7976-h.htm
13. Jerome Gray and James U. Blacksher, "The *Dillard* Cases and Grassroots Black Political Power," *Cumberland Law Journal* 46 (2016): 311.
14. James U. Blacksher and Larry Menefee, "From *Reynolds v. Sims* to *City of Mobile v. Bolden*: Have the White Suburbs Commandeered the Fifteenth Amendment?" *Hastings Law Journal* 34 (1982): 1, cited with approval in Thornburg v. Gingles, 478

U.S. 30, 47 n.13, 49, 51, 57, 68 (1986); see Daniel P. Tokaji, "*Realizing the Right to Vote: The Story of* Thornburgh v. Gingles," in *Election Law Stories*, ed. Joshua A. Douglas and Eugene D. Mazo (Foundation Press, 2016), 127, 168; Pamela S. Karlan, "The Alabama Foundations of the Law of Democracy," *Alabama Law Review* 67 (2015): 415.

15 Judge Higginbotham was born and raised in McCalla, Jefferson County, Alabama, but he was teaching at SMU law school when he was appointed to the Fifth Circuit bench.

16 In the 1985 trial before Judge Clemon, Auburn's history expert, Dr. William Warren Rogers, based on a 1960 article he had written in the *Alabama Review*, testified that race had played no role in the Alabama legislature's decision to award the 1862 Morrill Act funds to Auburn's predecessor. But preparing for the 1991 trial, we had discovered a revision of Dr. Rogers's 1960 article he had published in 1987. The revision said race was a central issue in the 1872 assignment of all land grant funds to Auburn. Judge Murphy's findings were much influenced by Dr. Rogers's explanation: "In his 1991 testimony, Dr. Rogers stands by the opinions expressed in the 1987 article, saying it 'is by far the superior article.' The professor candidly admits that, given the political milieu of the state in 1960, the Alabama Review would not have published his 1987 version of the 1872 events. In Dr. Rogers's own words: 'There was not a great deal of interest in it. It was just starting, the historical research in black history and in the reconstruction period in education, and . . . in 1960 . . . an editor would not necessarily have been impressed with an article that did that.'" Dr. Rogers is a native of Butler County, Alabama, and professor emeritus at Florida State University. He is a highly respected southern historian, whose works we have cited in many voting rights cases.

17 Dr. Anderson's work was completed by the detailed land grant remedy set out in the 1995 decree.

6

New Delivery Systems

Life after Passage of the 1964 Civil Rights Act

Robert L. Wiggins Jr.

Growing Up in the South

I was born and raised in upstate South Carolina where my family lived and worked in and around Easley for generations. Although my dad moved us to Akron, Ohio, to find work as a machinist in 1951, we returned to South Carolina to spend time with family twice a year during the next ten years and moved back to Easley permanently in the spring of 1963.

I first became interested in the civil rights movement in high school in May 1963, when the TV networks' nightly newscast brought Birmingham's racial problem into everyone's homes showing firehoses and snarling police dogs attacking schoolchildren for marching peacefully for civil rights. Those events had an electrifying effect on many of my generation who were just coming to grips with the question of equal rights and the South's racial history. Birmingham rocketed the rest of 1963 through six months of racial violence and debate mixed with fleeting moments of hope for change—President Kennedy's first major speech on civil rights in early June, Medgar Evers's assassination on June 12, introduction of the first major Civil Rights Act in Congress in nearly a century in mid- to late June, the March on Washington for Jobs and Freedom and the "I Have a Dream" speech on August 28, the Sunday morning bombing of Birmingham's Sixteenth Street Baptist church that killed four young girls on September 15, and the assassination of President Kennedy on November 22, 1963.

Civil rights remained a dominant issue throughout the South for the next ten years or more thanks to Birmingham, Selma, Mississippi, and too many other racial tragedies to count or reconcile. It was in those years that Congress created a series of new civil rights to redress some of the more obvious racial and sexual inequalities that had been accumulating over the past century. Congress started with the Civil Rights Act of 1964. I've spent the last 50 years litigating claims seeking to enforce the civil rights created by that act.

Undoing the Continuing Effects of Jim Crow

The role of civil rights lawyers dramatically changed once Congress got around to passing the Civil Rights Act of 1964. Not only did the act outlaw racial and sexual discrimination by private individuals and corporations for the first time in 100 years,[1] but it also delegated the principal responsibility for civil enforcement of the act to lawyers in private practice who were willing to handle civil rights cases at their own expense as so-called private attorney generals.[2] That was a questionable means of enforcement at best. There were far too few lawyers practicing law in the South who had any experience or interest in handling civil rights cases compared with the overwhelming need for such legal representation, as well as the enormity of the task of dismantling nearly 100 years of virulent racial prejudice and Jim Crow segregation throughout the region. The rising tide of racial segregation and white supremacy had gone unredressed in the South since the end of Reconstruction in 1876.

Once it gradually became clear in 1963 that Congress might actually pass a new civil rights act after nearly a century of inaction, there was a rush to adopt new practices and reinforce old policies aimed at freezing the status quo and carrying forward the effects of the past century of racial segregation for as long as possible. Throughout the South, the ravages of the past century of Jim Crow segregation of jobs, schools, and communities were being perpetuated by a battery of practices that appeared to be "race-neutral" and apply equally to both races on their face, but carried forward the effects of past racial prejudice and white privilege as applied.

That was a particular problem in getting a job or promotion. Black applicants and employees had first been denied the opportunity to obtain the job experience and training that was the key to hiring or promotion and were then told that they were "unqualified" or "less qualified" than their white peers because they lacked the very qualifications that they had been denied because of their race. Most of such practices were based on "prior experience" or educational factors that were proxies for race in one form or another, such as seniority, length-of-service and line-of-progression factors, pencil-and-paper tests, age restrictions, departmental service or experience requirements, and so on, which carried forward the effects of past racially segregated jobs and schools whether intended or not.

The first wave of civil rights cases filed in the mid-1960s sought to outlaw and undo the continuing effects of such past racial and sexual inequalities. Those cases gradually established the principle that practices or decisions that carry forward the effects of past discrimination or otherwise have "disparate impact" on one race or sex more than another violate the 1964 Civil Rights Act, and that corporations and entities applying such practices are liable for the natural consequences of their actions regardless of whether intended or not.[3] Establishing that principle, however, proved not to be nearly as difficult as implementing it. Many of those cases were still being litigated years later in the mid-1970s and had just begun to reach the far more difficult stage of dismantling and replacing the practices that were perpetuating the South's segregationist past.

How My Law Practice Began

My law practice grew out of that first wave of civil rights cases. After several years organizing public housing tenants in Alabama in the early 1970s, I was asked in June 1975 to represent a large class of several thousand black employees who were challenging the present effects of a long history of racial segregation at one of Birmingham's oldest and largest iron and steel foundries—the American Cast Iron Pipe Company (ACIPCO). *See Pettway v. American Cast Iron Pipe Co.,* 576 F.2d 1157 (5th Cir. 1978), *cert denied,* 439 U.S. 1115 (1979).

What happened in *Pettway* is a good example of the protracted litigation that became necessary to gain any meaningful relief against the present effects of past racial segregation. Like the rest of Birmingham, ACIPCO had been racially segregated since it first began producing cast iron pipe in 1905. In June 1975, Rush Pettway and the other leaders of the Committee for Equal Job Opportunity (CEJO) asked me to attend a mass meeting of ACIPCO's black employees at the Sixteenth Street Baptist church to discuss whether I would be willing to represent them in challenging a new round of plant policies and rules that would continue to carry forward the effects of the past if not enjoined. See *Pettway,* 576 F.2d at 1185–86 (describing such practices and how they made matters worse rather than better).

After ten years of litigation, ACIPCO had just substituted a new set of racially discriminatory policies and rules to replace the ones that the Court of Appeals found to have perpetuated past racial discrimination and required to be dismantled in 1974. *Id.* Rather than complying with the Court of Appeals' mandate on remand, however, the district judge in Birmingham entered an order that approved ACIPCO's new set of policies that entrenched the effects of its segregated past even more than the departmental seniority system that the Court of Appeals condemned.[4]

The new policies approved by the district judge substituted position in departmental lines of progression that were the product of the same racial segregation and discriminatory tests that had already been found to violate the Civil Rights Act. By carrying forward the effects of that past discrimination, ACIPCO's new lines of progression blocked black employees' access to historically white jobs and departments even more than the pre-1975 departmental seniority system that the lines of progression replaced. *Id.*[5] As a result, white employees were put at higher levels of the new lines of progression while black employees were simultaneously locked into the lower-paying, dirtier, and less opportune lines of progression in traditionally black departments. The black employees in those departments were not even considered for jobs in the historically white departments until *after all* the white incumbents in those departments had gotten the jobs and promotions they wanted. That meant they could only compete for the leftover entry-level jobs at the bottom of the white department's line of progression and were deterred from even seeking those few leftover entry-level jobs by a parallel policy that automatically cut their pay to the entry-level wage rate if they transferred. Mass picketing of the Birmingham federal courthouse immediately broke out in protest of the district judge's order approving that new round of discriminatory policies. Hundreds of ACIPCO's black employees picketed every day during the hottest part of the summer and fall of 1975.

During the next eight years, between 800 and 1,000 class members met with me once each month on a Sunday afternoon at the Sixteenth Street Baptist church as we worked our way through three more appeals and two more remands to the same district judge from 1975 to 1983. In 1978, the Court of Appeals agreed with us that ACIPCO's new policies discriminated on the basis of race *even more* than its pre-1975 policies that the court had previously condemned and ordered to be enjoined. The court determined that "[t]he requirement that jobs be held in a sequential order in any line of progression tends to 'lock in' formerly victimized blacks, thereby perpetuating the effects of past discrimination and prolonging the journey of class members to their rightful place within the company" (*Pettway*, 576 F.2d at 1191–94), that "[t]he superior position of white employees vis-à-vis blacks is a direct result of the earlier opportunities for whites in the more desirable departments and of the illegal testing and education requirements for promotion" (*id.*), that "[a]ll job vacancies are offered first to employees within the department in the position below the vacancy" (*id.*), that "class members, even if plant senior, may not bid against employees occupying a higher position on the line" (*id.*), and that "[e]ven vacancies in entry level positions are not posted plantwide until workers within the line of progression, or laid-off from it, decline the position" (*Id.*).[6]

Absent that appeal, ACIPCO's latest iteration of its discriminatory practices would have been allowed to continue with impunity for many years to come. It was only with the eight years of additional litigation and appeals that ACIPCO's persistent effort to lock in and perpetuate the effects of its past racial segregation was eventually enjoined and replaced with a nondiscriminatory promotion and transfer system, and each class member was awarded back pay with interest to compensate them for the economic losses they suffered from 1965 through 1983. See *Pettway v. American Cast Iron Pipe Co.*, 681 F.2d 1259 (11th Cir. 1982) (Tuttle, J.).[7]

The continuing effect of past segregation or bias has also been a problem for women. At the same time as the *Pettway* case, I represented a class of female employees who challenged ACIPCO's segregation of male and female jobs in a case that began before a different district judge in 1972. See *Cox v. American Cast Iron Pipe Co.*, 784 F.2d 1546, 1551–52 (11th Cir.), *cert. denied,* 479 U.S. 883 (1986). The Court of Appeals found that "the defendant had a policy of overt workforce sex segregation" until December 1973, that "[o]nly after this suit was filed did defendant allow a few women to make their way into the plant," and that in jobs "[o]utside the plant, women were also kept on the lowest levels of the workforce and paid the least." *Id.* at 1551–1552. It also found that ACIPCO had a "policy of paying men's clerical jobs and women's clerical jobs on two entirely different compensation schemes is discriminatory"—that "traditionally male jobs in the manufacturing division are compensated 'objectively' based on a system of detailed job descriptions, standardized evaluations, and publicly known job classifications, pay scales and review provisions, while compensation for non-manufacturing women's jobs is subjectively determined." *Id.* at 1560–1561.

Traced to their source, white or male employees' "qualifications" often came from prior experience and training in jobs and departments that were previously segregated and not available to black or female employees, or at least not equally available.[8]

Growth into a Larger Civil Rights Litigation Practice

The *Pettway* case and others like it dominated my practice for the first ten years. During those years the practice slowly grew to the point that we had to decide in 1985 whether to limit cases to just what two to three lawyers could handle personally or find a way to expand the practice to allow for continued growth.[9] Staying the same size was not really an option because we were litigating a significant number of class actions, like *Pettway,* that required more lawyers and a substantial investment of time and money to be successful.

The first ten years showed that a practice devoted to civil rights litigation was viable for the lawyers personally handling such cases, but would require spreading the risk and cost to a larger number of lawyers with established practices in order to grow through hiring and paying the salaries, overhead, and litigation expenses of a group of young lawyers until they could carry their own weight as part of a larger law firm. Experience also told us that it was unlikely that such a larger practice could survive the boom-and-bust income cycles of a strictly contingent-fee practice—that a blend of both contingent-fee and noncontingent-fee practices would be needed to be able to expand the civil rights and class action practice by hiring and supporting younger lawyers. To be able to attract young lawyers with a genuine interest in civil rights litigation required that we have sufficient resources to provide a place for them to practice without the risks and anxieties of being on their own. Very few young lawyers were in a position to litigate civil rights cases at their own expense on the chance that they might be paid a contingent fee someday if they ever prevailed. But those same young lawyers could often thrive in a firm that spread such risks and anxieties across a larger number of experienced lawyers willing to support them while they learned and helped with the firm's growing caseload.

That is what led us to eventually merge our contingent-fee practice with a firm of five partners with noncontingent-fee practices in 1985. That merger added one more experienced litigator, Dennis Pantazis, and gave us sufficient size and income to begin hiring younger lawyers interested in handling civil rights cases and related litigation. Over the next several years we gradually grew into a firm that has averaged 35 to 40 lawyers for the past 30 years, with the majority handling civil rights litigation of one sort or another on a contingent-fee basis. Although that growth and size is not typical of practices that primarily handle civil rights cases, it does show that such a practice is viable despite the financial risks and difficulties that civil rights attorneys ordinarily face.

How I Became Involved in Civil Rights Litigation

My work handling civil rights litigation has not been limited to cases challenging race and sex discrimination under the 1964 Civil Rights Act. I began practicing law in Birmingham after spending several years organizing public housing tenants in Alabama in the early 1970s. The steady drumbeat of events from 1963 to 1965 had propelled the civil rights movement in several directions, including organizing the Poor People's Campaign to push for "economic justice"; organizing tenants to oppose oppressive housing and community conditions; organizing low-wage laborers to push for better pay and working conditions; joining in the growing opposition to the Vietnam War; challenging environmental racism and so-called urban renewal projects that disproportionately impacted and degraded African American neighborhoods; organizing resistance to jail and prison conditions, death penalty sentences, and a racially oppressive criminal justice system that was rapidly incarcerating an ever larger prison population of young black men, and so on.

My initial work organizing tenants in 1972–74 led to formation of a statewide tenant organization—the Alabama State Tenants Organization—and a tenant campaign to stop an elevated expressway in downtown Birmingham that was slated to destroy 1,200 tenants' homes in the Central City Public Housing Project that occupied twelve city blocks in the center of downtown. The Red Mountain Expressway was being built to speed commuters downtown from the "white flight" suburbs that rapidly surrounded Birmingham "over the mountain" once desegregation began in earnest a few years earlier in the mid-1960s.

The organizing campaign against the expressway continued through the next several years and was supplemented by a federal lawsuit we filed in early 1975 to enjoin the expressway on behalf of the tenants and State Tenants Organization. That case was brought against George Wallace, the Alabama Highway Department, and the applicable federal highway agencies and was based on violation of nine federal statutes, including the 1964 Civil Rights Act, the 1969 National Environmental Policy Act, and several federal housing and highway-related statutes. Once the complaint was filed, the Federal Highway Administration (FHWA) reversed its position and conceded that work on the expressway must stop until an environmental impact statement and additional public hearings were completed. In June 1975, the federal district court assigned the case found that the expressway "was completely dormant, if not dead" and it was therefore premature to consider any other counts of the complaint unless work on the expressway resumed.

The court, nevertheless, ordered that the State Highway Department consider alternative routes for the expressway that would avoid destruction of the public housing project if design of the expressway ever resumed.[10] At that point the expressway abruptly ended on Third Avenue just two blocks from where it would have collided with the Central City Public Housing Project. It sat that way without any further construction for the next eight years (1975–83). New design work began in 1977, and over the slow course of the next six years we were able to negotiate an agreement with the state to abandon the expressway's original route and not to pursue any alternative route that would destroy any part of the existing housing project. The settlement was finalized in 1983 and saved twelve city blocks of federally assisted public housing that still remains there today, nearly 50 years after we first filed suit to oppose tearing that housing down just to build another highway.

The Continuing Struggle to Undo the Effects of Past Discrimination

The use of practices that exploit the present effects of past discrimination like that in *Pettway* was not an uncommon or isolated problem in the South. The right to challenge and undo the present effects of past discrimination, however, has been under assault for more than 40 years. For example, a case we handled for Lucy Walker challenged past racial discrimination from 1972 that was used in 1974 to deny her promotion to supervisor. *Walker v. Jefferson County Home*, 726 F.2d 1554, 1557–58 (11th Cir. 1984). The trial court found that the decision in 1974 was based on "prior supervisory experience" that was denied to her in 1972 during the period that the defendant had "a general policy, practice, or pattern of favoring whites over blacks for movement into supervisory positions." *Id.* The court held against her, however, by ruling that it was too late to challenge a decision in 1974 that incorporated past intentional discrimination that had occurred in 1972.

That ruling struck at the heart of the right to challenge *current* decisions or policies that are based on experience and qualifications that were intentionally denied to African Americans on a racial basis more than 180 days ago. Clients, however, often had no means to challenge *past* racial discrimination or segregation until its effect was carried forward to apply to them personally by denying them a *current* job opportunity or benefit. The Court of Appeals agreed with us, holding that individual decisions or policies are racially discriminatory and violate the act when they are based on criteria or reasons that incorporate past discrimination, or otherwise perpetuate its effect into the present, regardless of how long ago such past discrimination occurred or whether there was any current intent to discriminate. *Id.* at 1557–58. As Judge Tuttle said in the court's decision, black employees "were first denied the opportunity to obtain experience, and then were told they were 'unqualified' for promotion because they lacked the very quality that had intentionally been denied to them," and thereby "served to freeze the status quo of prior discriminatory employment practices." *Id.* at 1558.

The precedent established in Lucy Walker's case gave civil rights litigants an important right to challenge the disparate impact of qualifications like "prior experience" to prove *individual* claims of racial and gender discrimination. Before her case, there was a widespread but mistaken belief that disparate impact claims were only permissible in class actions. That allowed employers to avoid liability in an individual case by merely saying, not proving, that the plaintiff was not qualified or "best qualified" without any inquiry into whether such qualifications were themselves discriminatory because they had been spawned by the continuing effects of the defendant's past racial or sexual discrimination. Lucy Walker's case changed the focus of such cases by first examining the source of any differences in qualifications articulated by the defendant and whether they were merely the continuing effects of the defendant's past discriminatory practices.[11]

The Battle to Save Disparate Impact Cases from the Statute of Limitations

Corporate employers, however, did not quit there. They continued to push courts to do away with such claims by ruling that practices that perpetuate the effects of past discrimination that occurred more than 180 days ago are untimely notwithstanding the fact that the continuing effects of that past discrimination were *currently* being used to deny jobs and other opportunities. For over 30 years we successfully overcame that argument in cases like *Walker v. Jefferson County Home,* which held in 1984 that the present effects of past discrimination violate the 1964 Civil Rights Act even if that past discrimination occurred years earlier.

We faced that argument again in 1992 when the Court of Appeals similarly held that the present effects of past discrimination violate the act—that "a policy of denying insurance coverage to children who do not reside with their employee-parent . . . constitutes a continuing violation" regardless of whether it had been adopted years earlier. *Beavers v. American Cast Iron Pipe Co.*, 975 F.2d 792, 797–98 (11th Cir. 1992). A year later we faced another defendants' identical effort to dodge liability for the present effects of its past discrimination that the Court of Appeals rejected, holding once again that "this Circuit distinguishes between 'the present consequence of a one-time violation, which does not extend the limitations period, and the continuation of the violation into the present, which does.'" *Calloway v. Partners Nat'l Health Plans*, 986 F.2d 446, 448–49 (11th Cir. 1993).

That remained the law for the next twelve years until we faced yet another three-judge panel of the Eleventh Circuit in Lillie Ledbetter's case. See *Ledbetter v. Goodyear Tire*, 421 F.3d 1169 (11th Cir. 2005), *affirmed*, 550 U.S. 618 (2007). My partner, Jon Goldfarb, persuaded the jury to award Lillie $3 million as vindication for the years of wage discrimination she suffered, and Jon asked me to handle the appeal defending that verdict. This time the Court of Appeals went in the opposite direction from its prior decisions by vacating the jury's verdict that Goodyear was liable for paying her less than her male peers for the same job. The court ruled for the first time that the present effects of past discrimination are washed clean and are no longer discriminatory if that discrimination *began* more than 180 days before she filed an EEOC charge notwithstanding the fact that such past inequality in wages continued to be the basis for the same unequal wages that she was paid *within* that 180-day period and she first learned of that discrimination *within* that same 180 days. *Id.*

The Supreme Court granted our petition to hear Lillie Ledbetter's case, but it, too, held on a 5 to 4 vote that the present effects of past discrimination no longer violate the Civil Rights Act after 180 days. *Ledbetter v. Goodyear Tire & Rubber, Co.*, 550 U.S 618 (2007). Justice Ginsburg, however, read a stinging dissent from the bench, joined by three other justices, which documented the flaws in that decision and called for Congress to reverse it. A broad-based protest against the court's decision over the next 18 months led Congress to reverse the *Ledbetter* decision and pass the Lillie Ledbetter Fair Pay Act. President Obama signed that amendment of the 1964 Civil Rights Act as one of his first acts in office in January 2009. Lillie's Fair Pay Act adopted the legal standard that we had argued in her appeal and other cases throughout the prior 30 years—that the present effects of past discrimination violate the Civil Rights Act regardless of when that past discrimination occurred or was first discovered. That continues to be the law today.

Other Practices Challenged Because of Their Disparate Impact

Over the years we also challenged and obtained relief against an assortment of other practices that appeared to be nondiscriminatory on their face, but which adversely affected one race or sex at a substantially greater rate than anyone else. That included disparate impact claims brought against a "policy of denying insurance coverage to children who do not reside with their employee-parent" that discriminated on the basis of race and sex[12]; a policy granting a hiring preference to incumbent employees on study leave that was racially discriminatory[13]; a pay-raise policy based on annualized steps in a pay range that perpetuated past gender disparities in starting wages that were not protected by a "bona fide seniority system"[14]; a promotion rating policy based on a combination of racially discriminatory factors, such as sequential experience in lines of progression, "experience ratings," length of service, ranks on registers and performance evaluation scores[15]; a sexually discriminatory compensation scheme that used different criteria and procedures for traditionally male clerical jobs than those used for traditionally female clerical jobs[16]; a no-posting and word-of-mouth hiring and promotion process and wage-increase policy that perpetuated past racial discrimination in starting wage rates[17]; and a subjective selection process that perpetuated an immediate past history of racial discrimination.[18]

We also brought claims against practices that perpetuated not just the continuing effects of a defendant's own past discrimination but also the continuing effects of past societal discrimination or even basic biological differences between one race or gender and another. That included the racially disparate false-positive rates of a marijuana test that we challenged on behalf of a Southern Railway police sergeant who had been discharged on that test,[19] the racially disparate rates of garnishment disciplines and discharges that we challenged on the basis of societal differences in wealth and debt collection,[20] the racially skewed rates of misdemeanor arrests that we challenged on behalf of a class of rejected law enforcement hiring applicants based on societal differences in such arrests, and the disparate impact of a broad assortment of hiring and promotion tests that perpetuated societal differences in the education afforded black and white students in the South's racially segregated school systems.

Why Civil Rights Lawyers Were Scarce in the Early Years

Civil rights lawyers were relatively scarce in the 1960s, 1970s, and 1980s. The need for additional lawyers willing to handle civil rights cases as a regular part of their practice was initially caused by the fact that providing equal civil rights to African Americans and prohibiting racial prejudice or white privilege was still controversial in the South. There were also relatively few black lawyers allowed to practice law in the South because of its historically segregated law schools.[21]

The courageous exceptions were the cadre of black attorneys in the South who litigated school desegregation and other civil rights cases in the 1950s and 1960s along with attorneys from the NAACP Legal Defense and Education Fund (LDF), and they were still hewing to the task in the 1970s. The relatively few black attorneys who were able to obtain a license to practice law in those years usually had to leave the South or pursue correspondence courses to get a legal education. If they ever returned with a law degree and obtained a license to practice, they often faced daunting obstacles to handling civil rights cases as part of their practice due to the well-known risks and dangers of opposing the apartheid conditions that dominated the Deep South in those years. Birmingham, for example, was known as "Bombingham"—one of the most segregated and racially fearsome cities in the United States.[22] The dearth of African American attorneys with experience litigating civil rights cases dwindled even more as the older generation of civil rights attorneys who started practicing law in the 1950s and 1960s began to be elected or appointed to public office or moved into academic or corporate careers that had not previously been open to them in the South.

The well-known difficulty and risk of contingent-fee litigation of civil rights cases also contributed to the relatively small number of lawyers willing to accept such cases. The few who did typically had a general practice that provided them other means of support and left little time to handle civil rights cases on anything more than a sporadic or pro bono basis.[23] That changed very little in the first two decades of the 1964 Civil Rights Act when the body of law and precedent necessary to prevail in such a new area of law was still being developed and constantly changing.

The risk and difficulty of contingent-fee litigation of civil rights cases was exacerbated by the fact that there was relatively little settled law or precedent to rely on to evaluate or prosecute such cases, and what precedent did exist frequently varied from one court to another over time.

Lawyers handling civil rights cases in those years often had to successfully navigate a barrage of previously undecided procedural issues and defenses over a period of years before they could even hope to reach a trial on the merits or a final resolution of the case. The frequent need to appeal also increased the time and expense necessary to prevail, sometimes for years. Civil rights cases were also notoriously difficult because they were limited to nonjury trials before local federal judges from 1965 to 1991. Bench trials proved to be a particularly difficult and risky means of trial in many district judges' courtrooms in the Deep South before 1991 when jury trials were first allowed.[24]

Mississippi Center for Justice: Building Homegrown Capacity to Dismantle Mississippi's Historic Culture of Injustice

MARTHA BERGMARK

The Mississippi Center for Justice originated in the hearts of Mississippi civil rights lawyers who never stopped mourning the loss of the state's homegrown capacity for legal advocacy to advance racial justice.

At the height of the civil rights movement in the 1960s, Farish Street in Jackson was home to the Mississippi offices of the NAACP Legal Defense and Educational Fund, Lawyers' Committee for Civil Rights under Law, and the Lawyers Constitutional Defense Committee. But by 1980, all had shut down their local offices.

In 1968, federally funded legal services programs in Oxford and Jackson began to supplement the work of the national civil rights groups, but the legal services programs' focus on school desegregation cases was soon cut short by congressional restrictions. In the late 1970s, a new Legal Services Corporation–funded state support center began a focus on voting rights litigation that helped give Mississippi the highest number of Black elected officials in the nation. But this work came to an end in 1995, when Congress's termination of funding for state support centers (and a new prohibition on representation in redistricting cases) caused this program, too, to close its doors.

Thus, Mississippi—with its centuries-long history of racial injustice and its unfinished business of the civil rights era—was left at the turn of the new century with no concerted capacity for legal advocacy to advance racial justice. In 2002, a group of civil rights lawyers and other state leaders filed nonprofit incorporation papers and developed a fundraising strategy to change that, and the Mississippi Center for Justice—with its mission to advance racial and economic justice through systemic change—was born.

We set the ribbon-cutting for June 12, 2003, the fortieth anniversary of the slaying of Medgar Evers, the Mississippi civil rights hero who was gunned down as he returned home from a voting rights rally. We dedicated ourselves to the unfinished business of the movement for which Evers gave his life. And in 2023, as we commemorate both the sixtieth anniversary of Evers's death and celebrate MCJ's twentieth, we confront the continuing racial and economic disparities that are the legacy of slavery and Jim Crow.

Today, more than half a century after the historic advances of the civil rights movement, Mississippi remains our nation's poorest state as well as the state with the highest proportion of African Americans (38 percent). Both the civil rights movement and the War on Poverty produced significant gains for Mississippians, but we still score abysmally low on every measure of human well-being from infant mortality to educational attainment to family income. So MCJ's dual lens—racial and economic—is historically rooted, and it still makes sense. But as a practical matter, how does it play out?

In the Beginning: The Dirty Dozen

In 2003, with a first-year budget of $350,000 and a beginning staff of four, MCJ's founding board identified the state's worst social injustices—a list of the "dirty dozen" that became our radar screen for assessing opportunities for systemic change. The board adopted a campaign style of work designed to offer the right legal strategy at the right time to advance the social justice goals of our community partners, as well as to leverage the resources of national and regional support organizations.

Examples of our early successes included passage of the Juvenile Justice Reform Act of 2005, which imposed community-based alternatives to mass incarceration of Mississippi children, and the 2004 reinstatement, through litigation and subsequent legislation, of Medicaid benefits for 50,000 elderly and disabled Mississippians whose eligibility category had been eliminated by the governor. These victories exemplified an emerging method of work that included strong community partnerships, policy advocacy, impact litigation, media advocacy, and aggressive leveraging of national and regional resources.

Nature Intervenes: Hurricane Katrina

When Hurricane Katrina devastated the Mississippi Gulf Coast in 2005, MCJ immediately opened an office in Biloxi to address the overwhelming legal needs of individual survivors as well as to ensure equity in the development and implementation of recovery policies. Here, the magnitude of the need, matched by a generous outpouring of offers of assistance from all over the country, enabled us to grow our community lawyering approach to include direct legal services to individuals and incorporate the volunteer services of pro bono lawyers and law students. Indeed, putting in place a delivery system with the capacity to say yes to the offers of pro bono assistance became one of our biggest challenges.

Direct representation of thousands of Katrina survivors provided the basis for understanding how policy decisions about disaster recovery were playing out to the systematic disadvantage of low wealth and Black people and communities. Across the board, in Federal Emergency Management Agency decisions, grant programs, insurance coverage decisions, and evictions from rental housing, MCJ identified distinct patterns of discrimination based on race, economic status, and disability. To respond to them, we called upon every weapon in our community lawyering arsenal.

As a founding member of Steps, a grassroots coalition of nonprofit organizations committed to a healthy, just, and equitable recovery, MCJ worked closely with the Biloxi chapter of the NAACP, Lawyers' Committee for Civil Rights under Law, and many others to investigate, organize, educate, advocate, and litigate. We sought to tell—and change the ending of—the story of "two recoveries" on the coast. As one example of our success in that regard, MCJ and our partners challenged Mississippi governor Haley Barbour's diversion of federal funds, appropriated for low- and moderate-income housing recovery, to expand the state port of Gulfport. MCJ's federal lawsuit resulted in a settlement that required the state to commit $172 million to rebuild the homes of 6,000 families—disproportionately African American, low-income, and elderly—who were previously excluded from eligibility for assistance.

In the aftermath of Katrina, MCJ grew to a 2007 operating budget of $1.6 million with 15 staff members at offices in Jackson and Biloxi. We established long-term relationships with national advocacy organizations and law firms, expanding our influence and reach within the state, and putting us in better position to turn our attention toward the most challenged region of our state, the Mississippi Delta.

Digging Deeper: A Home in the Delta and Growing Advocacy Capacity Statewide

Located in northwest Mississippi, the Mississippi Delta has the largest concentration of Black people in the country—nearly 60 percent of the population—and the region stands out from the rest of the state in other ways, too: more income and wealth disparity, more poverty, fewer opportunities for high-quality education, and worse health outcomes. While the wealth gap and the racial disparities are glaring, there is hope. This is a region with a long history of political activism and leadership, having produced such civil rights pioneers as Fannie Lou Hamer and Aaron Henry. As we traveled there from our Jackson office to provide legal representation and community legal education, we witnessed the strong commitment to fight for a future that bridges economic and educational gaps, and we yearned to have a real presence there as a partner in that fight. In October 2011, following many months of planning, advance work, and fundraising, MCJ achieved its long-term goal of opening an office in the Delta city of Indianola, county seat of Sunflower County, where staff members focused their initial efforts on education and health advocacy.

Improving Mississippi's public education system is the necessary prerequisite to reducing the state's persistent high poverty and pervasive racial inequities. Poor education performance accounts for over half the state's economic gap, according to a recent study. The test scores of Mississippi schoolchildren in reading, writing, and mathematics sharply trail national averages. Within Mississippi, the test scores of Black students lag behind those of white students by significant margins. Efforts at systemic improvement have been hampered by funding disparities and by the resegregation of many public schools.

Nowhere is this situation more dire than in the Delta. For this reason, our educational opportunities director was based in Indianola, and our education team of attorneys and a community organizer pressed forcefully on the levers of change to keep children in school despite discipline and special education practices that, without our representation, would have pushed them out; to engage parents and communities in preserving and improving their neighborhood schools; and to promote equity and adequacy in school funding. Their work was concentrated in the Delta, Jackson, and the Gulf Coast, but suffered a setback when the principal foundation funder of this work shifted priorities. Today, we are rebuilding our efforts with a focus on assessing and addressing the impact of the COVID-19 pandemic on educational outcomes.

Our advocacy to improve access to affordable health care presents comparable challenges. Mississippi has the dubious distinction of having the lowest life expectancy in the nation. There are many causes for low longevity, and Mississippi has them all: inaccessible health care, high rates of controllable disease, low levels of education, generational poverty, and embedded racism. The Delta, in particular, leads the nation in infant mortality, teen pregnancy, and heterosexually acquired HIV/AIDS.

In the 2010s, the center battled unnecessary and burdensome bureaucratic impediments to the enrollment of eligible Medicaid recipients. We commissioned research that documented the adverse impact, in particular, of face-to-face recertification—a requirement imposed only in Mississippi—and advocated forcefully but unsuccessfully for elimination of this provision. We then turned our attention to an advocacy campaign to assure full and timely implementation of the Affordable Care Act, which, among many other benefits for low-income Mississippians, finally prohibits the bureaucratic churn and inequitable impact of face-to-face recertification. Despite the unrelenting advocacy of MCJ and community partners, however, Mississippi is one of 11 states that has yet to expand Medicaid benefits that would make health care available to some 200,000 eligible Mississippians.

Advocacy to promote financial inclusion has been another mainstay of MCJ's work. Mississippi's legacy of economic injustice has its roots in slavery and the sharecropping economy. Predatory lending is a national problem, but it has caused particular damage in Mississippi, the state with the highest per capita concentration of payday lending stores in the nation and where predatory lending is a racial justice issue. Payday lending and its cousins—check-cashers, pawnshops, rent-to-own outlets, and car-title lenders—are modern-day versions of the sharecropper's plantation store, with their crushing cycle of debt. Under Jim Crow, Black people also suffered discrimination at the hands of mainstream financial institutions, and a legacy of distrust remains. Today, more than 16 percent of the state's residents lack a checking or savings account, the highest such rate in the nation.

When our efforts over several years to reform payday lending through policy change came up short, we decided we needed a new approach. New Roots Credit Partnership brings employers, community leaders, and financial institutions together to engage Mississippians who have been shut out of the economic mainstream for generations. The program combines public education, grassroots outreach, and workforce development with responsible and fair lending products, but it has not grown as fast as we would have liked for lack of adequate investment. In the meantime, we've developed "navigator programs" in Jackson and in several Delta counties to assist individual defendants in consumer debt cases to understand and exercise their rights in small claims courts.

MCJ provides direct services to individuals to secure their legal rights in the areas of fair housing, criminal record expungement, and heir property. We complement this direct services work with systemic advocacy and impact litigation under the auspices of our George Riley Impact Litigation Initiative. For example, in 2021, after the US Supreme Court reversed the conviction of Curtis Flowers for prosecutorial misconduct, MCJ represented Mr. Flowers to secure his release from prison after spending 23 years on death row for a crime he did not commit, and to secure dismissal of the charges against him. In *Dobbs v. Jackson Women's Health Organization*, the landmark 2022 US Supreme Court case that overturned women's longstanding constitutional right to abortion, MCJ was co-counsel for Mississippi's last remaining provider of abortion services.

Today, MCJ has an operating budget of $4 million, and our 30 staff members include lawyers, community organizers, communications professionals, policy analysts, and pro bono counsel at offices in Jackson, Biloxi, and Indianola.

The Backstory: Why Me?

This origin story of MCJ begs a more personal question: why did this project have *my* name on it? The decade I spent as MCJ's founding president and CEO (followed by another decade as an MCJ board member) marks the closing chapter of my lifelong interrogation of the question of race and my career-long commitment to building legal capacity to attack racial and economic injustice.

The opening chapter begins with my family's move in 1953 from the Texas Hill Country hamlet of Hunt—where my father pastored and my mother directed the choir of a small Methodist congregation of ranchers, ranch hands, and their families—to Jackson, Mississippi. I was four years old, and Mississippi became my broken home. It is the place that molded me, and I have spent a lifetime trying to understand and even to fix it. I grew up in Jackson in the 1950s and '60s, when divorce was becoming more common, and "coming from a broken home" captured the stigma that still clung to it. In my case, the divorce was not between my parents but between the safe and nurturing space they provided their three children and the entrenched culture of injustice and danger around us.

Awareness of the disconnect came early. At five, I rode along as we took Sue Harris across the railroad tracks to the unpainted shotgun house where she lived. I learned to call her Sue, though she was old enough to be my grandmother. She worked as a maid for the family of my father's new colleague in the philosophy department at Millsaps College. For a few months she came to our house—long enough for me to sense my mother's discomfort that despite her entreaties, Sue kept strictly to "her place"— eating in the kitchen, riding in the back seat of the car. Long enough for me to intuit that this had something to do with skin color, and that there was something deeply unjust about the stark disparity between Sue's all-black neighborhood of narrow, unpaved streets and dilapidated housing and my more prosperous, all-white one.

At ten, the situation was becoming clearer to me. Mrs. Massey, my fifth-grade teacher whom I adored, lectured us one day about why we didn't—and shouldn't want to—go to school with "colored children." Not as smart as us, not clean, all the racist stereotypes carefully enumerated. At the dinner table that night—sensing, I think, that I would get pushback—I said how glad I was I didn't have to go to school with colored children. My father asked why, and I repeated all the reasons Mrs. Massey had laid out. Rather than contradict me, he shared a story of his own—how honored he felt to attend a recent lunch meeting with Ralph Bunche, who was in town to meet with local civil rights activists. He pronounced Mr. Bunche, a Negro, one of the wisest, most impressive people he had ever met.

Galloway Memorial Methodist church—Mississippi's flagship, all-white United Methodist institution—deserves a mention here. As an ordained Methodist minister, my father had the option to maintain his conference membership in Texas or to move it to Mississippi, and he chose the former. But he and my mother were committed churchgoers, and the local church they chose for us was Galloway. Its imposing Greek Revival architecture and prime location adjacent to the state capitol grounds befitted its status as the church of choice for Jackson's Methodist elite. Jackson's Mayor Allen Thompson—soon to become a notorious enforcer of the city's rigid segregation laws—held court on Sunday mornings from his seat on the center aisle. My mother was the contralto soloist in the church choir, my father was frequently called upon to teach adult classes, and we children were faithful Sunday school, junior choir, and youth fellowship participants. This was all routine enough until I was about 12, when Galloway emerged as the main venue for my continuing education about race.

The policy issue that split Galloway's pastoral and lay leadership was whether to continue the church's historic practice of barring Black people from attending services. Over many months, weekly visits by integrated groups sought to test this local violation of national church policy. Church ushers assumed a new role as bouncers who summoned police to arrest these would-be worshippers on the front steps. We children entertained ourselves in the interim between Sunday school and the main service by watching the action. This went on for about a year before reaching a climax on Easter Sunday 1964 when two Methodist bishops, one Black and one white, were denied entry, prompting widespread national news coverage. I watched as a friend's father became enraged enough to attack a TV cameraman, hurling his camera to the ground, and chasing him out of the parking lot. The raw hatred I witnessed in that one incident made more of an impression on me than did the long series of tortured justifications our lay teachers offered, citing various biblical sources in defense of "our southern way of life."

By the time I was 14, in 1963, it required no breathtaking insight to appreciate that my home, Mississippi, was deeply broken by its centuries-long deal with the devil of white supremacy. The entrenched culture of injustice was coming face to face with a righteous and organized resistance. I was a white teenager, absorbed most of the time with the typical concerns of childhood. But when Medgar Evers—Jackson's own exemplar of civil rights leadership and courage—was murdered, I felt an impotent rage. As I learned only much later, his home—a small, ranch-style rambler—was almost identical to the one I grew up in just a few miles away. Almost identical, except that Mr. Evers built his home without a front door—a valiant but vain effort to shield his vulnerable family from danger.

Evers had fought in the US Army in Europe during World War II, only to return home to a state where slavery had been replaced by Jim Crow laws that institutionalized discrimination in every aspect of life. Before long, he applied unsuccessfully to become the first Black person to attend the law school at the University of Mississippi and led sit-ins and boycotts of businesses that practiced segregation, even though he knew that challenging the white power structure could cost his life.

For many of us in Jackson, white as well as Black, the assassination of Medgar Evers was a turning point. We were forced to ask ourselves with regard to the growing civil rights movement, "Where do I stand, and what am I willing to risk?" For me, it meant getting summer jobs as a teacher aide, first in Mississippi's first Head Start program and later in the first Upward Bound program at Tougaloo College. In this, my parents were entirely supportive—a situation I knew distinguished me from virtually all my peers, whose parents would never have countenanced such a thing. For a good while, I was able to wall off my budding civil rights activism from my life as a student at all-white Murrah High School.

The Murrah Eight

The life-changing moment for me came at 16, in 1965, when eight new classmates at Murrah instilled in me the idea that I could do something to fix my broken home and inspired in me the courage to try. The "Murrah Eight" followed in the footsteps of the more famous Little Rock Nine, who desegregated Little Rock's Central High School in 1957. This was almost a decade later because Mississippi officials more fiercely resisted the Supreme Court's mandate that separate was not equal.

That summer, the NAACP chapter president called to invite me to meet with the Murrah Eight before school started. They wanted to know what to expect, and frankly, I was terrified for them. The best they could expect was to be ostracized by almost everyone, to be excluded from all activities except their classes, to be ignored or bullied by some teachers who had made their racist views well known to us white students. I tried not even to imagine what might be the worst they could expect. This was barely a year after the murders and church bombings of the Freedom Summer, and just two years after Medgar Evers was murdered.

I could not imagine having their sheer courage. As the first day of school approached, I took to praying for them every night. I was praying for me too. I was praying I might have the courage—just a small fraction of theirs of course, but enough to stand up for my convictions on that first day of school. Enough to openly welcome my new classmates, to sit with them at lunch, to be shunned by my friends, and maybe worse.

I did muster the courage of my convictions that day, but as for my eight new classmates, they endured a miserably difficult senior year. My friend Brenda White Swaggard told me—a full half century later—that sometimes the psychic wounds still feel fresh. But Brenda and all the Murrah Eight persevered to become my high school's first black graduates. Their courage inspires me to this day. Indeed, I credit their example for setting me on my life course as a civil rights and civil legal aid lawyer.

Staying the Course

Undeniably, the heroic movement that Evers, the Murrah Eight, and many others inspired brought an end to legal apartheid and transformed my home state and our country in important ways.

I was fortunate to have a part in that. My connections to the people and events of the Mississippi civil rights movement put me on a path to Oberlin College and Michigan Law School. At law school and during summer internships at North Mississippi Rural Legal Services in Oxford, I prepared to return home as a civil rights lawyer, met my future husband Elliott Andalman, and persuaded him to join me. In 1973, we opened a civil rights law firm in Hattiesburg, successfully litigating cases to secure voting, employment, and fair housing rights, and starting the area's first civil legal aid program, where I was founding executive director. In 1987, we moved with sons Aaron and David to Washington, DC, where I served tenures as president of the Legal Services Corporation, administering federal funding to legal aid groups nationwide, and as senior vice president at the National Legal Aid & Defender Association, directing the Project for the Future of Equal Justice that sparked the creation of MCJ.

But our work as a nation to achieve racial and economic justice is far from done. It is not just that the right to vote is once again under attack in many states, including Mississippi, and even, shockingly, by the US Supreme Court's decisions to nullify the Voting Rights Act's most powerful enforcement tool and to diminish its force in other ways. More than that, de facto segregation and discrimination continue to threaten opportunities for access to education, health care, financial services, and the job market. Nationally, the unemployment rate is about twice as high for Blacks as for whites. On average, Black and Latino families have about one-sixth the wealth of white families. Fewer than half of Black males graduate from high school. Black people are incarcerated at nearly six times the rate of whites.

After Medgar Evers was killed, his widow Myrlie Evers offered consolation and hope to his grieving friends and family by telling them, "You can kill a man, but you can't kill an idea." Whenever I feel discouraged about the slow pace of change—or worse, the scary backsliding of recent years—I reflect on the courage of people like Medgar and Myrlie Evers and the Murrah Eight who challenged injustice no matter what the price. Because of them, I can continue to believe that though the arc of history is long it bends toward justice. The magnetic field of Mississippi still repels me with its brokenness but draws me to the possibility of its redemption.[25]

Notes

1. The Supreme Court essentially nullified the original ban on racial discrimination by private parties in the Civil Rights Act of 1866 by restricting it to "state action." Those decisions in the 1880s ushered in the Jim Crow era of racial segregation and violence that dominated the South for the next eight decades. It was not until 1964 that Congress eventually got around to passing legislation, from 1964 to 1972, that provided a means of combatting and undoing the prior century of Jim Crow segregation and racial bias in virtually every aspect of life—jobs, voting, housing, health care, unions and public places, services and accommodations.
2. Once the 1964 act became effective, the pent-up effects of the past century of racial segregation came rushing forward and quickly overwhelmed the EEOC and other civil rights agencies that Congress had just created to administer the act. Hundreds of thousands of discrimination charges flooded into those agencies each year and largely left them broken and ineffective for years to come. Even as late as 1975, I was being asked to represent individuals whose claims had been stuck in the EEOC since the late 1960s and early 1970s. See, e.g., Fowler v. Blue Bell, Inc., 596 F.2d 1276, 1278–79 (5th Cir. 1979), holding that a 1970 claim for hiring discrimination could not be dismissed because of the EEOC's inexcusable six-year delay in processing the charge. The 1964 act did not create or fund any public agencies with the authority to prosecute civil enforcement actions administratively or in federal courts similar to the enforcement powers that Congress provided for the National Labor Relations Act on which the 1964 act was modeled.
3. Because the Constitution prohibited ex post facto laws against pre-act conduct that did not carry forward into the post-1964 time period, lawyers filing the first wave of cases under the 1964 Civil Rights Act had to concentrate most of their resources and efforts on establishing a convincing body of precedent that Congress intended to prohibit practices that carry forward the effects of past discrimination into the post-act time period even if there is no present intent to discriminate. Corporate employers and unions argued that discriminatory policies that originated before Congress passed the 1964 act could not be challenged or declared illegal ex post facto based on the continuing effects of such pre-1964 discrimination in the post-1964 period. A substantial part of the first decade of the 1964 act was spent litigating such cases.
4. Judicial antipathy to civil rights was apparent in courtrooms across the South, and that was slow to change because the South's segregationist senators still had inordinate control over federal judicial appointments both before and after the 1964 Civil Rights Act became effective. The district judge in *Pettway* had been appointed in 1946 and was well thought of on issues other than civil rights. The nation's quest for equal opportunity and racial justice in the Deep South depended on a fairly small number of district court judges who were willing to faithfully follow the law, as well as a Court of Appeals that was dedicated to assuring impartial enforcement of civil rights throughout the circuit. Consequently, appeals were a critical component of civil rights litigation and often offered the only means for many meritorious civil rights cases to have any realistic hope of succeeding.

5 Before May 1975, employees in a department could bid on all departmental vacancies based on their department seniority, but the new system substituted in 1975 was based on sequential position in departmental lines of progression that restricted bidding to employees in the same or next-lower level of the line of progression who were almost invariably white in the historically white departments. ACIPCO's past tests for promotions were based on knowledge, skills, and abilities that were only obtainable in the historically white jobs and departments, not the predominantly black departments. Such tests also perpetuated the effect of the South's racially segregated schools that provided African Americans inferior education and training.
6 Black employees were also discouraged from bidding for transfer to the better-paying white departments by the fact that, once there, they would still be unable to compete equally with white employees who had gained greater seniority in the department and higher positions in the line of progression as beneficiaries of ACIPCO's past racial segregation and discriminatory testing practices. *Pettway*, 576 F.2d at 1185–86 (citing *Pettway III*, 494 F.2d at 223–24, 235–36).
7 During those same years, the early progress in dismantling the continuing effects of past discrimination began to suffer a gradual retrenchment. In 1977, the Supreme Court held that the discriminatory effect of a "bona fide seniority system" cannot be enjoined without evidence that its "genesis" was intended to discriminate based on race, sex, ethnicity, or another prohibited category. That ruling made it much more difficult to prevail in cases like *Pettway* that had held the exact opposite—that seniority policies that perpetuate *past intentional discrimination* violate the Civil Rights Act without proof of a *present intent* to discriminate. The Supreme Court's decision, however, was limited to "seniority systems" and did not apply to other practices that perpetuated the continuing effects of past discrimination, like the tests and "prior experience" requirements in *Pettway* and other cases. The Supreme Court did not attempt to curtail the right to challenge nonseniority practices that disproportionately affected black employees or women until a later series of controversial decisions in the mid- to late 1980s. Those decisions were so at odds with a large body of prior precedent and congressional intent that they spurred Congress to reverse them and amend the Civil Rights Act in 1991 for practices other than seniority systems.
8 Examples of cases in which we challenged prior experience that perpetuated past racial or sexual discrimination included Walker v. Jefferson County Home, 726 F.2d 1554, 1557–58 (11th Cir. 1984); Brown, et al. v. Nucor, 576 F.3d 149 (4th Cir. 2009); *cert. denied*, 559 U.S. 974 (2010); Brown v. Nucor, 785 F.3d 895 (4th Cir. 2015); 4th Scott, et al. v. Family Dollar Stores, Inc., 733 F.3d 105 (4th Cir. 2013), *cert. denied*, 134 S. Ct. 2871 (2014); Powers v. Alabama Dep't of Education, 854 F.2d 1285, 1292–93 (11th Cir. 1988); Harris v. Birmingham Bd. of Educ., 712 F.2d 1377, 1383 (11th Cir. 1983).
9 The initial growth beyond a single-lawyer practice came one lawyer at a time, starting with Mike Quinn joining with me in 1976, my brother, Greg, joining us in 1979 as a law clerk while he went to law school, and Bob Childs working with us on various cases in 1983–85 after having represented ACIPCO in the *Pettway* and *Cox* cases.

10 The district court ultimately dismissed the three counts of the complaint based on violations of the Federal-Aid Highway Act with prejudice, but the court of appeals vacated that ruling on appeal, holding that those claims must be restored "without prejudice . . . if the state and federal defendants do not comply with applicable state and federal laws"; see Alabama State Tenants Organization v. Bass, 549 F.2d 961, 963 (5th Cir. 1977). The Fifth Circuit affirmed that certain other claims were temporarily premature once work ceased after the complaint was filed. Id.
11 Even as late as the 1980s, the Reagan administration was doing everything it could to roll back many of the most important civil rights precedents, programs, and regulations from the prior 20 years. By 1989, those efforts had undermined sufficient precedent to force Congress to amend the Civil Rights Act in 1991 to undo several decisions that threatened the ability to effectively litigate disparate impact claims or otherwise challenge the present effects of past racial or sexual prejudice.
12 Beavers v. American Cast Iron Pipe Co., 975 F.2d 792, 797–98 (11th Cir. 1992).
13 Craig v. Alabama State University, 804 F.2d 682, 685–86 (11th Cir. 1986): "[W]here, as here, the employer in the past exercised a pattern of racial discrimination, the failure to consider outside applicants necessarily impacts more harshly on minorities because the preference operates to their total exclusion and to the benefit of the employer's racially skewed workforce. The utilization of a hiring preference in such circumstances, as we see it, is the plainest means possible of perpetuating the status quo of a racially imbalanced workforce."
14 Mitchell v. Jefferson County Bd. of Educ., 936 F.2d 539, 545–46 (11th Cir. 1991): "The effect of this [annual step pay increase] process was to perpetuate past wage discrepancies that were unrelated to seniority because of the manner in which each employee's original position on the schedule was determined."
15 Powers v. Alabama Dep't of Education, 854 F.2d 1285, 1292–93 (11th Cir. 1988): holding promotion process can be challenged for perpetuating past racial discrimination when based on sequential line-of-progression experience, length of service, training and experience ratings, register ranks, and performance evaluation scores.
16 Cox v. American Cast Iron Pipe Co., 784 F.2d 1546, 1560–61 (11th Cir. 1986): holding "policy of paying men's clerical jobs and women's clerical jobs on two entirely different compensation schemes is discriminatory" because "traditionally male jobs in the manufacturing division are compensated 'objectively' based on a system of detailed job descriptions, standardized evaluations, and publicly-known job classifications, pay scales and review provisions, while compensation for non-manufacturing women's jobs is subjectively determined." "At a minimum, this claim if proved entitles plaintiffs to injunctive relief against the disparate compensation schemes, and the trial court erred in failing to grant such an injunction," cert. denied, 479 U.S. 883 (1986).
17 Carmichael v. Birmingham Saw Works, 738 F.2d 1126, 1132–34 (11th Cir. 1984): "The defendant used no formal procedures for posting notice of available promotions or for determining who would be offered the promotion. Instead, the company relied on "word of mouth" and informal review procedures"; id. at 1136: "Once the court found that the defendant had a practice of initial wage discrimination this was enough to create an inference that all successive wage disparities were the product of racial discrimination."

18 Harris v. Birmingham Bd. of Educ., 712 F.2d 1377, 1383 (11th Cir. 1983): "The record reveals that no objective standards or policies were promulgated by the BOE regarding the hiring of head coaches within the Birmingham school system. [P]roof of an immediate past history of racial discrimination alone can be sufficient to shift . . . the burden of justifying its employment decisions by clear and convincing evidence."

19 Chaney v. Southern R. Co., 847 F.2d 718, 725 (11th Cir. 1988): "If the [marijuana] test in fact has a substantial adverse impact upon a protected group, whether or not Southern Railway intended it to do so, then Chaney would have stated a *prima facie* case."

20 Keenan v. American Cast Iron Pipe Co., 707 F.2d 1274, 1278 (11th Cir. 1983): holding reprimands and discharges based on garnishments can be challenged on disparate impact grounds and that "[t]he district court abused its discretion in refusing to certify a class of employees who had been reprimanded or discharged for violating ACIPCO's garnishment policy."

21 As late as 1970, only three black law students had ever been admitted to the University of Alabama Law School, and they had only been recently admitted and had a ways to go before graduating.

22 The experience of Oscar Adams as an African American attorney in the 1950s and 1960s in Birmingham is telling. He had to leave Alabama in the 1940s to get a legal education, and when he returned to practice law, he had to file a lawsuit just to be allowed inside the courtroom rail to approach the bench or to be addressed and respected on the same basis as the white attorneys in the same courtroom. Despite the obstacle of his race, he handled civil rights cases for many years with the NAACP Legal Defense and Education Fund in desegregating schools, employers, and other institutions in Alabama. After three decades, he left his law practice to become the first African American justice of the Alabama Supreme Court in 1980 as well as the first African American to win a statewide election in Alabama since Reconstruction.

23 Even when a client eventually prevailed, it was often still necessary to litigate whether the hours and hourly rates for such work were "reasonable." Traditional percentage-based fee contracts were not suited to most employment discrimination cases in those years because the 1964 Civil Rights Act did not allow compensatory or punitive damages, and back pay awards were almost always too small to justify the time and expense that such cases typically took to prevail in an individual case or even in many class actions.

24 The advent of jury trials in 1991 did not end the risk and difficulty of litigating civil rights cases as a regular part of a law practice. Once jury trials were allowed, defendants' use of summary judgment motions vastly increased to avoid juries. That made it nearly as difficult to prevail in cases before the same judges who had made it unduly difficult to prevail in the bench-trial era. Summary judgment motions had been rare before 1991 because bench trials gave district judges an easier means of disposing of cases and avoiding appellate reversal by basing their decision on credibility. That changed as soon as jury trials were allowed in 1991. From then on, summary judgment motions were routine in virtually every case—the rule, not exception.

25 The early sections of this piece are adapted from and expand on the author's 2013 article for the *Clearinghouse Review Journal of Poverty Law and Policy*, "Unfinished Business: The Mission of the Mississippi Center for Justice." The author gratefully acknowledges the assistance of Matt Williams, then a policy analyst at MCJ, with research and footnoting for that article.

Conclusion

Where Are We Going?

Imagine and Create the Third Reconstruction

BARBARA PHILLIPS

I was stunned by the loss of my first voting rights case in Mississippi. Every relevant case affirmed that Hinds County violated the rights of Black Mississippians when it moved numerous polling places only in Black communities right before an election. Defendants' opposing memorandum failed to cite even a single case. I dressed carefully for my first appearance in the federal court of the Southern District of Mississippi. My ophthalmologist sent flowers to bolster my resolve. Frank Parker, chief counsel of the Mississippi Office of the Lawyers' Committee for Civil Rights under Law, determined that I was well prepared. I wanted my clients to know the law affirmed their dignity and humanity as expressed through the right to citizenship. What could go wrong?

When I walked into the formal and imposing room in which federal district court judge Harold Cox heard motions, I took a seat opposite the attorney representing defendants, as was the custom, at the long conference table populated by white men. They looked. You could have heard a mouse tiptoeing through cotton. Judge Cox, looking like a racist judge from Hollywood central casting and a segregationist who referred to Blacks from the bench as "baboons," entered and sat at the head of the table. His gaze landed upon me, his eyes widened as if startled, and he shouted down the table "Where are you from?" I explained I was with the Lawyers' Committee and represented plaintiffs. To which he responded with louder amazement, "No, I mean where are you FROM?!" I repeated my answer word-for-word while breathing as slowly as I could and keeping my shaking hands under the table. Clearly dissatisfied, he nevertheless moved on. Judge Cox ruled against my clients.

Frank helped me recover by telling me three things: (1) "In the Southern District of Mississippi, consider yourself an audience in the theater of the absurd"; (2) "Our passion gives us 'staying power' that defense counsel can't match" and (3) "Never forget the Fifth Circuit Court of Appeals and the Supreme Court." (Actually, there was a fourth, "Be sure the scent of Magnolias wafts off the pages of your brief to the Fifth Circuit.") The next time Judge Cox ruled against me, he actually said with pride, "I know you'll take this down to the Fifth Circuit and they'll reverse. They've got a big 'ole bat down there to hit it right back to me." Of course, he was reversed—often.

When I appeared before Judge Cox in that 1978 case, I was asserting claims under Section 5 of the Voting Rights Act of 1965 and, when I appealed his decision, the Fifth Circuit Court of Appeals protected the rights of my clients. We won.

Voting rights lawyers today cannot prevent Hinds County from engaging in the same behavior. The legal protection provided for my clients in 1978 by the Voting Rights Act was found unconstitutional by the US Supreme Court in 2013. In addition to decisions affecting voting rights, the Supreme Court has now recognized corporations as "persons" with the First Amendment right to corrupt our democracy with political contributions. In *Dobbs v. Jackson Women's Health Organization*, the Supreme Court has stripped women of the fundamental right to abortion and the decision has far-reaching impacts upon the rights of everyone to dignity, autonomy, and privacy with an interpretation of the Constitution that foreshadows more demolition of personal freedoms and privacy protections.

I often wondered how people felt during the demise of the First Reconstruction after only a ten-year period of Reconstruction following the Civil War. Now, I know. Another Mississippi example: litigation under the Voting Rights Act of 1965 created the conditions for 27 Black Representatives (previously one) and one Black senator, Mr. Henry Kirksey, to be elected to the Mississippi legislature and the election of the first Black congressman from Mississippi since the First Reconstruction. Chief Counsel Frank Parker led this assault upon White supremacy, and later entitled his book "Black Votes Count" as the triumphant exclamation point to the success of these years of struggle to include Black citizens in the full citizenship of "We the People" with opportunities to elect candidates of their choice and to participate fully in the political process by influencing the laws under which they were governed. Now, those elected representatives have little to no influence in the legislation passed by the all-white, radical, right-wing Republican solid majority in the state legislature and approved of by a governor eager to enact legislation and policies hostile to the 1,124,000 Black residents (38 percent of the population) of the state, growing Latino population, and any group considered "Other." Now, I know.

While I had reason to be confident of prevailing whenever I took a civil rights case to the Fifth Circuit Court of Appeals, today's civil rights lawyers face a landscape in which the Supreme Court has shredded civil rights laws as well as what were established by previous Supreme Court decisions as protections of the Thirteenth, Fourteenth, and Fifteenth Amendments to the Constitution. The goal of full citizenship for Black folks, Latinos, other people of color, and LGBTQ people as well as constitutional protections for noncitizens are rendered virtually impossible by this Supreme Court. And yet I recently listened to younger civil rights lawyers at the Mississippi Center for Justice speak with passion and with such smarts about representing the interests of their clients in Mississippi. What is the future for their clients and communities when the federal judiciary is now loaded with judges who emulate Harold Cox; when the "old Fifth Circuit" judges like John Minor Wisdom, Elbert Tuttle, and John Brown have been replaced by right-wing ideologues. The US Supreme Court now has a radical, right-wing majority. What is the path forward when federal judges of district courts, courts of appeal, and the Supreme Court replicate the complicity of federal courts in the demise of the First Reconstruction with an ideology that returns us to the darkest days of the nineteenth and twentieth centuries?

I sat in the San Francisco garden of Denise Hulett, one of the best voting rights litigators in the country, when our conversation pondered today's civil rights crisis in the midst of serious threats to democracy. We looked back to the First Reconstruction following the Civil War that brought the Thirteenth, Fourteenth, and Fifteenth Amendments to the Constitution ending slavery, expanding citizenship and the equal protection and due process of law to formerly enslaved people, and reconfiguring the relationship of the federal government and the states. However, that Reconstruction was abandoned after only ten years, marked by the Supreme Court decision *Plessy v. Ferguson* in 1896 concluding that state-mandated racial segregation laws did not violate the Equal Protection Clause of the Fourteenth Amendment. The resulting retrenchment—embodied most visibly in Jim Crow laws and white terrorism—endured well into the 1960s.

The Second Reconstruction—generated by lawyers, advocates, and communities who formed the ideas, community action, and litigation that delivered the 1954 Supreme Court decision in *Brown v. Board of Education*—brought about federal legislation such as the Civil Rights Act of 1964, the Voting Rights Act of 1965, federal legislation prohibiting discrimination on the basis of sex and disability, and more. Supreme Court decisions interpreted those federal laws and the Constitution to embrace an ever-expanding circle of people previously excluded from those recognized by law, policy, and culture as being among "We the People" of the Preamble to the US Constitution. Now, we face a well-financed backlash to this Second Reconstruction from the same ideologies and political and economic interests that, with the complicity of federal courts, destroyed the First Reconstruction. Fortunately, we are ready to emulate the boldness of Charles Hamilton Houston by first imagining the world we want to live in and, then, developing our strategies to create that world.

Litigators and other advocates who together with courageous communities created the conditions for progressive advances of the Second Reconstruction must now sit with—literally sit with—today's civil rights lawyers, social justice advocates, and philanthropic leaders to discern a coherent strategy for the way forward in the spirit of Sankofa. The word "Sankofa" comes from the Akan people of Ghana and literally means "to go back and get it." One of the symbols for Sankofa depicts a mythical bird with its feet firmly planted forward and its head turned backward. To the Akan, it is this wisdom in learning from the past that ensures a strong future. We must imagine a third Reconstruction, and then craft how we get there together. The time is now.

As civil rights lawyers, social justice advocates, and the communities they serve discern the way forward, foundations and individual donors must support and engage with transformative thinking as well. Tinkering around the edges simply enables the advance of radical, right-wing ideology. As Paul DiDonato, president of Proteus Fund, has noted:

> [T]hink about some of the major challenges pro-justice, equality, democracy funders (and organizations on the ground) continue to grapple with around breaking out of silos and achieving intersectionality. The radical forces we are pushing back against today found intersectionality and successful strategies to rise above siloed tactics (and funding streams) before we did. And, they have effectively taken both approaches further than we have.
>
> The question and the challenge we are faced with at this moment is whether foundation and individual donors can ground their work

in more accurate and insightful historical and political analyses while figuring out—quickly—ways to make similar strategic progress so that we can effectively work with our partners to realize the world we desire before the vision is completely out of reach.

I want to highlight five prongs of "more accurate and insightful historical and political analyses" that should be considered in any meaningful effort to develop new and complementary visions and strategies for the third Reconstruction. First, community organizing and political participation. Second, analysis of all Supreme Court cases concerning race. Third, Professor John Brittain's call for lawyers to deprioritize litigation and prioritize policy advocacy and popular public education. Fourth, Thomas A. Saenz, president and general counsel of the Mexican American Legal Defense and Educational Fund (MALDEF) calls for Civil Rights 2.0 to take us beyond the Black/White paradigm for our multiracial present and future; to understand the totality of the Constitution as a tool to advance civil rights by developing strategic, creative litigation; and to recalibrate our understanding of "winning." Fifth, Denise Hulett suggests that we reimagine the War College as a space for annual, critical reflection, and intergenerational engagement assessing our vision and strategies. We must also reimagine how we do our work consistent with our values. Each of these aspects will be summarized below.

Community Organizing and Political Participation

Community organizing and political participation function generally as separate planets within a universe of civic engagement. However, in political jurisdictions where these two planets aligned, progressives made significant progress during the 2020 elections. By engaging with 26 of the organizers who made that happen, Linda Burnham, Max Elbaum, and Maria Pobley, editors of the recent book *Power Concedes Nothing: How Community Organizing Wins Elections*, show us a way to advance toward the world we want to live in with respect to heightened civic engagement and, equally significant, our understanding of the policies and procedures needed to sustain that world.

A Study of Every US Supreme Court Case Concerning Race

Legendary civil rights litigator Armand Derfner and historian Vernon Burton offer the first complete analysis of every Supreme Court case concerning race in their recent book *Justice Deferred: Race and the Supreme*

Court. Revealing that the court as an institution has been a source of oppression as well as liberation, Derfner and Burton explore not only the legal issues resolved in these cases but also illuminate the human beings and life of the communities that gave rise to these important landmarks of national jurisprudence. This study is a necessary foundation for a more visionary articulation of what the law ought to be.

Deprioritize Litigation and Prioritize Policy Advocacy and Education

In his thoughtful essay *Advocating for the People: The Role of Civil Rights Lawyers,* Professor John C. Brittain warns, "While Houston and Marshall were able to use well-conceived and well-litigated legal cases to expand the civil rights of people, the Houstonian approach should not be utilized to advance civil rights causes at this time," noting that today's Supreme Court is "vying for opportunities to restrict personal freedoms and civil rights."

Brittain proposes limiting the commencement of lawsuits except in certain state courts, and engaging in litigation only where necessary to defend attacks on civil rights laws, policies, and procedures; avoiding the Supreme Court unless defending major challenges to civil rights such as in the *Jackson Women's Health Organization* case.

He proposes what is known as the "Learned Hand approach" in determining whether to engage in litigation likely to reach the Supreme Court and for activists to consider in their deliberations a particular course of action. The approach "essentially seeks to define reasonable behavior as that which produces benefits in excess of costs." For lawyers, that evaluation should include the likelihood that others will be injured and balance the risks to not only the interest of their client but also of a host of others who seek to avoid further injury to proclaimed civil rights and entitlements. Activists should use the approach "so all actions in the name of civil rights advancement produce benefits that exceed the cost of engagement." He warns, "the failed attempt to eradicate the harm suffered by one person can cause the erosion of civil rights for all people." This approach requires reassessing not only the sacrifice of potential justice for plaintiff but also Tom Saenz's suggestion that we recalibrate "winning" (which makes the case that "losing" in the particular case may yet prove fruitful).

Brittain also illuminates the view of Wade Henderson, former president at the Leadership Conference for Civil and Human Rights, prioritizing public policy advocacy to change nominating and confirming federal judges and advocacy for the judiciary to be the apolitical branch it was created to be. Brittain argues for expansive civic engagement extending beyond Election Day voting to massive demonstrations as well as participating fully in the political process through every means of communication: letter writing, postcards, phone calls, and social media campaigns to influence legislation at the local, state, and national levels. Further, he focuses upon repealing the doctrine of qualified immunity as a step toward ensuring that laws are enforced. Popular education about civil rights, the history of discrimination, and the restorative right to reparations are important components of the programming Brittain suggests.

Civil Rights 2.0—What the Law Ought to Be—Coupled with Appreciation for Strategic, Creative Litigation and Recalibrating "Winning"

Thomas A. Saenz responds to the call from *Justice Deferred* to consider "what the law OUGHT to be" and opens a wide door to opportunity noting that the historical Black/white paradigm at the foundation of our civil rights jurisprudence no longer serves our interest in recognizing and deterring every form of irrational discrimination. With its experience of trying to fit challenges to the daily experience of discrimination into legal frameworks that were developed for the Black/white paradigm, the experience of the Latino community takes us to "the cutting edge in pursuit of a broader conception of civil rights law—encompassing not just the post–Civil War amendments, but structural provisions in the Constitution like the First Amendment, Supremacy Clause, the Contracts Clause, and the Tenth Amendment." Noting that the right wing has a comprehensive theory of the Constitution, Saenz asks that we also see the entire Constitution as a civil rights tool. Saenz recognizes this moment as one of opportunity:

> [W]e are situated to ensure that the civil rights laws and civil rights jurisprudence of the next 50 years will prevent the patterns of discrimination and exclusion we have seen, and ensure our nation's ability to thrive with a renewed commitment to the constitutional principles and values that tie us all together.

While we seize the opportunity presented in this moment to determine collectively what the law ought to be, including a coherent approach to intersectional discrimination, Saenz also suggests that we recalibrate our conception of winning—not as a matter of resilience—but as an acknowledgment that what looks like losing today may actually be a detour to winning in the future. For example, a loss may lay the groundwork for a future victory. Saenz points to MALDEF losing hard-fought litigation that challenged a redistricting plan in California. But, ten years later, the new State Redistricting Commission adopted the district for which MALDEF had advocated, adopting the language of MALDEF's advocacy in justifying the district. Or a loss may still inflict enough of a cost upon Defendant A to deter Defendant B from replicating the offending behavior. A loss may also clarify the law and thereby sharpen advocacy for a win in the political arena—strategically demonstrating costs to the Right. Placing "losing" as well as "winning" in a context both broader and more longitudinal should support litigators, advocates, community organizers, and funders in negotiating successfully the creation of a new jurisprudence as well as strategic practice of civil rights law in the future.

Reimagining the War College and Intergenerational Engagement

Denise Hulett suggests that we reimagine the Voting Rights Conferences once held when the voting rights bar consisted of MALDEF, ACLU, Lawyers' Committee, and a handful of attorneys in private practice throughout the South who practiced within the historic geographic reach of the Fifth Circuit Court of Appeals (Texas, Louisiana, Mississippi, Alabama, Georgia, and Florida). Litigators and subject-matter experts made a practice of coming together for true brainstorming sessions about litigation strategy and collective assistance with one another's specific cases. The twenty-first-century version would expand to include social justice issues affecting communities today, provide space for intergenerational engagement, and include mock trials and oral arguments. Further, together with the millennials now in the field, we need to bring creativity to how we make our work consistent with our purported values.

Conclusion

We don't have the luxury of indulging in recriminations about failures in the past to perfect the jurisprudence we need today, or about good intentions gone squirrely, or wasted resources, or the delusion that all we need to do is replicate the past, or waste our time with turf wars and allotting credit or blame. Armand Derfner shares a useful proverb: "The best time to plant a tree was 20 years ago, the second-best time is now."

ABOUT THE EDITOR

Kent Spriggs spent his career litigating civil rights cases, primarily class actions. Along the way he authored the treatise *Representing Plaintiffs in Title VII Actions* (2 volumes) and served on the executive committee of the National Employment Lawyers Association. He has also served as city commissioner and mayor of Tallahassee. In recent years he has represented detainees at Guantanamo. He is the editor of *Voices of Civil Rights Lawyers: Reflections from the Deep South, 1964–1980*.

CONTRIBUTORS

James B. Ayers, Albany, New York

Martha Bergmark, Takoma Park, Maryland

James U. Blacksher, Birmingham, Alabama

Kenneth Cloke, Santa Monica, California

Jack Drake, retired lawyer, Birmingham, Alabama

John W. Gresham, Tin Fulton Walker & Owen, PLLC, formerly with the Chambers Ferguson firm, Charlotte, North Carolina

Paul Harris, San Francisco, California

J. Gerald Hebert, J. Gerald Hebert, PC, Alexandria, Virginia

Kent Hull, semiretired public interest lawyer, adjunct law professor, South Bend, Indiana

Wilhelm H. Joseph, Baltimore, Maryland

David Kern, El Paso, Texas

Chevene King Jr., Albany, Georgia

Melvyn R. Leventhal, former LDF staff member in Mississippi and New York City

Alan Levine, Miami, Florida

Stephen H. Oleskey, Attorney at Law, of Counsel Barclay Damon LLP, Boston, Massachusetts

Barbara Y. Phillips, social justice feminist, Oxford, Mississippi

Charles Stephen (Steve) Ralston, Mi Wuk Village, California

Bruce Rogow, Cedar Mountain, North Carolina

Jim Rowan, Newton, Massachusetts

David Rudovsky, Kairys, Rudovsky, Messing, Feinberg & Lin, Senior Fellow, Penn Carey Law School, Philadelphia, Pennsylvania

Amy Ruth Tobol, Professor, SUNY Empire State University, Brooklyn, New York

Michael B. Trister, Partner, Trister, Ross, Schadler & Gold (d. 2018)

Robert L. Wiggins Jr., Wiggins Childs Pantazis Fisher & Goldfarb LLC, Birmingham, Alabama

INDEX

AALS. *See* American Association of Law Schools
AAMU. *See* Alabama A&M University
ABA. *See* American Bar Association
Abolitionists, 33
Abortions, 250, 261
Accreditation, higher education, 108–9
ACIPCO. *See* American Cast Iron Pipe Company
ACLU. *See* American Civil Liberties Union
Activists, civil rights, 11–16, 19, 31, 40–41, 48, 82n34, 145, 160n8, 172. *See also specific actions*
Adams, Oscar, 1, 189–90, 219, 258n22
ADC. *See* Alabama Democratic Conference
Advocating for the People (Brittain), 265
AFDC. *See* Aid to Families with Dependent Children
Affirmative litigation, 86, 164
The Affluent Society (Galbraith), 183
Affordable Care Act, US, 249
African Americans, Black people and, 2–3, 12; attorneys, 15–16, 34, 36–37, 42–46, 65–66, 78nn7–8, 83, 90, 165, 188, 200–201, 219, 244, 258n22; class action suits for, 235–36; deaths of, 16, 36, 38, 40–41, 66–67, 69, 165–66, 233, 246, 252–54; farmers, 113, 118, 201; sharecroppers, 52, 75–76, 113, 156, 218–19, 249; soldiers, 92–94, 97–98, 197; tenant farmers, 52, 55; veterans, 97–98, 197, 200; violence against, 11, 35, 41, 74–75, 172–73, 175; women, 1, 24, 30, 192, 200, 237. *See also* Employment discrimination; Students of color, Black students and
Agriculture, 52–57, 75–76, 86, 91, 113, 227–28

Agriculture Adjustment Act, US, 113
Aid to Families with Dependent Children (AFDC), US, 62, 106, 110
Air Force, US, 199–200
Alabama: Black students in, 198–201, 203–5, 212, 218–30; federal judges in, 134–48, 188, 191, 196, 215–16; LDF in, 187–92; racism in, 175, 191, 206–7; redistricting plans, 137, 213–14, 217; school desegregation in, 42–43, 133–34, 198–99, 201–5, 218–31, 239–41, 258n22; voting rights in, 42, 133–34, 138–47, 190, 198, 203, 205–17. *See also specific cities*
Alabama A&M University (AAMU), 218–25, 227–29
Alabama Democratic Conference (ADC), 201
Alabama New South Coalition, 201
Alabama State Tenants Organization, 239–40
Alabama State University (ASU) (formerly Alabama State College), 200, 218, 221–25, 227–29
Albany, Georgia, 2, 15–16, 35–40, 61–71, 73, 192–94
Alexander v. Board of Education of Holmes County, 54–55
Alexander v. Holmes County Board of Education, 114
Alex v. City of Chicago, 126–28
Ali, Muhammad, 163
Allison, Bill, 85
All-white schools, 54, 74, 203–4, 253
Amaker, Norman, 190–91
American Association of Law Schools (AALS), 25, 108
American Bar Association (ABA), 12–14, 17–18, 21–25, 115–16, 219

American Cast Iron Pipe Company (ACIPCO), 235–37, 256n9, 256nn5–6, 258n20
American Civil Liberties Union (ACLU), 12–13, 144–45, 161
American Indian Law Alliance, 30
Amsterdam, Anthony, 36–37, 165, 189
Andalman, Elliott, 254
Anderson, James D., 224
Anderson, Joan, 84
Antidemonstration laws, 182
Antioch Law School, 116
Antler, Steve, 15–16, 19
Apartheid, racial, 26, 76, 97, 244, 254
Appalachian State University, 148–52
Archer, Marlene, 30
Arendall, Charlie, 205–6
Army, US, 92–94, 194, 252; drafts, 62–64, 83, 85, 187; veterans, 97–98, 197, 200, 205–6
Army Corps of Engineers, US, 53–54
Arnow, Winston, 209–12, 215, 296
Aronson, Henry, 52, 58–60, 82n41, 165, 174
Arrests, 1, 10–13, 82n52, 90, 92, 192, 243; in Louisiana, 169–70; in Mississippi, 110, 157–59, 167, 182; SNCC, 36, 74
Askew, Reubin, 211
Assassinations, 16, 40–41, 61, 98, 233, 246, 252–54
ASU. *See* Alabama State University
Atlanta, Georgia, 13
Atlantic City, New Jersey, 155–57, 159
Auburn University, 218–19, 225–28
Autonomy, 223, 261
Ayer, James, 39–51
Ayers v. Allain, 224

Baeza, Louie, 123–33
Baeza et al. v. The City of El Paso, 129–33
Bailey, D'Army, 21, 28, 41
Baker, Jim, 219
Baker County, Georgia, 35–37, 73–75
Baldwin, James, 212
Barbour, Haley, 247
Bass, Jack, 115, 162, 202
Beavers v. American Cast Iron Pipe Co., 242
Bell, Derrick, 203
Bell, Griffin, 203

Bench-trials, 136–37, 258n24
Bergmark, Martha, 245–54
Berkeley Law School, 36, 61, 72, 185–87
Beyond Integration (Butler), 209–10
Billingsley, Orzell, 90
Birdie Mae Davis v. Board of School Comm'rs of Mobile County, 201–6
Birmingham, Alabama, 1–2, 15–16, 152–53, 189–90, 199, 204–5, 239, 258n22; desegregation of higher education in, 218–30; Sixteenth Street Baptist church bombing, 233, 235–36
Black Belt region, Alabama, 229–30
Black consciousness, 174, 179, 183
Black legislators, 4, 113. *See also specific legislators*
Black Panther Party, 86, 179
"Black Power," 181–83
Blacksher, James, 196–230
Black/White paradigm, 264, 266
Bloody Sunday march, 135, 168, 190
Board of directors, LSCRRC, 20–24
Bolden, Wiley, 203, 205–7, 209
Bolivar County, Mississippi, 166–68
Bombings, 40, 163, 166, 233, 244, 253
Bond, Julian, 144–46, 163
Bonds, 163–64, 167, 170
Bond v. Floyd, 145
Boston College Law School, 153
Boult, Reber, 90–92
Boycotts, bus, 3, 31–32, 39, 69, 184, 198, 203
Boyd, Henry, 104
Bradley, John Robin, 108
Bradley, Neil, 211
Brazil, 51
Brittain, John, 17, 22, 110, 264–66
Bronstein, Alvin, 162–65
Bronx High School of Science, 179
Browder v. Gayle, 199
Brown, John, 115, 262
Brown, R. Jess, 162–63, 165–66
Brown v. Board of Education, 3, 31–32, 54–55, 78n8, 198, 203, 262–63
Bunche, Ralph, 251
Bunkley, William, 109
Burnham, Linda, 264
Burnham, Margaret, 90

Burns, Haywood, 22
Burton, Vernon, 196, 230, 264–66
Burton v. Hobbie, 213–14
Busbee v. Smith, 144–45
Bus boycotts, 3, 31–32, 39, 69, 184, 198, 203
Bush, George W., 194–95
Butler, Michael J., 209–10
Buttigieg, Pete, 112

Cahn, Edgar, 116–17
Cahn, Jean, 116–17
California, 72, 117, 185–86, 195–96
Calloway v. Partners Nat'l Health Plans, 242
Camus, Albert, 58
Canton, Mississippi, 177, 180
Capps, Charlie, 167
Carmichael, Stokely, 52–53, 172–73, 177, 179–81, 183
Carter, Jimmy, 101, 213, 219, 222
CASL. *See* Committee to Assist Southern Lawyers
Catholicism, 197–98
CDGM. *See* Child Development Group of Mississippi
CEJO. *See* Committee for Equal Job Opportunity
Central High School, Little Rock, 253
Chachkin, Norman, 203
Chambers, Julius, 84, 86–87
Chambliss, Lorenzo Eric, 29–30
Chaney, James, 40, 61, 82n52, 176–77
Chicago, Illinois, 126–27, 179–80
Child Development Group of Mississippi (CDGM), 107
Children, 100, 110, 117–18, 157–59, 233, 242–43, 246, 248–51, 253. *See also* Students
Children's Defense Fund, 7, 40–41, 82n40
Christenberry, Herbert, 158
City of Greenwood (Mississippi) v. Peacock, 167
City of Mobile v. Bolden, 211, 216
City of Port Arthur, Texas v. United States, 144, 146
Civil disobedience, 3, 32. *See also specific forms of civil disobedience*
Civil Rights. *See specific topics*
Civil Rights Act (1866), US, 254, 255n1
Civil Rights Act (1964), US, 3, 28, 51, 176, 180, 233–45, 255nn3–4, 258n23, 263; Title VI, 193, 218; Title VII, 44, 109, 194, 202
Civil Rights Act (1966), US, 178, 180
Civil Rights Act (1991), 256n7, 257n11
Civil Rights Division, DOJ, 13–134, 187, 194
Civil War, US, 52, 261–62
Clark, Jim, 135–36, 175, 189
Clark, Robert, 113
CLAS. *See* Committee for Legal Assistance to the South
Class: middle, 21–22, 185–86, 210; race and, 22–23, 26–27, 31, 179, 185
Class action suits, 4–5, 35, 110–11, 117, 216, 235–38, 241, 258n23
Clayton, Claude F., 165
Clemon, U. W., 196, 199, 215, 218–23, 232n16
Clerks, law, 4, 25, 39–40, 73, 199, 219, 224, 256n9
Clinton, Bill, 117
Clinton, Hillary, 7–8
Cloke, Kenneth, 35, 71–77
Coar, David, 200
Collective action suits, 130–33
Colonialism, British, 97
Columbia University Law School, 15–16, 18, 39, 41, 172, 187
Committee for Civil Rights Under Law, US, 116
Committee for Equal Job Opportunity (CEJO), 235
Committee for Legal Assistance to the South (CLAS), 13
Committee to Assist Southern Lawyers (CASL), 13
Communism, 10–12, 14, 34, 71, 79n13, 91, 162
Community organizing, political participation and, 38, 41, 264
Condon, Aaron, 103
Congress, US, 32, 144, 233–34, 245, 255nn1–3
Congress of Racial Equality (CORE), 10–11, 72, 165, 172–73, 177, 179–80, 183
Connelly, Chuck, 15–16
Conscientious objectors, 1, 190
Consciousness: Black, 174, 179, 183; race, 9, 23, 26, 214
Constitution, US, 100, 209, 255n3, 261–66; rights under, 3, 32, 36–37, 85, 108, 150, 167, 175. *See also specific amendments*

Contingent-fee practices, 238–39, 244
Cooper, A. J., Jr., 200, 203
CORE. *See* Congress of Racial Equality
Corum, A1149–52
Council Elementary Magnet School, Alabama, 204
Court-martial, 93–94
Court of Appeals, US, 126, 150–51, 235–37, 241–42, 255n4, 257n10; Eleventh Circuit, 139, 141, 207, 219–22, 225–26, 229–30, 252; Fifth Circuit, 108–9, 114–15, 162–63, 192, 199, 202, 207–11, 224, 261–62, 267
COVID-19 pandemic, 248–49
Cox, Ancil, 166
Cox, Harold, 144, 165, 260–62
Cox v. American Cast Iron Pipe Co., 237, 256n9, 257n16
Crawford, Vernon, 41–50, 200–201, 203, 205–6
Criminal: defense cases, 33, 35, 37, 42, 86, 121; justice, 33, 37, 157, 239; prosecutions, 33, 36–37, 153–54
Crockett, George, 161–62
Cross-examinations, 68–69, 73, 135–36, 138–39, 146–48, 190–91, 193, 221
Cumberland Law Journal, 216

Dallas County, Alabama, 133–39
Daly, George, 86
Davidson, Joyce, 102
Davis, Ivy, 23–24
Davis, Samuel M., 104
Davis v. Schnell, 205
Dawson, Bill, 211
Days, Drew, 35, 207
Deacons for Defense and Justice, 169–70
Dean, George, 91, 198–99
Deaths, 36, 38, 75, 82n52, 176, 215, 233; assassinations, 16, 40–41, 61, 98, 233, 246, 252–54; infant mortality, 246, 249; of King, C. B., 66–67. *See also* Murders
Death sentences, 41–42, 239, 250
Declaration of Independence, US, 230
Deep South, US, 26, 34, 51, 133, 152, 180, 242–45, 255n4
De facto segregation, 254
De jure racial segregation, 196–98, 210, 223–24
Delaney, Sheila, 140–43

Delany, Joseph, 102
Dentler, Bob, 204
Department of Education, US, 218, 228
Department of Energy, US, 218
Department of Health, US, 114
Department of Justice (DOJ), US, 133–34, 140–43, 178, 180, 187, 194 204, 213–14, 218
Derfner, Armand, 101, 112, 167, 196, 208, 230, 264–65
Desegregation, 11, 174, 179–80, 197–98, 206
Desegregation, school, 3, 78n8, 82n47, 197, 244; in Alabama, 42–43, 133–34, 198–99, 201–5, 218–31, 239–41, 258n22; of higher education, 96–97, 148–52, 219–30; in Mississippi, 41, 54, 70–71, 105, 113–14, 245, 253. *See also* Integration
Detroit, Michigan, 112
DiDonato, Paul, 263–64
Dillard v. Crenshaw County, 215–17
Disabilities, disability rights and, 27, 114, 118–19, 198, 246–47, 263
Disabilities Act (1990), US, 118
Disaster recovery, 247
Discrimination, 8, 166, 263; intentional, 206, 208–12, 215, 240, 256n7; past, 207, 235–36, 240–43, 255n3, 256n7; sexual, 24, 234–35, 237, 241–42, 256n8, 257n16; wage, 242–43, 257n17. *See also* Employment discrimination
Discrimination, racial, 26, 102, 118, 202, 224–25, 235–36, 240–43, 255n1, 257n13, 257n15, 257n17, 258n18; in Alabama, 218–30; Army, 92–93; in civil rights arrests, 36; *Lee v. Macon* addressing, 220; in Mississippi, 215–16. *See also* Employment discrimination; Segregation, racial
Dixwell Legal Rights Association, 104
Dobbs v. Jackson Women's Health Organization, 207, 250, 261, 265
Dohrn, Bernardine, 84
DOJ. *See* Department of Justice
Dole, Bob, 214
Doyle, Bob, 205–6
Draft, military, 62–64, 83, 85, 187
Drake, Jack, 88–95
Drinan, Robert, 18, 153
Due process, 148–49, 151, 262

Duke, Brian Andrew, 204
Duke Law School, 83–84, 88
Durham, Harvey, 150
Dyer, David, 220

Easley, South Carolina, 233
Eastland, James O., 107
Eastland, John, 165
Economic justice, 25–26, 51, 239, 246, 254
Edelman, Marian Wright, 7, 15–17, 21–22, 40–41, 82n34, 82n40, 1730174
Education, legal, 7–11, 14–30, 99, 165, 177, 185–86, 248, 254, 258n22; curricula, 14–15, 20, 118; segregation in, 200, 244. *See also* Law Students Civil Right Research Council; *specific law schools*
Education, schools and, 232n16, 254, 256n5; all-white schools, 54, 74, 203–4, 253; Catholic, 197–98; elementary schools, 177–78, 204, 223; employment discrimination and, 202–5, 234–37, 258n18; expulsions from, 86, 100–101; HBCUs and, 40, 82n37, 96–99, 169, 200, 218–19, 222–28; high schools and, 97, 203, 253–54; public, 54, 114, 203–5, 219, 220, 230, 248–50, 264; white students and, 11, 21–22, 153, 203, 223, 225, 227, 243, 248, 253; white universities, 220–21, 223, 225, 228. *See also* Desegregation, school; Students of color, Black students and; *specific schools*
Education for All Handicapped Children Act, US, 118
EEOC. *See* Equal Employment Opportunity Commission
Eisenhower, Dwight D., 188
Elbaum, Max, 264
Electoral data, 138–39
Elementary schools, 177–78, 204, 223
Eleventh Circuit, US Court of Appeals, 139, 141, 207, 219–22, 225–26, 229–30, 252
Eliot, J. Robert, 193
El Paso, Texas, 121–24
Employment discrimination, 4, 41–42, 44–45, 85, 87, 109, 115, 194, 255n2, 258n23; Alabama, 201–5, 220; lines-of-progression in, 46–48, 82n36, 202, 234–37, 240–43, 256nn5–6, 257n1; seniority policies and, 234–36, 243, 256nn5–7, 257n14; wage discrimination in, 125–33, 242–43, 257nn16–17
Environmental issues, 31, 77, 112, 239–40
Equal access to the political process, 3, 14, 19, 207, 214, 255n4
Equal Employment Opportunity Commission (EEOC), 7–8, 44, 46, 80n22, 109, 194, 242
Equal protection of the law, 115, 149, 151, 196, 213, 262
Escambia County, Florida, 209–11
Escambia County v. McMillan, 215
European Jewish immigrants, 161, 164
Evers, Medgar, 15–16, 40, 246, 252–54
Evers, Myrlie, 254
Experts, court, 138–39, 146–48, 226
Expulsions, school, 86, 100–101
Exum, James, 149, 151

Fair Labor Standards Act (FLSA), US, 125–29
Fair Pay Act, US, 242–43
Farmer, James, 11
Farm Security Administration, US, 113
Faulkner, William, 112
FDP. *See* Freedom Democratic Party
Federal Emergency Management Agency (FEMA), US, 247
Federal government, US, 13, 100, 110, 155, 172, 202, 220, 262; freedom-of-choice plans by, 54; habeas proceedings, 38–39, 192; LDF taking on the, 194. *See also specific legislation*
Federal Highway Administration (FHWA), 112, 239–40
Federal judges, 4, 36, 114, 158, 207, 210, 218, 231n7, 244, 255n4, 262, 265; Alabama, 134–48, 188, 191, 196, 215–16; on school desegregation, 42
Federal lawsuits, 106, 205, 239–40, 247
Federal legislation, 2, 262–63. *See also specific legislation*
FEMA. *See* Federal Emergency Management Agency
FHWA. *See* Federal Highway Administration
Fields, Frankie, 200
Fifteenth Amendment, US Constitution, 178, 215–16
Fifth Amendment, US Constitution, 199–200

278 · Index

Fifth Circuit, US Court of Appeals, 108–9, 114–15, 162–63, 192, 199, 202, 207–11, 224, 261–62, 267
Figures, Michael, 200
Fingerhood, Shirley, 18
Firefighters, paramedics compared to, 126–33
Fires, arson and, 47–48
First Amendment, US Constitution, 12–13, 57–58, 166, 175, 189, 261
First Reconstruction, 261–63
Florida, 161–62, 209–11
Flowers, Curtis, 250
FLSA. *See* Fair Labor Standards Act
Folsom, Jim, 197
Food stamp program, US, 105
Ford Foundation, 80n22, 81n31
Foster, Marie, 135–36
Fournier, Hazel, 205
Fourteenth Amendment, US Constitution, 202, 214–16, 222, 229, 262
Fowler, Nancy, 88–89
Freedom of speech, 72, 92, 148–49, 151
Freedom Riders, 11, 15, 28, 32, 39, 72, 180, 186, 197
Freedom Summer of 1964, 152–57
"Freedom Vote Campaign," SNCC, 11
Frontiero v. Laird, 199
Frontiero v. Richardson, 199–200, 212
Full citizenship, 98, 261–2662
Fuller, Howard, 86
Funding, 87, 227, 229–30, 254, 263–64; federal, 101, 114, 117, 154, 193, 247; LSCRRC, 17–18, 20, 22, 25, 27, 80nn22–23, 81nn31–32; for the Mississippi Center for Justice, 245, 248; NMRLS, 100–101, 104, 106–7

Galloway Memorial Methodist church, 251–52
Galveston, Texas, 186
Garnishment policies, 243, 258n20
Gay/lesbian/bisexual movement, 27, 31, 77
Gender, 21–23, 26, 30–31, 71–72, 92, 233; discrimination, 24, 234–35, 237, 241–43, 256n8, 257n16
George Washington University, 200
Georgia, 144–45, 212
Gerrymandering, 213–14

GI Bill, US, 98, 149
Gideon v. Wainwright, 116
Gilhooly, Tom, 17
Gill v. Woods, 105
Ginger, Ann Fagan, 15–16
Ginsburg, Ruth Bader, 199–200
Gold, Jon, 242
Goldberg v. Kelly, 117
González, Carlos, 224, 226–27
Goodman, Andrew, 40, 61, 82n52, 176–77, 180–81
Granat, Richie, 19
Grassroots support and organizations, 4, 105, 150, 183–85, 203, 247
Graves, James E., Jr., 216
Gray, Fred, Jr., 188, 194–95, 200, 215, 219
Gray, Jerome, 216–17
Great Depression, US, 14, 71, 113
Greenberg, Jack, 1, 14, 18, 79n13, 190–91, 194
Greenberg, Richard, 61
Greenpoint, Mississippi, 101, 109–10
Greensboro, Alabama, 72–73
Greensboro, North Carolina, 10, 72
Green v. County School Board of New Kent County, 55
Greenville, Alabama, 189–90
Green v. New Kent County, 203, 209
Grenada, Mississippi, 57–61
Gresham, John, 148–52
Griggs v. Duke Power Co., 201
Grooms, Hobart, 219–20
Guinier, Lani, 197, 208, 216
Guns, shootings and, 1, 16, 36, 41, 57, 74–75, 82n49, 172–73, 190, 246
Gutman, Jeremiah, 17–18

Hamer, Fannie Lou, 99–100, 156–57, 161, 248
Hancock, Paul, 140–43
Hand, Brevard, 133–43, 146
Hand, Learned, 138, 201–2, 204–7, 231n7, 265
Handicappers Civil Rights Act, Michigan, 118
"Hardship discharge" claim, 62–64
Harness v. Watson, 111–12, 119, 215–16
Harrington, Michael, 116
Harris, Paul, 61–64
Harris, Sue, 251

Index · 279

Harris v. Siegelman, 217
Hastings Law Journal, 216
Hawes, Amanda, 28, 30
HBCU. *See* Historically black college or university
Head Start program, 71, 105, 107, 253
Health, 26, 67, 248–49; mental, 92, 115, 198–99
Health care, 110, 166, 249, 254, 255n1
Hebert, Gerry, 208
Heflin, Howell, 213
Henderson, Wade, 265
Henry, Aaron, 248
Henry Street Settlement House, 81n31
Herbert, Gary, 133–48
Hershkop, Phil, 19
Higginbotham, Patrick, 224, 232n15
Higgs, Bill, 13, 15–17, 29
Higher education, desegregation of, 96–97, 148–52, 219–30. *See also specific schools*
High schools, 97, 203, 253–54
Highway Department, Alabama, 239–40
Hiken, Luke, 28
Hiring discrimination, 243, 255n3, 257n13, 258n18
Historically black college or university (HBCU), 40, 82n37, 96–99, 169, 200, 218–19, 222–28. *See also specific HBCUs*
HIV/AIDS, 249
Hobbs, Truman, 218
Hoke County Board of Education v. North Carolina, 151
Holmes, Hamilton, 221
Holmes, Mary, 107
Holmes County, Mississippi, 111–19
Holocaust, 153
Holt, Len, 13, 78n8
Holtzman, Elizabeth, 16, 21–22, 24
Holy Cross College, 7–8
Homeowners insurance, 48
Hoover, J. Edgar, 33
Houseman, Alan, 25
House on Un-American Activities Committee (HUAC), US, 13
Houston, Charles Hamilton, 202, 263, 265
Howard University, 13, 179
Hren, Greg, 42, 47–49

HUAC. *See* House on Un-American Activities Committee
Hudspeth, Harry Lee, 129
Hulett, Denise, 262, 264, 267
Hull, Kent, 111–19
Hunger, 26
Hunter, Charlayne, 221
Hurder, Alex, 83–85
Hurricane Katrina, 247
Hustwit, William P., 113–14

ICC. *See* Interstate Commerce Commission
IDEA. *See* Individuals with Disabilities Act
"I Have a Dream" speech (King Jr.), 172, 233
Illinois, 112–13, 118, 126–27, 179–80
Imperialism, 17, 64
Inc. Fund. *See* Legal Defense and Education Fund
Indigent people, 100, 105–6, 116–18
Individuals with Disabilities Act (IDEA), US, 118
Infant mortality, 149, 246
Institutionalized segregation, 12, 252
Insurance, 48, 242–43, 247
Integration, 70–71, 75, 172, 179; resistance to, 22, 29, 32, 54, 114–15, 202–5, 210, 218–30, 235
Intentional discrimination, 206, 208–12, 215, 240, 256n7
International Union of Operating Engineers, 133
Interracial groups, 12–13, 22–31
Interstate Commerce Commission (ICC), US, 53
Irby, I. W., 60
Ivy League law schools, 22–23, 28–29

Jackson, Mississippi, 13, 34, 163–66, 245, 250–51; LSCRRC in, 40–42, 51–62; NAACP in, 15–16, 173
Jackson County, Florida, 69
Jackson State College, 40
Jail, 3, 28, 60, 64, 67–68, 163–70
James, Fob, 200
Javins v. First National Realty Co., 117
Jefferson, Thomas, 230

Jenkins v. City of Pensacola, 209
Jim Crow laws, 31–33, 98, 173, 246, 249, 255n1, 262; Evers addressing, 252; Figures addressing, 201; HBCUs addressing, 223–24; King C. B. addressing, 73; legislation addressing, 234–35; Thompson, M., and, 215; veterans opposing, 197, 200. *See also* Segregation, racial
Job discrimination. *See* Employment discrimination
Johnson, Douglas, 62–64
Johnson, Frank M., Jr., 172, 188, 191, 198–201, 212–14, 219
Johnson, Lula Mae, 62–64
Johnson, Lyndon, 33, 135, 157, 172, 175, 178, 180, 206, 209
Johnson, Nancy F., 80n29
Johnson, Paul, 175–78, 182
Johnson, Warren "Gator," 74–75
Johnson v. Zerbst, 162–63
Jones, Elaine, 7
Jones, Justin, 4
Joseph, Wilhem H., 27, 96–102, 110
Joyner, Bill, 105
Judicare programs, 103, 107
Juries, 3, 68–69, 93, 258n24
Justice Deferred (Derfner, Burton), 264–66
Juvenile Justice Reform Act (2005), Mississippi, 246

Kairys, David, 37
Karlan, Pam, 216
Katz, Al, 80n29
Keenan, Jim, 90–92
Kelly, Robert, 105
Kennedy, Cain, 200
Kennedy, John F., 13, 80n21, 81n31, 116, 198, 233
Kennedy, Marilyn, 80n29
Kennedy, Robert, 19, 61
Kent State University, 92
Kentucky, 197–98
Kern, David, 121–33
Kilgore, Catherine, 102
King, Allen, 69
King, C. B., 1–2, 15–16, 28–29, 31–39, 61–74, 192–94

King, Chevene, Jr., 64–72
King, Martin Luther, Jr., 32, 41, 61, 69 173–85, 82n42, 114; "I Have a Dream" speech by, 172, 233; on violence, 74–75
Kinoy, Arthur, 86
Kirksey, Henry, 261
KKK. *See* Ku Klux Klan
Knight, John F., Jr., 218, 226–29
Knight v. Alabama, 207, 221–22, 224–25
Knight v. James, 218
Kopit, Bill, 15
Kousser, Morgan, 208–9
Kravitch, Phyllis, 211–12
Ku Klux Klan (KKK), 36, 40, 72–73; in Alabama, 2, 48–49; in Louisiana, 158, 169–71; in Mississippi, 55–58, 61, 176, 180–81
Kunstler, Bill, 86

Labor unions, 46, 86, 133, 255n3
Lafayette County Legal Services. *See* North Mississippi Rural Legal Services
Landerman, Dick, 86
Land grants, 225–26, 232nn16–17
Landsberg, Brian, 142
Langan, Joe, 205
Latinos, 26–27, 123–33, 186, 254
Law clerks, 4, 25, 39–40, 73, 199, 219, 224, 256n9
Law firms. *See specific law firms; specific lawyers*
Law Students Civil Right Research Council (LSCRRC), 80n22, 80n29, 99, 101; funding, 17–18, 20, 22, 25, 27, 80nn22–23, 81nn31–32; origins of, 10, 15–24, 80n27; in the South, 4, 10, 18–28, 34–36, 39–46; summer internship program, 7–9, 18, 20–64, 81n33
Lawyers, Civil Rights. *See specific topics*
Lawyers' Committee for Civil Rights under Law (Lawyers' Committee), ABA, 13–14, 51–53, 144
Lawyers Constitutional Defense Committee (LCDC), 13–14, 34, 112, 153–54, 159n4, 161–62
LCDC. *See* Lawyers Constitutional Defense Committee

LDF. *See* Legal Defense and Education Fund
Ledbetter, Lillie, 242–43
Lee, Bill Lann, 194
Lee v. Macon, 199, 219–20, 230
Lefcourt, Carol, 85
LeFlore, John, 44, 49, 202–3, 205
Legal: representation, 33, 35, 41–42, 92, 190, 234, 247–48; segregation, 3–4, 31–32, 221, 251, 262
Legal Defense and Education Fund (LDF), NAACP, 1, 7, 12–14, 17–18, 24–25, 33–34, 52, 78n8, 79n13, 81nn31–32, 244, 258n22; in Alabama, 187–92, 198, 200–205; *Alexander v. Holmes County Board of Education*, 114; leaders of, 87, 173
Legal Services Corporation (LSC), 80n22, 101–2, 116–17, 154, 245, 254. *See also* North Mississippi Rural Legal Services
Lerner, Alan, 26
Leventhal, Melvyn R., 171–85
Levine, Alan, 2–3, 152–59
Levy, Loni, 85
Lewis, Jim, 101, 115
Lewis, John, 32, 72, 156–57, 179, 194–95
Libraries, 4, 80n29, 157–59
License to practice law, 12, 69, 82n51, 110, 244
Lichtman, Allan J., 138–39
Life expectancy, 249
Lines-of-progression, employment, 46–48, 82n36, 202, 234–37, 240–43, 256nn5–6, 257n1
Little Rock, Arkansas, 253
Liuzzo, Viola, 180–81
Locke, John, 230
Logan, Eddie W., 113
Long, James, 151
Louisiana, 157–59, 169–71. *See also specific cities*
Low-income people, 102–5, 110, 193–94, 247–49
Lowndes County Freedom Organization. *See* Black Panther Party
LSC. *See* Legal Services Corporation
LSCRRC. *See* Law Students Civil Right Research Council
Lynch, Robert, 114

Lynch v. Alabama, 229
Lynne, Seybourn, 199

Macdonald, Dwight, 116
MacManus, Susan, 146–48
Madlock, Jewell, 109
Magnet schools, 204–5
Malcolm X Liberation School, 83, 86
MALDEF. *See* Mexican American Legal Defense and Educational Fund
Malnutrition, 26
Malone, Vivian, 203
Manley, Rick, 213
March against Fear (Meredith March), Mississippi, 57, 171–85
March on Washington (1963), 10, 16–17, 32, 233
Marcuse, Herbert, 164
Marengo County, Alabama, 140–43
Marginalized communities, 15, 19, 31
Marijuana tests, 243, 258n19
Marine Corps, US, 129
Marshall, Thurgood, 3, 12–13, 202, 265
Marshall County, Mississippi, 104–6
Marshall County Legal Services, 104
Marshall Field Foundation, 17, 79n20
Marshals, US, 157–59
Mary Holmes College, 106–7, 111
Mass arrests, 36, 153, 182, 189–90
Mass incarceration, 33, 38, 46, 246
Maxey, John, 104–5
McCarthyism, 10
McCrary, Peyton, 208–9, 215
McDonald, Laughlin, 85, 144, 211
McDougal, Luther, 104, 107–8
McFadden, Frank, 199–200
McGregor, Malcolm, 121
MCJ. *See* Mississippi Center for Justice
McKissick, Floyd, 172–73, 177, 179–81, 183
McMillan v. Escambia County, 209
McNeal Elementary School for Negroes, Mississippi, 177
Medicaid program, 110, 117, 246, 249
Memphis, Tennessee, 173–74
Menefee, Larry, 215–16, 218, 222
Mental health, 26, 92, 115, 198–99
Meredith, James, 41, 57, 171–73, 178, 181

282 · Index

Meredith March (March against Fear), 57, 171–85
Methodist churches, 250–52
Mexican American Legal Defense and Educational Fund (MALDEF), 264, 266–67
Mexico, 117
MFDP. *See* Mississippi Freedom Democratic Party
MFY. *See* Mobilization for Youth
Miles, Robert, Sr., 52–53, 56–58
Military law, 85, 87, 90, 92
Milligan v. Merrill, 217, 231n19
Mills, C. Wright, 118
Millsaps College, 251
Mississippi, 30–31, 215–16, 224–25; Black students in, 70–71, 96–97, 109–10, 248; demographics, 166, 246, 247–48; KKK in, 55–58, 61, 176, 180–81; LSCRRC in, 40–42, 51–62; March against Fear, 57, 171–85; Mississippi Freedom Summer, 11, 24–25, 34, 52–53, 57; NAACP in, 15–16, 247; school desegregation in, 41, 54, 70–71, 105, 113–14, 245, 253; voting rights in, 11, 30, 57, 111–12 153–157, 174–79, 184, 245–46, 260–62. *See also specific cities*
Mississippi Center for Justice (MCJ), 245–54, 262
Mississippi Delta, 40, 96–101, 166–67, 247–50
Mississippi Freedom Democratic Party (MFDP), 113, 155–57, 161
Mississippi Highway Patrol, 175, 177–78
Mississippi Valley State University, 96–101, 110
Mobile, Alabama, 39–50, 141–43, 197–209
Mobilization for Youth (MFY) program, 26–27, 81n31
Montgomery, Alabama, 191; Montgomery bus boycott, 31–32, 39, 69, 184, 198, 203
Montreat, North Carolina, 89–90
Moore, Howard, 86
Moore, Roy, 229
Moore v. Harper, 151
Morgan, Chuck, 13, 90, 162–63
Morrill Act, US, 225–26, 232n16
Morrison's Cafeteria, Mobile, 49–50
Morse, Joshua, 103–4, 106–9
Moses, Clarence, 200

Murders, 16, 41–42, 92, 165–66, 233, 246, 252–54; of civil rights workers, 40, 61, 82n52, 176–77, 180–81
Murphy, Alberta, 88–89
Murphy, Harold L., 221–30, 232n16
Murphy, Jay, 88–89
Murrah High School, Mississippi, 253–54

National Association for the Advancement of Colored People (NAACP), 7, 10, 78n8, 202; in Mississippi, 15–16, 69, 253. *See also* Legal Defense and Education Fund, NAACP
National Environmental Policy Act (1969), 239–40
National Labor Relations Act, US, 255
National Lawyers Guild (NLG), 8, 12–14, 33–34, 78n7, 79n12, 84
National Office for the Rights of the Indigent (NORI), 193–94
Nation of Islam, 91
Native Americans, 26–27, 30, 77, 149, 187
Navy, US, 142, 149, 197–98, 200, 206
Nevett v. Sides, 211
New Deal reforms, 12, 33–34, 113, 206
New Hampshire, 51
New Haven Legal Assistance, 7–8
New Jersey, 155–57, 159
"New Left" movement, 34, 287
New Orleans, Louisiana, 157–59
New Roots Credit Partnership, 249–50
Newton, Demetrius, 222
New World Foundation, 17, 79n20
New York City, 17–18, 26, 27, 34, 81n31; LDF in, 193–94; LSCRRC office in, 9, 101; Occupy Wall Street in, 152, 159
New York Civil Liberties Union, 154
New York University (NYU), 16, 34, 51, 61
Nixon, Richard, 101, 114, 117, 201
NLG. *See* National Lawyers Guild
NMRLS. *See* North Mississippi Rural Legal Services
Noncontingent-fee practices, 238, 244
Nonjury trials, 245
Non-Partisan Voters League, 41, 44, 49, 202–3
Nonprofits, 17, 20–21, 246–47
Nonviolent protests, "nonviolent resistance" and, 11, 74–75, 175–76, 179, 233

NORI. *See* National Office for the Rights of the Indigent
The North, US, 25–26, 76, 80n29, 185; law students from, 10–11, 14, 21–23
North Carolina, 10, 72, 90, 148–52
North Mississippi Rural Legal Services (NMRLS), 4, 103–11
Norton, Eleanor Holmes, 16, 21–22
Norvell, Aubrey, 175
NYU. *See* New York University

Obama, Barack, 117, 194–95
Occupy Wall Street, 152, 159
O'Connor, Flannery, 212
Office of Economic Opportunity (OEO), US, 26–27, 104, 107, 116; War on Poverty, 103, 246
Oral history, 8–10, 78n3
The Other America (Harrington), 116
"Our Invisible Poor" (Macdonald), 116
Overtime pay, 125–29
Oxford, Mississippi, 106–12

Paducah, Kentucky, 197–98
Panola County, Mississippi, 51–61
Pantazis, Dennis, 238–39
Paramedics, wage discrimination for, 125–33
Park, Jack, 217
Parker, Frank, 16, 116, 260–61
Parker, Mack, 165–66
Paun, Jerome, 29
Payday lending, 249–50
Pay-raise policies, 243
Pearson, Conrad, 84
Pearson, J. Richmond, 219
Pearson, Justin, 4
Pemberton, Jack, 13–14
Pennington, Jesse, 109
Pensacola, Florida, 209–11
Percy, Walker, 95
Pettway, Rush, 235
Pettway v. American Cast Iron Pipe Co., 235–37, 255n4, 256n7, 257n9
Philadelphia, Mississippi, 176–77, 180–81
Philadelphia, Pennsylvania, 37–39
Phillips, Barbara, 5, 260–67
Pittman, Virgil, 206–10, 215

Plantations, 52, 55, 166–68, 249
Plessy v. Ferguson, 3, 78n8, 262
Pobley, Maria, 264
Police, 2, 35, 59–61, 67, 72–75, 93, 163–64; desegregation, 206; local, 73–74, 94, 176–77; March against Fear and, 175–78; marijuana testing by, 243, 258n19; violence, 57–58, 171–72, 175, 187, 190–92. *See also* Arrests
Policy advocacy, 246, 264–66
Poor Peoples' Campaign, 239
Popper, Martin, 78n7
Populism, 113
Poverty, 26, 62–63, 81n31, 86, 96–97, 100, 149, 185, 249; poverty law, 14–15, 80n29, 85, 104, 116; War on Poverty program, 103, 246
Power Concedes Nothing (Burnham, Elbaum, Pobley), 264
Predatory lending, 112, 249–50
Prejudice, 7, 76, 192, 206, 234, 244
Prisoners' rights, 29–30
Privacy, 261
Private attorneys, 103, 134, 234
Private right of action, 4, 149, 151
Private schools, 3
Privilege, 9, 17, 179; white, 44, 234
Pro bono counsel, 39, 244, 247, 250
Procedural issues for civil rights lawyers, 194, 245
Proctor, Lister Hill, 213
Proll, Leslie, 222
Promotion discrimination and, 46–48, 82n36, 202, 234–37, 240–43, 256nn5–6, 257n15, 257n17
Property taxes, 229
Prosecutorial misconduct, 37, 250
Providence Co-operative Farm, 113–14
Public: defenders, 37–38; education, 54, 114, 203–5, 219, 220, 230, 248–50, 264; housing, 116–17, 235, 239–40
Purposeful discrimination, 206, 208–12, 215, 240, 256n7

Rabinowitz, Victor, 85
Race, 10, 75–76, 181–83, 186, 232n16, 242–43, 250, 264–65; class and, 22–23, 26–27, 31, 179, 185; consciousness, 9, 23, 26, 214
"Race-neutral," 214, 224, 234

Racial: apartheid, 26, 76, 97, 244, 254; bias, 36, 255n1, 258n22; identity, 70–71, 224; justice, 34–35, 210, 245–46, 249, 254, 255n4; polarization, 148, 208. *See also* Discrimination, racial; Segregation, racial

Racism, 4, 21–22, 32, 36, 61–62, 75–76, 179, 181, 212, 249, 251, 260; in Alabama, 175, 191, 206–7; in Mississippi, 100, 174, 177–78

Railroads, 44–46, 53

Rains, Albert, 206

Raleigh, North Carolina, 10

Ralston, Charles Stephen "Steve," 185–96

Ray, Dennison "Denny," 51–52

Raymond, George, 182

Reagan, Ronald, 117, 208–9, 213–14, 257n11

Recognizance bonds, 163–64, 167

Reconstruction era, US, 3, 200, 207, 232n16, 234, 261–62

Redistricting plans: Alabama, 137, 213–14, 217; California, 266–67; congressional, 144–45, 213

"Red Scare," Communism and the, 34

Reed, Joe L., 213–14, 218

Reed, Roy, 176

Rehabilitation Act (1973), US, 118

Removal petitions, federal court, 36–37, 74, 158, 167, 169, 189

Reproductive rights, 217, 250, 261

Reservations, Native Americans, 26

Residency requirements, bar exam, 90

Reusch, Janet, 130

Reynolds v. Sims, 198, 213

Richey, Charles, 147–48

Ricks, Willie, 181

Right-to-travel, 106

Right-wing ideology, 262–63, 266

Rindskopf, Peter, 85

Risks taken on by lawyers and law students, 3, 10–12, 33–37, 48, 57–61, 73, 77, 238–39, 244

Rita Sanders Geier v. University of Tennessee, 218

Rives, Richard T., 115

Roberts, Dennis, 16, 29, 35, 73

Robinson, William, 23–24, 28–30

Roe v. Wade, 217

Rogers, William Warren, 232

Rogers v. Lodge, 211

Rogow, Bruce, 161–71

Roosevelt, Franklin D., 12, 119

Rosengart, Oliver, 58

Rowan, Jim, 83–87

Rudman, Warren, 117

Rudovsky, David, 31–39

Russell, Daniel, 143

Saenz, Thomas A., 264–67

Sankofa, 263

Satterfield, John C., 115–16

Sayre, Mike, 85

SCEF. *See* Southern Conference Education Fund

Schnapper, Eric, 207, 230

Schwarzschild, Henry, 161–62, 168, 259n4

Schwerner, Michael, 40, 61, 82n52, 176–77, 180–81

SCLC. *See* Southern Christian Leadership Conference

Screws v. United States, 36

SDS. *See* Students for a Democratic Society

Secession, 188

Second Reconstruction, 230, 262–63

Section 5, Voting Rights Act (1965), 213, 261

Sedler, Bob, 86

Segregation, racial, 1–2, 12, 184, 254, 255nn1–2, 260; de jure, 196–98, 210, 223–24; legal, 3–4, 31–32, 221, 251, 262; in public schools, 53–54, 219; in the South, 11, 22–23, 53–58, 113–14, 157–59, 165, 197, 203, 234–37, 251–52, 255n4, 256n5. *See also* Jim Crow laws

Segregation, sexual, 237

Seligman, Dan, 166–68

Selma, Alabama, 133–38, 140–42, 168–69, 171–75, 188–91, 194–95

Seniority policies, 234–36, 243, 256nn5–7, 257n14

Sessions, Jeff, 231n7

Seventh Circuit, US Court of Appeals, 126

Sexual discrimination, 24, 234–35, 241–42, 256n8, 257n16

Shapiro v. Thompson, 106

Sharecroppers, Black, 52, 75–76, 113, 156, 218–19, 249

Shaw, Mississippi, 166

Shaw University, 10

Shelby County v. Holder, 4
Sherrod, Charles, 74–75
Shofner, Jerrell, 211
Shropshire, Claudia, 13
Siegelman, Don, 217
Silver, Carol Ruth, 28, 30
Sims, Alease, 218
Sims v. Amos, 212–13, 219
Singleton v. Allen, 213
Sit-ins, 13, 32, 42, 72, 179–80, 186; by students, 10–11, 219, 252
Sixteenth Street Baptist church bombing, Birmingham, 233, 235–36
SLAM. *See* Southern Legal Action Movement
Slater, Howard, 16–19, 29
Slavery, US, 3, 52, 197, 231n10, 233, 249, 262
Smith, Ben, 13, 86
Smith, Hazel Brannon, 113–14
Smith, John Lewis, Jr., 147
Smith, Orma, 108, 110
SNCC. *See* Student Nonviolent Coordinating Committee
Sobol, Richard, 87, 115
Social Security Act, US, 110
Social workers, 103–4
South, US, 11–16, 73, 76–77, 153–54, 267; Deep South, 26, 34, 51, 133, 152, 180, 242–45, 255n4; LSCRRC operating in, 4, 10, 18–28, 34–36, 39–46; after passage of the 1964 Civil Rights Act, 233–45; SLAM operating in, 4, 83–95. *See also specific states*
South Carolina, 233
Southern Christian Leadership Conference (SCLC), 10, 58, 168, 172–73
Southern Conference Education Fund (SCEF), 85–86
Southern Legal Action Movement (SLAM), 4, 83–95
Southern Railway police sergeant, 243
Southern Student Organizing Committee (SSOC), 83–84
Spanish Civil War, 71–172
Sparer, Ed, 81n31
Spriggs, Kent, 18, 34, 86, 109, 201–2
SSOC. *See* Southern Student Organizing Committee

State troopers: Alabama, 135, 190–91; Mississippi, 135, 176
Statute of Limitations, 241–43
Stein, Adam, 84–85
Stein, Greg, 205
Stennis, John, 107
Stern Family Fund, 17–18
Stevenson v. International Paper Co., 201
Stigmas, 135–36, 223, 250–51
Still, Ed, 205, 215
"The Strange Career of Birdie Mae Davis" (Duke), 204
Strickler, George, 107–8, 114–15
Stroock & Stroock & Lavan, 152, 159n5
Student Nonviolent Coordinating Committee (SNCC), 10–11, 14, 33, 35–36, 52–53, 72–75, 168, 172–73; "Black Power" promoted by, 181, 183; Freedom Summer organized by, 153
Students: sit-ins by, 10–11, 219, 252; white, 11, 21–22, 153, 203, 223, 225, 227, 243, 248, 253
Students for a Democratic Society (SDS), 83
Students of color, Black students and, 10, 20n28, 41, 209–11; Alabama, 198–201, 203–5, 212, 218–30; law students, 20, 22–23, 81n32, 200–201, 252, 2258n21; Mississippi, 70–71, 96–97, 109–10, 248. *See also* Desegregation, school; Integration
Supreme Court, US, 3–4, 33, 36, 54–55, 250, 254, 255n1, 256n7, 261–65; on desegregation, 199, 203; on removal petitions, 167, 189; on Statute of Limitations, 242–43. *See also specific cases; specific judges*
Surveillance, 88
Swaggard, Brenda White, 253
Swann v. Charlotte-Mecklenburg Bd. of Education, 201, 224

Taconic Foundation, 17–18, 80n21
Tallulah, Louisiana, 169–71
Taxes, 136, 229–30
Taylor, Lee, 204
Taylor, Stanley, 104–5
Tear-gas, 177–78, 180, 190–91
Teiger, Joseph, 83
Television broadcasts, 152, 172, 233, 252
Templeton, Furman, 35

Tenant farmers, 52, 55
Tenant organizing, 239–40
Tennessee, 4, 173–74, 218
Tennessee State University, 218
Texas, 121–33, 159n2, 186
Thames, Sally, 103
Thernstrom, Abigail, 208
Third Reconstruction, 5, 230, 260–67
Thomas, Clarence, 7–8, 225
Thomas, Dan, 203, 206
Thomas, Roddy, 200
Thompson, Allen, 251
Thompson, Myron, 213–15, 217, 219
Thornburgh v. Gingles, 215–17
Thornton, J. Mills, 207, 224
Thurmond, Strom, 188, 197
Tieger, Jerome "Buddy," 88
Tigar, Michael, 86
Tougaloo College, 184, 253
Trinidad and Tobago, 96
Trister, Michael B., 103–11, 114–15
Trister v. University of Mississippi, 108
Troy, Alabama, 67–68
Truman, Harry S., 225
Tuskegee Institute, 51, 69, 82n37
Tuttle, Elbert, 115, 162–63, 237, 241, 262
Twenty-Sixth Amendment, US Constitution, 198

UC. *See* University of California
UCMJ. *See* Uniform Code of Military Justice
Unconstitutional practices, 32, 38, 42, 90–92, 94, 108, 209, 211, 213, 217, 261
Unemployment rate, 254
Uniform Code of Military Justice (UCMJ), 93
Unions, labor, 46, 86, 133, 255n3
United Kingdom, 97
United States (US), 53–54, 130, 187, 199; Civil War, 52, 261–62; Congress, 32, 144, 233–34, 245, 255nn1–3; full citizenship, 98, 261–2662; Great Depression, 14, 71, 113; Reconstruction era, 3, 200, 207, 232n16, 234, 261–62; slavery in, 3, 52, 197, 231n10, 233, 249, 262. *See also* Army; Constitution; Court of Appeals, US; Federal government; Supreme Court; *specific departments; specific laws; specific states*

United States v. Alabama, 218
United States v. Dallas County Commission, 133–34
United States v. Fordice, 225–26
United States v. Marengo County, AL, 140–43
University of Alabama, 85, 88, 92, 200–201, 206, 252n21
University of Buffalo, 8–9
University of California (UC) Berkeley, 36, 61, 72, 185–87
University of Georgia, 221
University of Miami, 149
University of Mississippi, 41, 57, 99, 103–11, 114–15, 172
University of Pennsylvania, 104
University of Utah, 197
Unlikely Heroes (Bass), 162, 202
US. *See* United States

Valentine, John White, 167
Veterans, 97–98, 197, 200, 205–6
Vietnam War, 32, 61–64, 77, 88, 92, 94, 97–98, 145, 163, 239
Violence, 2–3, 16, 32, 58–59, 66, 153–54, 167–69, 233, 255n1; against African Americans, 11, 35, 41, 74–75, 172–73, 175; police, 57–58, 171–72, 175–78, 190–92. *See also* Guns, shootings and
Voter: registration, 39, 41, 51, 57, 80n21, 135, 155–57, 174, 176, 205; repression, 36, 111
Voting rights, voting rights cases and, 1–4, 40–41, 171–72, 187–88; in Alabama, 42, 133–34, 138–47, 190, 198, 203, 205–17; in Georgia, 36, 144; in Mississippi, 11, 30, 57, 111–12 153–157, 174–79, 184, 245–46, 260–62
Voting Rights Act (1965), US, 3–4, 51, 172, 180, 263; Section 5 of the, 213, 261
Voting Rights Amendments/Act (VRA), 208–9, 214–17
Voyles, James, 138–39
VRA. *See* Voting Rights Amendment/Act

Wage discrimination, 125–33, 242–43, 257nn16–17
Wage-increase policies, 243
Walker, Lucy, 240
Walker v. Jefferson County Home, 240–41

Wallace, George, 42, 191, 199, 203, 221, 239
Wallace v. Brewer, 91–92
Wallis, Ken, 221
Waltzer, Bruce, 13
War on Poverty, OEO, 103, 246
Washington, Booker T., 69
Washington, DC, 118, 143–45, 254
Washington Research Project, 7, 87
Washington v. Davis, 207
Watkins, Donald, 218, 222
Watkins, Levi, 218
Watkins v. Scott Paper Co., 201–2
Welfare, 55–57, 116–17; AFDC program, 62, 106, 110; welfare rights movement, 25, 81n31, 83, 86, 106
Wesleyan University, 39, 51, 82n42
West Point, Mississippi, 101, 109–10
Wharton, A. C., 109
Whatley, Joe, 221
Where Do We Go from Here (King Jr.), 181, 183
White: flight, 3, 239; power structure, 35, 55, 252; privilege, 44, 234; students, 11, 21–22, 153, 203, 223, 225, 227, 243, 248, 253; supremacy, 196, 204, 206–7, 219, 221, 223–24, 230, 234, 252, 261; universities, 220–21, 223, 225, 228
White people, 9–10, 51, 179–83, 195; in Baker County, 36–37; in Mobile, 43–50; in Panola County, 55–57; white women, 1, 73, 165–66, 192
White University of Tennessee–Nashville, 218
White v. Regester, 208
White women, 1, 73, 165–66, 192
Wiggins, Robert L., Jr., 233–45

Wilkins, Roy, 179–80
Williams, Hosea, 58, 168, 191–92
Williams, John Bell, 107
Wilson, Ed, 61–63
Wisdom, John Minor, 115, 119, 202, 262
Witnesses, court, 68–69, 91, 94, 136–41, 144–48
Women: Black, 1, 24, 30, 192, 200, 237; white, 1, 73, 165–66, 192
Women, rights of, 24, 31, 77; abortion, 217, 250, 261
Woodward, C. Vann, 230
Woolworth's lunch counter sit-in, 10
World War II, 71–72, 209, 252; veterans, 197, 200, 205–6
Wright, Gail, 194
Wright, J. Skelly, 147
Wright, Marian, 52, 181
Wulf, Mel, 12–13, 21, 81n33, 165
Wyatt v. Stickney, 92, 198–99
Wyche, Zelma, 169–71

Yale Law School, 7–8, 15–17, 215
Yazoo City, Mississippi, 115, 182–83
Young, Andrew, 177
Young, Whitney, 179–80

Zaks, Stan, 35
Zimberoff, Diane, 103
Zimmerman, Joseph, 146–48
Zimmer v. McKeithen, 206–7, 211
Zoghby-Figures Act, Alabama, 201
Zone assignments, racial attendance, 203–4
Zuccotti Park (Occupy Wall Street), 152, 159

www.ingramcontent.com/pod-product-compliance
Lightning Source LLC
Chambersburg PA
CBHW030610230426
43661CB00053B/1916